INTERNATIONAL
ACCOUNTING

Recent Titles from QUORUM BOOKS

INTERNATIONAL ACCOUNTING

Issues and Solutions

AHMED BELKAOUI

Q

Quorum Books
Westport, Connecticut • London, England

Library of Congress Cataloging in Publication Data

Belkaoui, Ahmed, 1943-
   International accounting.

   Includes bibliographies and index.
   1. International business enterprises—Accounting.
2. Comparative accounting.   I. Title.
HF5686.I56B44   1985   657'.95   84-11514
ISBN 0-89930-089-8 (lib. bdg.)

Library of Congress Catalog Card Number: 84-11514
ISBN: 0-89930-089-8

First published in 1985 by Quorum Books

Greenwood Press
A division of Congressional Information Service, Inc.
88 Post Road West, Westport, Connecticut 06881

Printed in the United States of America

10 9 8 7 6 5 4 3 2 1

To all the Belkaouis
"Aux âmes bien nées, la valeur n'attends pas le nombre des années."

CONTENTS

EXHIBITS

PREFACE

A single set of generally accepted international accounting principles does not exist at this time and may not exist for a long time. The field of international accounting is characterized more by diversity than commonality. The diversity lies in the different approaches taken in the various countries in the world to solving financial and managerial accounting, auditing, and taxation issues and agreeing on the role of accounting in economic development. What results is a set of unique international accounting issues in need of more coherent and uniform solutions.

This book presents the principal issues and proposed solutions in the field of international accounting. Eleven important issues are identified and examined in the 11 chapters:

1. The nature of international accounting
2. Determinants of national differences
3. The search for an international accounting theory
4. Accounting in foreign currency
5. Accounting for inflation internationally
6. Managerial accounting issues facing multinational operations
7. Transfer pricing for multinational operations
8. Foreign exchange and political risk management
9. Capital budgeting for the multinational corporation
10. International taxation issues
11. Accounting and economic development.

This book has various roots. Not only from an accounting perspective, but also from financial and economic perspectives, it is intended to provide a more comprehensive view of the issues and solutions. It should be of interest to practicing accountants and financial managers involved in multinational operations. It is also intended for second-year master's degree candidates in business and accounting and for final-year students in undergraduate accounting or business programs.

Many people helped in the development of the book. John Parkinson of York University reviewed various chapters and provided very helpful comments and suggestions. Considerable assistance was received from University of Illinois at Chicago students and staff, especially Doris J. Harmon, Zelia Champ, and George Ribarchik. The typists from the secretarial pool at the College of Business Administration of the University of Illinois at Chicago—Regina Rees, Danguole Prismantas, Queen E. Sawyer, Geraldine Shehorn, and Paul Ragas—provided professional secretarial support. Financial assistance provided by Ralph Westfall, Dean of the College of Business Administration and the Department of Accounting at the University of Illinois at Chicago, provided both time and resources to ensure that the manuscript was completed in adequate time. Also, I wish to express appreciation to the institutions or individuals for their kind permission to reprint very "valuable" and original material.

Finally, I thank all the people at Greenwood Press for their cheerful and intelligent assistance.

INTERNATIONAL ACCOUNTING

1.

NATURE OF INTERNATIONAL ACCOUNTING

One may safely assume that international accounting is neither a new invention nor the invention of any one country. It is not new because as a subset of modern accounting it has existed as long as accounting has existed and as often as international trade has occurred. It is not the invention of any one country since all countries through their domestic systems and the interdependence of their economies and trade have made important contributions to international accounting. Therefore, at least three questions arise: (1) What is meant by international accounting? (2) What triggered the modern growth and importance of international accounting? and (3) Is there an international public accounting profession? Because these questions are important to understanding the nature of international accounting, this chapter provides some of the answers.

International Accounting: An Idea in Search of a Definition

The worst that can happen to any discipline is to be ill defined. Rather than being ill defined, international accounting is the subject of various definitions encompassing different scopes. A useful clarification of these definitions was provided by both Qureshi and Weirich et al. by their identifying three major concepts: Parent-foreign subsidiary accounting or accounting for subsidiaries, comparative or international accounting, and universal or world accounting.[1]

The concept of *universal* or *world accounting* is by far the largest in scope. It directs international accounting to the formulation and study of a universally accepted set of accounting principles. It aims for a complete standardization of accounting principles internationally. The definition of Weirich et al. is:

World Accounting. In the framework of this concept, international accounting is considered to be a universal system that could be adopted in all countries. A world wide set of generally accepted accounting principles (GAAP), such as the set maintained in the United States, would be established. Practices and principles would be developed which were applicable to all countries. This concept would be the ultimate goal of an international accounting system.[2]

While very commendable, this goal is unlikely to be reached in the near future and may be safely characterized as highly idealistic by some and even utopian by others. As will be seen in the rest of the book, pessimistic attitudes are based on the many obstacles to a complete standardization of accounting principles. Chapter 2 examines in detail some of the factors determining accounting differences internationally.

The concept of *comparative* or *international accounting* directs international accounting to a study and understanding of national differences in accounting. It involves "(a) an awareness of the international diversity in corporate accounting and reporting practices, (b) understanding of the accounting principles and practices of individual countries, and (c) ability to assess the impact of diverse accounting practices on financial reporting."[3] There is a general consensus in accounting literature that the term *international accounting* refers to "comparative accounting principles." The definition of Weirich et al. is:

International Accounting. A second major concept of the term international accounting involves a descriptive and informative approach. Under this concept, international accounting includes all varieties of principles, methods and standards of accounting of *all* countries. This concept includes a set of generally accepted accounting principles established for each country, thereby requiring the accountant to be multiple principle conscious when studying international accounting. . . . No universal or perfect set of principles would be expected to be established. A collection of all principles, methods and standards of all countries would be considered as the international accounting system. These variations result because of differing geographic, social, economic, political and legal influences.[4]

The concept of *parent-foreign subsidiary* accounting or *accounting for foreign subsidiaries* is by far the oldest and narrowest in scope. It reduces international accounting to the process of consolidating the accounts of the parent company and its subsidiaries and translating foreign currency in local currency. The definition of Weirich et al. is:

Accounting for Foreign Subsidiaries. The third major concept that may be applied to "international accounting" refers to the accounting practices of a parent company and a foreign subsidiary. A reference to a particular country or domicile is needed under the concept for effective internal financial reporting. The accountant is concerned mainly with the translation and adjustment of the subsidiary's financial statement. Different accounting problems arise and different accounting principles are to be followed depending upon which country is used as a reference for translation and adjustment purposes.[5]

What Triggered International Accounting?

Various factors have triggered the growth of international accounting, and the most important are explored hereafter.

THE EMERGENCE OF THE MULTINATIONAL CORPORATION

A new form of organization, called either a "multinational company" in a *Business Week* special report in April 1963 or a "trans-national enterprise" in the "Thinking Ahead" column of the *Harvard Business Review*, March-April 1964, is an acceptable feature of the world business scene. Mueller gives the following accurate characterization of this new form of business organization: "The international corporation is emerging. This is a corporation which is internationally owned and controlled. It is not a domestic corporation with some foreign business. It is a business organization with a truly international organization for all its business functions, including management, production, marketing and finance."[6] Or, more succinctly, a multinational corporation is a company which owns and manages business operations in two or more countries.[7] Most of the time a multinational corporation results from a firm's development from a domestic firm to a truly international operation by going through some or all of the following stages of development:

1. Development of a strong product for domestic sales
2. Import of raw materials or parts
3. Exports through brokers
4. Direct export sales
5. Foreign branch sales office
6. Licensing
7. Licensing with partial ownership
8. Joint ventures
9. Wholly owned manufacturing branch plants or subsidiaries
10. Multinational management organization
11. Multinational ownership of equity securities.[8]

While most multinational companies come from the developed countries, the fastest growing group of multinational companies in the past two decades has come from the new industrializing countries. Examples include The Birla Group of India, United Laboratories from the Philippines, Autlan of Mexico, and Caloi of Brazil. The new competitors can be tough opponents when proposals are being considered for new projects in developing countries. The multinational management organization stage may take one of two formats: (1) a *world corporation format* where the functions of research and development, manufacturing, marketing, and finance are merged for domestic and foreign operations, or an *international division format* where all foreign operations are separated from their domestic counterparts in an "international division."[9]

The multinational corporations create specific internal and external accounting problems of relevance to the field of international accounting. Internal accounting problems include transfer pricing, foreign exchange risk management, budgeting, performance evaluation, and capital budgeting as some of the main problems. External accounting problems include consolidations, foreign currency translation, and accounting for inflation, to name only a few. Each of these issues demands specific solutions different to a certain extent from the ones advocated for domestic operations.

Furthermore, multinational corporations face unique pressure for higher levels of accountability, especially from governments and trade unions, creating a need for more relevant information about multinational corporations as a basis for policy making at the national and international levels. The question is, given the differences between domestic and multinational corporations, whether there should be specific standards set for multinational corporations. Gray et al. argue that there is a case for standards applicable to multinational corporations (MNCs) as follows:

The present lack of consistency in MNC accountability and the proliferation of national standards may lead to the conclusion that worldwide harmonization of MNC reporting—disclosure and measurement—is needed. Equally, there may be a supportable argument that international harmonization should not be considered a major priority for international (domestic) enterprises with no foreign operations, because the needs of the international investment community, the main agency involved and relatively expert, could be met to a large extent by accounting policy disclosures. It is only when international companies become units of a supernatural economic ability, the MNC, that arguments of consistency and comparability in the interests of international consituencies of users become persuasive.[10]

FOREIGN INVESTMENT

The multinational corporation is the most developed form of foreign direct investment. The main characteristic is that the foreign segments of the operations are not only owned but managed by the parent firm. A direct foreign investment involves the transfer of capital, managerial, and technical assets of a firm from one country (the home country) to another (the host country) by (within) the same firm. The opposite of a direct foreign investment is a foreign portfolio investment. Although direct foreign investment implies control of assets transferred abroad and financial commitment and managerial control over the subsidiary, foreign portfolio investment implies purely a financial investment in foreign securities, either bonds or equities purchased in small amounts in order to create no controlling will in the (foreign) firms involved.

Direct foreign investment is undertaken after an evaluation of the role and return of the foreign project and of the potential managerial presence of the parent firm in the host country. Foreign portfolio investment limits the analysis to the risk/return considerations. Various models and theories have been proposed to explain the main, diverse aspects of foreign direct investment. These views include international trade theory, the location theory, the investment theory, the theory of the firm, and the industrial organization theory. A summary of these theories is provided in Exhibit 1.1.

EXHIBIT 1.1 FIVE VIEWS OF FOREIGN DIRECT INVESTMENT

---

(1) **International Trade Theory**
  (a) comparative cost view: emphasizes supply-side conditions; usually focuses on commercial policy constraints to exports and FDI (which are usually substitutes); usually emphasizes production costs rather than distribution costs; frequently has macroeconomic orientation.

  (b) product life cycle view: a descriptive, "stage" theory which considers both supply and demand explicitly; emphasizes the roles of technology and marketing in describing the sequence of FDI in different products into different countries.

(2) **Location Theory:** similar to trade theory in orientation toward the supply side and cost conditions; emphasizes transportation costs rather than commercial policy; often resource availability is a central variable in analysis.

(3) **Investment Theory**
  (a) imperfect capital markets view: one position is that an under-valued exchange rate (which allows production costs in the country to remain below those of other countries) attracts FDI if foreign firms also have a technological advantage over local firms; another position is that long-term investment in LDC's will often be FDI rather than purchase of securities, because no organized securities market exists; a third position is that lack of knowledge about host-country securities favors FDI instead, because FDI allows control of host-country assets.

  (b) portfolio-of-FDI view: similar to portfolio approach in securities analysis, except that risk is diversified across national economies; emphasizes risk reduction from commercial and exchange rate changes.

(4) **Theory of the Firm:** assumes imperfect information, and presents managerial models of firm behavior; descriptive, often historical view; emphasizes the individual firm, rather than the country; takes a microeconomic perspective; includes the 'internalization' view.

(5) **Industrial Organization Theory:** focuses on market inperfections that create oligopolies; emphasizes company-specific advantages such as technology and management know-how; explores inter-industry differences in FDI; attempts to show why FDI is used to exploit the company-specific advantages.

SOURCE: Reprinted with permission from Robert Grosse, *The Theory of Foreign Direct Investment*, Essays in International Business, College of Business Administration, The University of South Carolina, December 1981, pp. 10-11.

As with the multinational corporation, foreign investment, either direct foreign investment or foreign portfolio investment, creates specific accounting problems relevant to the field of international accounting. Examples of these problems include risk return identification and measurement, accounting for foreign exchange transactions, and foreign currency translation.

ABANDONMENT OF STABLE CURRENCY SYSTEMS IN INTERNATIONAL MONETARY SYSTEM

Fluctuations in the exchange rates (also referred to as "parity") can arise due to fundamental economic problems as well as to monetary problems. The fundamental economic problems affecting the demand/supply relationship among currencies are mostly caused by the long-run developments in a nation's balance of payments. Basically, surplus or deficit leads to situations resulting in parity changes through revaluations or devaluations.

The monetary problems affecting the exchange rate are linked particularly to the problems affecting the international monetary system. In effect, the international monetary system constitutes the structure within which foreign exchange rates are determined, international trade and capital flows are accumulated, and balance-of-payments adjustments are made.[11] An understanding of the problem of the international monetary system is at the core of the exchange rate fluctuations. Basically, the following historical events are indicative of the international monetary situation:

First, the gold standard was in operation until World War I. Basically, governments and central banks made their currency and gold freely interconvertible at a fixed price.

Second, because a nation's supply of gold could run out before a deficit corrected itself, the Bretton Woods Conference of 1944 created the International Monetary Fund (IMF).[12]

The primary objective of the IMF was to promote exchange stability. Article I of the IMF Articles of Agreement specified the five objectives of the IMF, excerpted here:

a. To promote international monetary cooperation through . . . consultation and collaboration.
b. To facilitate the expansion and balanced growth of international trade.
c. To promote exchange stability . . . and to avoid competitive exchange depreciation.
d. To assist in the establishment of a multilateral system of payments . . . and in the elimination of foreign exchange restrictions.
e. To give confidence to members by making the Fund's resources available to them . . . thus providing them with opportunity to correct [temporary] maladjustments in their balances of payments.

The basic feature of the IMF was to establish a fixed exchange rate system or par value based on gold and the U.S. dollar.

Third, the initial IMF system proved inadequate as some of the reserve currency countries ran deficits, especially the United States, the United Kingdom, and France, and as a credibility gap developed. There was truly a need for a modification of the gold exchange standard. This was accomplished in two steps:

1. Step No. 1 was to allow swap agreements whereby instant reserves were created by a swap of credit lines between central banks.
2. Step No. 2 was to provide a more lasting solution to the need for growth in world monetary reserves by the creation of new reserves called special drawing rights (SDRs). This system permitted countries to borrow or withdraw SDRs from the IMF to buy other countries' currencies.

Fourth, however, lack of confidence in the international monetary system, and the dollar in particular, precipitated a world monetary crisis, which was quieted by the Smithsonian Agreement of December 1971 establishing semi-fixed exchange rates and devaluing the U.S. dollar. Fifth, continued pressure on the dollar in 1973 caused another devaluation and showed that a fixed-rate system was no longer feasible given the extreme surges of speculative flows of currencies. Sixth, while awaiting further reform of the international monetary system, the IMF permits a country to select one of the following three systems to value its currency:

1. A first system where the value of a currency is *pegged* (fixed) to another currency
2. A second system used by the members of the European Economic Community to peg the value of their currencies to a *basket of currencies*, expressed in *European Currency Units*
3. A third system where the value of a currency is allowed to *float* freely against other currencies.

This international monetary stability and the monetary fluctuations of exchange rates create a fundamental need in international accounting for accounting in foreign currencies, both accounting for transactions and accounting for translation.

RISING RESOURCE AND COMMODITY PRICES AND MONOPOLIES

It is quite evident that no nation or continent is endowed with all the raw materials essential to its economic growth. World and community dependence, especially the new dependence of rich nations on poor ones, and the emergence of community monopolies and producers' associations are creating a new component in the world that rich nations have to deal with. This new phenomenon is eloquently described by Brown:

The rich countries, particularly the United States, Japan and those of Western Europe, with their steadily rising consumption of minerals required to support their affluence, are becoming increasingly dependent on the poor countries with their largely unexploited mineral reserves. In Western Europe, consumption of eleven basic industrial raw materials—bauxite, copper, lead, phosphate, zinc, chrome ore, manganese ore, magnesium, nickel, tungsten and tin—exceeds production. In the case of copper, phosphates, tin, nickel, manganese ore and chrome ore, nearly all needs must now be met from imports.[13]

This new dependence on poor countries is further complicated by the fact that most reserves of these minerals are concentrated in poor countries. For example, Chile, Peru, Zambia, and Zaire supply most of the world's copper. Morocco, Tunisia, Senegal, Togo, and the United States control most of the world's phosphates. Mexico, Peru, and Australia account for 60 percent of the world's traded supply of lead. Potash seems to be an exclusivity of Canada. Bolivia, Malaysia, and Thailand control most of the trade in tin. However, the most flagrant and potent example of the new commodity situation is the case of energy and the dependence of most of the world countries on the export of oil by the OPEC (Organization of Petroleum Exporting Countries) countries. OPEC, created in 1974, resulted in the member sellers' control of the energy market and in a tremendous increase in the cost of oil imports to both developed and developing countries. This new energy and raw material dependence creates a special need for international accounting to account for the commodity price fluctuations and the instability created.

GROWTH OF BROADLY BASED INTERNATIONAL CAPITAL MARKETS

In addition to national capital markets, a truly international capital market for external financing exists and is known as the Eurobond (or the Eurocapital) market. It arose in response to the numerous controls restricting foreign access to national capital markets. Furthermore, governments and corporate borrowers faced with either restricted borrowing opportunities at home and in foreign markets or relatively "thin" domestic capital markets have tapped the Eurobond market, leading to the development of a broadly based capital market in Europe. Unique features of this European capital market include:

(1) the market's operation and structure are subject to the regulations of no one country; (2) although evidence suggests that competition among borrowers for access to this market is keen, such access has not been subject to formal restrictions of any kind; (3) minimum information requirements, as typified by those prescribed by the Securities and Exchange Acts in the United States or the Companies Acts and Legislation of various European countries, are not mandatory; (4) listing activities, when undertaken, tend to be a rational response to the economic advantages of doing so and tend to be concentrated in those exchanges where disclosure requirements are least burdensome; and (5) this market, which took hold largely in the early 1960s, has expanded very rapidly and, in view of its broad base, continues to be responsive to the international demands placed upon it for capital financing.[14]

Another unique feature of this market is the heterogeneity of the participants and their information needs. One may safely assume that, first, the corporate reporting practices in this broadly based market will reflect the information needs of transnational investor groups, and second, firms entering this relatively unregulated and competitive market will increase their disclosure significantly upon entry. While the first assumption remains contested, Choi examined the second assumption empirically and presented results suggesting that firms seeking financing in the free, but competitive, Eurobond market increase their disclosure significantly upon entry.[15]

It seems, then, that financial disclosure is an important parameter in granting access to domestic or international capital markets. At least in the United States there is a widely held belief that financial disclosure reduces inaccuracies and contributes to the efficient operation of capital markets. This belief has led to the enactment of disclosure statutes, such as the U.S. Securities Act in 1968. Internationally, good disclosure habits will seem to play a major role in the development of domestic capital markets and broadly based international capital markets. As a recognition of the importance of disclosure to the functioning of the capital market, the Securities and Exchange Commission (SEC) requires foreign companies, as a condition for listing their shares on the major U.S. securities exchanges, to conform to the financial reporting requirements prevalent in the United States. Basically, registration requires disclosure of information such as the following:

1. A description of the issuer's management
2. A description of the security to be issued, its relationship to the other securities, and the trading market for and market price of the issuer's securities
3. Information about the issuer's management
4. Management's discussion and analysis of financial condition and results of operations
5. Financial statements, selected financial data, and other financial information.

This information is required in all 1933 Act filings on Form F 1, Form F 2, or Form F-3.[16] In fact, more recently, in 1983, the SEC approved a plan to increase the amount of information U.S. investors receive from foreign companies whose stock is traded over the counter. This new information will include more detailed annual and quarterly reports.

GROWING ECONOMIC ASPIRATIONS OF THE THIRD WORLD

After World War II, Third World countries began gaining their independence one by one and immediately started to develop their economies. In effect, their political independence could be secured only by developing their national economy.

To escape from the vicious cycle of underdevelopment, the Third World countries began searching for a new social and economic identity. Economic development became the primary goal in the developing economies. Various strategies were used to spur economic growth. In spite of these efforts, most of these countries are still confronted with many problems and difficulties in developing their economy. Some of these problems include unbalanced development, backward agriculture and food shortage, deteriorating trade conditions, heavy foreign borrowing, and a widening gap between the rich and the poor and between the towns and the countryside, aggravated by high unemployment.

Faced with this bleak situation, the Third World countries began asking for a New International Economic Order. Of the many aspects of a new international economic order, the demands of the developing countries are:

1. To raise the prices of raw materials and primary goods
2. To reform industrial and trade structure
3. The developed countries should increase their foreign debt
4. To reform the present international financial system, enabling it to provide capital for the developing countries
5. To reform the international economic structure and its decision-making structure.[17]

Whether the new international economic order can be implemented creates special problems of relevance to international accounting such as the role of accounting in economic development, the measurement and management of political and economic risks, and accounting for the social costs and benefits of the operations of the multinationals.

International Dimensions of Accounting

ANNUAL REPORTS GO INTERNATIONAL

There are clear indications that annual reports of large corporations all over the world are becoming internationally oriented. The early manifestation of this transnational reporting was the translation of annual reports into one or more foreign languages and the separate disclosure of the extent of international business engaged in by the reporting corporation.[18] The need now is to try to meet the informational needs of unique multiple audiences-of-interest. To accomplish this, three identifiable schools of thought have been developed or have been advocated:[19]

Primary and Secondary Financial Statement. This follows from a recommendation by the Accountants International Study Group (AISG) that multiple sets of statements, primary and secondary, need to be prepared by an enterprise with financial reporting audiences-of-interest in more than one country. Essentially, the primary financial statements are those prepared to meet the information needs of audiences-of-interest in other countries. Secondary financial statements will have one or more of the following characteristics:

- The reporting standards of a foreign country will have been followed.
- The statements will have been translated into a language that is not the language of the company's country of domicile.
- The auditor's report will have been expressed in a form not commonly used in the company's country of domicile.[20]

Single-Domicile Reporting. This school of thought argues that financial statements can reflect only one point of view, that of the company's country of domicile. Mueller gives the following explanation:

The notion of a single domicile for financial statements means that each set of financial statements necessarily has a nationality, reflects style and customs at a particular point of time and has an individual viewpoint or character. Financial statements are anchored in a single set of underlying account data prepared within a framework of quite specific accounting standards, methods and procedures. Restatement of financial statements to a different set of accounting principles produces different relationships between individual account balances and financial ratios. The meaning and implications of these new relationships may convey an entirely different financial substance to statement readers in other countries.[21]

International Reporting Standards. This school of thought argues that international reporting standards would be set and followed by all countries in the preparation of financial statements. This proposal assumes a complete and international "standardization" of accounting techniques and policies. Needless to say, this alternative would be difficult to reach given the complexity of the international political, economic, and social climate.

INTERNATIONAL AUDITING

One may logically ask why there is a need for international auditing rather than depending on the auditing techniques of each country. The following arguments in favor of international auditing may be advanced: First, the growth of broadly based international capital markets will depend increasingly on generally accepted auditing standards to assure consistent and complete financial reporting. Second, the accountant must be in a position to look after the needs of his or her client wherever in the world the client chooses to establish operations. This requires that the auditor both undertake to practice in a foreign country and, for the sake of conformity, rely on accepted international auditing standards. Third, given that the standards that exist in various countries in the areas of independence—audit procedures relating to inventory, accounts receivable, and reporting standards—differ from one country to another, a case can be made for international auditing for the sake of understandability and communication.

At present there is a wide diversity of audit requirements. Examine, for example, the following requirements of the source of the members of the European Economic Community:

1. United Kingdom: Each limited company must have an annual audit carried out by an independent public accountant.
2. Belgium: There are virtually no audit requirements.
3. Netherlands: Similar to the UK, with an exception for small, privately owned companies.
4. France: A statutory audit exists for all companies.
5. Germany: Only banks, large corporations, and insurance companies are required to have internal audits.[22]

There is obviously a need for some uniform international auditing standards. The most serious difficulty in establishing international auditing standards is the acceptance of such standards by the standards-setting bodies. Efforts to harmonize audit requirements and procedures are being made by the International Federation of Accountants (IFAC). Among the seven standing committees created by the IFAC to enable it to carry out its mission of harmonizing the accounting profession, there is an International Auditing Practices Committee whose charge is to develop guidelines on generally accepted auditing and reporting practices and to promote their voluntary acceptance. Notice the careful use of the two words, *guidelines* and *voluntary*. In fact, it was clearly specified that these guidelines should be adopted by the member bodies of the IFAC insofar as they do not conflict with local regulations (IFAC Constitution, Part 2, Section 6a). To date these guidelines include: (1) "Objective and Scope of the Audit of Financial Statements," (2) "Audit Engagement Letters," (3) "Basic Principles Governing an Audit," (4) "Planning," (5) "Using the Work of Another Auditor," and (6) "Controlling the Quality of Audit Work."

These attempts are a first step toward harmonizing international standards. Notice that the attempts are toward harmonization but not rigid harmonization:

Rigid standardization across national lines is simply out of the question. We know this instinctively from the sharp differences of opinion on accounting and auditing matters that divide members of the profession within their own nations. Can those divisions do anything but widen as debate becomes international? For this reason, the approval structure for issuance of guidelines allows for the possibility of some dissent among members of the International Auditing Practices Committee. Three quarters of the members must agree to the publication of a guideline, meaning that as many as one quarter can disagree and [still] be overruled.[23]

Besides the harmonization of international auditing standards, other issues remain of importance to international auditing. These include government roles in setting auditing standards, the question of statutory or voluntary audit, problems of quality control, the question of review, the question of ethical conduct of management, and an internal audit in a foreign operating environment.

INTERNATIONAL REPORTING PROBLEMS

Most accounting issues could qualify easily as international accounting issues, which may explain why international accounting is often referred to as a subarea of accounting. There are, however, some issues relevant to international business which create special accounting problems and which constitute the accepted domain of international accounting. These issues, in fact, make international accounting an essential functional area in international business. They have been effectively subdivided into several areas as follows:

A. Private Sector Accounting
   1. Comparative analysis—
      a) national accounting, reporting, and auditing *practice* (principles, procedures, standards and disclosure);
      b) national accounting *theory* (including historical dimensions).
   2. Policy at the international level (standardization).
   3. Accounting for multinational operations
      a) financial accounting (translation, consolidation, segmental reporting, inflation accounting, disclosure, auditing);
      b) managerial accounting (risk and exposure measurements, foreign investment analysis, information systems, transfer pricing, control and performance evaluation, operational auditing, behavioral dimensions).
   4. Taxation (of international operations in different countries).

B. Public Sector Accounting
   1. Comparative analysis of national systems (GNP measurement, balance of payments, balance of trade, employment statistics and so on).
   2. Accounting for governmental agencies and public not-for-profit organizations (overlap in the private sector accounting because certain industries are nationalized in some countries).[24]

Most of these areas, especially those related to private-sector accounting, are explored in the following chapters.

THE ROLE OF ACCOUNTING IN ECONOMIC DEVELOPMENT

Accounting has a dual function in the economic development process, with a role at the micro-level and a role at the macro-level. At the micro-level, accounting will be helpful to corporations and micro-governmental units in measuring, reporting, and disclosing information about their financial position and performance. It will also be helpful in collecting and transforming economic and social data and disseminating relevant data for decision making by the same micro units. At the macro-level, accounting will be helpful to governments and nations in measuring, reporting, and disclosing national economic performance. It will be also helpful in measuring social indicators to assess the adequacy of planning in all the national areas of concern to the country, i.e., education, health, etc.

In short, the role of accounting in economic development goes beyond the mere measurement of economic activity at the micro and macro levels, to acquire socioeconomic dimension; more explicitly, accounting is to serve in the full implementation of economic development planning by providing the relevant information for its execution. Enthoven suggests the following contributions which accounting can make to development planning.

1. Definition, classification and valuation of transactions and stocks for all social accounts, in particular the national income and input-output accounts;

2. Assessment of, and changes in, the components of input-output data, capital coefficients and shadow prices, the latter being the equilibrium or true factors of production;

3. A uniform and standardized system of industrial accounts that would assist in obtaining more comparable data and coefficients for different countries;

4. Up-to-date cost accounting procedures for cost-benefit calculations at various sector levels;

5. Assistance in estimating future financial results and determination of how these will affect investments and the planning pattern;

6. Assistance in devising economic policies, measures and programs; this may include help in elaborating tax or incentive provisions and other administrative policies to stimulate industrial growth;

7. Control and audit of the plan, and reporting its results.[25]

In fact, a review of the relevant international accounting literature suggests the following main roles accounting may hold with regard to economic development. First, the skills and techniques which make up accounting are essential to the development of commerce, industry, and public administration. Second, economic development rests on a successful industrialization and the efficient mobilization of capital. Accounting helps in evaluating the success of both endeavors, according to Seidler: "Enterprise accounting is a supplier of information, a device for increasing the efficiency of resource allocations and a mechanism for controlling productive operations. It seems logical that these skills, normally considered to be tools of private enterprise management, should be equally useful to the management of the development process."[26] Third, through the production of reliable and timely information, accounting is essential to the efficient functioning of a capital market necessary to channel funds for development and investment in the collection of taxes, and the efficient allocation of scarce resources. Fourth, accounting information is needed by developing nations' government, capital markets, and business firms. Government needs such information for implementing public policy, controlling and regulating private enterprise, controlling economic cycles, analyzing expenditures for social overhead, measuring national income, constructing input-output and flow-of-funds systems, disseminating information, and, finally, collecting income taxes. Fifth, accounting information is seen as vital to the emergence of a domestic private capital market, a domestic public capital market, an external private capital market, external public sources of capital, and a capital market consisting of funds from international agencies. Sixth, accounting information is necessary to assist management in their custodial functions, operating decisions, control of subsidiaries and branches, personnel control, real income measurement, budgeting and forecasting, and special management problems. Seventh, economic development depends on an efficient use of a country's economic resources. It rests on development planning to guide the efficient use of these resources. Finally, to be successful, development planning should be supported by an adequate supply of information, which is one of the prerogatives of accounting. The last point is eloquently addressed by Mirghani:

Since development planning represents a system of decision making under conditions of great uncertainty, it should be supported by an information system capable of generating the types of information necessary for reducing the amount of uncertainty surrounding the economic choices that must be made. The development planning process can be likened to the resource allocation process in a micro-organization. The management of any organization would attempt to select the package of alternative uses that would yield maximum benefits in view of the constraints operating in that organization's specific environment. Such an exercise would not be fruitful without an information system that would enable management to make rational choices among alternative uses.[27]

ACCOUNTING STANDARDS FOR THE MULTINATIONAL CORPORATIONS

Investors and creditors more and more are faced with the problem of making decisions based on financial statements that have been prepared using accounting principles which vary from country to country. Various groups have started suggesting international standards for reporting the results of the multinationals' operations and guidelines for their behavior. Examples of these groups include the Center on Transnational Corporations, the U.S. Council of the International Chamber of Commerce, the Organization for Economic Cooperation and Development, the European Economic Community, the International Accounting Standards

Committee, and the International Federation of Accountants. Questions which would immediately appear to users, multinationals, and these potential standards setters include the following: Should there be standards for MNCs? What should be required by standards? Who should set standards?[28]

The first question, whether there should be standards for MNCs, is usually answered in the affirmative. There are now identifiable international constituencies which demand specific information from multinational corporations. In fact, the existence of an international investor group from different countries has created various unique reporting audiences-of-interest. The following reasons have been proposed for such uniqueness.

- People living and working in different cultures have different characteristics, attitudes, life styles and general behavior patterns. These differences make for differing standards of comparison and possibly lead to different decision processes.

- Investment institutions differ from country to country, thus causing differing information wants and usage.

- Accounting principles, as financial statement users understand them, are different from country to country.[29]

The second question, What should be required by the standards, is more difficult to answer given the lack of knowledge of the decision requirements of the user groups involved. While a minimal list of items of disclosure may easily be determined, more cooperation from the accounting profession and a substantial research effort, as well as a political effort, will be needed to develop general accounting standards for the multinational corporations and to resolve various issues. Examples of financial accounting issues include:

1. Defining user information needs
2. The role of general-purpose reports versus special-purpose reports
3. Segmental information, particularly on a geographic basis, or multianalysis by activity and by country
4. Transfer pricing and its impact
5. Employment conditions and prospects
6. Foreign currency transactions and the translation of foreign currency financial statements
7. Accounting for groups and the consolidation of financial statements
8. Accounting for inflation
9. Accounting for taxation.[30]

Examples of managerial accounting issues would include:

1. Foreign exchange risk management
2. Consolidation of enterprise accounts
3. Investment planning
4. External financial sourcing
5. International taxation
6. Transfer pricing
7. Performance evaluation
8. Information control systems.[31]

The third question, Who should set the standards, is the most difficult and sensitive one. One alternative is to let the multinational corporations set the standards, assuming an existing enlightened self-interest of the management of multinational interest groups that establish claims to disclosure by the multinational corporation about its worldwide or local activities. The point was also made as follows:

Our suggestion to the multinational is to become involved in the setting of standards and guidelines and then use these harmonized reporting and guideline suggestions to more fully communicate your accomplishments to others. While we understand that such standardization of reporting will not solve all multinational/host country disputes or cause a totally rational discussion between labor and business, we do believe a more standardized reporting which addresses the information needs of each may improve the dialogue.[32]

If this first alternative is rejected, one is forced to consider the two alternative agencies—the political or the professional. While the professional route would be preferable, developments in international accounting seem to show that the political approach is meritable. Consider the following statement:

Matters of accountancy appear to have become too important to be left to accountancy bodies. If the levels of accountability are to be defined at the national level in the first instance and ultimately some form of supernational harmonization is to be achieved, then it is difficult to see any alternative to political agencies. At this stage, it also seems likely that such agencies will concentrate on the philosophy of information disclosure—why information is needed and in what form it is required—leaving detailed aspects to be worked out in cooperation with professional accountancy organizations.[33]

IS THERE AN INTERNATIONAL INFORMATION SEEKER?

The rise of the multinational, the internationalization of the capital market, the growing cosmopolitanism of investors, and the internationalization of annual reports suggest that there is a new type of information seeker, the international information seeker. The international information seeker, whether individual investor, institutional investor, labor union, or government to name a few, is interested in the international performance of the multinational company for investment or political reasons. Unlike the "domestic" investor, the international information seeker is interested in the impact of political and environmental roles on his or her foreign-investment portfolio. Information needs include not only conventional accounting information (balance sheet, profit and loss statement, and statement of changes in financial position) but also nonaccounting information or information about political risks, economic and political systems, foreign exchange, among others.

The Internationalization of the Accounting Profession

One important result of the rise of international accounting is the internationalization of the accounting profession. It can be seen in the development of international and regional accounting bodies making their entrance in the standards-setting arena and in the growing network of international firm partnerships or liaisons. In effect, various organizations have in recent years made some efforts to harmonize accounting standards. These organizations include the Accounting International Study Group (AISG), the International Accounting Standards Committee, the European Economic Community (EEC), the United Nations, the International Federation of Accountants, and the Union of European Accountants. The role of these organizations in the harmonization of accounting standards is explored in Chapter 3.

The internationalization of the accounting profession can be seen in the growing network of international firm partnerships and liaisons. This is evident by the internationalization of the so-called Big Eight: Arthur Andersen & Co.; Arthur Young & Company; Coopers & Lybrand; Deloitte Haskins & Sells; Peat, Marwick, Mitchell & Co.; Price Waterhouse; Touche Ross & Co.; and Whinney Murray Ernst and Ernst (the international arm of Whinney Murray & Co. of the United Kingdom and Ernst & Whinney of the United States).

Other European firms are presenting a credible international challenge to the "Big Eight": Binder Dijker Otte, Klynveld Main Goerdeler, Interfides, McLintoech Main La Frentz, and Alexander Grant Tansley Witt.

What firms are auditing the world? A recent study conducted by Vinod B. Bavisli and Harold E. Wyman reveals that, while no one firm was world-dominant, 13 occupy a substantial portion of the market: Arthur Andersen & Co.; Arthur Young & Company; Coopers & Lybrand; Deloitte Haskins & Sells; Ernst & Whinney; Klynveld Main Goerdeler; Peat, Marwick, Mitchell & Co.; Price Waterhouse; Touche Ross & Co.; Binder Dijker Otte

& Co.; Fox Moore International; Grant Thornton International; and Horwath & Horwath International.[34]

These international accounting firms have developed for the most part to meet the needs of affiliates or subsidiaries of multinational companies. Marshall proposes the following reasons for this.[35]

Common bases of reporting: The foreign subsidiary is concerned not only with meeting the accounting requirements of the host nation but also with showing consistent application of principles required by the parent company. An international accounting firm has the capability to secure both objectives.

Common auditing standards: Again, the parent company would prefer to have its own international operations examined by firms applying similar standards and methods of auditing and to be judged by professionals applying common criteria and demands for accuracy. An international accounting firm can satisfy these requirements.

Reliance on the work of other auditors: Because of the future of achieving common standards of reporting and auditing, the auditors of parent companies have to be careful in their reliance on the work of a foreign auditor, especially when they have to assume responsibility for all subsidiary companies included in the consolidation, irrespective of whether they have examined the accounts themselves or have relied on the work of other auditors. To correct this problem, accounting firms may decide to go international, choosing one of two options: "First, impose their own auditing standards on the foreign professionals by issuing very specific instructions and requirements, with annual or at least periodic checks to insure compliance; second, assign the audit work to a firm with established standards equal to their own (an associated firm or possibly an associated firm of another international firm with an acknowledged reputation or capability)."[36]

International financing requirements: International financial institutions lend funds provided that borrowers' financial statements are audited by firms whose auditing and reporting standards and professional training and judgment are reliable. However, the international lenders prefer only international accounting firms because of their reputations, known standards of work, and previous experience with the requirements of international lenders.

These international firms have, however, several problems. One serious problem is the result of an outcry of nationalism and the call for local control of all foreign operations. Marshall, for instance, shows concern for the situation in most Latin American countries:

The professions in most Latin American countries exhibit extremely strong rationalistic feelings and, except for specific arrangements made under a very few international treaties, non-nationals generally are refused international recognition of their qualifications as well as their right to practice. In particular, international firms based in English speaking countries have been under severe attack in respect of their rights to practice and to assign and transfer non-national personnel to countries as the needs arise.[37]

A second problem of these new international firms is to maintain good standards of fieldwork and quality-control procedures through careful international coordination. A third problem arises from the need to find high-caliber local staff in each country. A more serious problem arises from the antagonistic attitudes of some of the governments of these developing countries toward enterprise accounting generally. For example, Enthoven has stated:

Effective dialogue and coordination between the enterprise accountancy profession and the governmental and economic agencies tend to be slow. Government and other agencies often accuse professional institutes and their members of being unaware of the larger needs or of being disinterested in serving broader purposes. But in turn we may find that certain governmental agencies would like to see the accountancy profession completely in their own image and fully at their service. Concurrently, the government may not always grasp the tasks the accountancy profession is to serve and its independence of work as a discipline.[38]

An additional problem faced by these firms as by other service firms is the national restrictions on gambling, insurance, construction, engineering, consulting, data processing, tourism, shipping, and other activities that are included under the common heading of "service." What may be needed is regulation to eliminate some of the barriers on service exports. In short, a General Agreement on Tariff and Trade (GATT) for services is needed. In fact, with $350 billion a year international trade in services, the U.S. took an important step when the Office of the U.S. Trade Representative (Bill Brock at the time) drafted the U.S. National Study on Trade and Services. The study has been submitted to the 89-nation Council of GATT to provide a point of discussion.[39] The problem of restrictions on service exports is deeply felt by American industry. In fact, a Price Waterhouse study, conducted among companies included in the *Fortune* services 500 directory, revealed the following findings:

1. Seventy-two percent believe foreign countries are taking unfair advantage of the U.S.'s open services trade policies.
2. Eighty-two percent believe that the U.S. shouldn't become more restrictive in its services trade policies.
3. Eighty-six percent believe that other countries will retaliate if the U.S. institutes new restrictions on services trade.

4. Sixty-eight percent believe that the use of trade as a foreign-policy mechanism (for example, Soviet pipeline sanctions and grain embargoes) is counterproductive.

5. Seventy-three percent believe the needs and problems of service organizations trading abroad are not adequately recognized by the U.S. government.[40]

In spite of these problems, the international accounting firms have been making an effort at adaptive transfers of accounting technology. Needles emphasizes that adaptive transfers of accounting technology can only be successful when they take as their starting point the social and economic objectives of the transferee nation.[41] Needles argues that national goals of countries combine with the social, political, and economic environment and general resources and constraints to influence the economic plan with a strategy for the transfer of accounting technology as a specific subplan of the overall economic plan. As a result, the international accounting firms should recognize the national economic goals of host countries in their adaptive transfer of accounting technology.

Conclusions

This chapter has explored the nature of international accounting by focusing on crucial issues. For the issue of a definition of international accounting, distinctions were made among the major concepts of parent-foreign subsidiary accounting for subsidiaries, comparative or international accounting, and universal or world accounting. For the issue of what triggered the sudden growth and importance of international accounting, the following six factors were examined: emergence of the multinational corporation, foreign investment, abandonment of stable currency systems in the international monetary system, rising resource and commodity prices and monopolies, the growth of broadly based international capital markets, and growing economic aspirations of the Third World.

The following six dimensions were examined in viewing the issue of the international dimensions of accounting: annual reports going international, international auditing, international reporting problems, the role of accounting in economic development, the need for accounting standards for the multinational corporations, and the possible presence of an international information seeker.

With regard to the issue of the internationalization of the accounting profession, this chapter has also examined the growth and problems of international public accounting firms. All of these issues and answers point to the growing role and importance of international accounting and to the urgent problems that are examined in the rest of this book.

Notes

1. Mahmoud Qureshi, "Pragmatic and Academic Bases of International Accounting," *Management International Review* 2 (1979), pp. 61-68.

   Thomas R. Weirich, Clarence G. Avery, and Henry R. Anderson, "International Accounting, Education and Research (Fall 1971), pp. 79-87.

2. Ibid., p. 9.

3. Qureshi, "Pragmatic and Academic Bases of International Accounting," p. 62.

4. Ibid.

5. Ibid.

6. Gerhard G. Mueller, "Whys and Hows of International Accounting," *The Accounting Review* (April 1965), p. 386

7. Neil H. Jacoby, "The Multinational Corporation," *The Center Magazine* 3 (May 1970), p. 38.

8. Ibid., p. 256.

9. J. Fred Weston, and Bart W. Sorge, *International Managerial Finance* (Homewood, Ill.: Richard D. Irwin, Inc., 1972), p. 249.

10. S. J. Gray, J. C. Shaw, and B. McSweeney, "Accounting Standards and Multinational Corporations," *Journal of International Business Studies* (Spring/Summer 1981), p. 127.

11. D. K. Eiteman, and A. I. Stonehill, *Multinational Business Finance*, 2d ed. (Reading, Mass.: Addison-Wesley Publishing Company, 1979), p. 26.

12. The International Bank for Reconstruction and Development (World Bank) was also created at this conference.

13. Lester Brown, *World without Borders* (New York: Random House, 1972), p. 193.

14. Frederick D. S. Choi, "Financial Disclosure and Entry to the European Capital Market," *Journal of Accounting Research* (Autumn 1973), pp. 161-62.

15. Ibid.

16. Form F-3 is available to foreign private issuers who have a consistent record of financial stability. Form F-2 is available to a middle tier of foreign private issuers who do not meet all the criteria for using Form F-3. Finally, Form F-1 is available to all foreign private issuers who do not qualify or choose not to use other registration forms and is the only form that may be used for exchange offers.

17. Zhao Fu San, "The Winding Road to Growth with Social Justice," *South* (December 1982), p. 26.

18. Kenneth B. Berg, Gerhard G. Mueller, and Lauren M. Walker, "Annual Reports Go International," *The Journal of Accountancy* (August 1967).

19. Gerhard G. Mueller, and Lauren M. Walker, "The Coming of Age of Transnational Financial Reporting," *The Journal of Accountancy* (July 1976).

20. Accountants International Study Group, *International Financial Reporting* (London, 1975), para. 39.

21. Gerhard G. Mueller, "To International Significance of Financial Statements," *Illinois CPA* (Spring 1965), pp. 1-10.

22. "Current Composites Cited in Audits of Multinationals," *Journal of Accountancy* (January 1984), p. 36.

23. Robert L. May, "The Harmonization of International Auditing Standards," in

The Internationalization of the Accountancy Profession, ed. W. John Brennan (Toronto: CICA, 1979), pp. 63-64.

24. Hanns-Martin W. Schoenfeld, "International Accounting: Development, Issues, and Future Directions," *Journal of International Business Studies* (Fall 1981), pp. 83-84.

25. Adolph J. H. Enthoven, *Accountancy and Economic Development Policy* (Amsterdam: North Holland Publishing Company, 1973), pp. 168-69.

26. Lee J. Seidler, *The Function of Accounting in Economic Development: Turkey As a Case Study* (New York: Frederick A. Praeger, 1967).

27. Mohamed A. Mirghani, "A Framework for a Linkage between Microaccounting and Macroaccounting for Purposes of Development Planning in Developing Countries," *The International Journal of Accounting, Education and Research*, 18, 1 (Fall 1982), pp. 57-68.

28. Gray et al., "Accounting Standards and Multinational Corporations," p. 122.

29. Gerhard G. Mueller, and Lauren M. Walker, "The Coming of Age" (July 1976).

30. Ibid., pp. 128-29.

31. Frederick D. S. Choi, "Multinational Challenges for Managerial Accountants," *Journal of Contemporary Business* (Autumn 1975), p. 10.

32. Joseph Cummings, and William L. Rogers, "Developments in International Accounting," *The CPA Journal* (May 1978), p. 12.

33. Gray et al., "Accounting Standards and Multinational Corporations," p. 130.

34. Vinod B. Bavisli, and Harold E. Wyman, *Who Audits the World: Trends in Worldwide Auditing Profession* (Stones, Conn. Center for Transnational Reporting, 1984).

35. A. J. Marshall, "Public Accounting and Multinationalism," *Chartered Accountant Magazine* (December 1974).

36. Ibid.

37. Ibid.

38. A.J.H. Enthoven, *An Evaluation of Accountancy Systems, Developments and Requirements in Asia* (New York: Ford Foundation, 1975). Used with permission.

39. The study shows that, of the 20 million jobs created in the U.S. in the last decade, 90 percent were in services—chiefly information services with high technological requirements.

40. "'Fair Trade' Supported in Export Services," *The Journal of Accountancy* (February 1984), p. 32.

41. Belverd E. Needles, Jr., "Implementing a Framework for the International Transfer of Accounting Technology," *International Journal of Accounting, Education and Research* (Fall 1976), pp. 45-62.

Bibliography

Becker, H. "Is There a Cosmopolitan Information Seeker?" *Journal of International Business Studies* (Spring 1976), pp. 77-90.

Benson, Sir Henry. "International Accounting: The Challenge of the Future," *The Journal of Accountancy* (November 1977), pp. 93-96.

Brennan, W. John, ed. *The Internationalization of the Accountancy Profession* (Toronto: CICA, 1979), pp. 63-64.

Brummet, R. Lee. "Internationalism and the Future of Accounting Education," *The International Journal of Accounting, Education and Research* (Fall 1975), pp. 161-66.

Chastney, John G. "On to International Accounting," *Accountancy* (July 1976), pp. 76-80.

Choi, Frederick D. S. "The Development of Nascent Capital Markets," *Management Accounting* (September 1975), pp. 18-20.

_____. "Financial Disclosure and Entry to the European Capital Market," *Journal of Accounting Research* (Autumn 1973), pp. 159-75.

_____. "Financial Disclosure in Relation to a Firm's Capital Costs," *Accounting and Business Research* (Autumn 1973), pp. 272-83.

_____. "Multinational Financing and Accounting Harmony," *Management Accounting* (March 1974), pp. 14-17.

Dufey, Carter. "Recent Developments in International Money and Capital Markets," *The International Journal of Accounting, Education and Research* (Spring 1972), pp. 77-90.

Enthoven, Adolf J. H. "The Unity of Accountancy in an International Context," *The International Journal of Accounting Education and Research* (Fall 1973), pp. 113-34.

Gray, S. J., J. C. Shaw, and B. McSweeney. "Accounting Standards and Multinational Corporations," *Journal of International Business Studies* (Spring/Summer 1981), pp. 121-36.

Keyserlingle, Alexander N. "International Public Accounting: An Underdeveloped Profession," *The International Journal of Accounting, Education and Research* (Fall 1975), pp. 15-22.

Maus, William J. "The Monetary Side of International Trade," *Management Accounting* (April 1974), pp. 13-17.

Mendelson, Morris. "The Euroland and Capital Market Integration," *Journal of Finance* (March 1972).

Mueller, Gerhard G. "Accounting for Multinationals," *Accountancy* (July 1975), pp. 68-75.

_____. "The Dimensions of the International Acounting Problem," *The Accounting Review* (January 1963), pp. 142-47.

_____. "Whys and Hows of International Accounting," *The Accounting Review* (April 1965), pp. 386-94.

Needles, Belverd E., Jr. "Implementing a Framework for the International Transfer of Accounting Technology," *International Journal of Accounting, Education and Research* (Fall 1976), pp. 45-62.

Nobes, Christopher. "Why International Accounting Is Important," *The Accountant* (September 8, 1977), pp. 277-78.

Parker, R. H. "Some International Aspects of Accounting," *Journal of Business Finance* (November 8, 1971), pp. 29-35.

Qureshi, Mahmoud. "Pragmatic and Academic Bases of International Accounting," *Management International Review* 2 (1979), pp. 61-68.

Savoie, Leonard M. "Financial and Accounting Aspects in International Business," *The International Journal of Accounting Education and Research* (Fall 1973),

Schoenfeld, Hanns-Martin W. "International Accounting: Development, Issues, and Future Directions," *Journal of International Business Studies* (Fall 1981), pp. 83-100.

Weinstein, Arnold K., Louis Corsini, and Ronald Pawliczek. "The Big Eight in Europe," *The International Journal of Accounting, Education and Research* (Spring 1978).

Weirich, Thomas R., Clarence G. Avery, and Henry R. Anderson. "International Accounting: Varying Definitions," *The International Journal of Accounting, Education and Research* (Fall 1971), pp. 79-87.

Wu, Frederick H., and Donald W. Hackett. "The Internationalization of U. S. Public Accounting Firms: An Empirical Study," *The International Journal of Accounting, Education and Research* (Spring 1977), pp. 81-92.

2.

DETERMINANTS OF NATIONAL DIFFERENCES IN INTERNATIONAL ACCOUNTING

That accounting objectives, standards, policies, and techniques differ among various countries is an established and proven fact in international accounting. A recent survey of the financial statements and explanatory notes appearing in the 1980 annual reports issued by the U.S. and non-U.S. companies in our sample reveals again a diversity in financial accounting principles and techniques.[1] These differences are shown in Exhibit 2.1. Major differences appear to revolve around such issues as consolidation and accounting for goodwill, deferred taxes, long-term leases, discretionary reserves, inflation, and foreign exchange translation gains and losses. Given these differences, the comparative accounting literature includes various attempts to classify the accounting patterns in the world of accounting in different historical "zones of accounting influence," examples of which are provided by DaCosta, Bourgeois, and Lawson[2] and depicted in Exhibit 2.2; Frank[3] and depicted in Exhibit 2.3; and Nair and Frank[4] and depicted in Exhibits 2.4-2.7.

A general explanation for the various zones of accounting influence is that the accounting objectives, standards, policies, and techniques result from environmental factors in each country; if these environmental factors differ significantly between countries, it would be expected that the major accounting concepts and practices in use in various countries would also differ. It is generally accepted in international accounting that accounting objectives, standards, policies, and techniques reflect the particular environment of the standards-setting body. Various attempts have been made to identify the environmental conditions likely to affect the determination of national accounting principles. Two major comments may be made about these studies. First, it is implicitly assumed that cultural, social, and economic factors may explain the differences in accounting principles and techniques among the various countries. Second, various important environmental factors which may affect business behavior in general and accounting development in particular have not been included in these studies. This chapter intends to fill the void first by presenting the most important determinants of national differences in international accounting and second by presenting an international accounting contingency framework to explain these differences. These determinants and main elements of the framework include cultural relativism, linguistic relativism, political and civil relativism, economic and demographic relativism, and legal and tax relativism.

Cultural Relativism

Cultural relativism refers to the need to judge any behavior in terms of its own cultural contract, and not from another cultural context. Applied to accounting, cultural relativism rests on the fundamental assumption that accounting concepts in any given country are as unique as any other cultural traits. Thus the study of cultural issues, cross-cultural research, and their impact on accounting research is fundamental to an understanding of the determinants of national differences in international accounting.

CONCEPT OF CULTURE

No consensus exists on the definition of culture. After reviewing more than 150 years' uses of the concept, Kroeber and Kluckhorn proposed the following definition.

Culture consists of patterns, explicit and implicit, of and for behavior acquired and transmitted by symbols, constituting the distinctive achievements of human groups, including their embodiments in artifacts; the essential core of culture consists of traditional (i.e., historically derived and selected) ideas and especially their attached values; cultural systems may on the one hand be considered as products of action, on the other as conditioning elements of further action.[3]

The distinctive achievements constituting culture include both physical objects (or physical culture), which are man-made, and subjective objects (or subjective culture), which are the subjective response to what is man-made. This last point was made by Triandis, who elaborates on the concept:

Subjective culture refers to variables that are attributes of the cognitive structures of groups of people. The analysis of subjective culture refers to variables extracted from consistencies in their responses and results in a kind of "map" drawn by a scientist which outlines the subjective culture of a particular group. In short, when we observe consistent response to classes of stimuli that have some quality in common, we assume that some "mediators" ((attitudes, norms, values, etc. . . .) are responsible for their consistencies. It is the cognitive structures which "mediate" between stimuli and responses in different cultural settings that we wish to study.[6]

EXHIBIT 2.1 SYNTHESIS OF ACCOUNTING DIFFERENCES

Accounting principles	U.S.	Canada	Brazil	Mexico	U.K.	West Germany	France	Belgium	Netherlands
1 **Marketable securities recorded at the lower of cost or market?**	Yes	Yes	Yes (A)	Yes	Yes	Yes	Yes	Yes	Yes
2 Provision for uncollectible accounts made?	Yes	Yes	Yes	Yes	Yes	Yes	No	No	Yes
3 **Inventory costed using Fifo?**	Mixed	Mixed	No (F)	Mixed	Yes	Yes	Mixed	Mixed	Mixed
4 Manufacturing overhead allocated to year-end inventory?	Yes	NF	Yes	Yes	Yes	Yes	NF	Yes	Yes
5 **Inventory valued at the lower of cost or market?**	Yes	Yes	Mixed	Mixed	Yes	Yes	Yes	Yes	Yes
6 Accounting for long-term investments: less than 20% ownership—cost method?	Yes	Yes	Yes	Yes	Yes	Yes	Yes*	Yes	No (K)
7 **Accounting for long-term investments: 21-50% ownership—equity method?**	Yes	Yes	Yes	Yes	Yes	No (B)	Yes*	No (B)	Yes
8 Accounting for long-term investments: more than 50% ownership—full consolidation?	Yes	Yes	Yes	Yes	Yes	Yes	Yes*	Yes	Yes
9 **Both domestic and foreign subsidiaries consolidated?**	Yes	Yes	Yes	Yes	Yes	No**	Yes	Yes	Yes
10 Acquisitions accounted for under the pooling-of-interest method?	Yes	No (C)	NF	NF	No (C)	No (C)	No (C)	No (C)	No (C)
11 **Intangible assets: goodwill amortized?**	Yes	Yes	NF	Yes	No**	No	Yes	Yes	Mixed
12 Intangible assets: other than goodwill amortized?	Yes	Yes	Yes	Yes	No**	Yes	Yes	Yes	Yes
13 **Long-term debt includes maturities longer than one year?**	Yes	Yes	Yes	Yes	Yes	No (D)	Yes	Yes	Yes
14 Discount-premium on long-term debt amortized?	Yes	Yes	NF	Yes	No	No	No	No**	NF
15 **Deferred taxes recorded when accounting income isn't equal to taxable income?**	Yes	Yes	Yes	Yes	Yes	Yes	Yes	No**	Yes
16 Financial leases (long-term) capitalized?	Yes	Yes	No	Yes	No	No	No	No**	No
17 **Company pension fund contribution provided regularly?**	Yes	Yes	Yes	Yes	Yes	Yes	Yes	Yes	Yes
18 Total pension fund assets and liabilities excluded from company's financial statement?	Yes	Yes	Yes	Yes	Yes	No	Yes	Yes	Yes
19 **Research and development expensed?**	Yes	Yes	Yes	Yes	Yes	Yes	Yes	No**	Yes
20 Treasury stock deducted from owners' equity?	Yes	Yes	No**	NF	NF	No	Yes	NF	Mixed
21 **Gains or losses on treasury stock taken to owners' equity?**	Yes	Yes	No**	NF	NF	No	Yes	NF	Mixed
22 No general purpose (purely discretionary) reserves allowed?	Yes	Yes	No	Yes	Yes	No	No	No	No
23 **Dismissal indemnities accounted for on a pay-as-you-go-basis?**	Yes	Yes	No**	Yes	Yes	Yes	Yes	NF	NF
24 Minority interest excluded from consolidated income?	Yes	Yes	Yes	NF	Yes	No	Yes	Yes	Yes
25 **Minority interest excluded from consolidated owners' equity?**	Yes	Yes	Yes	NF	Yes	No	Yes	Yes	Yes
26 Are intercompany sales-profits eliminated on consolidation?	Yes	Yes	Yes	Yes	Yes	Yes	Yes	Yes	Yes
27 **Basic financial statements reflect a historical cost valuation (no price level adjustment)?**	Yes	Yes	No	No	No	Yes	No	No	No**
28 Supplementary inflation-adjusted financial statements provided?	Yes	No**	No	No	Yes	No	No	No	No**
29 **Straight-line depreciation adhered to?**	Yes	Yes	Yes	Yes	Yes	Mixed	Mixed	Mixed	Yes
30 No excess depreciation permitted?	Yes	Yes	No	No	No	Yes	No	No	Yes
31 **Temporal method of foreign currency translation employed?**	Yes	Yes	N/A	Mixed	No (E)	No (E)	No (E)	Mixed	No (E)
32 Currency translation gains or losses reflected in current income?	Yes	Yes	N/A	Mixed	No	Mixed	Mixed	Mixed	No (J)

Key: Yes—Predominant practice. Yes*—Minor modifications, but still predominant practice. No**—Minority practice. No—Accounting principle in question not adhered to. NF—Not found. N/A—Not applicable. Mixed—Alternative practices followed with no majority.

Notes: A—Adjusted for monetary correction. B—Cost method is used. C—Purchase method is used. D—Long-term debt includes maturities longer than four years. E—Current rate method of foreign currency translation. F—Weighted average is used. G—Cost or equity. H—Translation gains and losses are deferred. I—Market is used. J—Owners' equity. K—Equity.

													South Korea	South Africa
Switzerland	*Ireland*	*Austria*	*Sweden*	*Denmark*	*Finland*	*Norway*	*Italy*	*Spain*	*Japan*	*Australia*	*Malaysia*	*India*		
Yes	Yes	Yes	Yes	No (I)	Yes	Yes	Yes	Yes	Yes	Yes	Yes	Yes	Yes	Yes
Yes	Yes	Yes	Yes	Yes	Yes	Yes	Yes	No**	Yes	Yes	Yes	No	Yes	No**
Yes	Yes	Mixed	Yes	Yes	Yes	Yes	Mixed	Yes	Mixed	Yes	Mixed	Mixed	Mixed	Mixed
No	Yes	Yes	Yes	Yes	Yes	Yes	Yes	Yes	NF	Yes	No	No	Yes	Yes
Yes	Yes	Yes	Yes	Yes	Yes (B)	Yes	Yes	Yes	Yes	Yes	Yes	Yes	Yes	Yes
Yes	Yes	Yes	Yes	NF	No**	Yes	Yes	Yes	Yes	Yes	Yes	Yes	Yes	Yes
No (B)	Yes	No (B)	No (B)	NF	No**	No (B)	No (B)	No (B)	No (B)	No (G)	Yes	No (B)	No (B)	No (G)
Yes	Yes	Yes	Yes	Yes	No**	Yes	No**	Yes	Yes	Yes	Yes	No (B)	No	Yes
Yes	Yes	Yes	Yes	Yes	No**	Yes	No**	Yes	Yes	Yes	Yes	No	N/A	Yes
NF	No (C)	NF	No (C)	No (C)	No (C)	No (C)	No (C)	NF	NF	No (C)	No (C)	NF	No (C)	No (C)
No**	No**	NF	Yes	Yes	No**	No**	No**	No	Yes	Yes	No	NF	Yes	No**
No**	NF	NF	Yes	NF	Yes	NF	Yes	Yes	Yes	Yes	Yes	NF	Yes	Yes
Yes	Yes	Yes	Yes	Yes	Yes	Yes	Yes	Yes	Yes	Yes	Yes	Yes	Yes	Yes
NF	No	NF	No	Yes	NF	No	Yes	Yes	Yes	Yes	Yes	Yes	Yes	Yes
No	Yes	No	No	Yes	No	No	No	No	Yes	Yes	Yes	No	No	Yes
No	No	No	No	No	No	No	No	No	No	No	No	No	No	No
Yes	Yes	Yes	Yes	Yes	Yes	Yes	Yes	Yes	Yes	Yes	Yes	Yes	Yes	Yes
Yes	Yes	Yes	Yes	Yes	Yes	Yes	Yes	Yes	Yes	Yes	Yes	Yes	Yes	Yes
Yes	Yes	Yes	Yes	Yes	NF	Yes	No**	No	Yes	Yes	No**	Yes	No	Yes
NF	NF	No	NF	Yes	NF	NF	Mixed	Yes	Yes	NF	NF	NF	Yes	NF
NF	NF	No	NF	Yes	NF	NF	Mixed	Yes	No**	NF	NF	NF	Yes	NF
No	Yes	Yes	No	No	No	No	No	No	No	Yes	No	No	Yes	Yes
NF	Yes	Yes	Yes	Yes	Yes	Yes	Yes	Yes	Yes	Yes	Yes	Yes	No	Yes
Yes	Yes	NF	Yes	Yes	Yes	Yes	No	NF	Yes	Yes	Yes	NF	NF	Yes
Yes	Yes	NF	Yes	Yes	Yes	Yes	No	NF	Yes	Yes	Yes	NF	NF	Yes
Yes	Yes	NF	Yes	Yes	Yes	Yes	No**	Yes	Yes	Yes	Yes	NF	Yes	Yes
No	No	No	No	No	No	No	No	No	Yes	Yes	No	No	No	No
No**	Yes	No	No	No	No**	No**	No	No	No	No**	No	No	No	No
Yes	Yes	Mixed	Yes	Yes	Yes	Yes	Yes	Mixed	Mixed	Yes	Yes	No	No	Yes
No	No	Yes	No	No	No	No	No	No	Yes	No	No	No	No	No
No (E)	No (E)	NF	No	No	No	No	NF	No	No	Mixed	N/A	No	No	No
No (H)	No	NF	Mixed	No	Mixed	Mixed	NF	No	Mixed	Mixed	N/A	No	Yes	No

SOURCE: Frederick D. S. Choi and Vinod B. Bavishi, "International Accounting Standards: Issues Needing Attention," *Journal of Accountancy* (March 1983), pp. 66-67. Reprinted with permission.

EXHIBIT 2.2 DACOSTA-BOURGEOIS-LAWSON ACCOUNTING GROUPS

GROUP I	GROUP II	UNCLASSIFIABLE
Japan	United Kingdom	Netherlands
Philippines	Eire	Canada
Mexico	Rhodesia	
Argentina	Singapore	
West Germany	South Africa	
Chile	Australia	
Bolivia	Jamaica	
Panama	Kenya	
Italy	New Zealand	
Peru	Fiji	
Venezuela		
Colombia		
Paraguay		
United States		
Pakistan		
Spain		
Switzerland		
Brazil		
France		
Uruguay		
Sweden		
India		
Ethiopia		
Belgium		
Trinidad		
Bahamas		

SOURCE: R. C. DaCosta, J. C. Bourgeois, and W. M. Lawson, "Linkages in the International Business Community: Accounting Evidence," *International Journal of Accounting Education and Research* (Spring 1978), p. 79. Reprinted with permission.

EXHIBIT 2.3 FRANK ACCOUNTING GROUPS

GROUP I	GROUP II	GROUP III	GROUP IV
Australia	Argentina	Belgium	Canada
Bahamas	Bolivia	Colombia	West Germany
Ethiopia	Brazil	France	Japan
Eire	Chile	Italy	Mexico
Fiji	India	Spain	Netherlands
Jamaica	Pakistan	Sweden	Panama
Kenya	Paraguay	Switzerland	Philippines
New Zealand	Peru	Venezuela	United States
Rhodesia	Uruguay		
Singapore			
South Africa			
Trinidad & Tobago			
United Kingdom			

SOURCE: Werner G. Frank, "An Empirical Analysis of International Accounting Principles," *Journal of Accounting Research*, Autumn 1979, p. 596. Reprinted with permission.

EXHIBIT 2.4 NAIR-FRANK 1973 MEASUREMENT GROUPS

GROUP I	GROUP II	GROUP III	GROUP IV
Australia	Argentina	Belgium	Canada
Bahamas	Bolivia	Colombia	Japan
Ethiopia	Brazil	France	
Eire		West Germany	Mexico
	Chile	Italy	Panama
Fiji	Columbia	Spain	Philippines
Jamaica	Ethiopia	Sweden	United States
Kenya	India	Switzerland	
Netherlands	Paraguay	Venezuela	
New Zealand	Peru		
Rhodesia	Uruguay		
Singapore			
South Africa			
Trinidad & Tobago			
United Kingdom			

SOURCE: R. D. Nair and Werner G. Frank, "The Impact of the Disclosure and Measurement Practices on International Accounting Classifications," *The Accounting Review* (July 1980), p. 429. Reprinted with permission.

EXHIBIT 2.5 NAIR-FRANK 1973 DISCLOSURE GROUPS

I	II	III	IV	V	VI	VII
Australia	Bolivia	Belgium	Canada	Argentina	Sweden	Switzer-
Bahamas	West Ger-	Brazil	Mexico	Chile		land
Fiji	many	Colombia	Netherlands	Ethiopia		
Jamaica	India	France	Panama	Uruguay		
Kenya	Japan	Italy	Philippines			
New Zealand	Pakistan	Paraguay	United			
Eire	Peru	Spain	States			
Rhodesia		Venezuela				
Singapore						
South Africa						
Trinidad						
United Kingdom						

SOURCE: Nair and Frank, "The Impact of the Disclosure and Measurement Practices," p. 431. Reprinted with permission.

EXHIBIT 2.6 NAIR-FRANK 1973 MEASUREMENT GROUPS

GROUP I	GROUP II	GROUP III	GROUP IV	GROUP V
Australia	Argentina	Belgium	Bermuda	Chile
Bahamas	Bolivia	Denmark	Canada	
Fiji	Brazil	France	Japan	
Iran	Columbia	West Germany	Mexico	
Jamaica	Ethiopia	Norway	Philippines	
Malaysia	Greece	Sweden	United States	
Netherlands	India	Switzerland	Venezuela	
New Zealand	Italy	Zaire		
Nicaragua	Pakistan			
Erie	Panama			
Rhodesia	Paraguay			
Singapore	Peru			
South Africa	Spain			
Trinidad	Uruguay			
United Kingdom				

SOURCE: Nair and Frank, "The Impact of the Disclosure and Measurement Practices," p. 433. Reprinted with permission.

EXHIBIT 2.7 NAIR-FRANK 1973 DISCLOSURE GROUPS

I	II	III	IV	V	VI	VII
Belgium	Australia	Bahamas	Bermuda	Argentina	Denmark	Italy
Bolivia	Ethiopia	West Ger-	Canada	India	Norway	Switzer-
Brazil	Fiji	many	Jamaica	Iran	Sweden	land
Chile	Kenya	Japan	Netherlands	Pakistan		
Colombia	Malaysia	Mexico	Eire	Peru		
France	New Zea-	Panama	Rhodesia			
Greece	land	Philippines	United			
Paraguay	Nigeria	United	Kingdom			
Spain	Singapore	States				
Uruguay	South Africa	Venezuela				
Zaire	Trinidad					

SOURCE: Nair and Frank, "The Impact of the Disclosure and Measurement Practices," p. 436. Reprinted with permission.

Subjective culture refers then to the cognitive structures used by individuals in their information processing in a particular world setting. Understanding how these cognitive structures affect the information processing of individuals from different cultures is the subject of cross-cultural research.

CROSS-CULTURAL RESEARCH

The basic objective of cross-cultural research is to test the generalisability of psychological laws in order to understand whatever cultural differences are observed. Berry elaborates on the concept:

Cross-cultural psychology seeks to comprehend the systematic covariation between cultural and behavioral variables. Included within the term *cultural* are ecological and societal variables, and within the term *behavioral* are inferred variables. Thus the purpose is to understand how two systems, at the levels of group and individual analyses, relate to each other. Ideally, of course, more than covariation is sought; under some conditions *causal* relations may be inferred as well.[7]

Central to cross-cultural psychology is the idea that cultures differ and humans in different cultures develop different degrees of cognitive complexity. As a result, cultures may be differentiated along the degree of cultural complexity. One way to measure this degree of complexity was accomplished by Murdock and Provost when they used the following 10 scales to rate societies:

1. *Writing and records*: a high score when there is an indigenous system of writing; a zero score when there are no records of such a system

2. *Fixity of residence*: differentiating between permanent residence (high longevity) and nomadic existence

3. *Agriculture*: focusing on the importance of agriculture to the culture's food supply

4. *Urbanism*: focusing on the size of settlements

5. *Technical specialization*: focusing on the number of different crafts and skills

6. *Land transport*: focusing on automotive versus human means of transport

7. *Money*: focusing on an indigenous currency versus barter

8. *Population density*

9. *Level of political integration*

10. *Degree of social stratification.*[8]

While societies were found to differ along the variable of cultural complexity, the question remains to test the generality of psychological laws. One approach was attempting to generalize theories originating in western cultures, showing a distinctly ethnocentric bias. Another approach was more interested in attempting to account for cross-cultural differences and similarities. The second approach has generated various findings on cross-cultural differences of interest to international accounting.

CROSS-CULTURAL DIFFERENCES

Lonner identifies four consistent bases for making comparisons across cultures within a universalistic framework:

Biologically, we are all of the same species; *socially*, the species is governed by generalized functional prerequisites; and *ecologically*, the species must adapt to a limited range of geographic and environmental conditions (ecosystems). These three bases likely converge in various patterns to form a finite number of culture types. Once this is done the behavior of individuals within the culture can be compared along a fourth baseline, the *psychological*, which would assume an interspecies commonality of processes.[9]

While acknowledging that a finite number of culture types may be differentiated on the basis of the first three bases, this section emphasizes the cross-cultural differences arising from the psychological base. In effect, culture does play a role in the psychological makeup of individuals. This is illustrated in the area of cultural differences in motivation to work, values and orientations to work, job satisfaction, managerial needs satisfaction, management goals, attitudes toward compensation, motivations, norms and attitudes, effects of values on organizational efficiency and work habits, management and supervision, managerial styles, the meaning of authoritarianism, the concept of participation, the distribution of control in organizations, and perception and cognition.[10] The cultural differences found in each of these areas may have an impact on the acceptance and conduct of accounting in various cultures. Accounting researchers interested in the cultural relativism may find in this list of areas and others interesting research questions which may lead to a better understanding and conduct of international accounting. Before engaging in cross-cultural research, they should be warned of a debate with both serious theoretical and methodological implications which centers on the contrast between "emic" and "etic" orientations in cross-cultural research. The emic orientation is that cultures can be understood only in their own terms. It assumes that cultural traits cannot be compared. In contrast, the etic orientation is that cultures can be understood if one uses a universal perspective and thinks panculturally. In brief, accounting researchers may have to avoid using the emic concepts of one culture to explain characteristics of another. Various solutions to the etic-emic issue have been proposed by Davidson et al.[11] and Berry.[12]

ACCOUNTING RESEARCH OF RELEVANCE TO CULTURAL RELATIVISM

One anthropological study relevant to cultural relativism in accounting explores the degree to which accounting systems influence perceptions of opportunities by comparing the local view of business possibilities derived from the native system of accounts in Cuanago, a Tarascan village in Mexico, with more formal accounting methods.[13] In this study, Acheson found that while the native accounting system, a crude cash flow-based system, does not permanently block responsiveness to opportunities where they exist; it confuses, however, the view of opportunities, leading to many poor business decisions, and hence plays a critical role in influencing further business decisions.

Accounting research relevant to cultural relativism in accounting is in its infancy and has not yet reached a high level of theoretical and methodological rigor. Various accounting issues have been examined. First, the issue of whether the same accounting information may be perceived differently by different cultural groups was examined by Chevalier using French Canadians and English Canadians.[14] Perceptions were found not to differ with regard to the importance of conventional published financial information, which had been expected to differ with the French Canadians placing more importance on additional and nonconventional information such as data on human resources, earnings forecasts, and management philosophy.

Chevalier's subjects were essentially Canadian students from the Francophone and Anglophone sections of Canada. Other groups examined, however, include investors and financial analysts from various cultural settings. Chang and Most investigated the uses of financial statements by individual investors, institutional investors, and financial analysts from three countries—the United States, the United Kingdom, and New Zealand—all three of which have large capital markets and well-organized stock exchanges which tend to function in a similar manner.[15] The results showed a strong belief in the importance of corporate annual reports as a source of information for investment decisions and a stronger belief that the most important parts of the corporate annual report for this purpose were those pertaining to the financial data. The study also examined the composition of the three financial user groups and found the institutional investors and financial analysts comprised homogeneous groups while the individual investors were a diverse group.

Because the decisions of most investors in any country are greatly influenced by the opinions held by financial analysts, Belkaoui et al. examined the differential needs of financial analysts in Canada, the United States, and Europe.[16] Any differences in perception were hypothesized to be primarily due to the differences in the European and American methods of investing. The European approach has been more debt-oriented, with analysis concentrated on the balance sheet. In brief, the method requires the preparation of three reports: profit and loss account, financing table, and balance sheet. These reports are presented in vertical form highlighting a set of totals and subtotals deemed to be of interest to the financial analysts. The reports offer a convenient means of achieving European comparisons of European accounting information. In contrast, the American method is oriented more toward equity investment, the income statement, and corporate earning power. As expected, the study demonstrates that there is a high degree of consensus by North American financial analysts on the informational items of value to equity investors but there is quite a divergence of opinion when the North Americans are compared with their European counterparts. This difference was attributed to institutional differences in the accounting and investment environments of Europe and North America, as well as to differences in outlook, with Europeans more interested in balance sheet information while North Americans tended to be more concerned about the income statement.

In addition, two hypotheses on the issue of the impact of the cultural environment and individual value orientations on financial disclosures were developed by Jaggi.[17]

Hypothesis 1: The reliability of disclosures in financial statements is likely to differ with differences in the value orientations of managers from different countries. Accounting principles and procedures will vary to respond to the needs of individual countries and to ensure reliability in a given set of cultural environments.

Hypothesis 2: As a result of the prevailing cultural environment in the developing countries, the reliability of financial disclosure is not expected to be high unless legal disclosure standards are set.[18]

Without empirically testing these two important hypotheses, Jaggi goes on to suggest that the procedures for developing accounting principles should be modified to suit the cultural environments.

Linguistic Relativism

THE NATURE OF LINGUISTIC RELATIVISM

Because language mediates our world view, it plays a central role in the development of cognition and perception. Individuals, as they learn a language, acquire not only a store of lexical and grammatical characteristics but also a linguistic mode of cognition and perception.

Anthropologists have always emphasized the role of language in their studies of culture. Sapir's investigations of the linguistic symbolism of a given culture view language both as an instrument and as communication of thought. A given language predisposes its users to a distinct belief. The idea that language is an active determinant of thought forms the basis of the principle of linguistic relativism. According to the Whorfian version of the principle, ways of speaking are reflections of the metaphysics of a culture. These metaphysics constitute the unstated promises which shape the perception and thought of those who participate in that culture and predispose them to a given method of perception.

Fishman's work is an attempt to systematize this set of assumptions, known as the "Sapir-Whorf Hypothesis."[19] Fishman's fourfold analytical scheme (Exhibit 2.8) distinguishes between two levels of language (lexical and grammatical) and two types of behavior (linguistic and nonlinguistic). The lexical level refers to all words which compose a language. Languages differ in the number of terms they possess to describe phenomena. The grammatical level refers to the manner in which the structural units of a language are organized. Linguistic behavior refers to choices among words. Nonlinguistic behavior refers to choices among objects. These distinctions are clarified in the following explanation of the cells in Exhibit 2.8.

1. Cell 1 posits a relationship between the lexical properties of a language and the speaker's linguistic behavior. Linguistic behavior, the choice of words for describing a particular phenomenon, differs from one language to another.

2. Cell 2 posits a relationship between the lexical properties of a language and the nonlinguistic behavior of the users of that language. This refers to the idea that speakers of a language that makes certain lexical distinctions will be able to perform tasks better and more rapidly than speakers of languages that do not make such distinctions.[20]

3. Cell 3 posits a relationship between grammatical characteristics and linguistic behavior. This refers to the idea that speakers of a language with specific grammatical rules acquire a world view quite different from that of speakers of languages that do not employ such rules.[21]

4. Cell 4 posits a relationship between grammatical characteristics and nonlinguistic behavior. This refers to the idea that speakers of a language with certain grammatical characteristics will perform nonlinguistic tasks differently from speakers of languages that do not have these characteristics.[22]

EXHIBIT 2.8 FISHMAN'S SCHEMATIC SYSTEMATIZATION OF THE SAPIR-WHORF HYPOTHESIS

Data of Language Characteristics	Data of Cognitive Behavior	
	Language Data ("Cultural Themes")	Nonlinguistic Data
Lexical or "semantic" Characteristics	Level 1	Level 2
Grammatical Characteristics	Level 3	Level 4

ACCOUNTING AS A LANGUAGE

Accounting has been often called the language of business. It is one means of communicating information about a business. What makes accounting a language? To answer this question, let us look at the possible parallels existing between accounting and language. There are two components to a language, namely, symbols and grammatical rules. Thus, the recognition of accounting as a language rests on the identification of these two components as the two levels of language. It may be argued: (1) The symbols or lexical characteristics of any language are its identifiable "meaningful" units or words. These symbols are linguistic objects used to identify particular concepts. Symbolic representations do exist in accounting. For example, McDonald identifies numerals and words, and debits and credits, as the only symbols respectively accepted and unique to the accounting discipline.[23] (2) The grammatical rules of any language refer to its existing syntactical arrangements. Such rules exist in accounting. They refer to the general set of procedures used for the creation of all financial data for the business. Jain establishes the following parallel between grammatical rules and accounting rules:

The CPA (the expert in accounting) certifies the correctness of the application of the accounting rules as does an accomplished speaker of a language for the grammatical correctness of the sentence. Accounting rules formalize the structure of accounting in the same way as grammar formalizes the inherent structure of a natural language.[24]

Given the existence of the components identified—symbols and grammatical rules—accounting may be defined a priori as a language. Consequently, according to the Sapir-Whorf Hypothesis, both its lexical and grammatical characteristics will shape the world view held by users of accounting: that accounting influences thinking.

ACCOUNTING RESEARCH OF RELEVANCE TO LINGUISTIC RELATIVISM

Belkaoui argues that accounting is a language and, according to the Sapir-Whorf hypothesis, its lexical characteristics and grammatical rules will affect the linguistic and nonlinguistic behavior of users.[25] Four propositions derived from the linguistic-relativism paradigm were introduced to conceptually integrate research findings on the impact of accounting information on the user's behavior. These are:

1. The users that make certain lexical distinctions in accounting are enabled to talk and/or solve problems that cannot be solved by users that do not.
2. The users that make certain lexical distinctions in accounting are enabled to perform (nonlinguistic) tasks more rapidly or more completely than those users that do not.
3. The users that possess the accounting (grammatical) rules are predisposed to different managerial styles or emphasis than those that do not.
4. The accounting techniques may tend to facilitate or render more difficult various (nonlinguistic) managerial behaviors on the part of users.[26]

These propositions were empirically tested and verified in two studies pointing to the importance of linguistic considerations in the use of accounting information and in international standards setting.[27]

Within the linguistic-relativism school, the role of language is emphasized as a mediator and shaper of the environment. This would imply that accounting language may predispose "users" to a given method of perception and behavior. Furthermore, the affiliation of users with different professional organizations or communities with their distinct interaction networks may create different accounting language repertoires. Accountants from different professional groups may use different linguistic codes because of different organizational constraints and objectives. At worst, a confounding lack of communication may emerge. Using a "sociolinguistic thesis," Belkaoui empirically shows that various affiliations in accounting create different linguistic repertoires or codes for intra- or intergroup communications.[28] The sociolinguistic construct was used to justify the possible lack of consensus on the meaning of the accounting concepts. As a result, specific issues identified which need further research include (1) the presence and the nature of the "institutional language" within each accounting professional group, (2) the presence of a profession-linked linguistic code in the accounting field composed of a "formal language" and a "public language," and (3) a test of whether the public language is understood by users of public data (for example, financial analysts) and whether the formal language is understood by users of formal data (for example, students).[29]

Other studies investigated the linguistic effects of accounting data and techniques without relying on the linguistic-relativism thesis or the sociolinguistic thesis. Instead, they focus on the difference on the intra- and intergroup communication of accounting data or techniques among the users and producers of accounting data. To prove these differences they relied on various techniques including a semantic differential technique,[30] the antecedent-consequent technique,[33] multidimensional scaling techniques,[32] and the Cloze procedure.[33]

Political and Civil Relativism

Political and civil relativism refers to the need to judge any behavior in terms of its own political and civil context and not from any other context. Applied to accounting, political and civil relativism rests on the fundamental assumption that accounting concepts in any given country rest on the political and civil context of that country.

POLITICAL AND CIVIL INDICATORS

Although political rights and civil liberties are abstract concepts without natural units of measurement, various attempts are made by sociologists and political scientists to rank countries in terms of the degree of political rights and civil liberties that they offer and to construct appropriate indexes.[34] These indexes are intended to measure political democracy rather than some particular aspects connected with the real level of freedom. A good definition of political democracy is: "a political system which supplies regular constitutional opportunities for changing the governing officials, and a social mechanism which permits the largest possible part of the population to influence major decisions by choosing among contenders for political office."[35]

With the same emphasis on freedom to connote political democracy, Dr. Raymond Gastil, director of Freedom House, has constructed and published since 1973 indexes of political rights and civil liberties.[36] Gastil defines civil liberties as the rights of the individual against the state and the rights to freedom of expression and a fair trial. He then develops a civil-liberties index composed of seven levels:

- Level 1 for states where the rule of the law is not mistaken and which include various news media and possible and evident freedom of expression.
- Level 2 for states where civil liberties are less effective than in states ranked (1) because of violence and ignorance or lack of sufficient or free media of expression, created either by special laws that restrain rights or authoritarian civil tradition or by the influence of religion.
- Level 3 for states where civil liberties exist but are hampered by serious imperfections such as repeated reliance on martial law, jailing for sedition, or suppression of publications.
- Level 4 for states where there are broad areas of freedom and free publication along with broad areas of repression.
- Level 5 for states where civil liberties are often denied and complaints of violation are ignored because of weak government-controlled or frequently censored media.
- Level 6 for states where the rights of the state and the government are given legal priority over the rights of groups and individuals, although a few individuals are allowed considerable freedom.
- Level 7 for states where citizens have no rights vis-à-vis the state and where internal criticism is only known to the outside world because of the government's condemnation of it.[37]

Gastil defines political rights as the right to play a part in determining the laws and the government of the community. He then develops a political-rights index composed of seven levels:

- Level 1 for states where almost everybody has both rights and opportunities to participate in the political process, to compete for political office, and to join freely formed political parties.
- Level 2 for states where the effectiveness of the open electoral processes is reduced by factors such as extreme poverty, a feudal social structure, violence, or agreements to limit opposition.
- Level 3 for states where the effectiveness of the open electoral processes is reduced by nondemocratic procedures, such as coups.
- Level 4 for states where there is either a constitutional block to the full democratic significance of elections or the power distribution is not affected by the elections.
- Level 5 for states where either elections are closely controlled or limited or the results have very little significance.
- Level 6 for states where either there is no operational electoral system or opposition candidates are not allowed to compete.
- Level 7 for states which may be characterized as tyrannies with little legitimacy either in a national tradition or a modern ideology.[38]

The political-structure index suggested by Gastil ranks countries as (1) for multiple-party systems, (2) for dominant-party systems, (3) for one-party systems, (4) for military dictatorships, and (5) for traditional monarchies. The higher the level of political freedom, the lower the rank of a country.

Another useful and sophisticated classification of political systems is provided by Edward Shils.[39] He presents five different types of political systems: political democracy, tutelary democracy, modernizing oligarchy, totalitarian oligarchy, and traditional oligarchy. The distinguishing characteristics of these different types of political systems are summarized in Exhibit 2.9. Shils' classifications, like Gastil's classifications, result from an association among the complex and dynamic factors which form political systems.

POLITICAL AND CIVIL RELATIVISM IN ACCOUNTING

The political freedom of a country is important to the development of accounting in general and reporting and disclosure in particular. When people cannot choose the members of a government or influence government policies, they are less likely to be able to create an accounting profession based on the principle of full and fair disclosure. Political repression involves a general loss of freedom which may hinder to some extent the development of such a profession of accounting. There is likely to be a negative relationship between accounting freedom to report or to disclose and political freedom. The degree of political freedom in a given country is generally assumed to depend on the degree of political rights, the civil liberties, and the type of political system. Violations of political rights and civil liberties associated with various forms of political structure restrict political freedom in general and may act as a hindrance to the tradition of full and fair disclosure. While these propositions may be viewed as intuitive and hardly self-evident, one of the objectives of international accounting research would be to empirically test their validity.

Economic and Demographic Relativism

Economic and demographic relativism refers to the need to judge any behavior in terms of its own economic and demographic context. Applied to accounting, economic and demographic relativism rests on the fundamental assumption that accounting concepts in any given country rest on the economic and demographic context of that country.

TYPES OF ECONOMIC SYSTEMS

Gastil makes a distinction among the following four economic systems: capitalist, capitalist-statist, capitalist-socialist, and socialist. Capitalist states are those states that "rely on the operation of the market and on

EXHIBIT 2.9 A CLASSIFICATION OF POLITICAL SYSTEMS

Systems Properties	POLITICAL DEMOCRACY	TUTELARY DEMOCRACY	MODERNIZING OLIGARCHY	TOTALITARIAN OLIGARCHY	TRADITIONAL OLIGARCHY
Legislature	Representative, elected. "Parliament" is center of partisan decision-making.	"Rubber-stamp" parliament or none at all. But there is the appearance of representation.	Is advisory or serves in ratification mode.	Acclamatory & ceremonial functions.	Not needed, function performed as needed by executive ("monarch").
Executive	Shares power with the legislature. Actions are modified by party ideology, opposition & electorate.	Personality-oriented. Greater preponderance of the executive.	Centralized powers, strong control by power elite.	Strong, limited sharing of power, and autocratic.	Supreme power, divine right to rule.
Judiciary	Constitutional and independent.	Constitutional & generally independent but subject to corruption by the executive.	Controlled by the executive.	No independent judiciary. Supports & enforces executive decrees.	No independent judiciary, instead there is usually a hand-picked retinue of advisers.
Power Elite	Exist in diverse fields, e.g., industrial, political, professional. Are not coalesced.	Coalesced, stable, competent & politically active.	Well-organized, cohesive, closed military-civilian clique.	Party-oriented. Stringent restrictions on membership. Loyalty, coherence and discipline.	Dynastic, coherent, extremely conservative, fraternal, lineal & reactionary.
Opposition	Multi-partied structure. Coherent, articulate & responsible.	Benign, but "visible" opposition. Restrictions on press.	Suppressed in political form. Contrary views may surface in press, but they are censored.	Suppressed in all phases of society. "States of crises" are used to induce cooperation & stifle opposition.	Opposition is not tolerated. Moral as well as legal pressures are used to secure cooperation & stifle opposition.
Mechanism of Authority	Politically-detached civil service; independent judiciary; police, secret-service & military.	Competent and detached civil service. Police/military are used to discourage dissatisfaction.	Bureaucratic, entrenched civil service. Police/military are used to discourage dissatisfaction.	Party supervision over members, non-members, & government leaders & bureaucracy.	Lineal relationships, fraternal, rudimentary and incapable of dealing with social change.
Public Opinion	Self-confident and self-sustaining public institutions: press, universities, special interests.	Feeble public institutions: press, universities and special interest groups. A-political or compliant.	Feeble, suppressed interest groups, or used to support government.	Loyal intelligensia substitutes for civic & special interest groups. Extensive propaganda.	Absent. Confined to advisory function of the monarchal retinue.
Civil Order	Homeostatic. Self-disciplining. Common belief in political order.	National rather than political loyalties, supine & antitumultous.	Strong dependence on police & military. Absence of civility & public opinion forums.	Unity behind party. Party policies are enforced. Prospect of party membership provides incentive to social order as does the possibility of dis-membership.	Maintained by encouraging ignorance, illiteracy, and poverty. None or poor education for the masses. Rural subsistence.

SOURCE: "Report of the Committee on International Accounting Operations and Education, 1975-1976," The Accounting Review, Supplement to Vol. 52 (1977), p. 94. Reprinted with permission.

45

private provision for individual welfare."[40] Capitalist-statist states are those states that have "very large government productive enterprises, either because of an elitist development philosophy or a major dependence on a key resource such as oil."[41] Capitalist-socialist states are those states that "provide social services on a large scale through governmental or other nonprofit institutions, with the result that private control over property is sacrificed to egalitarian purposes."[42] Finally, socialist states are those states that "strive programmatically to place an entire national economy under direct or indirect control."[43]

ECONOMIC AND DEMOGRAPHIC RELATIVISM ACCOUNTING

The economic environment is important to the development of accounting in general and reporting and disclosure in particular. Economic development constitutes economic growth and various structural and social changes. One such change is the need for financial and reporting devices to measure the performance of each sector of the economy in terms of efficiency and productivity. Lowe notes that, from a historical point of view, accounting development is an evolutionary process dependent upon and interwoven with economic development.[44] Similarly, Elliot et al. state that the "social function of accounting, to measure and communicate economic data, cannot be considered simply as the effect of economic development, but should be considered a valuable tool for promoting the development process."[45] However, economic development may be achieved by various forms of economic policies depending on the type of economic system chosen, the level and growth rate of income, the extent of government intervention and expenditures, and the level of exports. Each of these factors may imply a specific impact on accounting development which needs to be investigated. The following discusses possible impacts.

All things being equal, a capitalist system may be more favorable to accounting development than other economic systems may be. In a capitalist economic system the survival of private enterprises depends on not only the production of goods and services but adequate information to various interest groups from investors and creditors to the capital market in general. Qureshi draws attention to the relationship among financial accounting, capital formation, and economic development as follows.

The choice is based on the idea that financial reporting, capital markets and capital formation interrelate. Capital formation, a strategic formation in economic development, is closely dependent upon financial mechanisms and institutions. Studies by such eminent monetarists as Kuznets, Goldsmith and McKinnon provide a convincing evidence of the parallel between the development of capital market and economic growth. The development and proper functioning of capital markets in turn is ultimately related to the availability of financial information which is provided by the accounting function of reporting.[46]

The higher the level and growth of income, the higher the political and economic freedom and the better the adequacy of reporting and disclosure. This may apply to any economic system, since economic growth in some socialist countries was often followed by an effort to liberalize the regimes.

The higher the level of government expenditures, the higher the level of government intervention and the better the adequacy of reporting and disclosure. Government intervention is dictated by a need to provide economic security to all classes of society and takes the form of industry and opportunity creation. Because government is assumed to be account-able to the people, its intervention may be followed by an effort to report and disclose and may be favorable to the development of an accounting program and a reporting and disclosure tradition. This is applicable to any economic system. In the U.S., a capitalist economic system, governmental agencies all employ accounting as a tool to accomplish the regulatory mandate placed upon them by Congress.[47] Socialist countries have developed unique accounting systems and procedures in the furtherance of their own centrally managed economies. Finally, the role of governments in developing accounting principles and providing legal authority is assumed to result in a higher reliability of financial disclosures in the developing countries. As stated by Jaggi, the "interference of governments may be essential to ensure higher reliability (which is vital for the expansion of industries in these countries), for creating public confidence and trust corporations, for creating an atmosphere where industrialization can progress, and for making economic and social decisions."[48]

The higher the level of exports and imports, the higher the need for better reporting and disclosure. Free-trade policies in general and export promotion in particular increase cooperation with other countries, the flows of human and physical capital, and the need for comparable reporting and adequate disclosure. For example, Kraayenhof argues that the international flow of capital for financing and investment participation creates more interest in the soundness of financial presentations and the intelligibility of the explanatory notes.

The number of people in a given country may also be important to the development of accounting. The larger the population, the higher the number of people to be interested in the accounting profession, and the greater the need for a well-developed accounting profession and the need for full and fair disclosure. India, Egypt, and Pakistan, for example, which are usually classified as developing countries, have developed accounting professions and also well-developed systems for accounting education.[49]

Legal and Tax Relativism

Legal and tax relativism refers to the need to judge any behavior in terms of its own legal and tax context. Applied to accounting, legal and tax relativism rests on the fundamental assumption that accounting concepts in any given country rest on the legal and tax context of that country.

THE LEGAL ENVIRONMENT AND ACCOUNTING

Countries have different national legal systems. The national law of each country defines most directly and most frequently the conduct of business and hence the practice of accounting. Given that there are differences in the national legal systems of different countries implies by definition that there will be differences in their accounting systems. The differences in national legal systems include, for example, the difference between the Roman, or "civil," law and the common law. While civil law is a *legislative* system, common law is basically nonlegislative. Other general differences include the size and sophistication of government and the proliferation of regulatory agencies and commissions. In the U.S. examples of regulatory agencies include the Food and Drug Administration, the Federal Trade Commission, and the U.S. Tariff Commission; British examples include the Board of Trade and the Prices and Incomes Board. Other differences are in the nature of legal entities, welfare policy, property-ownership restrictions, monopoly policy, and applicability of national laws.

All these legal differences imply different accounting practices internationally since accounting may be used to implement some of these laws. In fact, the legalistic approach to accounting is predominant in most countries, with some countries completely relying on it and others permitting other approaches. In the countries relying completely on the legalistic approach, accounting becomes effectively a process of compliance with the laws of the country. Similarly, official audits are performed by statutory auditors to certify that financial statements have been prepared in accordance with the law.

THE TAX ENVIRONMENT AND ACCOUNTING

Countries have different national tax systems. The tax system of each country defines most directly and most frequently the conduct of business and hence the practice of accounting. Seidler makes this point:

Worldwide tax collections constitute the greatest source of demand for accounting services. The tax on income, both on the individual and business enterprise level, is the largest source of revenue for governments of countries with literate populations. Clearly, the collection of tax revenues, the life-blood of government, outweighs the niceties of accounting theory. Income tax evasion is frequently grounded in distortions of records or in absence of records. Therefore, tax collecting governments initially become involved in the bookkeeping and accounting procedures followed by individuals and companies, to provide some assurance of collecting taxes.[50]

Given the differences in the tax systems and collection methods of different countries, it is fair to expect differences in their accounting systems. The differences in the tax systems involve differences in personal income taxes, corporation income taxes, and indirect taxes. An example of a clear difference between the European Economic Community and the U.S. is in the area of the value-added tax. It was first introduced in France as the *taxe sur la valeur ajoutée*. A tax on value added (VAT) is levied at each stage of the production process, but only on the value added at that specific stage. It is basically passed on until it is eventually paid for by the final consumer. Another example of a clear difference in taxation is presented by the tax incentives used in poorer nations to attract new capital and new businesses.

Conclusion: A Contingency Framework for International Accounting

The development of accounting may be viewed in terms of the development of an accounting profession and systems of accounting education, or in terms of the development of adequate reporting and disclosure traditions. Both features of accounting development are positively related. One may expect and safely assume that a well-developed accounting profession and system of accounting education in a given country will lead to a tradition or effort of providing adequate reporting and disclosure. Therefore, in attempting to identify the elements influencing the development of accounting, the reporting and disclosure system may be considered as representative of the state of accounting development in a given country.[51] If we also view the reporting and disclosure system as an expression of social behavior (based on a well-accepted thesis in sociology that social structure determines social behavior), it may be advanced that the reporting and disclosure system is a direct product of its environment.[52] Based on the contents of this chapter and as shown in Exhibit 2.10, the system of reporting and disclosure of a given country may then be represented as being influenced by the cultural, linguistics, political and civil rights economic and demographic characteristics, and legal and tax environment in a given country. In other words, based on cultural relativism, linguistic relativism, political and civil relativism, economic and demographic relativism, and legal and tax relativism, the accounting concepts and the reporting and disclosures system in any given country rest on the varying aspects of that country.

Notes

1. Frederick D. S. Choi, and Vinod B. Bavishi, "International Accounting Standards: Issues Needing Attention," *Journal of Accountancy* (March 1983), pp. 62-68.

2. R. C. Da Costa, J. C. Bourgeois, and W. M. Lawson, "Linkages in the *International Journal of Accounting* (Spring 1978), pp. 92-102.

EXHIBIT 2.10 MODEL OF ACCOUNTING DEVELOPMENT

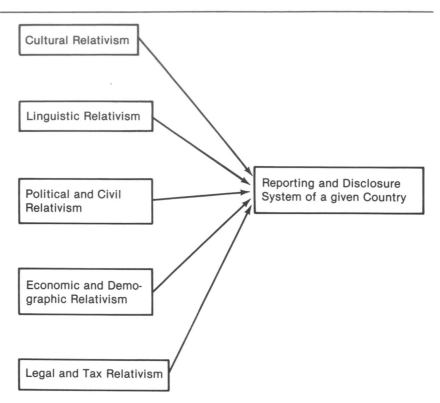

3. Werner G. Frank, "An Empirical Analysis of International Accounting Principles," *Journal of Accounting Research* (Autumn 1979), pp. 593-605.

4. R. D. Nair and Werner G. Frank, "The Impact of Disclosure and Measurement Practices on International Accounting Classifications," *The Accounting Review* (July 1980), pp. 462-50.

5. A. L. Kroeber and C. Kluckhorn, *Culture: A Critical Review of Concepts and Definitions* (Cambridge, Mass.: Peabody Museum, 1952), p. 181.

6. H. Triandis, *the Analysis of Subjective Culture* (New York: Wiley, 1972), p. 3.

7. J. Berry, "An Ecological Approach to Cross-Cultural Psychology," *Netherlands Journal of Psychology* 30 (1973), pp. 379-92.

8. G. P. Murdock, and C. Provost, "Measurement of Cultural Complexity." *Ethnology* 12 (1973), pp. 379-92.

9. W. J. Lonner, "The Search for Psychological Universals," in *Handbook of Cross-Cultural Psychology*, ed. Harry C. Triandis and W. W. Lambert (Boston: Allyn and Bacon, Inc., 1980), p. 146.

10. A survey of findings for each of these areas is available in G. V. Barrett and R. M. Bass, "Cross-Cultural Issues in Industrial and Organizational Psychology,"

Handbook of Industrial and Organizational Psychology ed. M. Dunnette (Chicago: Rand McNally, 1976), pp. 1639-86.

11. A. J. Davidson, J. Jaccard, J. Triandis, J. Morales, and R. Diaz-Guerrero, "Cross-Cultural Model Testing: Toward a Solution of the Emic-Etic Dilemma," *International Journal of Psychology* 11 (1976), pp. 1-13.

12. J. Berry, "An Ecological Approach to Cross-Cultural Psychology," *Netherlands Journal of Psychology* 30 (1975), pp. 51-84.

13. J. Acheson, "Accounting Concepts and Economic Opportunities in a Tarascan Village: Emic and Etic Views," *Human Organization* (Spring 1979), pp. 83-91.

14. G. Chevalier, "Should Accounting Practices Be Universal?" *CA Magazine* (July 1977), pp. 47-50.

15. L. S. Chang and K. S. Most, "An International Comparison of Investor Uses of Financial Statements," *The International Journal of Accounting Education and Research* (Fall 1981), pp. 43-60.

16. A. Belkaoui, A. Kahl, and J. Peyrard, "Information Needs of Financial Analysts: An International Comparison," *The International Journal of Accounting Education and Research* (Fall 1977), pp. 19-27.

17. B. Jaggi, "The Impact of the Cultural Environment on Financial Disclosure," *The International Journal of Accounting Education and Research* (January 1975), pp. 75-84.

18. Ibid., p. 83.

19. J. A. Fishman, "A Systematization of the Whorfian Hypothesis," *Behavioral Science* (1960), pp. 323-35.

20. E. H. Lenneberg, "Cognitions in Ethnolinguistics," *Language* (1973), pp. 463-71; R. W. Brown, and E. H. Lenneberg, "A Study in Language and Cognition," *Journal of Abnormal and Social Psychology* (1954), pp. 454-62; D. L. Lantz, "Language and Cognition Revisited," *Journal of Abnormal and Social Psychology* (1953), pp. 454-62.

21. H. Hoijer, "Cultural Implications of the Navaho Linguistic Categories," *Language* (1951), pp. 111-20; S. Erwin-Tripp, "Sociolinguistics," in *Advances in Experimental Social Psychology* ed. L. Berkovitz (New York: Academic Press, 1969), pp. 91-165.

22. J. B. Carol and J. B. Casagrande, "The Functions of Language Classification in Behavior," in *Readings in Social Psychology*, 3d ed., ed. E. E. Macoby, T. M. Newcomb, and E. L. Hartley (New York: Holt, Rinehart, and Winston, 1958).

23. D. McDonald, *Comparative Accounting Theory* (Reading, Mass.: Addison-Wesley Publishing Company, 1972).

24. T. H. Jain, "Alternative Methods of Accounting and Decision Making: A Psycholinguistic Analysis," *The Accounting Review* (January 1973), p. 101.

25. A. Belkaoui, "Linguistic Relativity in Accounting," *Accounting, Organizations and Society* (October 1978), pp. 97-104.

26. Ibid., p. 103.

27. A. Belkaoui, "The Impact of Socio Economic Accounting Statements on the Investment Decision: An Empirical Study," *Accounting, Organizations and Society* (September 1980), pp. 263-84. Janice Belkaoui and A. Belkaoui, "Bilingualism and the Perception of Professional Concepts," *Journal of Psycholinguistic Research* 12, 2 (1983), pp. 111-27.

28. A. Belkaoui, "The Interprofessional Linguistic Communication of Accounting

Concepts: An Experiment in Sociolinguistics," *Journal of Accounting Research* (Autumn 1980), pp. 362-74.

29. Ibid., p. 371.

30. A. Haried, "The Semantic Dimensions of Financial Statements," *Journal of Accounting Research* (Autumn 1979), pp. 376-91; B. Oliver, "The Semantic Differential: A Device for Measuring the Interprofessional Communication of Selected Accounting Concepts," *Journal of Accounting Research* (Autumn 1974), pp. 299-316; E. Flamholtz and E. Cook, "Connotive Meaning and Its Role in Accounting Change: A Field Study," *Accounting, Organizations and Society* (October 1978), pp. 115-39.

31. A. Haried, "Measurement of Meaning in Financial Reports," *Journal of Accounting Research* (Spring 1973), pp. 117-45.

32. R. Libby, "Bankers' and Auditors' Perceptions of the Message Communicated by the Audit Report," *Journal of Accounting Research* (Spring 1973), pp. 99-122.

33. A. Adelberg, "A Methodology for Measuring the Understandability of Financial Report Messages," *Journal of Accounting Research* (Autumn 1979), pp. 565-92.

34. K. A. Bollen, "Issues in the Comparative Measurement of Political Democracy," *American Sociological Review* (June 1980), pp. 290-370; G. Lenski, "The Need for Reader-Access to the Measures of Variables Used in Quantitative Cross-National Studies," *American Sociological Review* (1976), pp. 741-51.

35. S. Lipset, *Political Man* (Garden City, N.Y.: Anchor Books, 1963).

36. R. D. Gastil, *Freedom in the World-Political Rights and Civil Liberties 1978* (New York: Freedom House, 1978).

37. Ibid., p. 19.

38. Ibid.

39. Edward Shils, *Political Development in the New States* (The Hague: Morton & Co., 1966).

40. Gastil, R. D., *Freedom in the World-Political Rights and Civil Liberties 1978*, Op. cit., p. 46.

41. Ibid.

42. Ibid., p. 47.

43. Ibid.

44. Howard D. Lowe, "Accounting Aid for Developing Countries," *The Accounting Review* (April 1967), p. 360.

45. Edward L. Elliot, Jose Larrea, and Juan M. Rivera, "Accounting Aid to Developing Countries: Some Additional Considerations," *The Accounting Review* (October 1968), p. 764.

46. Mahmoud A. Qureshi, "Economic Development, Social Justice and Financial Reporting: Pakistan's Experience with Private Enterprise," *Management International Review* 6 (1975), p. 71.

47. James P. Bedingfield, *Accounting and Federal Regulation* (Reston, Va.: Reston Publishing Company, 1982).

48. B. L. Jaggi, "The Impact of the Cultural Environment on Financial Disclosures," *The International Journal of Accounting Education and Research* (Spring 1975), p. 84.

49. American Accounting Association, Committee on International Accounting,

Operations and Education, 1976-1978, *Accounting Education and the Third World* (Sarasota, Fla., August 1978), p. 6.

50. Lee J. Seidler, "Technical Issues in International Accounting," in *Multinational Accounting: A Research Framework for the Eighties,* ed. F.D.S. Choi (Ann Arbor, Mich.: UMI Research Press, 1981), p. 41.

51. Mueller takes the other viewpoint and calls for a study of the factors or variables which produce an efficient and effective public accounting profession and the possible construction of a "professional accounting development index." G. G. Mueller, "The State of the Art of Academic Research in Multinational Accounting," *Canadian Chartered Accountant Magazine* (February 1977).

52. This thesis derives from the sociological paradigm of structural functionalism, which holds that structural determinants, i.e., social facts, constitute the primary methodological foci for explanation of social behavior. T. Parsons, *The System of Modern Societies* (Englewood Cliffs, N.J.: Prentice Hall, 1971).

Bibliography

Acheson, J. "Accounting Concepts and Economic Opportunities in a Tarascan Village: Emic and Etic Views," *Human Organization* (Spring 1972), pp. 83-91.

Barrett, G. V., and R. M. Bass. "Cross-Cultural Issues in Industrial and Organization Psychology." In *Handbook of Industrial and Organizational Psychology,* ed. M. Dunnette (Chicago: Rand McNally, 1976), pp. 1639-86.

Belkaoui, A. "Economic, Political and Civil Indicators and Reporting and Disclosure Adequacy," *Journal of Accounting and Public Policy* 2 (1983).

——. "The Interprofessional Linguistic Communication of Accounting Concepts: An Experiment in Sociolinguistics," *Journal of Accounting Research* (Autumn 1980), pp. 362-74.

Belkaoui, A., A. Kahl, and J. Peyrard. "Information Needs of Financial Analysts: An International Comparison," *The International Journal of Accounting Education and Research* (Fall 1977), pp. 19-27.

Belkaoui, Janice, and A. Belkaoui. "Bilingualism and the Perception of Professional Concepts," *Journal of Psycholinguistic Research* 12, 2 (1983), pp. 111-27.

Chang, L. S., and K. S. Most. "An International Comparison of Investor Uses of Financial Statements," *The International Journal of Accounting Education and Research* (Fall 1981), pp. 43-60.

Chevalier, G. "Should Accounting Practices Be Universal?" *CA Magazine* (July 1977), pp. 47-50.

Davidson, A. J., J. Jaccard, J. Triandis, J. Morales, and R. Diaz-Guerrero. "Cross-Cultural Model Testing: Toward a Solution of the Emic-Etic Dilemma," *International Journal of Psychology* 11 (1976), pp. 1-13.

Frank, Werner G. "An Empirical Analysis of International Accounting Principles," *Journal of Accounting Research* (Autumn 1979), pp. 593-605.

Jaggi, B. "The Impact of the Cultural Environment on Financial Disclosure," *The International Journal of Accounting Education and Research* (January 1975), pp. 75-84.

Jain, T. H. "Alternative Methods of Accounting and Decision Making: A Psycholinguistic Analysis," *The Accounting Review* (January 1973), pp. 95-104.

Lowe, Howard D. "Accounting Aid for Developing Countries," *The Accounting Review* (April 1967), pp. 350-61.

Seidler, L. J. "International Accounting—The Ultimate Theory Course," *The Accounting Review* (October 1967), pp. 775-81.

Triandis, Harry C., ed. *Handbook of Cross-Cultural Psychology* (Boston: Allyn and Bacon, Inc., 1980).

Parkinson, J., "Economic, Political and Civil Indicators and Reporting and Disclosure Adequacy", *Journal of Accounting and Public Policy* 2 (1984).

APPENDIX 2.1

RELIGIOUS RELATIVISM IN ACCOUNTING

Religion may also affect the conduct of accounting in a given country by restricting or forbidding certain kinds of transactions. The most evident case in today's world is the impact of the moslem religion on the ways Islamic Banks can conduct their affairs. As an example the following table shows the similarities and differences among Islamic and business banks.

SIMILARITIES AND DIFFERENCES AMONG ISLAMIC AND BUSINESS BANKS

Banking Activities	Business Bank	Islamic Banks
1. Sources of funds		
a. Capital and R.E.	yes	yes (common stocks)
b. Deposits	yes (fixed interest)	yes (participating in profit)
c. Loans and Bonds	yes	No
2. Use of funds		
a. Investments in loans	yes (main field)	No
b. Investments in securities	yes, all kinds	yes (excluding fixed interest)
c. Participation in business projects	yes, sometimes	yes, (main field of invest.)
d. Investments in foreign currencies	yes	yes
3. Services rendered		
a. Current Accounts	yes	yes
b. Letters of Credit	yes	yes (100% down payment)
c. Letters of Guarantees	yes	yes
d. Purchasing for others on a preagreed profit basis.	No	yes
e. Bills discounted	yes	No
f. Collection of checks	yes	yes
g. Collection & payment of bills for their clients	yes	yes
h. Investment in securities for their clients	yes	yes (common stock only)
i. Leasing lock boxes	yes	yes
j. Underwriting in securities	yes	yes (common stock only)
k. Forward rate and Arbitrage	yes	No
l. Credit Cards	yes	yes (no over-draft)
m. Carrying out feasibility studies	yes (for bank projects)	yes (for bank projects and for clients)
n. Other services	yes	yes (provided no interest)
4. Cost of Capital		
a. Expected return on Cap.	yes (Stockholders)	yes (Stockholders)
b. Interest on loans & Bn.	yes (Creditors)	No
c. Interest on deposits	yes (Depositors)	No
d. Expected return to dep.	No	yes

SOURCE: Nidal R. Sabri and M. Hisham Jabr. "Accounting Information System for Banks Without (Islamic Bank)." A research paper was presented at International Accounting Seminar held by Center for International Education and Research in Accounting, University of Illinois at Urbana Champaign, March 1984.

3.

TOWARD AN INTERNATIONAL ACCOUNTING THEORY

The Need for an International Accounting Theory

There are basic differences in the accounting systems of countries throughout the world. Most of these differences result from a felt need for an identifiable national accounting system reflecting local information demands. The growing internationalization of trade and local economies is creating great pressure for more uniformity in the accounting and auditing system and frequent calls for accounting harmonization. As a result, various national and international bodies have started a drive toward reconciling some of the accounting differences. At the same time the standards-setting bodies of various countries have begun developing a conceptual framework as a guide to developing accounting techniques. All these efforts are contributing in a piecemeal approach to the emergence of various elements of an international accounting theory. This chapter elaborates on these developments and pinpoints the need for a coordination of all these efforts toward the emergence of an international accounting theory.

Harmonization of Accounting Standards

THE NATURE OF HARMONIZATION OF ACCOUNTING STANDARDS

Harmonization has for a long time been erroneously associated with complete standardization. It is in effect different from standardization. Wilson presents this useful distinction:

The term harmonization as opposed to standardization implies a reconciliation of different points of view. This is a more practical and conciliatory approach than standardization, particularly when standardization means that the procedures of one country should be adopted by all others. Harmonization becomes a matter of better communication, of information in a form that can be interpreted and understood internationally.[1]

This definition of harmonization is more realistic and has a greater likelihood of being accepted than standardization. Every host country has its sets of rules, philosophies, and objectives at the national level aimed at protecting or controlling the national resources. This aspect of nationalism gives rise to particular rules and measures which ultimately affect a country's accounting system. Harmonization consists of recognizing these national idiosyncracies and attempting to reconcile them with other countries' objectives as a first step. The second step is to correct or eliminate some of these barriers in order to achieve an acceptable degree of harmonization.

MERITS OF HARMONIZATION

There are various advantages to harmonization. The most often cited favorable arguments include the following: First, for many countries, there are still no adequate codified standards of accounting and auditing. Internationally accepted standards not only would eliminate the set-up costs for those countries but would allow them to immediately be part of the mainstream of accepted international accounting standards. Some of this work is already being accomplished by the major accounting firms in their international practice. For example, Macrae states: "Each of these firms of course has only been able to set and enforce the standards for its own organization, but combined, they determine the standards followed in a substantial portion of international audit engagements."[2]

Second, the growing internationalization of the world's economies and the increasing interdependency of nations in terms of international trade and investment flows act as a major argument for some form of internationally accepted standards of accounting and auditing. Such internationalization will also facilitate international transactions, pricing, and resource allocation decisions and may render the international financial markets more efficient.

Third, the need for companies to raise outside capital given the insufficiency of retained earnings to finance projects and the availability of foreign loans has increased the need for accounting harmonization. In effect, supplies of capital, here and abroad, tend to rely on financial reports to make the best investment and loan decisions and tend to show preference for comparable reporting.

LIMITS TO HARMONIZATION

Current trends seem to indicate that there is little chance of ever achieving international harmonization. The following arguments are usually advanced to justify this pessimistic attitude: First, tax collections in all countries are one of the greatest sources of demand for accounting services. Because tax-collection systems vary internationally, it can be easily expected that it will lead to a diversity in the accounting principles and systems used internationally. As an emphasis Seidler states: "Since tax collection systems vary widely between countries, and since governments show little sign of desiring to harmonize tax systems (except in the collection of maximum amounts from multinational corporations), there is little reason to expect that this barrier to international accounting harmonization will disappear."[3]

Second, accounting policies are known to be fashioned sometimes to achieve either political or economic goals compatible with the economic or political system espoused by a given country. Since there is little hope of having a single political or economic system internationally, it can be expected that the differences in political and economic systems will continue to act as a barrier to international accounting harmonization.

Third, some of the obstacles to international harmonization are created by accountants themselves through national strict licensing requirements. An extreme example occurred in 1976, when the French profession required foreign accountants practicing in France to sit for an oral examination. As a result of the French experience, the EEC became involved with the qualifications of auditors. The first published version of the draft Eight Directive created several restraints on the ability of foreign accountants to practice in the EEC member countries. Consider the following paragraphs from the first version of the draft of the Eight Directive:

The partners, members, persons responsible for management, administration direction or supervision of such professional companies or associations who do not personally fulfill the Directive (i.e., non-EEC qualified accountants) shall exercise no influence over the statutory audits carried out under the auspices of such approved professional companies or associations.

The law shall, in particular, ensure:

—that the above mentioned persons may not participate in the appointment or removal of auditors and that they may not issue to the latter any instructions regarding the carrying out of audits; . . .

—that the confidentiality of audit reports produced by the auditors and all documents relating thereto are protected and that these are withheld from the knowledge of the above-mentioned persons.

Actors Involved in the Harmonization Drive

ACCOUNTANTS INTERNATIONAL STUDY GROUP (AISG)

The AISG was formed as a three-nation group to study accounting and auditing requirements and practices in the United States, the United

Kingdom, and Canada. Its terms of reference were as follows: "To institute comparative studies as to accounting thought and practice in participating countries, to make reports from time to time, which, subject to the prior approval of the sponsoring Institutes, would be issued to members of those Institutes." Before being disbanded, the AISG issued 18 studies, which are listed in Exhibit 3.1. Most of the studies were comparative and were not binding on the sponsoring institutes.

EXHIBIT 3.1 STUDIES PRODUCED BY THE AISG

---

1. Accounting and Auditing Approaches to Inventories in Three Nations—1968
2. The Independent Auditor's Reporting Standards in Three Nations—1969
3. Using the Work and Report of Another Auditor—1970
4. Accounting for Corporate Income Taxes—1971
5. Reporting by Diversified Companies—1972
6. Consolidated Financial Statements—1972
7. The Funds Statement—1973
8. Materiality in Accounting—1974
9. Extraordinary Items, Prior Period Adjustments, and Changes in Accounting Principle—1974
10. Published Profit Forecasts—1975
11. International Financial Reporting—1976
12. Comparative Glossary of Accounting Terms in Canada, the United Kingdom and the United States—1975
13. Accounting for Goodwill—1975
14. Interim Financial Reporting—1975
15. Going Concern Problems—1976
16. Independence of Auditors—1977
17. Audit Committees—1976
18. Accounting for Pension Costs—1977
19. Related Party Transactions—1978
20. Revenue Recognition—1978

INTERNATIONAL FEDERATION OF ACCOUNTING COMMITTEE (IFAC)

Various international organizations preceded the creation of the IFAC. First, the International Congress of Accounts (ICA) was founded in 1904 with the general objective of increasing interaction and exchange of ideas between accountants of different countries. Second, in 1972 the ICA founded the International Coordination Committee for the Accounting Profession (ICCAP) with the objectives to conduct specific studies of professional accounting ethics, education and training and the structure of regional accounting organizations. Third, the ICCAP dissolved in 1976 to be reconstituted as the International Federation of Accounting Committee (IFAC). The goals of the IFAC are best expressed by the following 12-point program to guide its efforts:

1. Develop statements that would serve as guidelines for international auditing practices.

2. Establish a suggested minimum code of ethics to which it is hoped that member bodies would subscribe and which could be further refined as appropriate.

3. Determine the requirements and develop programs for the professional education and training of accountants.

4. Evaluate, develop, and report on financial management and other management accounting techniques and procedures.

5. Collect, analyze, research and disseminate information on the management of public accounting practices to assist practitioners in conducting their practices more effectively.

6. Undertake other studies of value to accountants such as, possibly, a study of the legal liability of auditors.

7. Foster closer relations with users of financial statements, including preparers, trade unions, financial institutions, industry, government, and others.

8. Maintain close relations with regional bodies and explore the potential for establishing other regional bodies as well as for assisting in their organization and development, as appropriate. Assign appropriate projects to existing regional bodies.

9. Establish regular communication among the members of IFAC and with other interested organizations through the medium of a newsletter.

10. Organize and promote the exchange of technical information, educational materials, and professional publications and other literature emanating from other bodies.

11. Organize and conduct an International Congress of Accountants approximately every five years.

12. Seek to expand the membership of the IFAC.[4]

As of 1984, IFAC's membership reached 85 professional accountancy bodies from 63 countries. Its governing bodies consist of (1) an assembly comprising one representative designated as such by each member of the IFAC and (2) a council comprising 15 representatives of member bodies from 15 countries. The agenda of the IFAC is set by the following seven standing committees: education, ethics, international auditing practices, international congresses, management accounting, planning, and regional organizations. As seen in Chapter 1, the International Auditing Practices Committee (IAPC) of the IFAC is the most active and most important.[5]

INTERNATIONAL ACCOUNTING STANDARDS COMMITTEE (IASC)

The IASC was founded in 1973 with the following objectives contained in its constitution:

a. to formulate and publish in the public interest accounting standards to be observed in the presentation of financial statements and to promote their worldwide acceptance and observance;

b. to work generally for the improvement and harmonization of regulations, accounting standards and procedures relating to the presentation of financial statements.[6]

This translates into a goal of developing a common international approach to standards setting in accounting aimed at a worldwide harmonization and improvement of accounting principles used in the preparation of financial statements for the benefit of the public.

The IASC has an operating structure composed of the IASC board, the consultative group, and various steering committees. Its procedure of exposure and comment is as follows:

a. After discussion, the IASC Board selects a topic that is felt to need an International Accounting Standards, and assigns it to a Steering Committee. All IASC member bodies are invited to submit material for consideration.

b. The Steering Committee, assisted by the IASC Secretariat, considers the issues involved and presents a point outline on the subject to the Board.

c. The Steering Committee receives the comments of the Board and prepares a preliminary draft on the proposed standard.

d. Following review by the Board, the draft is circulated to all member bodies for their comments.

e. The Steering Committee prepares a revised draft, which, after approval by at least two-thirds of the Board, is published as an Exposure Draft. Comments are invited from all interested parties.

f. At each stage in the consideration of drafts, member bodies refer for guidance to the appropriate accounting research committees in their own organizations.

g. At the end of an exposure period (usually six months) comments are submitted to IASC and are considered by the Steering Committee responsible for the project.

h. The Steering Committee then submits a revised draft to the Board for approval as an International Accounting Standard.

i. The issue of a Standard requires approval by at least three-quarters of the Board, after which the approved text of the Standard is sent to all member bodies for translation and publication.[7]

As of 1984 the following fiscal standards have been produced.

- IAS1, Disclosure of Accounting Policies, 1975
- IAS2, Valuation and Presentation of Inventories in the Context of the Historical Cost System, 1975
- IAS3, Consolidated Financial Statements, 1976
- IAS4, Depreciation Accounting, 1976
- IAS5, Information to Be Disclosed in Financial Statements, 1976
- IAS6, Accounting Responses to Changing Prices
- IAS7, Statement of Changes in Financial Position, 1977
- IAS8, Unusual and Prior Period Items and Changes in Accounting Policies, 1978
- IAS9, Accounting for Research and Development Activities, 1978
- IAS10, Contingencies and Events Occurring after the Balance Sheet Date, 1978
- IAS11, Accounting for Construction Contracts, 1979
- IAS12, Accounting for Income Taxes, 1979
- IAS13, Presentation of Current Assets and Current Liabilities, 1979
- IAS14, Preparing Financial Information by Segment, 1981
- IAS15, Information Reflecting the Effects of Changing Prices, 1981
- IAS16, Accounting for Property, Plant and Equipment, 1982
- IAS17, Accounting for Leases, 1982
- IAS18, Revenue Recognition, 1983
- IAS19, Accounting for Retirement Benefits in Financial Statements of Employers, 1983
- IAS20, Accounting for Government Grants and Disclosure of Government Assistance, 1983
- IAS21, Accounting for the Effects of Changes in Foreign Exchange Rates, 1983
- IAS22, Accounting for Business Combinations, 1983
- IAS23, Capitalization of Borrowing Costs, 1984
- IAS24, Disclosure of Related Party Transactions, 1984

The success of the IASC's efforts naturally rests on acceptance of the standards by member countries and recognition and support internationally. Noncompliance with international standards has been attributed to the following reasons by Sir Henry Benson, the founder of IASC:

Some countries take the view that they cannot require compliance locally until they are satisfied that the Standards are internationally acceptable. Some see local legislation as an obstacle to the introduction of international standards. Some accounting bodies do not have the power to discipline over their members, and cannot therefore impose compliance with either national or international standards. Some countries have not yet overcome stubborn local resistance from the business community.[8]

Besides these obstacles there is definite evidence that effort toward harmonization is not equally shared by all members of IASC. Douglas summarized the situation as follows:

Some accountancy bodies have declared to their members that international accounting standards are to be accorded the same status as domestic accounting standards. Each IAS is accompanied by an explanation of the relationship between the international standard and any domestic standard dealing with the same subject.

Other accountancy bodies have issued statements declaring support for the concept of international standards and strongly encouraging their members to accept them. Some of these bodies indicate the extent to which an international standard differs from the related domestic standard. They often offer to review, or encourage the relevant body to review, the basis of the domestic standard, with the objective of eliminating any differences.

There are some member countries, however, that have not yet presented any format statement of the status of IASs to the members of the accountancy profession.[9]

One good evidence, however, of increasing compliance and national support of IASC pronouncements is a letter written in November 1980 by member bodies in Canada to the 300 largest companies quoted on the Toronto Stock Exchange, urging them to include a reference such as: "The accompanying financial statements are prepared in accordance with accounting principles generally accepted in Canada and conform in all material respects to International Accounting Standards."[10] In fact, the IASC's success rests on the "best efforts of local professional organizations to ensure that published financial statements in their countries comply with the IASs in all material respects."[11]

A second good evidence has been provided by the International Finance Corporation (IFC), which is an investment institution established by its member governments to further economic development by encouraging the growth of productive private enterprise in developing member countries.[12] In effect, a recent publication of IFC "Financial Reporting Requirements (Manufacturing and Commercial Enterprises)" contains the following statement.

IFC recognizes that accounting policies vary from country to country. This could result in IFC receiving financial statements which are based on differing accounting policies. Hence, it is essential to include a summary of accounting policies applied as the first note to the financial statements as is adherence, in general, to generally accepted standards of reporting and disclosure. In deciding on accounting policies reference should be made, whenever applicable and practicable, to International Accounting Standards Issued by the International Accounting Standards Committee (IASC). The IASC formulates and publishes basic standards to be observed in the presentation of audited accounts and financial statements.

The International Accountancy Profession Agreement and the list of IASC members are shown in the Appendix at the end of the chapter.

THE UNITED NATIONS (UN)

The United Nations became interested in accounting and the need for improved corporate reporting when the Group of Eminent Persons appointed to study the impact of multinational corporations advocated the formulation of an international, comparable system of standardized accounting and reporting.[13] It also recommended the creation of a Group of Experts on International Standards of Accounting and Reporting. The group was created in 1976 with the following objectives.

a. To review the existing practice of reporting by transnational corporations and reporting requirements in different countries;

b. To identify gaps in information in existing corporate reporting and to examine the feasibility of various proposals for improved reporting;

c. To recommend a list of minimum items, together with their definitions, that should be included in reports by transnational corporations and their affiliates, taking into account the recommendations of various groups concerned with the subject matter.[14]

As a result the group issued a report which included a 34-page list of recommended items to be disclosed (1) by the "enterprise as a whole," that is, consolidated data, and (2) by individual member companies, including the parent company. Following issuance of the report an Intergovernmental Working Group of Experts on International Standards of Accounting and Reporting was formed with the objective of contributing to the harmonization of accounting standards. It does not function as a standards-setting body; its mandate is to review and discuss accounting and reporting standards. The group expects to publish a comprehensive report in 1985. The group will consider, among other issues, whether the UN should promulgate accounting standards.[15] Needless to say, this effort by the UN has created mixed international reaction. Most of the concerned institutions have expressed the feeling that accounting standards at the domestic or the international level are best set in the private sector. These same institutions are united in their support for the work of the IASC and national accountancy groups.

THE ORGANIZATION FOR ECONOMIC COOPERATION AND DEVELOPMENT (OECD)

The OECD is an organization whose members include 24 relatively industrialized noncommunist countries in Europe, Asia, North America, and Australia. A Declaration on International Investment and Multinational Enterprises was issued in 1976, including an annex titled "Guidelines for Multinational Enterprises," a section of which is subtitled "Disclosure of Information."[16] The major elements suggested to be disclosed are listed below:

Enterprises should publish within reasonable time limits, on a regular basis, but at least annually, financial statements and other pertinent information relating to the enterprise as a whole comprising in particular:

- the structure of the enterprise, showing the name and location of the parent company, its main affiliates, its percentage ownership, direct and indirect, in these affiliates, including shareholdings between them;
- the geographical areas (1) where operations are carried out and the principal activities carried on therein by the parent company and the main affiliates;
- the operating results and sales by geographical area and the sales in the major lines of business for the enterprise as a whole;
- significant new capital investment by geographical area and, as far as practicable, by major lines of business for the enterprise as a whole;
- a statement of the sources and uses of funds by the enterprise as a whole;
- the average number of employees in each geographic area;
- research and development expenditure for the enterprise as a whole;
- the policies followed in respect of intra-group pricing;
- the accounting policies, including those on consolidation, observed in compiling the published information.[17]

THE EUROPEAN ECONOMIC COMMUNITY (EEC)

The EEC has also been active in achieving regional harmonization of accounting principles through a series of directives which, within the treaty of Rome, are not as binding as regulations. The directive anticipates given results but the mode and means of implementation are left to the member countries. The EEC is in fact the first supranational body to have an important authority in the area of financial reporting and disclosure. Its influence is so pervasive that its directives are perceived to have important effects on non-EEC-based multinationals operating in the community. Particularly relevant to international accounting are the fourth, fifth, and seventh directives.

The Fourth Directive

The fourth directive, formally adopted in 1978, deals with the annual financial statements of public and private companies, other than banks and insurance companies.[18] Its purposes have been summarized as follows:

1. Coordinating national laws for the protection of members and third parties relating to the publication, presentation, and content of annual accounts and reports of limited-liability companies, and the accounting principles used in their preparation.
2. Establishing in the EEC minimum equivalent legal requirements for disclosure of financial information to the public by companies which are in competition with one another.
3. Establishing the principle that annual accounts should give a true and fair view of a company's assets and liabilities, and of its financial position and profit or loss.
4. Providing the fullest possible information about limited companies to shareholders and third parties (with some relief to smaller companies).[19]

The major aspects relevant to international accounting were Articles 1 and 2 on types of companies covered by the directive and the general reporting requirements; Articles 3-27 on the format of annual reports; Articles 28-39 on the valuation rules; Articles 44-50 on publication requirements; and Articles 51-52 on the procedural, statutory changes in national laws required for compliance.

The Fifth Directive

The proposed fifth directive, revised in 1984, deals with the structure, management, and external audits of limited-liability corporations. In the revised draft, the directive proposes to require a company that employs more than 1,000 workers in the EEC (or is part of a group of companies that employs more than 1,000 workers in the EEC) to allow the employees to participate in the company's decision-making structure. In addition, the proposal specifies certain rules concerning annual meetings of shareholders, the adoption of the company's annual financial statements, and the appointment, compensation, and duties of the company's auditors.

The Seventh Directive

The seventh directive, issued in June 1983, addresses the issue of consolidated financial statements and offers some guidelines for more standardization of accounting reporting. Companies in EEC member countries and non-EEC corporations with subsidiaries in a member country are required to file consolidated financial statements in that country. However, each of the 10 EEC countries has five years to pass legislation to implement the directive, and annual reports do not have to conform until 1990.

OTHER ACTORS

The preceding sections identify the most important actors involved in the harmonization drive. Various other national, regional, and international groups are emerging as active in the same drive. They include basically the following.

1. ASEAN Federation of Accountants (AFA)[20]
2. African Accounting Council (AAC)[21]
3. Union Européenne des Experts Comptables Economiques et Financiers (UEC)
4. Association Interamericana de Contabilidad (AIC)
5. Confederation of Asian and Pacific Accountants (CAPA)
6. Nordic Federation of Accountants (NFA)
7. Association of Accountancy Bodies in West Africa (ABWA)
8. American Accounting Association (AAA)
9. Canadian Association of Academic Accountants (CAAA)
10. European Accounting Association (EAA)
11. Japan Accounting Association (JAA)
12. Association of University Instructors in Accounting (AUIA)[22]
13. Financial Analysts Federations (FAF)
14. Financial Executives Institute (FEI)
15. Arab Society of Certified Accountants (ASCA)[23]

Given the proliferation of actors involved or willing to be involved in the harmonization drive, one would expect some interrelationships among these bodies and cross-representation in an attempt to excercise some influence in the international accounting arena. The results are best illustrated by Exhibits 3.2, 3.3, and 3.4. Exhibit 3.2 lists the countries most often represented in the international bodies ranked by incidence of international representation. Exhibit 3.3 examines the geographical distribution of the membership of the major international groups. Finally, Exhibit 3.4 examines the cross-representation among some major international accounting bodies. Only the future will tell whether this is a situation favorable or unfavorable to the harmonization drive.

Toward an International Conceptual Framework

NATURE OF AN INTERNATIONAL CONCEPTUAL FRAMEWORK

The credibility of international financial reporting has eroded and is subject to various criticisms. To correct the situation and provide a more rigorous way of setting standards and increasing financial statement users' understanding and confidence in financial reporting, an international

EXHIBIT 3.2 SELECTED REPRESENTATION OF INTERNATIONAL STANDARDS-SETTING BODIES BY INDIVIDUAL COUNTRY

Country	AAC	AFA	CAPA	EEC	UEC	AIC	IASC	IFAC	OECD	UN**	
Canada	-	-	X	-	-	X	X	X	X	X	**6 Group representation**
France	-	-	-	X	X	-	X	X	X	X	
Germany	-	-	-	X	X	-	X	X	X	X	
Italy	-	-	-	X	X	-	X	X	X	X	
Netherlands	-	-	-	X	X	-	X	X	X	X	
Great Britain	-	-	-	X	X	-	X	X	X	X	
United States	-	-	X	-	-	X	X	X	X	X	
Belgium	-	-	-	X	X	-	X	X	X	-	**5 Group representation**
Denmark	-	-	-	X	X	-	X	X	X	-	
Ireland	-	-	-	X	X	-	X	X	X	-	
Japan	-	-	X	-	-	-	X	X	X	X	
Luxembourg	-	-	-	X	X	-	X	X	X	-	
Norway	-	-	-	-	X	-	X	X	X	X	
Philippines	-	X	X	-	-	-	X	X	-	X	
Australia	-	-	X	-	-	-	X	X	X	-	**4 Group representation**
Brazil	-	-	-	-	-	X	X	X	-	X	
Finland	-	-	-	-	X	-	X	X	X	-	
Greece	-	-	-	-	X	-	X	X	X	-	
India	-	X	X	-	-	-	-	X	-	X	
Malaysia	-	X	X	-	-	-	X	X	-	-	
Mexico	-	-	-	-	-	X	X	X	-	X	
New Zealand	-	-	X	-	-	-	X	X	X	-	
Nigeria	X	-	-	-	-	-	X	X	-	X	
Panama	-	-	-	-	-	X	X	X	-	X	
Pakistan	-	-	X	-	-	-	X	X	-	X	
Portugal	-	-	-	-	X	-	X	X	X	-	
Singapore	-	X	X	-	-	-	X	X	-	-	
Spain	-	-	-	-	X	-	X	X	X	-	
Sweden	-	-	-	-	X	-	X	X	X	-	
Argentina	-	-	-	-	-	X	-	X	-	X	**3 Group representation**
Bangladesh	-	-	X	-	-	-	X	X	-	-	
Cyprus	-	-	-	-	-	-	X	X	-	X	
Dominican Republic	-	-	-	-	-	X	-	X	-	X	
Fiji	-	-	X	-	-	-	X	X	-	-	
Iceland	-	-	-	-	X	-	-	X	X	-	
Sri Lanka	-	-	X	-	-	-	X	X	-	-	
Thailand	-	X	X	-	-	-	-	X	-	-	
Representatives	1	5	14	9	16	7	32	37	21	19	
Total number of representations in body	23	5	18	9	18	21	42	53	23	30	

NOTE: Adapted from United Nations Report E/C.10/AC.3/7 of September 9, 1980. Second session of the Ad Hoc Intergovernmental Working Group on International Standards of Accounting and Reporting Commission on Transnational Corporations—UN Economic and Social Council.

*Member of the UN intergovernmental working group.

EXHIBIT 3.3 REPRESENTATION OF INTERNATIONAL STANDARDS-SETTING BODIES BY CONTINENT

Body	Africa	Asia	Middle East	Europe	North America	Latin America	Australia/ New Zealand	Total
AAC	23	--	--	--	--	--	--	23
AFA	--	5	--	--	--	--	--	5
CAPA	--	13	1	--	2	--	2	18
EEC	--	--	--	9	--	--	--	9
UEC	--	--	--	18	--	--	--	18
AIC	--	--	--	--	2	19	--	21
IASC	5	9	1	16	2	7	2	42
IFAC	4	11	3	18	2	13	2	53
OECD**	2	1	--	15	2	2	1	23
UN**	8	4	1	9	2	6	--	30

NOTE: Adapted from United Nations Report E/C.10/AC.3/7 of September 9, 1980. Second session of the Ad Hoc Intergovernmental Working Group on International Standards of Accounting and Reporting Commission on Transnational Corporations—UN Economic and Social Council.

*Member of the UN intergovernmental working group.

EXHIBIT 3.4 INTERREPRESENTATION AMONG MAJOR INTERNATIONAL STANDARDS-SETTING BODIES

Body	AAC	AFA	CAPA	EEC	UEC	AIC	IASC	IFAC	OECD	UN**
AAC	23	---	----	---	---	---	1	1	----	3
AFA	--	5	5	---	---	---	3	5	----	1
CAPA	--	5	18	---	---	2	13	16	5	5
EEC	--	---	----	9	9	---	9	9	9	5
UEC	--	---	----	9	18	---	16	16	17	5
AIC	--	---	2	---	---	21	5	11	2	7
IASC	1	3	13	9	16	5	42	39	20	17
IFAC	1	5	16	9	16	11	39	53	22	21
OECD**	--	---	5	9	17	2	20	22	23	8
UN**	3	1	5	5	5	7	17	21	8	30

NOTE: Adapted from United Nations Report E/C.10/AC.3/7 of September 9, 1980. Second session of the Ad Hoc Intergovernmental Working Group on International Standards of Accounting and Reporting Commission on Transnational Corporations—UN Economic and Social Council.

*Member of the UN intergovernmental working group.

conceptual framework may be needed. A good definition suitable to the international conceptual framework follows:

A conceptual framework is a *constitution*, a coherent system of interrelated objectives and fundamentals that can lead to consistent standards and that prescribes the nature, function, and limits of financial accounting and financial statements. The objectives identify the goals and the purposes of accounting. The fundamentals are the underlying concepts of accounting, concepts that guide the selection of events to be accounted for, the measurement of those events, and the means of summarizing and communicating them to interested parties. Concepts of that type are fundamental in the sense that other concepts flow from them and repeated reference to them will be necessary in establishing, interpreting, and applying accounting and reporting standards.[24]

A conceptual framework, therefore, is intended to act as a constitution for the international standards-setting process. It would guide in resolving disputes in the standards-setting process by narrowing the question to whether specific standards conform to the conceptual framework. In fact, five specific benefits that would result from any conceptual framework have been identified. A conceptual framework, when completed, will (1) guide the standards-setting body in establishing accounting standards, (2) provide a frame of reference for resolving accounting questions in the absence of specific promulgated standards, (3) determine the bounds for judgments in preparing financial statements, and (4) enhance comparability by decreasing the number of alternative accounting methods.[25]

At this time there is no international conceptual framework project. Instead, we are witnessing separate national efforts at creating a national conceptual framework in countries like the U.S., Canada, Great Britain, and Australia. Whether these separate efforts will lead ultimately to a final harmonization in the form of an international conceptual framework is either a long-term goal or merely wishful thinking, depending on one's perceptions of the likelihood of an international consensus on such theoretical projects as an international conceptual framework for accounting. The separate efforts are examined as a first step in an international conceptual framework.

U.S. EFFORTS

The U.S. efforts to formulate a conceptual framework started first with the publication by the AICPA of APB Statement No. 4, *Basic Concepts and Accounting Principles Underlying Financial Statements of Business Enterprises*. Although it was basically descriptive, which diminished its chances of providing the first accounting conceptual framework, the Statement did influence most subsequent attempts to formulate the objectives of financial statements and to develop a basic conceptual framework for the field of accounting. In response to the criticisms of corporate financial reporting and the realization that a conceptual framework for accounting is needed, in April 1971 the board of directors of the AICPA announced the formation of two study groups. The study group on the establishment of accounting principles, known as the "Wheat Committee," was charged with the task of improving the standards-setting process. Its report resulted in the formation of the Financial Accounting Standards Board (FASB). A second study group, known as the "Trueblood Committee," was charged with the development of the objectives of financial statements. It published the *Report of the Study Group on the Objectives of Financial Statements* which presented 12 objectives of accounting. Following the publication of this report the FASB began its work on the conceptual framework. It first identified nine important issues:

Issue 1: Which view of earnings should be adopted?

Issues 2 through 7: What are the definitions of assets, liabilities, earnings, revenues, expenses, and gains and losses?

Issue 8: Which capital maintenance or cost recovery concepts should be adopted for a conceptual framework for financial accounting and reporting?

Issue 9: Which measurement method should be adopted?

Exhibit 3.5 illustrates the overall scope of the conceptual framework and lists the related documents issued thus far by the FASB.

EXHIBIT 3.5 U.S. CONCEPTUAL FRAMEWORK FOR FINANCIAL ACCOUNTING AND REPORTING

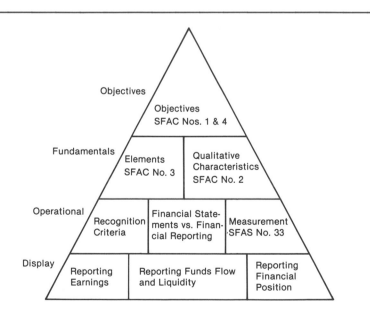

1. At the first level the *objectives* identify the goals and purposes of accounting. Statement of Financial Accounting Concepts No. 1, *Objectives of Financial Reporting by Business Enterprises*, presents the goals and purposes of accounting for business enterprises. Statement of Financial Accounting Concepts No. 4, *Objectives of Financial Reporting by Nonbusiness Organizations*, presents the goals and purposes of accounting for nonbusiness organizations.

2. At the second level the *fundamentals* identify and define the *qualitative characteristics* of accounting information (Statement of Financial Accounting Concepts No. 4) and the *elements* of financial statements (Statement of Financial Accounting Concepts No. 3, *Elements of Financial Statements of Business Enterprises*).

3. At the third level the *operational guidelines* that the accountant uses in establishing and applying accounting standards include the recognition criteria, financial statements versus financial reporting, and measurement (Statement of Financial Accounting Standards No. 33, *Financial Reporting and Changing Prices*).

4. At the fourth level the *display* mechanisms that accounting uses to convey accounting information include reporting earnings, reporting funds flow and liquidity, and reporting financial position.

CANADIAN EFFORTS

The Canadian Institute of Chartered Accountants (CICA) published a research study in June 1980, *Corporate Reporting: Its Future Evolution*, written by Edward Stamp and hereafter referred to as the Stamp Report.[26] The main motivations behind this effort are first, the FASB conceptual framework is not suitable for Canada given the environmental, historical, political, and legal differences between the U.S. and Canada and, second, it will provide a Canadian solution to the problem of improving the quality of corporate financial accounting standards.

The approach advocated in the Stamp Report is an evolutionary one. It identifies problems and conceptual issues and provides solutions in terms of identification of the objectives of corporate financial reporting, the users of corporate reports, the nature of the users' needs, and the criteria for assessment of the quality of standards and of corporate accountability as the possible components of a Canadian conceptual framework. Unlike the FASB's conceptual framework, which is deemed too normative (if not axiomatic) and too narrow in its scope (its primary concern is with investors), the Canadian conceptual framework would be based on an evolutionary (rather than revolutionary) approach and would be less narrow in its scope (its primary concern is with the reasonable needs of the legitimate users of published financial reports). Furthermore, a public justification and explanation of the standards is suggested to win general acceptance of the framework.

It is now up to the CICA to evaluate the recommendations of the Stamp

Report and develop a truly Canadian conceptual framework. The report is truly successful in listing major conceptual problems in developing any framework.

Reactions to the report have been mixed. It has been perceived as an opinion document: "In the final analysis, *Corporate Reporting* is an opinion document. It is not, nor do I believe it attempts to be, a classic inquiry type research study. Rather, it is based on the informed opinion of a group of experienced and capable accountants."[27] It has also been characterized as confusing before finally opting for a socioeconomic political world view. "We might conclude that the Stamp Report, though arriving at many blind alleys, going through several iterations, and making several detours, does arrive at a position on a world view that might prove to be very fruitful in the development of public accounting theory and standards—the socio-economic-political world view."[28] Finally, practitioners found the study's recommendations as either far from practical or too costly to implement.[29]

BRITISH EFFORTS

In July 1976, The Accounting Standards Steering Committee of the Institute of Chartered Accountants in England and Wales published its *Corporate Report* as a discussion paper intended as a first step toward a major review of users, purposes, and methods of modern financial reporting in the United Kingdom.[30] The paper's major findings and recommendations follow. First, the basic philosophy and starting point of *Corporate Report* is that financial statements should be appropriate to their expected use by the potential users. In other words, they should attempt to satisfy the informational needs of users. Second, the report assigns responsibility for reporting to the "economic entity" having an impact on society through its activities. Economic entities are itemized as limited companies, listed and unlisted, pension schemes, charitable and other trusts, and not-for-profit organizations; noncommercially oriented central government departments and agencies; partnerships and other forms of unincorporated business enterprises; trade unions and trade and professional associations; local authorities; and national industries and other commercially oriented public-sector bodies.[31]

Third, the report defines users as those having a reasonable right to information and whose information needs should be recognized by corporate reports. The users are identified as the equity investor group, the loan creditor group, the employee group, the analyst-advisor group, the business contact group, the government, and the public.[32] Fourth, to satisfy the fundamental objectives of annual reports set by the basic philosophy, seven desirable characteristics are cited, namely, that the corporate report be relevant, understandable, reliable, complete, objective, timely, and comparable. Fifth, after documenting the limitations of current reporting practices, the report suggests the need for the following additional statements:

1. *A statement of value added,* showing how the benefits of the efforts of an enterprise are shared among employees, providers of capital, the state, and reinvestment. Exhibit 3.6 is an example of a statement of value added.

EXHIBIT 3.6 A MANUFACTURING COMPANY STATEMENT OF VALUE

	Year to Dec. 31, 1974, thousands of pounds	Preceding Year, thousands of pounds
Turnover	£ 203.9	£ 202.3
Brought-in material and services	67.6	72.1
Value added	£ 136.3	£ 130.2
Applied the following way		
To pay employees, wages, pensions and fringe benefits	125.9	117.3
To pay providers of capital		
Interest on loans	0.8	0.6
Dividends to shareholders	0.9	0.9
	1.7	1.5
To pay government		
Corporation tax payable	3.9	3.1
To provide for maintenance and expansion of assets		
Depreciation	2.0	1.8
Retained profits	2.8	6.5
	4.8	8.3
Value added	£ 136.3	£ 130.2

SOURCE: The Accounting Standards Steering Committee, *The Corporate Report* (London: The Institute of Chartered Accountants in England and Wales, 1975). Reprinted with permission.

2. *An employment report,* showing the size and composition of the work force relying on the enterprise for its livelihood, the work contribution of employees, and the benefits earned.

3. *A statement of money exchange with government,* showing the financial relationship between the enterprise and the state.

4. *A statement of transactions in foreign currency,* showing the direct case dealings between the United Kingdom and other countries.

5. *A statement of future prospects,* showing likely future profit, employment, and investment levels.

6. *A statement of corporate objectives,* showing management policy and medium-term strategic targets.

Finally, after assessing six measurement bases (historical cost, purchasing power, replacement cost, net realizable value, value to the firm, and net present value) against three criteria (theoretical acceptability, utility, and practicality), the report rejected the use of historical cost in favor of current values accompanied by the use of general index adjustment.

Conclusions

In spite of the basic differences in the accounting systems internationally, an effort is made toward a harmonization of accounting systems and the development of conceptual frameworks to guide the development of accounting techniques. Such efforts would surely produce better results from an international perspective if they were coordinated by a single international unit.

Notes

1. John A. Wilson, "The Need for Standardization of International Accounting," *Touche Ross Tempo* (Winter 1969), p. 40.

2. Edwin W. Macrae, "Impediments to a Free International Market in Accounting and the Effects on International Accounting Firms," in *The International World of Accounting: Challenges and Opportunities,* ed. John C. Burton (N.Y.: Arthur Young, 1981), p. 150.

3. Lee J. Seidler, "Technical Issues in International Accounting," in *Multinational Accounting: A Research Framework for the Eighties,* ed. Frederick D. S. Choi (Ann Arbor, Mich. UMI Research Press, 1981), p. 41.

4. Joseph P. Cummings, and Michael N. Chetkovich, "World Accounting Enters a New Era," *The Journal of Accountancy* 145 (April 1978), p. 52.

5. The IFAC newsletter can be obtained free by writing to the International Federation of Accountants, 540 Madison Avenue, New York, N.Y. 10022.

6. IASC, *Objectives and Procedures* (London: IASC, January 1983), par. 8.

7. Ibid., par. 27.

8. Sir Henry Benson, "The Story of International Accounting Standards," *Accountancy* 87 (July 1976), p. 34.

9. T. R. Douglas, "International Accounting Standards," *CA Magazine* (October 1977), pp. 49-50.

10. "The Time Is Now," *CA Magazine* (November 1980), p. 68.

11. The IASC newsletter can be obtained free by writing to IASC, 41 Kingsway, London, WC2BGYU, England.

12. It is affiliated with the World Bank.

13. *The Impact of Multinational Corporations on Development and on International Relations*, UN Publication, Sales No. E.74.II.A.5 (v), p. 95.

14. Group of Experts on International Standards of Accounting and Reporting, *International Standards of Accounting and Reporting for Transnational Corporations* (New York: United Nations, 1977), p. 17.

15. Another UN group, the UN Commission on Transnational Corporations, continues developing a code of conduct for transnational corporations. The most recent draft of the code addresses numerous facets of multinational companies' activities, including trade unions, research and development, finance marketing policies, transfer pricing, and accounting disclosures.

16. OECD, *International Investment and Multinational Enterprises* (Paris; 1976), pp. 14-16.

17. OECD, "Declaration on International Investment and Multinational Enterprises," *The OECD Observer* 82 (July/August 1976), p. 14.

18. Commission of the European Communities, *Amended Proposal for a Fourth Council Directive for Co-ordination of National Legislation regarding the Annual Accounts of Limited Liability Companies* (Brussels, 1974).

19. *The Fourth Directive* (London: Deloitte, Haskins & Sells, 1978), p. 1.

20. Frederick D. S. Choi, "ASEAN Federation of Accountants: A New International Accounting Force," *Intrernational Journal of Accounting* (Fall 1979), pp. 53-75.

21. "Accounting Council Aiming for Far-Ranging Impact," *World Accounting Report* (August 1979), p. 18.

22. There is one each in the United Kindgom and Australia-New Zealand.

23. A very recent creation (1984).

24. FASB, *Conceptual Framework for Financial Accounting and Reporting: Elements of Financial Statements and Their Measurement* (Stamford, Conn., December 2, 1976), p. 2.

25. FASB, *Scope and Implications of the Conceptual Framework Project* (Stamford, Conn., December 2, 1976), pp. 6-8.

26. E. Stamp, *Corporate Reporting: Its Future Evolution* (Toronto: CICA, 1980).

27. T. R. Archibald, "A Research Perspective on Corporate Reporting: Its Future Evolution," in *Research to Support Standard Setting in Financial Accounting: A Canadian Perspective*, ed. S. Basu and J. Alex Milburn (Toronto: The Clarkson Gordon Foundation, 1982), p. 229.

28. J. F. Dewhirst, "An Evaluation of *Corporate Reporting: Its Future Evolution* Based on Different World Views," in Basu and Milburn, *Research to Support Standard Setting*, p. 253.

29. R. W. Park, "Is *Corporate Reporting* Asking Too Much?," *The Chartered Accountant Magazine* (December 1981), pp. 34-37.

30. The Accounting Standards Steering Committee, *The Corporate Report* (London: The Institute of Chartered Accountants in England and Wales, 1975), p. 50.

31. Ibid., p. 16.

32. Ibid., p. 17.

Bibliography

AlHashim, Dhia D. "Accounting Control through Purposive Uniformity: An International Perspective," *The International Journal of Accounting Education and Research* 8 (Spring 1973), pp. 21-32.

_____. "Regulation of Financial Accounting: An International Perspective," *The International Journal of Accounting Education and Research* 16 (Fall 1980), pp. 47-62.

Bartlett, Ralph T. "Current Developments of the IASC," *The CPA Journal* 51 (May 1981), pp. 20-27.

Belkaoui, Ahmed, Alfred Kahl, and Josette Peyrard. "Information Needs of Financial Analysts: An International Comparison," *The International Journal of Accounting Education and Research* 13 (Fall 1977), pp. 19-28.

Benson, Sir Henry. "The Story of International Accounting Standards," *Accountancy* 87 (July 1976), pp. 34-39.

Brown, Jan Giannini. "The Development of International Accounting Standards," *The Woman CPA* 39 (October 1977), pp. 9-12.

Chetkovich, Michael N. "An Appeal for Unity in Establishing Financial Accounting Standards," *The International Journal of Accounting Education and Research* 8 (Fall 1972), pp. 99-107.

Choi, Frederick D. S. "A Cluster Approach to Accounting Harmonization," *Management Accounting* 63 (August 1981), pp. 26-31.

Corbett, P. Graham. "International Accounting Standards: The Impact on Practicing Firms," *The Accountant* 176 (May 26, 1977), pp. 602-3.

_____. "Why International Accounting Standards?" *CA Magazine* 111 (July 1978), pp. 36-39.

Cowperthwaite, Gordon H. "Prospectus for International Harmonization," *CA Magazine* 108 (June 1976), pp. 22-31.

Cummings, Joseph P. "The International Accounting Standards Committee: Current and Future Developments," *The International Journal of Accounting Education and Research* 11 (Fall 1975), pp. 31-37

_____. "The International Accounting Standards Committee—Its Purpose and Status," *The CPA Journal* 44 (September 1974), pp. 50-53.

Cummings, Joseph P., and Michael N. Chetkovich. "World Accounting Enters a New Era," *The Journal of Accountancy* 145 (April 1978), pp. 52-62.

Cummings, Joseph P., and William L. Rogers. "Developments in International Accounting," *The CPA Journal* 48 (May 1978), pp. 15-19.

DaCosta, Richard C., Jacques C. Bourgeois, and William M. Lawson. "A Classification of International Financial Accounting Practices," *The International Journal of Accounting Education and Research* 13 (Spring 1978), pp. 73-86.

deBruyne, D. "Global Standards: A Tower of Babel?" *Financial Executive* 48 (February 1980), pp. 30-37.

Elsea, Carole Ann. "Progress toward International GAAP," *The Woman CPA* 41 (July 1979), pp. 22-23.

Feldman, Stewart A., and LeRoy J. Herbert. "The International Accounting Standards Committee," *The CPA Journal* 47 (January 1977), pp. 17-21.

Firth, Michael A. "An Empirical Examination of the Applicability of Adopting the AICPA and NYSE Regulations on Free Share Distribution in the U.K.," *Journal of Accounting Research* 11 (Spring 1973), pp. 16-24.

Fitzgerald, Richard D. "International Disclosure Standards—The United Nations Position," *Journal of Accounting, Auditing and Finance* 3 (Fall 1979), pp. 5-20.

_____. "International Harmonization of Accounting and Reporting," *The International Journal of Accounting Education and Research* 17 (Fall 1981), pp. 21-32.

Gaertner, James F., and Norlin Rueschhoff. "Cultural Barriers in International Accounting Standards," *CA Magazine* 113 (May 1980), pp. 36-39.

Gray, S. J. "The Impact of International Accounting Differences from a Security-Analysis Perspective: Some European Evidence," *Journal of Accounting Research* 18 (Spring 1980), pp. 64-76.

_____. "Multinational Enterprises and the Development of International Accounting Standards," *The Chartered Accountant in Australia* 52 (August 1981), pp. 24-25.

Hampton, Robert, III. "World of Difference in Accounting and Reporting," *Management Accounting* 62 (September 1980), pp. 14-18.

Harvey, Iain. "International Standards—Why We Need Them," *Accountancy* 88 (March 1977), pp. 96-98.

Hauworth, William P. "Problems in the Development of Worldwide Accounting Standards," *The International Journal of Accounting Education and Research* 9 (Fall 1973), pp. 23-24.

Hayes, Donald J. "The International Accounting Standards Committee—Recent Developments and Current Problems," *The International Journal of Accounting Education and Research* 16 (Fall 1980), pp. 1-10.

Howe, Wong Eng. "International Standards of Accounting and Reporting," *The Australian Accountant* 50 (August 1980), pp. 435-40.

Hussein, Mohamed Elmutassim. "Translation Problems of International Standards," *The International Journal of Accounting Education and Research* 17 (Fall 1981), pp. 147-56.

Kanaga, William. "International Accounting: The Challenge and the Changes," *The Journal of Accounting* 150 (November 1980), pp. 55-61.

Lamond, Robert A. "The Role of the International Practices Committee," *The Chartered Accountant in Australia* 49 (March 1979), pp. 12-14.

McComb, Desmond. "The International Harmonization of Accounting: A Cultural Dimension," *The International Journal of Accounting Education and Research* 14 (Spring 1979), pp. 1-16.

McKenzie, Alec. "The Progress of the International Accounting Standards Committee: The First Two Years," *The Accountant's Magazine* 80 (April 1976), pp. 137-39.

McMonnies, P. N. "EEC, UEC, ASC, IASC, IASG, AISG, ICCAP, IFAC, Old Uncle Tom Cobbleigh and All," *Accounting and Business Research* 7 (Summer 1977), pp. 162-67.

Mason, Alister K. "International Reporting of Inventories: Potential Impact of IAS 2," *The Accountant* 174 (October 7, 1976), pp. 410-13.

Miles, J.N. "The Development of International Accounting Standards," *The Chartered Accountant in Australia* 49 (August 1978), pp. 26-32.

_____. "The Development of International Accounting Standards, Part 2," *The Chartered Accountant in Australia* 49 (September 1978), pp. 33-37.

Mueller, G. G. "International Accounting Standards and Problems," *The Accountant* 177 (October 13, 1977), pp. 446-49.

Mueller, Gerhard G., and Lauren M. Walker. "The Coming of Age of Financial Transnational Reporting," *The Journal of Accountancy* 142 (July 1976), pp. 67-74.

Nair, R. D., and Werner G. Frank. "The Harmonization of International Accounting Standards, 1973-79," *The International Journal of Accounting Education and Research* 17 (Fall 1981), pp. 61-78.

_____. "The Impact of Disclosure and Measurement Practices on International Accounting," *The Accounting Review* 55 (July 1980), pp. 426-50.

Needles, Belverd E., Jr. "Implementing a Framework for the International Transfer of Accounting Technology," *The International Journal of Accounting Education and Research* 12 (Fall 1976), pp. 45-62.

Nobes, C. W. "An Empirical Analysis of International Accounting Principles: A Comment," *Journal of Accounting Research* 19 (Spring 1981), pp. 268-70.

Owles, Derrick. "Foreign Affairs—International Harmonisation," *The Accountant, Annual Review 1979-1980* (supplement to *The Accountant* 182 [April 3, 1980]), pp. 4-6.

Pomeranz, Felix. "Prospects for International Accounting and Auditing Standards—The Transnationals in Governmental Regulations," *The International Journal of Accounting Education and Research* 17 (Fall 1981), pp. 7-20.

Previts, Gary John. "On the Subject of Methodology and Models for International Accountancy," *The International Journal of Accounting Education and Research* 10 (Spring 1975), pp. 1-12.

Schieneman, Gary S. "International Accounting: Issues and Perspective," *Journal of Accounting, Auditing and Finance* 3 (Fall 1979), pp. 21-30.

Schwartz, Ivo. "The Harmonization of Accounting and Auditing in the European Community," *The Accountant's Magazine* 81 (December 1977), pp. 508-10.

Smith, Willis A. "International Accounting Standards—An Update," *The CPA Journal* 50 (June 1980), pp. 22-27.

Stillwell, M. I. "'Generally Accepted Accounting Principles . . .': Why the Americans Report as They Do," *The Accountant* 175 (November 25, 1976), pp. 607-8.

Thomas, R. D. "The Closer We Get the Better We'll Look," *The Australian Accountant* 46 (August 1976), pp. 400-4.

Vincent, Geoff. "Australia's International Involvement," *The Australian Accountant* 50 (August 1980), pp. 441-48.

_____. Geoff. "Towards International Standards for Accountants," *The Australian Accountant* 51 (March 1981), pp. 98-99.

Watt, George C. "Toward Worldwide Accounting Principles," *The CPA Journal* 42 (August 1972), pp. 651-53.

APPENDIX 3A

INTERNATIONAL ACCOUNTANCY PROFESSION AGREEMENT

1. Whereas the International Accounting Standards Committee (IASC) was formed in 1973 with the function of formulating and publishing in the public interest standards to be observed in the presentation of audited financial statements and

2. Whereas the International Federation of Accountants was formed by professional accounting bodies in 1977 with the broad objective of developing and enhancing a coordinated worldwide accountancy profession with harmonised standards and

3. Whereas the sponsoring professional accountancy bodies

   (a) acknowledge that both IASC and IFAC are operating within the common framework of the internationally organized accountancy profession and are sponsored by and report to the same professional accountancy bodies

   (b) recognize that IASC has full and complete autonomy in the setting of international accounting standards and in the issue of discussion documents on international accounting issues

   (c) recognize the necessity of involving other interested parties in the accounting standard setting process to widen input and encourage acceptance and adoption of such standards.

4. The professional accountancy bodies which are listed in Appendix A (see Appendix 5) hereby collectively agree to

   A. Maintain an International Federation of Accountants with the objectives, powers, membership, and obligations of membership set out below. (IFAC Constitution).

   B. Maintain an International Accounting Standards Committee, with the objectives, powers, membership, and obligations of membership set out below. (IASC Constitution-Appendix 2)

Ratified by member bodies of
IFAC and Board Members and member
bodies of IASC
Mexico City, Mexico
October 1982

APPENDIX 3B

LIST OF MEMBERS OF IASC (AT JANUARY 1983)

Argentina
  Federacion Argentina de Colegios de Graduados en Ciencias Economicas
† * Australia
  Australian Society of Accountants
  The Institute of Chartered Accountants in Australia
Austria
  Institut Osterreichischer Wirtschaftsprufer
Bahamas
  Bahamas Institute of Chartered Accountants
Bangladesh
  The Institute of Chartered Accountants of Bangladesh
Barbados
  The Institute of Chartered Accountants of Barbados
  * Belgium
  College National des Experts Comptables de Belgique
  Institut des Reviseurs d'Entreprises, and Institut
  Belge des Reviseurs de Banques
Brazil
  Instituto Brasileiro de Contadores
† * Canada
  Canadian Institute of Chartered Accountants
  Certified General Accountants Association of Canada
  The Society of Management Accountants of Canada
Chile
  Colegio de Contadores de Chile A.G.
Columbia
  Instituto Nacional de Contadores Publicos de Colombia
Cyprus
  The Institute of Certified Public Accountants of Cyprus
Denmark
  Foreningen af Statsautoriserede Revisorer
Dominican Republic
  Instituto de Contadores Publicos Autorizados de la Republica Dominicana
Egypt
  The Egyptian Society of Accountants and Auditors
† * Federal Republic of Germany
  Institut der Wirtschaftsprufer in Deutshland e.V.
  Wirtschaftpruferkammer
Fiji
  The Fiji Institute of Accountants
Finland
  KHT-Yhdistys Foreningen CGR

† * France
    Compagnie Nationale des Commissaires Aux Comptes
    Ordre des Experts Comptables et des Comptables Agrees
  Ghana
    The Institute of Chartered Accountants (Ghana)
  Greece
    Association of Certified Accountants & Auditors of Greece
    Institute of Certified Public Accountants of Greece
    Institute of Incorporated Public Accountants in Greece
  * Hong Kong
    Hong Kong Society of Accountants
  Iceland
    Felag Loggiltra Endurkodenda
  * India
    The Institute of Chartered Accountants of India
    The Institute of Cost and Works Accountants of India
  Indonesia
    Indonesian Institute of Accountants
  * Israel
    The Institute of Certified Public Accountants in Israel
† * Italy
    Consiglio Nazionale dei Dottori Commercialisti
  Jamaica
    The Institute of Chartered Accountants of Jamaica
† * Japan
    The Japanese Institute of Certified Public Accountants
  Kenya
    Institute of Certified Public Accountants of Kenya
  Korea
    Korean Institute of Certified Public Accountants
  Lebanon
    The Lebanese Association of Certified Public Accountants
    The Middle East Society of Associated Accountants
  Luxembourg
    Ordres des Experts Compatables Luxembourgeois
  Malawi
    The Society of Accountants in Malawi
  * Malaysia
    Malaysian Institute of Accountants
    The Malaysian Association of Certified Public Accountants
  Malta
    The Malta Institute of Accountants
† * Mexico
    Instituto Mexicano de Contadores Publicos A.C.
† * Netherlands
    Nederlands Instituut van Registeraccountants
  New Zealand
    New Zealand Society of Accountants
† * Nigeria
    The Institute of Chartered Accountants of Nigeria
  Norway
    Norges Statsautoriserte Revisorers Forening
  * Pakistan
    Institute of Chartered Accountants of Pakistan
    Institute of Cost and Management Accountants of Pakistan
  Paraguay
    Colegio de Contadores de Paraguay
  * Philippines
    Philippine Institute of Certified Public Accountants
  Portugal
    Associacao Portuguesa de Contabilistas
    Sociedade Portuguesa de Contabilidade

Appendix 3B (con't)

   Republic of China
      National Federation of Certified Accountants Association of
      the Republic of China
   Republic of Panama
      Colegio de Contadores Publicos Autorizados de Panama
      Asociacion de Mujeres Contadores de Panama
   Sierra Leone
      The Association of Accountants in Sierra Leone
 * Singapore
      Singapore Society of Accountants
† * South Africa
      The South African Institute of Chartered Accountants
   Spain
      Instituto de Censores Jurados de Cuentas de Espana
   Sri Lanka
      Institute of Chartered Accountants of Sri Lanka
 * Sweden
      Foreningen Auktoriserade Revisorer FAR
   Switzerland
      Schweizerische Treuhand-und Revisionskammer
   Thailand
      The Institute of Certified Accountants and Auditors of Thailand
   Trinidad and Tobago
      The Institute of Chartered Accountants of Trinidad and Tobago
   Turkey
      Expert Accountants' Association of Turkey
† * United Kingdom and Ireland
      The Association of Certified Accountants
      The Chartered Institute of Public Finance and Accountancy
      The Institute of Certified Public Accountants in Ireland
      The Institute of Chartered Accountants in England and Wales
      The Institute of Chartered Accountants in Ireland
      The Institute of Chartered Accountants of Scotland
      The Institute of Cost and Management Accountants
† * United States of America
      American Institute of Certified Public Accountants
      National Association of State Boards of Accountancy
   Uruguay
      Colegio de Doctores en Ciencias Economicas y Contadores del Uruguay
   Venezuela
      Associacion de Contadores (CNTC) de Venezuela
      Federacion de Colegio de Contadores Publicos de Venezuela
   Yugoslavia
      Social Accounting Service of Yugoslavia
      Yugoslav Association of Accountants and Financial Experts
   Zambia
      The Zambia Association of Accountants
 * Zimbabwe
      The Institute of Chartered Accountants of Zimbabwe

* Countries who have participated in Steering Committees

† Members of the Board of IASC at January 1983

4.

ACCOUNTING FOR FOREIGN CURRENCY: TRANSACTIONS AND TRANSLATION

One important accounting problem resulting from multinational operations is the translation of transactions of a reporting firm that are denominated in a foreign currency (foreign currency transactions) and of financial statements of a foreign operation for incorporation into the financial statements of a reporting firm. This problem has been a hot issue throughout the 1970s and 1980s. Both the Financial Accounting Standards Board (FASB) in 1975 and the Canadian Institute of Chartered Accountants (CICA) in 1978 advocated the temporal method of translation. This position created so much controversy that both standards setting bodies issued new Statements, FASB Statement No. 52 in 1981 and CICA Section 1650 in 1983, advocating a more complex approach to accounting for foreign currency transactions and translation. Accordingly, this chapter explores the issues and solutions to the problem.

The World of Foreign Exchange

Each country has its own national currency. Therefore, foreign exchange refers to the national currency of another country. Each national currency has its own relative value or exchange rate. An exchange rate of a currency is initially determined as a function of its direct or indirect precious metal content or by the reserves of other currencies held in the central bank to be used as a support for its international exchangeability. To facilitate the determination of the values of foreign exchange and its sales and purchases, foreign exchange markets have been organized. These markets include mainly the foreign exchange traders of commercial banks, the International Money Market Division of the Chicago Mercantile Exchange which specializes in trading currency futures, and so-called exchange clubs such as the Hague Club and the Paris Club. These markets establish foreign exchange as an economic commodity whose value is subject to the laws of supply and demand. Basically, the foreign exchange market determines the rate at which one national currency is exchanged for another national currency. The resulting exchange rates are the basis for the exchange prices used for international business transactions. Within these foreign exchange markets is the forward market used to hedge against the exchange rate risks arising from holding open-ended account balances.

There are basically two types of foreign exchange rates: the *spot rate* and the *forward rate*. The spot rate is the rate quoted for currency transactions to be delivered within two days. The spot rate is determined by trade flows, inflation, seasonal demands for a currency, and arbitrage. The forward rate is the rate quoted for forward exchange contracts. These are contracts between a foreign exchange trader and a customer or between two foreign exchange traders which specify the delivery of a certain sum in foreign currency at a future date and at a given rate. Various reasons motivate the use of a forward contract: to hedge a transaction, to speculate on currency movements, to hedge a net investment in a foreign entity, and to hedge a foreign currency commitment. The designated rate in the forward contracts is the forward rate.

The forward rate may be equal to or different from the spot rate at the time the contract is made. The difference between the two rates is known as the *spread*. If the forward rate is superior to the spot rate, the currency is selling at a discount. If the forward rate is less than the spot rate, it is selling at a premium. The discount and the premium are normally quoted at the number of points above or below the spot rate. They may also be quoted in annualized percentage terms computed as follows:

$$\text{Premium (discount)} = \frac{FR - SR}{SR} \times \frac{12}{N}$$

where:
  FR = forward rate on the day the contract is entered into
  SR = spot rate on the same day
  N = number of months forward

The above formula may be used as a way of determining the forward rate. Assuming the premium or discount is due to the interest rate differential between two countries—the local country (LC) and the foreign country (FC)—then:

$$r_{LC} - r_{FC} = \frac{FR - SR}{SR} \times \frac{12}{N}$$

$$\text{and } FR = SR\,(r_{LC} - r_{FC})\left(\frac{N}{12}\right) + SR$$

where:
^{r}LC $=$ interest rate in the local country
^{r}FC $=$ interest in the foreign country

Accounting for Foreign Currency Transactions

Various transactions by corporations require the flow of money worldwide. These transactions include the import or export of merchandise, the sale or purchase of services, the payment or receipt of dividends, royalties and management fees, and borrowing and lending money. They are called foreign currency transactions because they require settlement in a currency other than the functional currency of the reporting entity. The functional currency of an entity is the currency used in the economic environment in which that entity operates. For a U.S.-based corporation, accounting for foreign currency transactions is covered in FASB Statement No. 52 (FAS 52). For the sake of clarity, this chapter divides the process of accounting for foreign transactions into two major categories. The first is the accounting for foreign currency transactions that are not the result of foreign exchange contracts. The second is the accounting for foreign currency transactions involving forward exchange contracts.

FOREIGN CURRENCY TRANSACTIONS NOT INVOLVING
FORWARD EXCHANGE CONTRACTS

For those foreign currency transactions not involving forward exchange contracts, the following treatments apply:

1. At the time of the transaction, the asset, liability, revenue, or expense is recorded in the functional currency of the recording entity by use of the current exchange rate on that date.
2. At the balance sheet date and at the date of the settlement of the foreign currency translation, recorded balances in the foreign currency transaction accounts are adjusted to reflect the current exchange rate.
3. With two exceptions, gains and losses resulting from the restatement are reflected in the current period's income statement.
4. The two exceptions are foreign currency transactions that are the result of an economic hedge of a net investment in a foreign entity, and long-term intercompany foreign currency transactions when the entities to the transaction are consolidated, combined, or accounted for by the equity method in the reporting enterprise's financial statements. In both these cases, the gains and losses are reported as translation adjustments in a separate component of the stockholder's equity account.

Two examples illustrate these treatments: one involving export of goods to illustrate the treatment of transaction gains and losses in current net income and one involving an intercompany foreign currency transaction to illustrate the treatment of transaction gains and losses and translation adjustments to stockholders' equity.

Foreign Exchange Transaction Involving Imports or Exports of Goods

Let's suppose the following events:

1. The American National Company sold on December 21, 19X3, merchandise to a foreign supplier—the Foreign National Company—billed and valued for FC1,000,000, on "net 30" terms.

2. Information about exchange rates between U.S. dollar and the foreign currency (FC) of the seller follows:

> December 21, 19X3: FC1 = $.50
> December 31, 19X3: FC1 = $.55
> January 20,   19X4: FC1 = $.45

The entries for this foreign exchange transaction follow:

1. At the date of the foreign exchange transaction: December 21, 19X3
   Accounts Receivable $500,000
   Sales   500,000
   To record the purchase of goods for $500,000 (FC1,000,000 $\times$ .50).

2. At the balance sheet date: December 31, 19X3
   Accounts Receivable $50,000
   Exchange Gain $50,000
   To record the exchange gain equal to FC1,000, 000 (.55 − .50). This exchange gain will be included in the 19X3 income statement of American National Company as a nonoperating item.

3. At the date of the settlement: January 20, 19X3.
   Cash $450,000
   Exchange Loss   100,000
   Accounts Receivable $550,000
   To record the amount received on settlement equal to FC1,000,000 (.45) and the exchange loss equal to FC1,000,000 (.55 − .45).
   This exchange loss will be included in the 19X4 income statement of American National Company as a nonoperating item.

Foreign Exchange Transaction Involving Intercompany Items

Let's hypothesize further:

1. The American National Company made on December 21, 19X3, an advance of FC1,000,000 to the "Other National Company," which is now a subsidiary of the American National Company. This advance is considered to be long-term in nature.

2. Information about the exchange rates between the U.S. dollar and the foreign currency (FC) of the subsidiary follows:
   December 21, 19X3:   FC1 = $.50
   December 31, 19X3:   FC1 = $.55

The entries for this foreign exchange transaction follow:

1. At the date of the foreign exchange transaction: December 21, 19X3
   Investment in Other National Company $500,000
      Cash $500,000
2. At the balance sheet date, no exchange gains and losses are recognized in the current net income but enter into the determination of the translation adjustment as a component of stockholders' equity. It is determined accordingly:
   Amount Used in Translation Adjustment = FC1,000,000 ($.55 − .50) = $50,000

FOREIGN CURRENCY TRANSACTIONS INVOLVING FORWARD EXCHANGE CONTRACTS

A forward exchange contract is defined as an agreement to exchange different currencies at a specified future date and at a specified rate (the forward rate). Firms enter in a forward exchange contract with a third-party broker to guarantee a fixed exchange price for the transaction. Three adjustments have to be computed and accounted for.

The first adjustment is the *gain or loss (whether or not deferred) on a forward contract.* It is equal to the foreign currency amount of the forward contract multiplied by the difference between the spot rate at the balance sheet date and the spot rate at the inception of the forward contract (or the spot rate last used to measure a gain or loss on that contract for an earlier period).

The second adjustment is the *discount or premium on a forward contract.* It is equal to the foreign currency amount of the contract multiplied by the difference between the contracted forward rate and the spot rate at the date of the inception of the contract.

The third adjustment is the *gain or loss on a speculative forward contract.* It is equal to the foreign currency amount of the contract multiplied by the difference between the forward rate available for the remaining maturity of the contract and the contract forward rate (or the forward rate last used to measure a gain or loss on that contract for an earlier period).

The accounting treatment of a foreign currency transaction involving foreign exchange contracts will be different whether the forward exchange contract is intended as a hedge of an identifiable currency speculation or a hedge of an exposed net asset or liability position.

A forward exchange contract is considered a hedge of an identifiable foreign currency commitment if (1) the foreign currency transaction is designated as, and is effective as, a hedge of a foreign currency commitment and (2) the foreign currency commitment is firm. In such a case the gain on the forward contract will be deferred and accounted for in the cost basis of the object of the foreign currency commitment. Any loss is recognized currently rather than deferred.[1] In addition, the discount or premium on a forward contract will be deferred and included in the cost basis.

A forward exchange contract that serves as a hedge of an exposed net asset or liability position is accounted for differently. Hence, the gain or loss is recognized in the current accounting period, while the discount or premium is accounted for separately over the life of the contract.

A forward exchange contract that serves as a hedge of an exposed net asset or liability position is also accounted for differently. Hence, all gains and losses, premiums, and discounts are recognized currently.

Examples involving the hedge of an identifiable foreign currency commitment, the hedge of an exposed net asset or liability position, and foreign currency speculation are presented to illustrate these treatments.

Hedge of an Identifiable Foreign Currency Commitment

Let's suppose the following events:

1 . The American National Company agreed to buy on December 1, 19X3, merchandise from a foreign supplier—the Foreign National Company—for FC2,000,000, on "net 90" terms.

2. The American National Company entered on December 1, 19X3, in a forward contract for the delivery of FC200,000 in 90 days.

3. Information about the exchange rates between the U.S. dollar and the foreign currency (FC) of the seller follows:

    December 1, 19X3, Forward Rate: FC1 = $.50
    December 1, 19X3, Spot Rate: FC1 = $.45
    December 31, 19X3, Spot Rate: FC1 = $.55
    March 1, 19X3, Spot Rate: FC1 = $.60

Because the contract qualifies as an identifiable foreign currency commitment, the entries will be as follows;

1. At the date of the inception of the forward exchange contract: December 1, 19X3
    Foreign Currency Receivable from Exchange Broker $90,000
    Premium on Forward Exchange Contract   10,000
        Payable to Exchange Broker $100,000

To record the receivable and payable relating to the forward exchange contract. The premium is equal to ($.50 − .40) × FC200,000.

2. At the balance sheet date: December 31, 19X3
    Foreign Currency Receivable from Exchange Broker $20,000
        Deferred Gain on Forward Exchange Contract $20,000

To record the gain from the forward exchange contract. The gain is equal to ($.55 − .45) X FC200,000.

3. At the date of the settlement, March 1, 19X3, we have three entries.

Entry No. 1: To record the gain from the forward exchange contract.
Foreign Currency Receivable from Exchange Brokers $10,000
    Deferred Gain on Forward Exchange Contract $10.000
Where the gain equals ($.60 − .55) × 200,000.

Entry No. 2: To record the payment of the obligation to the exchange broker and the receipt of the foreign currency.

Payable to Exchange Broker	$100,000	
Cash		$100,000
Foreign Currency	$120,000	
Foreign Currency Receivable from Exchange Broker		$120,000

Entry No. 3: To record the cost of the merchandise received and the payment of the foreign currency to the supplier.

Deferred Gain on Forward Exchange Contract	$30,000	
Equipment	100,000	
Foreign Currency		$120,000
Premium on Forward Exchange Contract		10,000

Hedge of an Exposed Net Asset or Liability Position

Let's suppose the following events:

1. To hedge against an exposed liability position, the American National Company entered on December 1, 19X3, into a forward exchange contract with an exchange broker for the delivery of FC2000,000 in 90 days.

2. Information about the exchange rates between the U.S. dollar and the foreign currency (FC) of the seller follows:

December 1, 19X3, Forward Rate:	FC = $.48
December 1, 19X3, Spot Rate:	FC = $.45
December 31, 19X3, Spot Rate:	FC = $.55
March 1, 19X3, Spot Rate:	FC = $.60

Because the contract qualifies as a hedge of an exposed liability position, the entries will be as follows:

1. At the date of the inception of the forward exchange contract: December 1, 19X3

Foreign Currency Receivable from Exchange Broker	$90,000	
Premium on Forward Exchange Contract	$ 6,000	
Payable to Exchange Broker		$96,000

To record the receivable and payable dating to the forward contract.

2. At the balance sheet date, December 31, 19X3, the gain from the forward contract and the amortization of premium will be recognized by the following two entries:

Entry No. 1:

Foreign Currency Receivable from Exchange Broker	$20,000	
Gain on Forward Exchange Contract		$20,000

Entry No. 2:

Amortization of Premium on Forward Exchange Contract	$2,000	
Premium on Forward Exchange Contract		2,000

3. At the date of settlement, March 1, 19X3, we have three entries.

Entry No. 1: To recognize the gain from the forward exchange contract:

Foreign Currency Receivable from Exchange Broker	$10,000	
Gain on Forward Exchange Contract		$10,000

Where the gain equals ($.60 − .55) X FC200,000.

Entry No. 2: To record the payment of the obligation to the exchange broker and the receipt of the foreign currency.

Payable to Exchange Broker	$96,000	
Cash		$96,000
Foreign Currency	$120,000	
Foreign Currency Receivable from Exchange Broker		$120,000

Entry No. 3: To record the amortization of the premium.

Amortization of Premium or Forward Exchange Contract	$4,000	
Premium on Forward Exchange Contract		$4,000

Foreign Currency Speculation

Let's suppose the following events:

1 . To speculate in the foreign currency market, the American National Company entered on December 1, 19X3, into a forward contract with an exchange broker for the delivery of FC200,000 in 60 days.

2. Information about the exchange rates between the U.S. dollar and the foreign currency (FC) follows:
   December 1, 19X3, 60-Day Forward Rate: FC1 = $.50
   December 31, 19X3, 30-Day Forward Rate: FC1 = $.60

Because the contract qualifies as foreign currency speculation, the entries will be as follows:

1. At the date of the inception of the forward exchange contract, December 1, 19X3

Foreign Currency Receivable from Exchange Broker	$100,000	
Payable to Exchange Broker		$100,000

   To record the receivable and payable relating to the forward contract.

2. At the balance sheet date, December 31, 19X3

Foreign Currency Receivable from Exchange Broker	$10,000	
Gain on Forward Exchange Contract		$10,000

   To record the gain on the foreign exchange contract. The gain is computed as ($.55 − .50) X FC200,000.

3. At the date of settlement, January 30, 19X3, we have three entries:
   Entry No. 1: To recognize the gain from the forward exchange contract.

Foreign Currency Receivable from Exchange Broker	$10,000	
Gain on Forward Exchange Contract		$10,000

   Where the gain equals ($.60 − .55) X FC200,000.

   Entry No. 2: To record the payment of the obligation to the exchange broker and the receipt of foreign currency.

Payable to Exchange Broker	$100,000	
Cash		$100,000
Foreign Currency	$120,000	
Foreign Currency Receivable from Exchange Broker		$120,000

   Entry No. 3: To record the sale of foreign currency.

Cash	$120,000	
Foreign Currency		$120,000

Translating Foreign Currency Financial Statements

THE CURRENT-NONCURRENT METHOD

Under the current-noncurrent method of translation, current assets and liabilities are translated at the current exchange rate (the actual exchange rate in effect at the balance sheet date), and noncurrent assets and liabilities are translated at historical exchange rates (the rates in effect when those assets were acquired and liabilities incurred). Income statement items are translated at the average exchange rate, except for depreciation and amortization charges, which are translated at the historical rates in effect when the assets are acquired.

The current-noncurrent method (fully described in Chapter 12 of the AICP's Accounting Research Bulletin No. 43) was a popular method in the United States until its replacement by FAS 8. This method, however, suffers from the following basic limitation: The assumptions that accounts should be first grouped according to maturity and then translated accordingly lack conceptual justification. Balance sheet presentation according to maturity does not justify the choice of a translation rate.

THE MONETARY-NONMONETARY METHOD

Under the monetary-nonmonetary method of translation, the monetary assets and liabilities are translated at current rates, while the nonmonetary assets and liabilities are translated at historical rates. Income statement items are translated in the same manner as in the current-noncurrent method. Basically, monetary assets and liabilities are those representing rights to receive obligations to pay a fixed number of foreign currency units. Examples of monetary assets and liabilities include cash, receivables, payables, and long-term debt. Examples of nonmonetary assets and liabilities include fixed assets, long-term investment, and inventories.

The monetary-nonmonetary method was introduced by Hepworth as a way of correcting some of the limitations of the current-noncurrent method.[2] The rationale behind the method was that monetary assets and liabilities represent fixed amounts of money whose parent-currency equivalent changes each time the exchange rate changes. The method gained immediate acceptance. First, the National Association of Accountants (NAA) published a monograph which praised the relevance of the monetary-nonmonetary method.[3] Second, the Accounting Principles Board (APB) gave official recognition to the method in APB Opinion No. 6 by allowing long-term debt to be translated at current rates.[4]

It is evident, however, that the monetary-nonmonetary method suffers from the same conceptual limitation as the current-noncurrent method. In effect, the monetary-nonmonetary classification scheme does not present any conceptual ground for the choice of the translation rates. A good criticism of the method follows:

. . . no comprehensive principle of translation can be derived solely from the monetary-nonmonetary distinction. Nonmonetary assets and liabilities are measured on different bases (for example, past prices or current prices) under different circumstances, and translation at a past rate does not always fit. Translating nonmonetary items at a past rate produces reasonable results if the items are stated at historical cost but not if they are stated at current market price in foreign currency.[5]

THE CURRENT-RATE METHOD

Under the current-rate method of translation, all assets and liabilities are translated at the current exchange rate. The method was first introduced and supported by the Institute of Chartered Accountants in England and Wales in their 1968 Statement No. 25.[6] It was also heavily advocated in a study by Parkinson, under the auspices of the CICA's Accounting and Auditing Research Committee.[7]

The principal advantage of the current-rate method is that it reflects, in the translation of accounts, the economic situation and perspective of the local country. Basically, the ratios and relationships existing in a local currency do not change after translation to the parent currency. The maintenance of the local perspective after translation is seen as a positive factor.

A problem arising from the use of the current-rate method is in the choice between the market exchange rate and the official exchange rate. The problem is aggravated by the degree of fluctuations in currency values in a world of floating exchange rates. One way to get out of this dilemma, according to Parkinson, is to use a standard bookkeeping rate which will approximate actual exchange rates:

As a general rule, the accounts of a foreign subsidiary should be translated to Canadian currency at bookkeeping rates of exchange which need only approximate actual rates for converting the foreign currency. Once established, a bookkeeping rate should not be changed until, because of changes in actual exchange rates, it becomes clearly inappropriate; a new translation rate should be selected as soon as practical after a currency revaluation, as distinct from a mere currency fluctuation.[8]

A better choice would be the market exchange rate quoted for spot transactions in the country where the accounts to be translated originate, given that it is readily available and that it gives a better measure of the economic value of the local currency. Choi and Mueller see an exception to the use of the free-market rate where specific exchange controls are in effect:

For instance, if a Latin American subsidiary of a United States parent has received permission to import certain goods from the United States at a favorable rate and has set aside certain cash funds to do so, the earmarked funds should be translated to dollars at the special preference rate. The current year-end free-market rate should, of course, be applied to the balance of the foreign cash account. This procedure has the effect of translating portions of a foreign currency cash account at two or more different translation rates. Nothing is wrong as long as economic reality is properly and fully reflected thereby.[9]

A second problem which may arise from the use of the current-rate method is the possibility of having "abnormal" exchange gains and losses when the foreign currency is subject to strong fluctuation. A third problem arises from the use of foreign currency rather than the parent currency as the unit of measure. The parent firm may object to the situation while the subsidiary may argue that the local perspective allows it to see in parent-currency units the same relationships seen in the local currency. The situation is basically a plus from the subsidiary's point of view and a minus from the parent's.

Finally, the current-rate method may be considered a partial departure from the cost principle. In effect, it becomes a revaluation of assets expressed in foreign currencies while those assets expressed in local currencies are kept at cost.

THE TEMPORAL METHOD

The temporal method was first introduced by Lorenson in AICPA Account Research Study No. 12.[10] The purpose of the method was to use translation as a measurement process which does not change the attribute of the item being measured but changes only the unit of measure. Basically, accounts carried at past exchange rates are translated at historical rates while accounts carried at current purchase or sale exchange prices or future exchange prices are translated at current rates. Thus, under the temporal method cash, receivables, and payables (both current and noncurrent) are translated at current rates. Other assets and liabilities are translated at either the current rate or their historical rates depending upon whether these are carried at current values or historical values. In other words, the temporal method retains the accounting valuation bases used to measure the foreign currency items. It should be noted that similar results may be obtained under both the monetary-nonmonetary and the temporal methods if the historical cost valuation basis is applied to all accounts. It should also be noted that the temporal method may be adapted to all other forms of asset valuation bases, such as replacement cost, net realizable value, or discounted cash flows. Finally, the temporal method appears to avoid most of the limitations of the other translation methods. A comprehensive tabulation of the rates at which balance sheet items are to be translated under the current method, the current-noncurrent method, the monetary-nonmonetary method, and the temporal method is presented as Exhibit 4.1.

EXHIBIT 4.1 RATES USED TO TRANSLATE ASSETS AND LIABILITIES

Balance Sheet Accounts*	Current Rate Method	Current-Noncurrent Method	Monetary-Nonmonetary Method	Temporal Method
Cash	c	c	c	c
Marketable equity securities				
Carried at cost	c	c	h	h
Carried at current market price	c	c	h	c
Accounts and Notes Receivable	c	c	c	c
Inventories				
Carried at cost	c	c	h	h
Current at market	c	c	h	c
Prepaid Expenses	c	c	h	h
Property, Plant and Equipment	c	h	h	h
Accumulated Depreciation	c	h	h	h
Other Intangible Assets	c	h	h	h
Liabilities and Equities				
Accounts and notes payable	c	c	c	c
Bonds payable or other long term debt	c	h	c	c
Common stock	h	h	h	h
Paid-in surplus	h	h	h	h
Retained Earnings	amount used to balance the balance sheet			

NOTE: Exchange rate used:
        h = historical exchange rate;
        c = current exchange rate.

FINANCIAL STATEMENT EFFECTS

To illustrate the application of the translation method a simple balance sheet example is used.[11] A U.S. firm has a foreign subsidiary whose year-end balance sheet appears as Exhibit 4.2. Relevant exchange rates appear as Exhibit 4.3.

Exhibit 4.4. illustrates the balance sheet of the foreign subsidiary after translation using each of the known translation methods. The different translation methods offer a rich variety of results. In addition, Exhibit 4.5 shows the different balance sheet exposures to foreign exchange risks under the four translation methods.

This wide array of results and exposures may call for a choice of one of the methods on the basis of conceptual reasons and in order to provide some uniformity in the translation process by multinational companies. This choice has been made over the years and has covered each of the translation methods. More recently, official pronouncements in the United States, England, and Canada have been reduced to either the temporal method or the current-rate method for various conceptual and practical reasons. Accordingly, in what follows, the official positions on foreign currency translation in the United States, Great Britain, and Canada are examined.

EXHIBIT 4.2 RELEVANT INFORMATION FOR THE TRANSLATION PROCESS (YEAR-END BALANCE SHEET)

Cash	FC 2,000	Accounts payable	FC 3,000
Accounts Receivable	3,000	Long term debt	6,000
Marketable equity securities		Common stock	9,000
(at cost)	8,000	Retained earnings	7,000
Inventories (at Market)	7,000		
Property, Plant and Equipment	5,000		
	FC 25,000		FC 25,000

B.   End of the Year Income Statement

EXHIBIT 4.3 RELEVANT EXCHANGE RATES FOR THE TRANSLATION PROCESS

Current Exchange Rate (End of the Year)	FC 1 = $1.60
Historical Exchange Rate for the Marketable Equity Securities	FC 1 = $1.80
Historical Exchange Rate for Inventories (End of the Year)	FC 1 = $1.90
Historical Exchange Rate for Property, Plant and Equipment	FC 1 = $2.30
Historical Exchange Rate for Long Term Debt	FC 1 = $2.30
Historical Exchange Rate for Common Stock	FC 1 = $2.30
Historical Exchange Rate for Inventories (Beginning of the year)	FC 1 = $2.40
Average Current Exchange Rate	FC 1 = $2.00

The U.S. Position on Foreign Currency Translation

As mentioned earlier in this chapter, Accounting Research Study No. 12 recommended the use of the temporal method. Later, in October 1975, the FASB issued Statement No. 8, *Accounting for the Translation of Foreign Currency Transactions and Foreign Currency Financial Statements*, which also recommended the use of the temporal method. According to FAS 8, the objective of translation is: "For the purpose of preparing an enterprise's financial statements, the objective of translation is to measure and express (a) in dollars and (b) in conformity with U.S. generally accepted accounting principles [GAAP] the assets, liabilities, revenue, or expenses that are measured or denominated in foreign currency."[12] The temporal method advocated by FAS 8 was unique, however, in that foreign exchange gains and losses were to be recognized in the income statement in the period in which they occur. FAS 8 generated a lot of debate and criticisms, especially with regard to the translation of inventory and long-term debt and the recognition of exchange gains and losses. For example, the 1978 Exxon annual report mentions the problem as follows:

EXHIBIT 4.4 BALANCE SHEET EXPRESSED IN U.S. CURRENCY

Balance sheet Items	Current Rate Method		Current Noncurrent Method		Monetary Nonmonetary Method		Temporal Method	
	Rate	$	Rate	$	Rate	$	Rate	$
Assets								
Cash	$1.60	$ 3,200	$1.60	$ 3,200	$ 1.60	$ 3,200	$1.60	$ 3,200
Accounts Receivable	1.60	4,800	1.60	4,800	1.60	4,800	1.60	4,800
Marketable Equity Securities (cost)	1.60	12,800	1.60	12,800	1.80	14,400	1.80	14,400
Inventories (Market)	1.60	11,200	1.60	11,200	2.40	16,800	1.60	11,200
Property, Plant and Equipment	1.60	8,000	2.30	11,500	2.30	11,500	2.30	11,500
TOTAL		$40,000		$43,500		$50,700		$45,100
Liabilities and Equities								
Accounts Payable	1.60	$ 4,800	1.60	$ 4,800	1.60	$ 4,800	1.60	$ 4,800
Long Term Debt	1.60	9,600	2.30	13,800	1.60			
Common Stock	1.60	14,400	2.30	20,700	2.30			
Retained Earnings		11,200*		4,200*				
TOTAL		$40,000		$43,500		$50,700		$45,102

*Exchange gains and losses are included in the income figure.

98

EXHIBIT 4.5 BALANCE SHEET EXPOSURE TO FOREIGN EXCHANGE RISK

	Current Rate Method	Current Noncurrent Method	Monetary Nonmonetary Method	Temporal Method
Cash	FC 2,000	FC 2,000	FC 2,000	FC 2,000
Accounts Receivable	3,000	3,000	3,000	3,000
Marketable Equity Securities (cost)	8,000	8,000	--------	
Inventories (Market)	7,000	7,000	--------	
Property, Plant and Equipment	5,000	--------	--------	--------
TOTAL	FC 25,000	FC 20,000	FC 5,000	FC 12,000
Accounts Payable	FC 3,000	FC 3,000	FC 3,000	FC 3,000
Long Term Debt	6,000	----------	6,000	6,000
Common Stock	9,000	----------	---------	---------
TOTAL	FC 18,000	FC 3,000	FC 9,000	FC 9,000

Under these presently prescribed accounting procedures, essentially all of Exxon's foreign liabilities, including short-term and long-term debt obligations, are measured in terms of year-end exchange rates. As the dollar has weakened, these liabilities, translated at the year-end rates of exchange, are equivalent to greater U.S. dollar obligations. In contrast, a relatively small portion of the corporation's foreign assets—essentially only cash, marketable securities and receivables—are measured using year-end exchange rates. The balance of the corporation's foreign assets—mainly inventory, plant and equipment—are not included in the calculation and continue to be measured in terms of their equivalent dollar value at the time these assets were acquired. As a consequence of using the Standard No. 8 definition, Exxon continued to show a net liability exposure which creates currency translation losses during periods of U.S. dollar weakness.[13]

In reaction to these criticisms and debate, in December 1981 the FASB issued Statement No. 52 (FAS 52).[14] The FAS 52 requirements follow:

1. Foreign currency financial statements must be in conformity with GAAP before being translated to the reporting currency.
2. Foreign currency financial statements must be expressed and, if necessary, remeasured in the functional currency before being translated to the reporting currency. The Statement provides some guidelines based on certain indicators to be used in determining the functional currency. These indicators are as follows:

   a. Cash flow indicators
   b. Sales price indicators
   c. Sales market indicators

    d. Expense indicators

    e. Financing indicators

    f. Intercompany transactions and arrangements indicators

    Basically, if the foreign operation's cash flows are usually in foreign currency and do not affect the parent's cash flows, if the sales price of its products depends on local conditions rather than on fluctuations in the exchange rates, if it has an active local sales market for its product, if most of its costs are incurred locally, if it services its debt obligations through local resources, and if it has little relationship with the parent company except for competitive advantages, then the functional currency is the foreign currency. Otherwise, the functional currency is the parent company's currency.

3. The translation process may be divided in two categories. Category one is where the U.S. dollar is the functional currency. In that case the temporal method of FAS 8 will be used, with one major exception: While deferred taxes are translated in FAS 8 using the historical exchange rates, they are translated in FAS 52 using the current rate. In addition, the translation gains or losses are reported in the income statement as a nonoperating item. Category two is where the foreign currency is the functional currency. In that case the current method will be used. In addition, the translation gains or losses are reported in the stockholders' equity section of the balance sheet as a *translation adjustment*. The translation rates for both categories are shown as Exhibit 4.6.

4. The only exception to the above translation process relates to the financial statements of a foreign entity in a country that has had cumulative inflation of approximately 100 percent or more over a three-year period (highly inflationary). In this case the reporting currency is the functional currency.

Illustration of the Translation Process under FASB Statement No. 52

    As was mentioned earlier the translation rates used to translate the assets and liabilities under FASB Statement No. 52 depend on whether the U.S. dollar or the foreign currency is the functional currency. To illustrate the translation process under FASB 52, it is desirable to examine both cases.

    Let's assume that the first financial statements of a subsidiary, named the Foreign Company, for the period ending December 31, 19X1, are as shown in Exhibits 4.7, 4.8, and 4.9 and have been prepared in accordance with U.S. generally accepted accounting principles. To facilitate the translation process, selected foreign exchange rates are provided as Exhibit 4.10. As suggested earlier, the translation process is examined first under the assumption of the U.S. dollar as the functional currency and next under the assumption of the foreign currency as the functional currency.

TRANSLATION PROCESS WHEN THE U.S. DOLLAR
IS THE FUNCTIONAL CURRENCY

    Exhibit 4.6 shows the rates to be used when the U.S. dollar is the functional currency. When applied to the balance sheet items, they will

EXHIBIT 4.6 RATES USED IN THE TRANSLATION OF BALANCE SHEET ITEMS

	U.S. Dollar Is Functional Currency Translation Rates		Foreign Currency Is Functional Currency Translation Rates	
	Current	Historical	Current	Historical
ASSETS				
Cash on hand and demand and time deposits	X		X	
Marketable equity securities:				
Carried at cost		X	X	
Carried at current market price	X		X	
Accounts and notes receivable and related unearned discount	X		X	
Allowance for doubtful accounts and note receivable	X		X	
Inventories:				
Carried at cost		X	X	
Carried at current replacement price or current selling price	X		X	
Carried at net realizable value	X		X	
Carried at contract price (produced under fixed price contracts)	X		X	
Prepaid insurance, advertising, and rent		X	X	
Refundable deposits	X		X	
Advances to unconsolidated subsidiaries	X		X	
Property, plant, and equipment		X	X	
Accumulated depreciation of property, plant, and equipment		X	X	
Cash surrender value of life insurance	X		X	
Patents, trademarks, licenses, and formulas		X	X	
Goodwill		X	X	
Other intangible assets		X	X	
LIABILITIES				
Accounts and notes payable and overdrafts	X		X	
Accrued expenses payable	X		X	
Accrued losses on firm purchase commitments	X		X	
Refundable deposits	X		X	
Deferred income		X	X	
Bonds payable or other long-term debt	X		X	
Unamortized premium or discount on bonds or notes payable	X		X	
Convertible bonds payable	X		X	
Accrued pension obligations	X		X	
Obligations under warranties	X		X	

EXHIBIT 4.7 BALANCE SHEET IN FOREIGN CURRENCY—FOREIGN COMPANY, DECEMBER 31, 19X1 (in thousands)

Current Assets	19X1
Cash	478.15
Accounts receivable-Trade	1,221.85
Accounts receivable-intercompany	0.00
Notes receivable	500.00
Inventories	3,950.25
Prepaid expenses	0.00
Accrued interest on notes receivable	5.70
Total Current Assets	6,155.95
Long Term Notes Receivable	3,000.00
Property, Plant and Equipment	
Land	8,500.00
Buildings	74,905.50
Equipment	16,313.00
Total Property, Plant and Equipment	99,718.50
Accumulated depreciation	(5,632.60)
Net Property, Plant and Equipment	94,085.90
Total Assets	103,241.85

Current Liabilities	
Accounts payable	1,814.00
Accrued interest on long term debt	225.00
Income tax payable	383.25
Dividends payable	125.00
Current portion of long term debt	1,250.00
Total Current Liabilities	3,797.25
Long Term Debt	33,750.00
Deferred Income Taxes	548.10
Stockholders' Equity	
Common stock	25,000.00
Contributed capital in excess of par	38,591.20
Retained earnings	1,555.30
Total Stockholders' Equity	65,116.50
Total liabilities and Stockholders' Equity	103,241.85

EXHIBIT 4.8 INCOME STATEMENT IN FOREIGN CURRENCY—FOREIGN
COMPANY, DECEMBER 31, 19X1 (in thousands)

		19X1
Sales		36,638.00
Costs and Expenses		
Cost of goods sold:		
Inventory-January 1	0.00	
Production costs	24,982.80	
Goods available for sale	24,982.80	
Inventory-Dec. 31	3,950.25	
Cost of goods sold		21,032.55
General and Administrative		4,122.50
Advertising and selling		2,335.75
Depreciation		5,632.60
Total costs and expenses		33,123.40
Net income from operations		3,514.60
Other income (expenses)		(339.10)
Net income before taxes		3,175.50
Income taxes		
Current		572.10
Deferred		548.10
Total taxes		1,120.20
Net Income		2,055.30

EXHIBIT 4.9 STATEMENT OF RETAINED EARNINGS IN FOREIGN CURRENCY
—FOREIGN COMPANY, YEARS ENDED DECEMBER 31, 19X1 AND 19X2

	19X2	19X1
Retained earnings-January 1	1,555.30	0
Add net income for the year	1,429.60	2,055.30
Deduct dividends for the year	(1,000.00)	(500.00)
Retained earnings-December 31	1,984.90	1,555.30

EXHIBIT 4.10 FOREIGN CURRENCY RATES

Rates	U.S. Dollar is Functional Currency FC1 19X1	Foreign Currency is Functional Currency FC1 19X1
1. Current rate at March 31	$2	NA
2. Current rate at September 30	$1.98	NA
3. Current rate at June 30	$1.96	NA
4. Current rate at December 31	$1.92	$1.92
5. Average rate for the year	$1.964	$1.964
6. Historical rate when stock was issued and land purchased	$2.04	$2.04
7. Historical rate when property, plant and equipment were purchased	$2	NA
8. Average historical rate applicable to inventories on hand at December 31	$1.94	NA

result in the balance sheet of the Foreign Company expressed in U.S. dollars as shown in Exhibit 4.11. Although the translation of the balance sheet items is straightforward, it is important to note that the retained earnings figure is determined as a "plug" figure. The computation of the retained earnings is made as follows:

Total dollar value of assets translated	$206,170.22
Total dollar value of liabilities and equities translated (other than retained earnings)	202,869.11
Retained earnings balance, December 31, 19X1	3,301.11

The translation of the income statement will proceed in phases: a first to determine the net income translated before finding the translation gains or losses, a second to determine the translation gains or losses, and a third to combine both results. The first phase of the translation of the income statement before finding the translation gains or losses is shown as Exhibit 4.12. The second phase includes the determination of the translation gains or losses as a "plug" figure.[15] the computation of the translation gains or losses will be as follows:

Retained earnings—January 1, 19X1	0.0000
Add net income	$2,756.5298
Minus retained earnings, December 31, 19X0 (See Exhibit 4.11)	3,301.1100
Translation gains	$ 544.5802

The third phase incorporates the translation gains as a nonoperating item in the income statement, as shown in Exhibit 4.13.

TRANSLATION PROCESS WHEN THE FOREIGN CURRENCY IS THE
FUNCTIONAL CURRENCY

When the foreign currency is the functional currency, FASB Statement No. 52 advises the use of the current method. Basically, most balance sheet accounts are translated using the current exchange rate; most revenues and expenses are translated using the average exchange rate for the period.

EXHIBIT 4.11 BALANCE SHEET IN U.S. DOLLARS—FOREIGN COMPANY,
DECEMBER 31, 19X1 (in thousands)

	FC	Translation Rate	$
Current Assets			
Cash	FC478.15	1.92	$ 918.048
Accounts receivable-trade	1,221.85	1.92	2,345.952
Accounts receivable-intercompany	0.00	1.92	0.000
Notes receivable	500.00	1.92	960.000
Inventories	3,950.25	1.94	7,663.485
Prepaid expenses	0.00	1.92	0.000
Accrued interest on notes receivable	5.70	1.92	10.944
Total Current Assets	6,155.95	1.92	$ 11,898.429
Long Term Notes Receivable	3,000.00		5,760.000
Property, Plant and Equipment			
Land	8,500.00	2.04	17,340.000
Buildings	74,905.50	2	149,811.000
Equipment	16,313.00	2	32,626.000
Total Property, Plant and Equipment	99,718.50		$199,777.000
Accumulated depreciation	(5,632.60)	2	(11,265.200)
Net Property, Plant and Equipment	94,085.90		$188,511.800
Total Assets	103,241.85		$206,170.220
Current Liabilities			
Accounts payable	1,814.00	1.92	$ 3,482.88
Accrued interest on long term debt	225.00	1.92	432.00
Income tax payable	383.25	1.92	735.84
Dividends payable	125.00	1.92	240.00
Current portion of long term debt	1,250.00	1.92	2,400.00
Total Current Liabilities	3,797.25		$ 7,290.72
Long Term Debt	33,750.00	1.92	64,800.00
Deferred Income Taxes	548.10	1.92	1,052.352
Stockholders' Equity			
Common stock	25,000.00	2.04	51,000.00
Contributed capital in excess of par	38,591.20	2.04	78,726.048
Retained earnings	1,555.30		3,301.11
Total Stockholders' Equity	65,146.50		133,027.15
Total liabilities and Stockholders' Equity	103,241.85		$206,170.220

EXHIBIT 4.12 INCOME STATEMENT IN U.S. DOLLARS—FOREIGN COMPANY, DECEMBER 31, 19X1 (in thousands)

	FC	Rate	$
Sales			
Costs and expenses	36,638.00	1.964	$ 71,957.032
Costs of goods sold			
Inventory-January 1	0.00		0.000
Production costs	24,982.80	1.964	49,066.219
Goods available for sale	24,982.80		49,066.219
Inventory, December 31	(3,950.25)	1.94	(7,663.485)
Cost of goods sold	21,032.55		41,402.734
General and Administrative	4,122.50	1.964	8,096.59
Advertising and selling	2,335.75	1.964	4,587.413
Depreciation	5,632.60	2	11,265.200
Total costs and expenses	33,123.40		65,351.937
Net income from operations	3,514.60		6,605.095
Other income (expenses)	(339.10)	1.964	(665.9924)
Net income before taxes	3,175.50		5,939.1026
Income taxes			
Current	572.10	1.964	1,123.6044
Deferred	548.10	1.964	1,076.4684
Total taxes	1,120.20		2,200.0728
Net income before dividends	2,055.30		3,739.0298
Dividends			
1st quarter	125	2	250.00
2nd quarter	125	1.98	247.50
3rd quarter	125	1.96	245.00
4th quarter	125	1.92	240.00
Total dividends	500		982.50
	1,553.3		2,756.5298

EXHIBIT 4.13 INCOME STATEMENT IN U.S. DOLLARS—FOREIGN COMPANY, DECEMBER 31, 19X1 (in thousands)

Sales		$71,957.032
Costs and expenses		
Costs of goods sold		
Inventory-January 1	$ 0.00	
Production costs	49,066.219	
Goods available for sale	$49,066.219	
Inventory, December 31	(7,663.485)	
Cost of goods sold		41,402.734
General and Administrative		8,096.590
Advertising and selling		4,587.413
Depreciation		11,265.200
Total costs and expenses		$65,351.937
Net income from operations		$ 6,605.095
Nonoperating items		
Other income (expenses)		(665.9924)
Translation gain		554.5802
Net income before taxes		$ 6,493.6828
Income taxes		
Current		1,123.6044
Deferred		1,076.4684
Net income		$ 4,293.61
Add Retained Earnings-Jan. 1, 19X1		0.00
Decust Dividends for the year		$ 4,293.61
Retained earnings-Dec. 31, 19X1		982.50
		$ 3,301.11

Thus, the translation process is more straightforward. Exhibit 4.14 shows the income statement of the Foreign Company in U.S. dollars. All income statement items have been translated using the average exchange rate of 1.964. Notice the absence of translation gains and losses in the income statement given that they now will appear in the stockholders' equity section of the balance sheet as a translation adjustment. In fact, the translated balance sheet appears as Exhibit 4.15. With the exception of common stock and contributed capital in excess of par, all balance sheet items have been translated using the current exchange rate of 1.92. The common stock and the contributed capital are translated at the historical rate of 2.04. The translation adjustment of $(7,698.8698) appears as a "plug" figure. However, for the sake of reconciling the figures and checking on the accuracy of the computation, the determination of the translation adjustment is also show as Exhibit 4.16.

The Canadian Position on Foreign Currency Translation

The Canadian position on foreign currency translation is expressed in Section 1650 of the Accounting Standards Committee Handbook.[16] The Canadian position does not use the term *functional currency*, but instead classifies foreign operations as either "integrated" or "self-sustaining." Whether a foreign operation is classified as integrated or self-sustaining

EXHIBIT 4.14 INCOME STATEMENT IN U.S. DOLLARS—FOREIGN COMPANY, DECEMBER 31, 19X1 (in thousands)

	FC	Rate	$
Sales	36,638.00	1.964	$71,957.032
Costs and expenses			
Costs of goods sold			
Inventory-January 1	000.00	1.964	0.000
Production costs	24,982.80	1.964	49,066.219
Goods available for sale	24,982.80		49,066.219
Inventory, December 31	(3,950.25)	1.964	(7,750.291)
Cost of goods sold	21,032.55		41,307.928
General and Administrative	4,122.50	1.964	8,096.59
Advertising and selling	2,335.75	1.964	4,587.413
Depreciation	5,632.60	1.964	11,062.426
Total costs and expenses	33,123.40		65,054.357
Net income from operations	3,514.60		6,902.675
Other income (expenses)	(339.10)	1.964	(665.9924)
Net income before taxes	3,175.50		6,236.6826
Income taxes			
Current	572.10	1.964	1,123.6044
Deferred	548.10	1.964	1,076.4684
Total taxes	1,120.20		2,200.0728
Net income before dividends	2,055.30		4,036.6098
Deduct Dividends	500		982.50
Retained Earnings-Dec. 31	1,553.3		3,054.1098

EXHIBIT 4.15 INCOME STATEMENT IN U.S. DOLLARS—FOREIGN COMPANY, DECEMBER 31, 19X1 (in thousands)

	FC	Rate	$
Current Assets			
Cash	478.15	1.92	$ 918.048
Accounts receivable-trade	1,221.85	1.92	2,345.952
Accounts receivable-intercompany	0.00	1.92	0.000
Notes receivable	500.00	1.92	960.000
Inventories	3,950.25	1.92	7,584.48
Prepaid expenses	0.00	1.92	0.00
Accrued interest on notes receivable	5.70	1.92	10.944
Total Current Assets	6,155.90		$ 11,819.424
Long Term Notes Receivable	3,000.00	1.92	5,760.000
Property, Plant and Equipment			
Land	8,500.00	1.92	16,320.00
Buildings	74,905.50	1.92	143,818.56
Equipment	16,313.00	1.92	31,320.96
Total Property, Plant and Equipment	99,718.50		191,459.52
Accumulated depreciation	(5,632.60)	1.92	(10,814.592)
Net Property, Plant and Equipment	94,085.90		180,644.93
Total Assets	103,241.85		198,224.35
Current Liabilities			
Accounts payable	1,814.00	1.92	$ 3,482.88
Accrued interest on long term debt	225.00	1.92	432.00
Income tax payable	383.25	1.92	735.84
Dividends payable	125.00	1.92	240.00
Current portion of long term debt	1,250.00	1.92	2,400.00
Total Current Liabilities	3,797.25		$ 7,290.72
Long Term Debt	33,750.00	1.92	64,800.00
Deferred Income Taxes	548.10	1.92	1,051.352
Stockholders' Equity			
Common stock	25,000.00	2.04	51,000.00
Contributed capital in excess of par	38,591.20	2.04	78,726.048
Retained earnings	1,555.30		3,054.1098(1)
Translation Adjustment			(7,698.8698)(2)
Total Stockholders' Equity	365,146.50		125,081.29
Total liabilities and Stockholders' Equity	103,241.85		198,224.36

(1)See Exhibit 4.14

(2)See Exhibit 4.16 for a reconciliation of this result

EXHIBIT 4.16 RECONCILIATION OF TRANSLATION ADJUSTMENT FOR 19X1

Total Assets-Foreign Currency		103,241.85
Total Liabilities-Foreign Currency		
Current	3,797.25	
Long-term debt	33,750.00	
Deferred income taxes	548.10	
Total Liabilities-Foreign Currency	38,095.35	38,095.35
Net Assets-Foreign Currency		65,146.50
End of the Period Exchange Rate		1.92
Net Assets in Dollars		$125,081.28
Stockholders' Equity Dollars		
Common stock	$ 51,000.00	
Contributed capital in excess of par	78,726.048	
Retained earnings	3,054.1098	
Total Stockholders' Equity in Dollars	$132,780.16	$132.780.16
Translation Adjustment		7,698.8698

108

depends on the exposure of the reporting firm to exchange rate changes as determined by the economic facts and circumstances. Matters which would be taken into consideration include basically the same indicators as those used in FAS 52, namely, cash flow indicators, sales price indicators, and intercompany transactions and arrangement indicators. Basically, an integrated foreign operation is a foreign operation that is financially or operationally interdependent with the reporting firm such that the exposure to exchange rate is similar to the exposure that would exist had the transactions and activities of the foreign operation been undertaken by the reporting enterprise. Similarly, a self-sustaining foreign operation is a foreign operation which is financially and operationally independent of the reporting firm such that the exposure to exchange rate changes is limited to the reporting firm's net investment in the foreign operation.[17]

Given this differentiation between foreign operations, the Canadian position recommends: (1) foreign currency-denominated transactions and related financial statement items of the reporting firm are to be translated using the temporal method, as are financial statements of integrated foreign operations; (2) financial statements of self-sustaining foreign operations are to be translated using the current-rate method, unless the economic environment of the foreign operations is highly inflationary, in which case the temporal method is used; (3) exchange gains and losses of the reporting firm that arise on translation or settlement of a foreign currency-denominated item or a nonmonetary item carried at market should be included in the determination of net income for the current period; (4) exchange gains and losses of the reporting firm relating to the translation of foreign currency-denominated monetary items that have a fixed or ascertainable life extending beyond the end of the following fixed year should be deferred and amortized on a systematic basis over the remaining life of the monetary item;[18] (5) exchange gains or losses arising on the translation of financial statements of integrated foreign operations and on those of self-sustaining operations in highly inflationary environments are also deferred and amortized on a systematic basis over the remaining life of the monetary item; and (6) exchange gains and losses arising from the translation of the financial statements of a self-sustaining foreign operation should be deferred and included in a separate component of shareholders' equity.[19]

Two major differences with FASB Statement No. 52 arise: First, Section 1650 requires deferral and amortization of exchange gains and losses relating to long-term foreign currency-denominated monetary items of the reporting firm and adjustments arising on translation of long-term monetary items of integrated foreign operations while FAS 52 requires recognition of such amounts in the determination of net income. Second, Section 1650 requires translation of deferred income tax balances of integrated foreign operations at historical rates while FAS 52 requires translation at current rates. These two differences force Canadian SEC registrants to report still another difference between Canadian and U.S. generally accepted accounting principles.

British Position on Foreign Currency Translation

The last British position on foreign currency translation is expressed in Statement of Standard Accounting Practice No. 20 (SSAP 20), issued in April 1983. The objectives of translation are to produce results which are generally compatible with the effects of rate changes on a firm's cash flows and its equity and to ensure that the financial statements present a true and fair view of the results of management actions. To do so, two-stage procedures are adopted, namely, preparation of the financial statements of an individual company and preparation of the consolidated financial statements.

THE INDIVIDUAL COMPANY STAGE

For a company which undertakes transactions denominated in a foreign currency the following guidelines are provided:

1. Translate transaction values in local currency at transition date rates, and use an average rate for periods where there is little fluctuation.
2. If there is a contracted rate, use that; if there is a matching forward contract covering the transaction, the rate specified in the contract should be used.
3. At balance sheet date, monetary assets and liabilities denominated in a foreign currency are to be translated using that date's exchange rate or the rates specified by any binding contract.
4. All exchange gains and losses on either settled or unsettled transitions should be reported in the current income statement.

THE CONSOLIDATED FINANCIAL STATEMENTS STAGE

The method used to translate financial statements for consolidation purposes should reflect the financial and operational relationships which existed between an investment company and its foreign enterprises. Basically, two methods may be used: either the *closing rate/net investment method* or the *temporal method*.

The closing rate/net investment method is used when the investment of a company is in the net worth of its foreign enterprise rather than a direct investment in the individual assets and liabilities of that enterprise. Under this method, financial statement items should be translated at the closing rate or at an average rate for the period. Exchange differences are dealt with as adjustments to reserves.

The temporal method is used when the affairs of a foreign enterprise are so closely interlinked with those of the investing company that its results may be regarded as being more dependent upon the economic environment of the investing company's currency than on that of its own reporting currency. The factors taken into account to determine whether the currency of the investing company is the dominant currency in the economic environment in which the foreign enterprise operates include (1) the extent to which the cash flows of the enterprise have a direct impact upon those of the investing company, (2) the extent to which the functioning of the enterprise is dependent upon the investing company, (3) the currency in which the majority of the trading transactions are denominated, and (4) the major currency to which the operation is exposed in its financing structure.[20]

International Position on Foreign Currency Translation

In 1983, the International Accounting Standards Committee issued International Accounting Standard 21 (IAS 21), *Accounting for the Effects of Changes in Foreign Exchange Rates.* It deals with both accounting for transactions in foreign currencies in the financial statements of an enterprise and with translation of the financial statements of foreign-based operations into a single reporting currency for the purpose of including them in the financial statements of the foreign firm. The Statement's recommendations were practically similar to those of FAS 52. The major difference between IAS 21 and FAS 52 is that IAS 21 permits exchange gains and losses on long-term foreign currency monetary items to be deferred and amortized over the remaining lives of the related monetary items unless it is reasonable to expect that recurring exchange losses on the items will arise in the future.

Conclusions

This chapter has examined the issues and solutions surrounding the problem of accounting for foreign currency—transactions and translation. Foreign currency transactions are examined in cases involving and not involving forward exchange contracts. Foreign currency transaction methods are presented: the current-noncurrent method, the monetary-nonmonetary method, the current-rate method, and the temporal method. Finally, both the U.S. and Canadian positions on the problem have been examined.

Notes

1. In addition, the amount of the contract must not be more than the amount of the total hedge on an after-tax basis.
2. Samuel R. Hepworth, *Reporting Foreign Operations* (Ann Arbor: University of Michigan, 1966).

3. NAA, *Accounting Problems in Foreign Operations,* Research Report No. 36 (New York, 1960).

4. APB Opinion No. 6, *Status of Accounting Research Bulletins* (New York: AICPA, 1965), par. 5.

5. FASB Statement No. 8, *Accounting for the Translation of Foreign Currency Transactions and Foreign Currency Financial Statements,* Statement of Financial Accounting Standards No. 8 (Stamford, Conn., October 1975), par. 126.

6. Institute of Chartered Accountants in England and Wales, *Member's Handbook, Statement No. 25* (London, 1968), par. 14.

7. MacDonald R. Parkinson, *Translation of Foreign Currencies* (Toronto; CICA, 1972).

8. Ibid., p. 26.

9. F.D.S. Choi, and G. G. Mueller, *An Introduction to Multinational Accounting* (Englewood Cliffs, N.J.: Prentice Hall, 1978), p. 79.

10. AICPA Accounting Research Study No. 12, *Reporting Foreign Operations of U.S. Companies in U.S. Dollars* (New York, 1972), by Leonard Lorensen.

11. A more exhaustive example is used later in the chapter to illustrate the requirements of FASB Statement No. 52.

12. FASB Statement No. 8, par. 6.

13. The 1978 Exxon annual report.

14. FASB Statement No. 52 *Foreign Currency Translation* (Stamford, Conn., December 1981).

15. Ibid, p. 3.

16. Accounting Standards Committee, *Accounting Recommendations* (Toronto: CICA, 1983), pp. 4, 5.

17. Jonathan M. Kligman, "Foreign Currency Translation: From Exposure Draft to Standard," *Chartered Accountant Magazine* (June 1983), p. 57.

18. Such an exchange gain or loss is considered an element of the cost or benefit of holding a foreign currency-denominated monetary item related to the period of time during which the item is unsettled.

19. In such circumstances, the reporting firm's exposure to exchange-rate changes is limited to its net investment in the foreign operation, and the exchange gain or loss arising on translation has no direct effect on the reporting firm's activities.

20. Examples of situations provided where the temporal method may be used include situations where the foreign firm:

1. Acts as a selling agency receiving stocks of goods from the investing company and remitting the proceeds back to the company
2. Provides a raw material or manufactures parts or subassemblies which are then shipped to the investing company for inclusion in its own products
3. Is located overseas for tax, exchange control, or similar reasons to act as a means of raising funds for other companies in the group.

Bibliography

Aggarwal, Raj, and James C. Baker. "Using Foreign Subsidiary Accounting Data: A Dilemma for the Multinational Corporation," *Columbia Journal of World Business* (Fall 1975), pp. 83-92.

Aliber, Robert Z., and Clyde P. Stickney. "Accounting Measures of Foreign Exchange Exposure," *The Accounting Review* (January 1975), pp. 44-57.

Armstrong-Flemming, Nigel. "Multicurrency Accounting: Dispelling the Mystique," *Accountancy* (March 1981), pp. 118-20.

Barrett, M. E., and L. Spero. "Foreign Exchange Gains and Losses," *Financial Analysts Journal* (March/April 1975), pp. 26-31.

Bilson, John F. O. "Leading Indicators of Currency Devaluation," *Columbia Journal of World Business* (Winter 1979), pp. 62-76.

Bradford, Samuel R. "Exchange Rate—Factors Determining Trends," *Accountancy* (May 1976), pp. 44-46.

Carstairs, Rolf. "Accounting and Management Aspects of Foreign Exchange Transactions," *The Australian Accountant* (August 1979).

Christofides, N., R. D. Hewins, and G. R. Salkin. "Graphic Theoretic Approaches to Foreign Exchange," *Journal of Financial and Quantitative Analysis* (September 1979), pp. 481-500.

Clark, F. L. "Patz on Parities, Exchange Rates and Translation," *Accounting and Business Research* (Winter 1978), pp. 73-77.

Connor, Joseph E. "Accounting for the Upward Float in Foreign Currencies," *The Journal of Accountancy* (June 1972), pp. 39-44.

Cooper, J.R.H. "Foreign Exchange Operations," *Accountancy* (August 1974), pp. 54-58.

Cornell, Bradford. "The Denomination of Foreign Trade Contracts Once Again," *Journal of Financial and Quantitative Analysis* (November 1980), pp. 933-45.

Cornell, Bradford, and Marc R. Reinganum. "Forward and Future Prices: Evidence from the Foreign Exchange Markets," *The Journal of Finance* (December 1981), pp. 1035-46.

Duangploy, Orapin. "The Sensitivity of Earnings per Share to Different Foreign Currency Translation Methods," *The International Journal of Accounting Education and Research* (Spring 1979), pp. 121-34.

Earl, Michael, and Dean Paxson. "Value Accounting for Currency Translations," *Accounting and Business Research* (Spring 1978), pp. 92-100.

Evans, Thomas G. "Diversity in Foreign Currency Translation Methods—A Proposal for Uniformity," *The CPA Journal* (February 1974), pp. 41-45.

Fekrat, M. A. "Multinational Accounting: A Technical Note," *The International Journal of Accounting Education and Research* (Fall 1979), pp. 95-103.

Flower, John. "A Price Parity Theory of Translation: A Comment," *Accounting and Business Research* (Winter 1978), pp. 64-65.

Frenkel, Jacob A. "The Efficiency and Volatility of Exchange Rates and Prices in the 1970's," *Columbia Journal of World Business* (Winter 1979), pp. 15-27.

Garman, Mark B., and Steven W. Kohlhagen. "Inflation and Foreign Exchange Rates under Production and Monetary Uncertainty," *Journal of Financial and Quantitative Analysis* (November 1980), pp. 949-67.

Giddy, Ian H. "Research on the Foreign Exchange Markets," *Columbia Journal of World Business* 14 (Winter 1979), pp. 4-6.

Giddy, Ian H., and Gunter Dufey. "The Random Behavior of the Flexible Exchange Rates: Implications for Forecasting," *Journal of International Business Studies* (Spring 1975), pp. 1-32.

Gray, John Y. "Translating Foreign Currency Transactions and Financial Statements," *The CPA Journal* 47 (June 1977), pp. 31-36.

Hayes, Donald J. "Translating Foreign Currencies," *Harvard Business Review* 50 (January-February 1972), pp. 6-18.

Houghton, John W., Jr. "Foreign Long-Term Debt Translation," *Management Accounting* 56 (September 1974), pp. 17-18.

Jackson, Peter D., and Michael B. Meagher. "The New Foreign Currency Recommendations," *CA Magazine* 111 (December 1978), pp. 47-53.

Jacobi, Michael H. "The Unit of Account in Consolidated Financial Statements of Multinational Enterprises," *The International Journal of Accounting Education and Research* 15 (Spring 1980), pp. 17-34.

Jansz, Rodney. "Foreign Currency Translation," *The Australian Accountant* 51 (February 1981), pp. 18-21.

Klein, Richard B. "Inter-Country Purchasing Power Index Numbers," *Management Accounting* 54 (August 1972), pp. 28-32.

Kligman, Jonathan M. "Foreign Currency Translation: From Exposure Draft to Standard," *Chartered Accountant Magazine* (June 1983), pp. 57-62.

Konrath, Larry F. "Foreign Exchange versus Purchasing Power Gains and Losses," *Management Accounting* 53 (May 1972), pp. 41-43.

Leighton, G. R. "Exchange Control in Australia," *The Australian Accountant* 46 (November 1976), pp. 600-612.

Leighton, G. R. "Exchange Control in Australia," *The Australian Accountant* 46 (November 1976), pp. 600-612.

Leighton, G. R. "Exchange Control in Australia 1980," *The Australian Accountant* 50 (August 1980), pp. 465-71.

Leo, K., and G. Grundy. "Foreign Currency Translation—The Key Issues," *The Chartered Accountant in Australia* 50 (February 1980), pp. 23-28.

Lewis, Kenneth A., and Francis F. Breen. "Empirical Issues in the Demand for Currency: A Multinational Study," *The Journal of Finance* 30 (September 1975), 1065-79.

Lorensen, Leonard. "Misconception about Translation," *CA Magazine* 102 (March 1973), pp. 20-25.

———. "The Temporal Principle of Translation," *The Journal of Accountancy* 134 (August 1972), pp. 48-54.

McMonnies, Peter N., and Bryan J. Rankin. "Accounting for Foreign Currency Translation," *The Accountant's Magazine* 81 (June 1977), pp. 241-43.

McMonnies, Peter N., and Bryan J. Rankin. "Accounting for Foreign Currency Translation—II," *The Accountant's Magazine* 81 (July 1977), pp. 285-88.

McMonnies, Peter N., and Bryan J. Rankin. "Accounting for Foreign Currency Translation—III: ED 21," *The Accountant's Magazine* 81 (November 1977), pp. 460-61.

McMonnies, Peter N., and Bryan J. Rankin. "Accounting for Foreign Currency Translation—IV: IASE 11," *The Accountant's Magazine* 82 (January 1978), pp. 16-17.

Marthur, Ike, and David Loy. "Foreign Currency Translation: Survey of Corporate Treasurers," *Management Accounting* 63 (September 1981), pp. 33-42.

Mensah, Yaw M., and Louis F. Biagioni. "The Predictive Ability of Financial Ratios Using Alternative Translation Methods for Foreign Currency Financial Statements: A Simulation Study," *The International Journal of Accounting Education and Research* 16 (Fall 1980), pp. 221-45.

Messier, William F., Jr. "SFAS No. 8: Some Implications for MNCs," *The International Journal of Accounting Education and Research* 14 (Spring 1979), pp. 101-20.

Munter, Paul. "Currency Strategies under FASB 8: An Empirical Analyis," *The International Tax Journal* 6 (December 1979), pp. 85-89.

Nobes, C. W. "A Review of the Translation Debate," *Accounting and Business Research* 10 (Autumn 1980), pp. 421-31.

Norr, David. "Currency Translation and the Analyst," *Financial Analysts Journal* 32 (July/August 1976), pp. 46-54.

Pakkala, A. L. "Accounting of Multinational Companies," *Financial Analysts Journal* 31 (March/April 1975), pp. 32-41.

Parkinson, MacDonald R. "Whose Misconceptions," *CA Magazine* 102 (March 1973), pp. 26-29.

Patz, Dennis H., "A Price Parity Theory of Translation," *Accounting and Business Research* 8 (Winter 1977), pp. 14-24.

_____. "A Price Parity Theory of Translation: A Reply," *Accounting and Business Research* 9 (Winter 1978), pp. 66-72.

_____. "Price Parity Translation: Methodology and Implementation," *Accounting and Business Research* 11 (Summer 1981), pp. 207-16.

_____. "The State of the Art in Translation Theory," *Journal of Business Finance & Accounting* 4 (Autumn 1977), pp. 311-25.

Piper, Andrew. "Accounting for Overseas Currencies," *The International Journal of Accounting Education and Research* 15 (Fall 1979), pp. 46-52.

Pleak, Ruth E. "An Analysis of the FASB's Treatment of Foreign Currency Translation," *Management Accounting* 59 (September 1977), pp. 29-32.

Polimeni, Ralph S. "Accounting for Forward Exchange Contracts," *The International Journal of Accounting Education and Research* 13 (Fall 1977), pp. 159-68.

Portington, Michael. "Foreign Currency Translation: The New Accounting Approach," *Accountancy* 92 (February 1981), pp. 105-7.

Price, Claudia I. "The Multinational Corporation and SFAS No. 8," *The Woman CPA* 42 (October 1980), pp. 26-30.

Radebaugh, Lee. "Accounting for Price-Level and Exchange Rate Changes for U.S. International Firms: An Empirical Study," *Journal of International Business Studies* 5 (Fall 1974), pp. 41-56.

_____. "The International Dimension of the Financial Accounting Standards Board: Translation and Disclosure of Foreign Operations," *The International Journal of Accounting Education and Research* 10 (Fall 1974), pp. 55-70.

Reckers, Philip M. J., and Martin E. Taylor. "FASB No. 8—Does it Distort Financial Statements?" *The CPA Journal* 48 (August 1978), pp. 31-34.

Rickard, D. R. "Currency Translation," *The Australian Accountant* 50 (January/February 1980), pp. 10-11.

Rodriguez, Rita M. "FASB No. 8: What Has It Done To Us?" *Financial Analysts Journal* 33 (March/April 1977), pp. 40-47.

Rogalski, Richard J., and Joseph D. Vinso. "Price Level Variations as Predictors of Flexible Exchange Rates," *Journal of International Business Studies* 8 (Spring/Summer 1977), pp. 71-82.

Rosenfield, Paul. "Accounting for Foreign Branches and Subsidiaries," *The Inter-*

national Journal of Accounting Education and Research (Spring 1972), pp. 35-44.

Scott, David A., and Bryan C. Walker. "Foreign Currency Translation in Canada and the US," *CA Magazine*, 110 (November 1977), pp. 48-53.

Scott, George M. "Currency Exchange Rates and Accounting Translation: A Mismarriage?" *Abacus* 11 (June 1975), pp. 58-70.

Seidler, Lee J. "An Income Approach to the Translation of Foreign Currency Financial Statements," *The CPA Journal* 42 (January 1972), pp. 26-35.

Shank, John K. "How Good Is FASB Statement No. 8?" *Financial Analysts Journal* 32 (July/August 1976), pp. 55-61.

Shank, John K., Jesse F. Dillard, and Richard J. Murdock. "FASB No. 8 and the Decision-Makers," *Financial Executive* 48 (February 1980), pp. 18-23.

Shank, John K., and Gary S. Shamis. "Reporting Foreign Currency Adjustments: Disclosure Perspective," *The Journal of Accountancy* 147 (April 1979), pp. 59-67.

Shwayder, Keith R. "Accounting for Exchange Rate Fluctuations," *The Accounting Review* 47 (October 1972), pp. 747-60.

Sibley, Angus. "Exchange Control: The Cage Opens," *The Accountant's Magazine*, 83 (December 1979), pp. 509-12.

Smith, Alan F. "Temporal Method: Temporary Mode?" *Management Accounting* 59 (February 1978), pp. 21-26.

Stanley, Marjorie, and Stanley B. Block, "Response by United States Financial Managers to Financial Accounting Standard No. 8," *Journal of International Business Studies* 9 (Fall 1978), pp. 89-99.

Stanley, Marjorie T., and Stanley B. Block, "Accounting and Economic Aspects of SFAS No. 8," *The International Journal of Accounting Education and Research* 14 (Spring 1979), pp. 135-55.

Steinle, Kurt. "Currency Translation—A German View," *Accountancy* 87 (March 1976), pp. 42-45.

Stern, Michael. "When to Discount Your Bills of Exchange," *Accountancy* 88 (October 1977), pp. 60-64.

Teck, Alan. "Beyond FAS No. 8: Defining Other Exposures," *Management Accounting* 60 (December 1978), pp. 54-57.

Willey, Russell W. "In Defense of FAS No. 8," *Management Accounting* 61 (December 1979), pp. 36-40.

_____. "Foreign Currency Translation on the Shelf," *CA Magazine* 112 (April 1979), pp. 54-57.

Wyman, Harold E. "Analysis of Gains or Losses from Foreign Monetary Items: An Application of Purchasing Power Parity Concepts," *The Accounting Review* 51 (July 1976), pp. 545-58.

Appendix 4A

ANOTHER ILLUSTRATION OF FASB STATEMENT NO. 52

The example given in the chapter pertains to the first year of inception of the subsidiary named the Foreign Company. To illustrate the translation process for year 19X2, let's assume that the second financial statements of the Foreign Company, for the period ending December 31, 19X2, are as shown in Exhibits 4.17, 4.18, and 4.19 and that they have been prepared in accordance with U.S. generally accepted accounting principles. To facilitate the translation process, selected foreign exchange rates are provided as Exhibit 4.20. As suggested earlier, the translation process is examined first under the assumption of the U.S. dollar as the functional currency and second under the assumption of the foreign currency as the functional currency.

The translated statements of the Foreign Company for 19X2 and supporting schedules when the U.S. dollar is the functional currency are shown as Exhibits 4.21, 4.22, 4.23, 4.24, 4.25, 4.26, 4.27, and 4.28.

The translated statements of the Foreign Company for 19X2 and supporting schedules when the foreign currency is the functional currency are shown as Exhibits 4.29, 4.30, 4.31, 4.32, and 4.33.

	19x2 (Thousands)
Current Assets:	
Cash	FC 625.00
Accounts Receivable-Trade	1,951.25
Accounts Receivable-Intercompany	471.25
Notes Receivable	1,485.00
Inventories	4,550.00
Prepaid Expenses	212.65
Accrued Interest on Notes Receivable	17.90
Total Currrent Assets	FC 9,313.05
Long Current Assets	FC 3,000.00
Property Plant and Equipment:	
Land	8,500.00
Buildings	78,384.00
Equipment	19,966.00
Total Property, Plant & Equipment	FC 106,850.00
Accumulated Depreciation	FC (11,633.60)
Net Property, Plant and Equipment	FC 95,216.40
Total Assets	FC 107,529.45
Current Liabilities:	
Accounts Payable	1,387.275
Accrued Interest on Long Term Best	255.00
Income Tax Payable	381.625
Dividends Payable	250.00
Current Portion of Long Term Debt	1,250.00
Total Current Liabilities	FC 3,523.90
Long Term Debt:	37,500.00
Deferred Income Taxes	929.45
Stockholders' Equity:	
Common Stock	25,000.00
Contributed Capital in Excess of Par	38,591.20
Retained Earnings	1,984.90
Total Stockholder's Equity	FC 65,576.10
Total Liabilities and Stockholders' Equity	FC 107,529.45

EXHIBIT 4.18 INCOME STATEMENT IN FOREIGN CURRENCY—FOREIGN COMPANY, DECEMBER 31, 19X2 (in thousands)

	19x2 (Thousands	
Sales		FC 42,037.75
Cost and Expenses:		
Cost of Goods Sold		
Inventory - January 1	3,950.25	
Production Costs	24,231.25	
Goods Avaiable for Sale	28,181.50	
Inventory - December 31	(4,550.00)	
Cost of Goods Sold:		23,631.50
General and Administrative		4,865.70
Advertising and Selling		3,663.00
Depreciation		6,001.00
Total Costs and Expenses		FC 38,161.20
Net Income From Operations:		3,876.55
(Other Income (Expenses)		(1,493.75)
Net Income Before Taxes:		2,382.80
Income Taxes		
Current		571.85
Deferred		381.35
Total Taxes		FC 953.20
Net Income		FC 1,429.60

EXHIBIT 4.19 STATEMENT OF RETAINED EARNINGS IN FOREIGN CURRENCY—FOREIGN COMPANY, YEAR ENDED DECEMBER 31, 19X2

	19x2
Retained Earnings - January 1	FC 1,555.30
Add Net Income for the year	1,429.60
Deduct Dividends for the year	(1,000.00)
Retained Earnings - December 31	1,984.90

EXHIBIT 4.20 FOREIGN CURRENCY RATES (19X2)

	U.S. Dollar is Functional Currency	Foreign Currency is Functional Currency
	FC1	FC1
Rates:	19x2	19x2
1. Current Rate at March 31	$1.96	NA*
2. Current Rate at June 30	$2.00	NA
3. Current Rate at September 30	$2.00	NA
4. Current Rate at December 31	$1.96	$1.96
5. Average Rate for the year	$1.98	$1.98
6. Historical Rate When Stock was Issued and Land Purchased	$1.96	
7. Historical Rate When Property Plant, and Equipment were Purchased	$1.96	NA
8. Average Historical Rate Applicable to Inventories on Hand at December 31	$2.00	NA

EXHIBIT 4.21 BALANCE SHEET—FOREIGN COMPANY, YEAR ENDED DECEMBER 31, 19X2

U.S. $ is Functional Currency (In Thousands)

Current Assets:	Foreign Currency	Translation Rate	Dollar Balance
Cash	FC 625.00	1.96	$ 1,225.00
Accounts Receivable - Trade	1,951.25	1.96	3,824.45
Accounts Receivable - Intercompany	471.25	--	105.00[3]
Notes Receivable	1,485.00	1.96	2,910.60
Inventories	4,550.00	2.00*	9,100.00
Prepaid Expenses	212.65	2.00**	425.30
Accrued Interest on Notes Rec.	17.90	1.96	35.08
Total Current Assets	FC 9,313.05		$ 17,625.43
Long Term Noted Receivable	FC 3,000.00	1.96	$ 5,880.00
Property, Plant & Equipment			
Land	8,500.00	2.04	17,340.00
Building	78,384.00		156,628.86[1]
Fixtures & Equipment	19,966.00		39,785.88[2]
Total Property, Plant & Equipment	FC 106,850.00		$ 213,754.74
Accumulated Depreciation	(11,633.60)	1.96	(23,252.46)[4]
Net Property, Plant & Equipment	FC 95,216.40		$ 190,502.28
Total Assets	FC 107,529.45		$ 214,007.71

[a]Used average historical rates for inventories on hand on December 31.
[b]Prepaid expenses assumed to be purchased on September 30, 19X2.
[c]Information given.
[d]See Exhibit 4.24.

120

EXHIBIT 4.22 BALANCE SHEET IN U.S. DOLLARS—FOREIGN COMPANY, YEAR ENDED DECEMBER 31, 19X2.

U.S. $ is Functional Currency (In Thousands)

Current Liabilities:	Foreign Currency		Translation Rate	Dollar Balance	
Accounts Payable	FC	1,387.27	1.96	$	2,714,04
Accrued Interest on Long Term Debt		255.00	1.96		499.80
Income Taxes Payable		381.62	1.96		747.97
Dividends Payable		250.00	1.96		490.00
Current Maturities on Long Term Term Debt		1,250.00	1.96		2,450.00
Total Current Liabilities	FC	3,523.90	1.96	$	6,906.81
Long Term Debt		37,500.00	1.96		73,500.00**
Deferred Income Taxes		929.45	1.96		1,784.54**
Stockholders' Equity:					
Common Stock		25,000.00	2.04		51,000.00
Contributed Capital in Excess of Par		38,591.20	2.04		78,726.04
Retained Earings		1,984.90			2,090.32*
Total Stockholders' Equity	FC	65,576.10		$	131,816.36
Total Liabilities and Stockholders Equity	FC	107,529.45		$	214,007.71

aSee Exhibit 4.24.
bSee Exhibits 4.25 and 4.26.

EXHIBIT 4.23 BALANCE SHEET IN U.S. DOLLARS—FOREIGN COMPANY, YEAR ENDED DECEMBER 31, 19X2

U.S. $ is Functional Currency (In Thousands)

Balance Sheet Calculations

1. **Property, Plant and Equipment**

Buildings Acquired in 19x1 (FC 74,905.50 x 2.00)	$ 149,811.00
Building Acquired in 19x2 (FC 3,478.50 x 1.96(	6,817.86
Translated Building Account	$156,628.86
Fixtures & Equipment Acquired in 19x1 (FC 16,313.00 x 2.00	$326,626.00
Fixtures & Equipment Acquired in 19x2 (FC 3653.00 x 1.96	7,159.88
Translated Fixtures & Equipment Account	$39,785.88

Accumulated Depreciation

Straight Line Depreciation for 19x1	FC	5,632.60
Straight Line Depreciation for 19x2 on Assets Acquired in 19x1	FC	5,632.60
Straight Line Depreciation for 19x2 on Assets Acquired in 19x2	FC	368.40
Foreign Currency Balance in Accumulated Depreciation Account		$11,633.60

121

EXHIBIT 4.24 BALANCE SHEET CALCULATIONS

U.S. $ is Functional Currency (In Thousands)

Depreciation on Assets Acquired in 19x1	
(FC 5632.6 x 2 Years x 2.00)	$ 22,530.40
Depreciation on Assets Acquired in 19x2	
(FC 368.40 x 1 Year x 1.96)	722.06
Accumulated Depreciation	$ 23,252.46
Deferred Income Taxes	
Deferred Taxes Resulting From 19x1	
(FC 548.10 x 1.92)	1,052.35
Deferred Increase Resulting From 19x2	
(FC 381.35 x 1.92)	732.19
Deferred Income Taxes in Dollars	$ 1,784.54
Stockholders Equity Section	
Current Liabilities	6,906.81
Long Term Debt	73,500.00
Deferred Income Taxes	1,784.54
Common Stock	51,000.00
Contributed Capital in Excess of Par	78,726.04
Total Liabilities & Equities Translated	$ 211,917.39

EXHIBIT 4.25 BALANCE SHEET CALCULATIONS

U.S. $ is Functional Currency (In Thousands)

Translated Value of Assets	$ 2,14,007.71
Translated Value of Liabilities and Equity	
Accounts Other Than Retained Earnings	2,11,917.39
Retained Earnings Balance, December 31, 19x2	$ 2,090.32
Dividend	
March 31 Dividend (FC 250.00 x 1.96	$ 490.00
June 30 Dividend (FC 250.00 x 2.00)	500.00
September 30 Dividend (FC 250.00 x 2.00)	500.00
December 31 Dividend (FC 250.00 x 1.96)	490.00
Dividends for 19x2	$ 1,980.00
Retained Earnings - January 1	$ 3,301.11
Add Net Income for the Year	2,974.36
Deduct Dividends for the Year	(1,980.00)
Retained Earnings - December 31	$ 4,295.47

EXHIBIT 4.26 BALANCE SHEET CALCULATIONS

U.S. $ is Functional Currency (In Thousands)

Net Income From Operations		$ 7,819.31
Non-operating Items:		
Other Income (Expense)	(2,957.62)	
Translation Loss	(2,205.15)*	(5,162.77)
		$ 2,656.54
Net Income Before Taxes		
Income Taxes		
Current	1,132.26	
Deferred	755.07	1,887.33
Net Income		$ 769.21

   Ret. Earn: Ret. Earn.
*-4295.47 + 2,090.32 = (2205.15)
Restating Net Income in Statement of Retained Earnings

Retained Earnings - January 1	$ 3,301.11
Add Net Income for the Year	769.21
Deduct Dividends for the Year	(1,980.00)
Retained Earnings - December 31	$ 2,090.32

EXHIBIT 4.27 INCOME STATEMENT IN U.S. DOLLARS—FOREIGN COMPANY, YEAR ENDED DECEMBER 31, 19X2

U.S. $ is Functional Currency (In Thousands)

	Foreign Currency	Translation Rate	Dollar Balance
Sales	FC 42,037.76	1.98	$83,234,74
Costs and Expenses			
Cost of Goods Sold:			
Inventory - January 1	3,950.25	1.94*	7,663.48
Production Costs	24,231.25	1.98	47,977.87
Cost of Goods for Sale	FC 28,181.50		$55,641.35
Inventory - December 31	(4,550.00)	2.00**	(9,100.00)
Cost of Goods Sold	FC 23,631.50		$46,541.35
General and Administrative	4,865.70	1.98	9,634.08
Advertising and Selling	3,663.00	1.98	7,252.74
Depreciation[1]	6,001.00		11,987.26[1]
Total Costs and Expenses	FC 38,161.20		$75,415.43
Net Income from Operations	3,876.55		7,819.31
Other Income (Expenses)	(1,493.75)	1.98	(2,957.62)
Net Income Before Taxes	FC 2,302.00		$ 4,861.69
Income Taxes			
Current	571.85	1.98	$ 1,132.26
Deferred	381.35	1.98	755.07
Total Taxes	FC 953.20		$ 1,887.33
Net Income	FC 1,429.60		$ 2,974.36

[a]See 19X1 income statement.
[b]See 19X2 balance sheet translation.
[c]See Exhibit 4.28.

EXHIBIT 4.28 CALCULATION OF DEPRECIATION EXPENSE FOR 19X2

U.S. $ is Functional Currency (In Thousands)

Straight Line Depreciation in 19x2 on Assets Acquired in 19x1 (FC 5,632.60 x 2.00)	$11,265.20
Straight Line Depreciation in 19x2 on Assets Acquired in 19x2 (FC 368.40 x 1.96)	722.06
Depreciation Expense for 19x2	$11,987.26

EXHIBIT 4.29 BALANCE SHEET—FOREIGN COMPANY, YEAR ENDED DECEMBER 31, 19X2

Foreign Currency is Functional Currency (In Thousands)

Current Assets:	Foreign Currency	Translation Rate	Dollar Balance
Cash	FC 625.00	1.96	$ 1,225.00
Accounts Receivable-Trade	1,951.25	1.96	3,824.45
Accounts Receivable-Intercompany	471.25	1.96	923.65
Notes Receivable	1,485.00	1.96	2,910.60
Inventories	4,550.00	1.96	8,918.00
Accrued Interest on Notes Rec.	17.90	1.96	35.08
Prepaid Expenses	212.65	1.96	416.79
Total Current Assets	FC 9,313.05		$ 18,253.57
Long Term Notes Receivable	3,000.00	1.96	5,880.00
Property, Plant & Equipment			
Land	8,500.00	1.96	16,660.00
Building	78,384.00	1.96	153,632.64
Fixtures & Equipment	19.966.00	1.96	39,133,36
Total Property, Plant and Equipment	FC 106,850.00		$ 209,426.00
Accumulated Depreciation	(11,633.60)	1.96	(22,801.85)
Net Property, Plant and Equipment	FC 95,216.40		$1,86,624.15
Total Assets	FC 107,529.45		$ 210,757.72

EXHIBIT 4.30 BALANCE SHEET—FOREIGN COMPANY, YEAR ENDED DECEMBER 31, 19X2

Foreign Currency is Functional Currency (In Thousands)

Current Liabilities		Foreign Currency	Translation Rate	Dollar Balance
Account Payable	FC	1,387.27	1.96	$ 2,719.04
Accrued Interest on Long Term Debt		255.05	1.96	499.00
Income Taxes Payable		381.62	1.96	747.97
Dividends Payable		250.00	1.96	490.00
Current Maturities on Long Term Debt		1,250.00	1.96	2,450.00
Total Current Liabilities	FC	3,523.90	1.96	$ 6,906.81
Long Term Debt		37,500.00	1.96	73,500.00
Deferred Income Taxes		929.45	1.96	1,821.72
Stockholders' Equity				
Common Stock		25,000.00	2.04	51,000.00
Contributed Capital in Excess of Par		38,591.20	2.04	78,726.04
Retained Earnings		1,984.90		3,904.73*
Translation Adjustment				(5,101.61)**
Total Stockholders Equity	FC	65,576.10		$128,529.16
Total Liabilities and Stockholders Equity	FC	107,529.45		$210,757.72

aTaken from statement of retained earnings (Exhibit 4.33).
bSee Exhibit 4.32.

EXHIBIT 4.31 INCOME STATEMENT—FOREIGN COMPANY, YEAR ENDED DECEMBER 31, 19X2

Foreign Currency is Functional Currency (In Thousands)

		Foreign Currency	Translation Rate	Dollar Balance
Sales	FC	42,037.75	1.98	$83,234.74
Costs and Expenses				
Cost of Goods Sold				
Inventory - January 1		3,950.25	1.98	7,821.49
Production Costs		24,231.25	1.98	47,977.87
Cost of Goods for Sales		28,181.50	1.98	$55,799.37
Inventory - December 31		(4,550.00)	1.98	(9,009.00)
Cost of Goods Sold	FC	23,631.50	1.98	$46,790.37
General and Administrative		4,865.70	1.98	9,634.08
Advertising Expense		3,663.00	1.98	7,262.74
Depreciation		6,001.00	1.98	11,881.98
Total Costs and Expenses	FC	38,161.20	1.98	75,559.17
Net Income from Operations		3,876.55	1.98	$ 7,675.57
Non-operating Items:				
Other Income (Expense)		(1,493.75)	1.98	(2,957.62)
Net Income Before Taxes	FC	2,382.80	1.98	$ 4,717.95
Income Taxes				
Current		571.85	1.98	1,132.26
Deferred		381.35	1.98	755.07
Total Taxes		953.20	1.98	$ 1,887.33
Net Income	FC	1,429.60	1.98	$ 2,830.62

EXHIBIT 4.32 COMPUTATION OF TRANSLATION ADJUSTMENT FOR 19X2

Foreign Currency is Functional Currency (In Thousands)

Total Assets - Foreign Currency		$ 107,529.45
Total Liabilities - Foreign Currency		
Current	3,523.90	
Long Term Debt	37,500.00	
Deferred Income Taxes	929.45	
Total Liabilities		41,953.35
Net Assets - Foreign Currency		$ 65,576.10
End of Period Exchange Rate		1.96
Net Assets in Dollars		$ 128,529.16
Stockholders Equity - Dollars		
Common Stock	51,000.00	
Contributed Capital in Excess of Par	78,726.04	
Retained Earnings	3,904.73	
Total Stockholders Equity in Dollars		133,630.77
Translation Adjustment		$ (5,101.61)

EXHIBIT 4.33 STATEMENT OF RETAINED EARNINGS, YEAR ENDED DECEMBER 31, 19X2

Foreign Currency is Functional Currency (In Thousands)

Retained Earnings - January 1	3,054.11[1]
Add Net Income for the Year	2,830.62[2]
Deduct Dividends for the Year	(1.980.00)[3]
Retained Earnings - December 31, 19x2	$3,904.73

---

[a]Taken from statement of retained earnings, 19X1.
[b]See 19X2 income statement, Exhibit 4.31.
[c]Dividends are computed in the same manner as in the section using the U.S.$ as the functional currency.

5.

ACCOUNTING FOR INFLATION INTERNATIONALLY

Inflation is here to stay internationally. Accounting does not create bad news but simply reports it. How to report the effects of inflation on the financial position, performance, and conduct of a firm is the issue. Various models have been advocated in the literature and in practice. This chapter explains the differences, advantages, and limitations of each of the proposals advocated in the literature before examining the solutions advocated in practice in the U.S., Great Britain, Canada, and the Netherlands.

The Concept of Income

Why measure income? Arguments in favor of measuring income could be extended ad infinitum. Income is a basic and important item of financial statements. It has various uses in various contexts. Income is generally perceived as a basis for taxation, a determinant of dividend payment policy, a guide for investment and decision making, and an element of prediction.

The most popular expression of income is the accounting income. It is operationally defined as the difference between the *realized revenues* arising from the transactions of the period and the *corresponding historical costs*. This definition suggests five characteristics of accounting income. First, accounting income is based on the actual transaction entered into by the firm, primarily revenues arising from the sales of goods or services minus the costs necessary to achieve these sales. Second, it is based on the period postulate, meaning that it refers to the financial performance of the firm for a given period. Third, it is based on the revenue principle in general and the realization test in particular for the recognition of revenues. Fourth, it requires the measurement of expenses in terms of the historical cost to the enterprise, constituting a strict adherence to the cost principle. Finally, it is based on the matching principle, which requires that the realized revenues of the period be related to appropriate or corresponding costs.

Accounting income has been the subject of compliments and criticisms. Among the advantages claimed for accounting income are the facts that it has survived the test of time, it is objective and verifiable, it meets the criterion of conservatism, and it is useful for control purposes and especially in reporting on stewardship. Among the criticisms are the facts that it fails to recognize unrealized increases in the values of assets held in a given period because of the application of the historical and realization principles, it makes comparability difficult given the different acceptable methods of computing "cost," it leads to misleading and irrelevant data given reliance on the realization, historical cost, and conservatism principles, and it may give the impression to the users that the balance sheet represents an approximation of value rather than merely a statement of unallocated cost balances.

Given the limitations of accounting income, especially its failure to account for the effects of inflation, various proposals have been considered in the literature and in practice. An understanding of all the proposals rests on an understanding of the economic concept of income which serves as a basis for all these proposals.

Hicks used concepts introduced by various economists such as Irving Fisher and Lindahl to develop a general theory of economic income.[1] He defined a person's personal income as "the maximum amount he can consume during a week, and still expect to be as well-off at the end of the week as he was at the beginning."[2] This definition has become the basis of many discussions on the concept of income. One problem raised by such a definition, however, is the lack of consensus on the interpretation of the term *as well-off*, or *welloffness*. The most accepted interpretation is that of "capital maintenance," in which case the "Hicksian" income is the maximum amount which may be consumed in a given period and still maintain the capital intact.

Concepts of Capital Maintenance

The concept of capital maintenance implies that income is recognized after capital has been maintained or costs have been recovered. Return on capital (income) is distinguished from return of capital (cost recovery). Two principal concepts of capital maintenance or cost recovery may be expressed both in terms of units of money and in terms of units of the same general purchasing power: financial capital and physical capital. We have, therefore, four concepts of capital maintenance.

1. Financial capital measured in terms of money (money maintenance), which implies that the financial capital invested or reinvested by the owners is maintained. *Conventional accounting*, as it relies on historical cost for the valuation of assets and liabilities, conforms to the money-maintenance concept.

2. Financial capital measured in units of the same purchasing power (general purchasing power money maintenance), which implies that the purchasing power of the financial capital invested or reinvested by the owner is maintained. *General price level-adjusted historical cost accounting* conforms to the general purchasing power money maintenance concept.

3. Physical capital measured in units of money (productive capacity maintenance), which implies that the physical productive capacity of the firm is maintained. Alternative definitions of capacity are:

   a. Productive capacity should be defined as the physical assets possessed by the company, so that profit would be the amount that could be distributed after making sufficient provision to replace the physical assets held by the company as they are consumed or wear out.

   b. Productive capacity should be defined as the capacity to produce the same *volume* of goods and services in the following year as could be produced in the current year.

   c. Productive capacity should be defined as the capacity to produce the same *value* of goods and services in the following year as could be produced in the current year.[3]

Productive capacity maintenance is the concept of capital maintenance used in current-value accounting, in which assets and liabilities are disclosed in the financial statements at their current values.

4. Physical capital measured in units of the same purchasing power (general purchasing power productive capacity maintenance), which implies that the physical productive capacity of the firm measured in units of the same purchasing power is maintained.

The following example illustrates the impact on income statements of each of the four concepts of capital maintenance. Let us suppose that a given firm has $4,000 of net assets at the beginning and $6,000 of net assets at the end of a given period. Let us also assume that $5,000 of net assets is required to maintain the actual physical productive capacity and that the general price level increased by 10 percent during the period. Income under each of the concepts of capital maintenance would be:

Money maintenance:
$6,000 − $4,000 = $2,000

General purchasing power money maintenance:
$6,000 − ($4,000 + 0.10 × $4,000) = $1,600

Productive capacity maintenance:
$6,000 − $5,000 = $1,000

General purchasing power productive capacity maintenance:
$6,000 − ($5,000 + 0.10 × $5,000) = $500

The accounting income, therefore, is $2,000, the general price level-adjusted accounting income is $1,600, the current value-based income is $1,000, and the general price level-adjusted current value-based income is $500. Each of these income concepts is discussed next.

Alternative Asset Valuation and Income Determination Models

To illustrate the different accounting models, let's consider the simplified case of the "Zribi Company," which was formed January 1, 19X6, to distribute a new product called HEDI. Capital is composed of 33,000 equity and $3,000 liabilities carrying a 10 percent interest. On January 1, the Zribi Company began operations by purchasing 600 units of HEDI at $10 per unit. On May 1, the company sold 500 units at $15 per unit. Changes in the general and specific price levels for the year 19X6 are as follows:

	January 1	May 1	December 31
Replacement cost	$ 10	$ 12	$ 13
Net realizable value	—	$ 15	$ 17
General price level index	$100	$130	$156

A brief description of each accounting model follows, accompanied by illustrations using the given data.

ALTERNATIVE ACCOUNTING MODELS EXPRESSED IN UNITS OF MONEY

To illustrate and isolate only timing differences, we present first the alternative accounting models which do not reflect changes in the general price level. These models are historical cost accounting, replacement cost accounting, and net realizable value accounting. The income statements and the balance sheets for 19X6 under the three accounting models are shown as Exhibits 5.1 and 5.2, respectively.

Historical Cost Accounting

Historical cost accounting, or conventional accounting, is characterized primarily by the use of historical cost as the attribute of the elements of financial statements, the assumption of a stable monetary unit, the matching principle, and the realization principle. Accordingly, historical cost income, or accounting income, is the difference between the realized revenues and the corresponding historical costs. As shown in Exhibit 5.1, accounting income is equal to $2,200. What does this figure represent for the Zribi Company? Generally it is perceived as a basis for the computation of taxes and dividends and for the evaluation of performance. Its possible

EXHIBIT 5.1 ZRIBI COMPANY INCOME STATEMENTS, DECEMBER 31, 19X6

	Historical Cost	Replacement Cost	Net Realizable Value
Revenues	$7,500a	$7,500	$9,200b
Cost Goods Sold	5,000c	6,000d	7,300e
Gross Margin	$2,500	$1,500	$1,900
Interest	300	300	300
Operating Profit	$2,200	$1,200	$1,600
Realized Holding Gains and Losses	Included above	1,000f	1,000
Unrealized Holding Gains and Losses	Not applicable	300g	300
General Price-Level Gains and Losses	Not applicable	Not applicable	Not applicable
Net Profit	$2,200	$2,500	$2,900

a500 × $15 = $7,500.
b7,500 + $17 (100) = $9,200.
c500 × $10 = $5,000.
d500 × $12 = $6,000.
e6,000 + $13 (100) = $7,300.
f500 ($12 − $10) = $1,000.
g100 ($13 − $10) = $300.

EXHIBIT 5.2 ZRIBI COMPANY BALANCE SHEETS, DECEMBER 31, 19X6

	Historical Cost	Replacement Cost	Net Realizable Value
Assets			
Cash	$7,200	$7,200	$7,200
Inventory	1,000	1,300a	1,700b
Total Assets	$8,200	$8,500	$8,900
Equities			
Bonds (10%)	$3,000	$3,000	$3,000
Capital	3,000	3,000	3,000
Retained Earnings			
Realized	2,200	2,200c	2,200c
Unrealized	Not applicable	300	700d
Total Equities	$8,200	$8,500	$8,900

a100 × ($13) = $1,300.
b100 × ($17) = $1,700.
cMay be divided into current operating profit ($1,200) and realized holding gains and losses ($1,000).
dUnrealized operating gain of $400 ($1,700 - $1,300) + unrealized holding gain of $300.

use in various decision models results from the unconditional and long-standing acceptance of this version of income by the accounting profession and the business world. This attachment to accounting income may be explained primarily by the fact that it is objective, verifiable, practical, and easy to understand. Accountants and business persons may prefer account-ing income over other measures of income for its practical advantages, and they may fear the confusion that could result from the adoption of another accounting model.

In spite of these practical advantages, the Zribi Company's $2,200 accounting income contains both timing and measuring unit errors—timing errors because it includes in a single figure operating income and holding gains and losses which are recognized in the current period and which occurred in the current period but which are recognizable in future periods, and measuring unit errors because it does not take into account changes in the general price level that would have resulted in amounts expressed in units of general purchasing power and, by relying on historical cost as the attribute of the elements of financial statements rather than either replacement cost or net realizable value, it does not take into account changes in the specific price level.

How, then, should we evaluate historical cost financial statements? First, they are interpretable. They are based on the concept of money mainten-ance. The attribute being expressed is the number of dollars (NOD). The balance sheet reports in NOD at December 31, 19X6, and the income statement reports the change in NOD during the year. Second, historical cost financial statements are not relevant because the command of goods (COG) is not measured. A measure of COG permits reflection of the changes in both the specific and general price levels, and, therefore, such a measure represents the ability to buy the amount of goods necessary for capital maintenance.

In summary, historical cost financial statements contain timing errors, contain measuring unit errors, are interpretable, and are not relevant.

Replacement Cost Accounting

Replacement cost accounting, as a particular case of current entry price accounting, is characterized primarily by the use of replacement cost as the attribute of the elements of financial statements, the assumption of a stable monetary unit, the realization principle, the dichotomization of operating income and holding gains and losses, and the dichotomization of realized and unrealized holding gains and losses.

Accordingly, replacement cost net income is equal to the sum of replacement cost operating income and holding gains and losses. Replace-ment cost operating income is equal to the difference between the realized revenues and the corresponding replacement costs. From Exhibit 5.1, the Zribi Company's replacement cost net income of $2,500 is composed of replacement cost operating income of $1,200, realized holding gains and losses of $1,000, and unrealized holding gains and losses of $300.

What do these figures represent for the Zribi Company? The replacement cost operating income represents the "distributable" income, or the maximum amount of dividends the company can pay and maintain its productive capacity intact. The realized holding gains and losses constitute an indicator of the efficiency of holding resources up to the time of sale. The realization holding gains and losses are an indicator of the efficiency of holding performances. In addition to these practical advantages, replacement cost net income contains timing errors on only operating profit. It does, however, contain measuring unit errors.

Replacement cost net income contains timing errors because it omits the operating profit that occurred in the current period but which is realizable in future periods, it includes the operating profit which is recognized in the current period but which occurred in previous periods, and it includes holding gains and losses in the same period as they occur.

In addition, replacement cost net income contains measuring unit errors because it does not take into account changes in the general price level which would have resulted in amounts expressed in units of general purchasing power and it does take into account changes in the specific price level, as it relies on replacement cost as the attribute of the elements of financial statements.

We may evaluate replacement cost financial statements as follows. First, they are interpretable. They are based on the concept of productive capacity maintenance. The attribute being expressed is still the NOD in the income statement. The asset figures, however, are interpretable as measures of COG. The asset figures shown in Exhibit 5.2 are expressed in terms of the purchasing power of the dollar at the end of the year. They reflect changes in both the specific and the general price levels, and, therefore, they represent the COG necessary for capital maintenance. Second, because COG is the relevant attribute, the replacement net income is not relevant, even though the asset figures are relevant.

In summary, replacement cost financial statements present the following characteristics: They contain operating profit timing errors, they contain measuring unit errors, they are interpretable as NOD for the income and COG for the asset figures, and only the asset figures are relevant as measures of COG.

Net Realizable Value Accounting

Net realizable value accounting, as a particular case of current exit price accounting, is characterized primarily by the use of net realizable value as the attribute of the elements of financial statements, by the assumption of a stable monetary unit, by the abandonment of the realization principle, and by the dichotomization of operating income and holding gains and losses.

Accordingly, under net realizable value accounting, net income is equal to the sum of the net realizable value operating income and holding gains and losses. Net realizable value operating income is equal to the operating income arising from sale and the net operating income on inventory. Operating income on sale is equal to the difference between the realized revenues and the corresponding replacement cost of the items sold. From Exhibit 5.1, the Zribi Company's net realizable value net income of $2,900 is composed of net realizable value operating income of $1,600, realized holding gains of $1,000, and unrealized holding gains and losses of $300.

Note that the net realizable value operating income is composed of operating income on sale of $1,200 and operating income on inventory of $400. Thus, in Exhibit 5.2, unrealized retained earnings equal the sum of the unrealized holding gains and losses of $300 and the operating income on inventory of $400.

What do these figures represent for the Zribi Company? They are similar to the figures obtained with replacement cost accounting, except for the operating income on inventory, which results from the abandonment of the realization principle and the recognition of revenues at the time of production and at the time of sale. Net realizable value net income indicates the firm's ability to liquidate and to adapt to new economic situations.

To these practical advantages we may add that net realizable net income contains no timing errors, but it does contain measuring unit errors. It does not contain any timing errors because it reports all operating profit and holding gains and losses in the same period in which they occur and it excludes all operating and holding gains and losses occurring in previous periods.

Net realizable value net income contains measuring unit errors because it does not take into account changes in the general price level (if it had, it would have resulted in amounts expressed in units of purchasing power) and it does take into account changes in the specific price level because it relies on net realizable value as the attribute of the elements of financial statements.

We may evaluate net realizable value financial statements as follows. First, they are interpretable. They are based on the concept of productive capacity maintenance. The attribute being measured is expressed in NOD in the income statement and COG in the balance sheet. Unlike replacement cost accounting, under net realizable value accounting, asset figures are expressed as measures of COG in the output market rather than the input market. Second, because COG is the relevant attribute, the net realizable value income is not relevant, while the asset figures are.

In summary, net realizable value financial statements present the following characteristics: They contain no timing errors, as shown in Exhibit 5.3; they contain measuring unit errors; they are interpretable as NOD for the net income and COG for the asset figures; and only the asset figures are relevant as measures of COG.

EXHIBIT 5.3 ZRIBI COMPANY TIMING ERROR ANALYSIS, 19X6

TOTAL OPERATING AND HOLDING GAINS	HISTORICAL COST Reported Income	Error	REPLACEMENT COST Reported Income	Error	NET REALIZABLE VALUE Reported Income	Error
$2,900	$2,000	$700	$2,500	$400	$2,900	0

ALTERNATIVE ACCOUNTING MODELS EXPRESSED IN UNITS
OF PURCHASING POWER

To illustrate both timing and measuring unit errors, we present in this section accounting models which reflect changes in the general price level. These models are general price level-adjusted historical cost accounting, general price level-adjusted replacement cost accounting, and general price level-adjusted net realizable value accounting. Continuing with our example of the Zribi Company, the income statements and the balance sheets for 19X6, under the three accounting models, are shown as Exhibits 5.4 and 5.5, respectively. The general price level gain or loss is shown as Exhibit 5.6.

General Price Level-Adjusted Historical Cost Accounting

General price level-adjusted historical cost accounting is characterized primarily by the use of historical cost as the attribute of the elements of financial statements, the use of units of general purchasing power as the unit of measure, the matching principle, and the realization principle. Accordingly, general price level-adjusted historical cost income is the difference between the realized revenues and the corresponding historical costs, both expressed in units of general purchasing power. From Exhibit 5.4, general price level-adjusted historical cost income is equal to $1,080. Included is a $180 general price level gain computed as shown in Exhibit 5.5. Again, what does the $1,080 figure represent for the Zribi Company? It represents accounting income expressed in dollars that have the purchasing power of dollars at the end of 19X6. In addition to the practical advantages listed for accounting income, general price level-adjusted historical cost income is expressed in units of general purchasing power. For these reasons, the use of such an accounting model may constitute a less radical change for those used to historical cost income than any model based on current value.

In spite of these practical advantages, the general price level-adjusted historical cost income of $1,080 contains the same timing errors as does historical cost income. It contains no measuring unit errors because it does take into account changes in the general price level. It does not, however, take into account changes in the specific price level because it relies on historical cost as the attribute of the elements of financial statements rather than on replacement cost or net realizable value.

EXHIBIT 5.4 GENERAL PRICE LEVEL INCOME STATEMENT, DECEMBER 31, 19X6

	Historical Cost	Replacement Cost	Net Realizable Value
Revenues	$9,000a	$9,000	$10,700b
Costs	7,800c	7,200d	8,500e
Gross Margin	$1,200	$1,800	$ 2,200
Interest	300	300	300
Operating Profit	$900	$1,500	$ 1,900
Real Realized Holding Gains and Losses	Included above	(600)f	(600)
Real Unrealized Holding Gains and Losses	Not applicable	(260)g	(260)
General Price-Level Gain or Loss	180h	180	180
Net Profit	$1,080	$ 820	$ 1,220

a$7,500 × $\dfrac{156}{130}$ = $9,000.

b$9,000 + ($17 × 100 units) = $10,700.

c$5,000 × $\dfrac{156}{100}$ = $7,800.

d$6,000 × $\dfrac{156}{130}$ = $7.200.

e$7,200 + ($13 × 100 units) = $8,500.

f $\left[\left(\$12 \times \dfrac{156}{130}\right) - \left(\$10 \times \dfrac{156}{100}\right)\right] \times 500 = (\$600)$

g $\left(\$13 - \$10 \times \dfrac{156}{100}\right) \times 100 \text{ units} = (\$260).$

hSee Exhibit 5.6.

Again, how should we evaluate the general price level-adjusted historical cost financial statements presented in Exhibits 5.4 and 5.5? First, they are interpretable. They are based on the concept of purchasing power money maintenance. The attribute being measured is NOD in some cases and COG in others. Hence, general price level-adjusted historical cost income and all balance sheet figures with the exception of cash (and monetary assets and liabilities) may be interpreted as NOD measures. Only the cash figure (and monetary assets and liabilities) may be interpreted as a COG measure. Second, only the cash figures (and monetary assets and liabilities) are relevant because they are expressed as COG measures.

In summary, general price level-adjusted historical cost financial statements present the following characteristics: They contain timing errors, they contain no measuring unit errors, they are interpretable, and only the cash figures (and monetary assets and liabilities) are relevant as COG measures.

EXHIBIT 5.5 GENERAL PRICE LEVEL BALANCE SHEET, DECEMBER 31, 19X6

	Historical Cost	Replacement Cost	Net Realizable Value
Assets			
Cash	$7,200	$7,200	$7,200
Inventory	1,560a	1,300	1,700
Total Assets	$8,760	$8,500	$8,900
Equities			
Bonds (10%)	$3,000	$3,000	$3,000
Capital	4,680b	4,680	4,680
Retained Earnings			
Realized	900	900	900
Unrealized	Not applicable	260	140c
General Price-Level			
Gain or Loss	180	180	180
Total Equities	$8,760	$8,500	$8,900

a$1,000 × $\frac{156}{100}$ = $1,560

b$3,000 × $\frac{156}{100}$ = $4,680.

cUnrealized operating gain of $400 ($1,700 - $1,300) + unrealized holding gain of ($260).

EXHIBIT 5.6 GENERAL PRICE LEVEL GAIN OR LOSS, DECEMBER 31, 19X6

	Unadjusted	Conversion Factor	Adjusted
Net Monetary Assets on			
January 1, 19X5	$ 3,000	156/100	$ 4,680
Add Monetary Receipts			
during 19X6 Sales	7,500	156/130	9,000
Net Monetary Items	$10,500		$13,680
Less Monetary Payments			
Purchases	6,000	156/100	9,360
Interest	300	156/156	300
Total	$6,300		$ 9,660
Computed Net Monetary			
Assets, December 31, 19X6			4,020
Actual Net Monetary			
Assets, December 31, 19X6			4,200
General Price-Level Gain			$ 180

General Price Level-Adjusted Replacement Cost Accounting

General price level-adjusted replacement cost accounting is characterized primarily by the use of replacement cost as the attribute of the elements of financial statements, by the use of units of general purchasing power as the unit measure, by the realization principle, by the dichotomization of operating income and real realized holding gains and losses, and by the dichotomization of real realized and real unrealized holding gains and losses. Accordingly, general price level-adjusted replacement cost income is equal to the difference between realized revenues and the corresponding replacement costs, both expressed in units of general purchasing power. Similarly, general price level-adjusted replacement cost financial statements eliminate the "fictitious" holding gains and losses to arrive at the "real" holding gains and losses. Fictitious holding gains and losses represent the general price level restatement necessary to maintain the general purchasing power of nonmonetary items. We see from Exhibit 5.4 that the general price level replacement cost net income is equal to $820. Included is a $180 general price level gain, computed as shown in Exhibit 5.5. Again, what does the $820 figure represent for the Zribi Company? It represents the replacement cost net income expressed in units of general purchasing power of the end of 19X7. Such a measure of income has the same advantages that we listed for replacement cost accounting income, with the added advantage of being expressed in units of general purchasing power. For these reasons, general price level restated replacement cost accounting constitutes a net improvement over replacement cost accounting. Not only does this accounting model use replacement cost as an attribute of the elements of financial statements, it also uses the units of general purchasing power as the unit of measure. In spite of these improvements, however, general price level-adjusted replacement cost income contains the same timing errors as replacement cost income, but it contains no measuring unit errors because it takes into account changes in the general price level. In addition, it takes into account changes in the specific price level because it adopts replacement cost as the attribute of the elements of financial statements.

How should we evaluate the general price level-adjusted replacement cost financial statements presented in Exhibits 5.4 and 5.5? First, they are interpretable. They are based on the concept of purchasing power productive capacity maintenance. The attribute we are expressing is COG in both the income statement and the balance sheet. Second, general price level-adjusted replacement cost financial statements are relevant because they are expressed as measures of COG. Note, however, that it is COG in the input market rather than the output market.

In summary, general price level-adjusted replacement cost financial statements contain timing errors, contain no measuring unit errors, are interpretable, and are relevant as COG measures in the input market.

General Price Level-Adjusted Net Realizable Value Accounting

General price level-adjusted net realizable value accounting is character-ized primarily by the use of net realizable value as the attribute of the elements of financial statements, the use of units of general purchasing power as the unit measure, the abandonment of the realization principle, the dichotomization of operating income and real holding gains and losses, and the dichotomization of real realized and unrealized gains and losses. Accordingly, general price level-adjusted net realizable value net income is equal to the sum of the net realizable value operating income and holding gains and losses, both expressed in units of general purchasing power. The general price level-adjusted net realizable value operating income is equal to the sum of operating income arising from sale and operating income on inventory, both expressed in units of general purchasing power. From Exhibit 5.4, the general price level-adjusted net realizable value net income of $1,220 is composed of general price level-adjusted net realizable value operating income of $1,900, real realized holding losses of $600, real unrealized holding losses of $260, and general price level gain of $180.

Note again that the general price level-adjusted net realizable value operating income on sale of $1,900 is composed of the general price level-adjusted net realizable value operating income on sale of $1,500 and general price level-adjusted net realizable value operating income on inventory of $400.

In addition to the advantages of net realizable value net income, general price level-adjusted net realizable value net income has the advantage of being expressed in units of general purchasing power. For these reasons, general price level-net realizable value accounting represents a net improvement on net realizable value accounting. Not only does it use net realizable value as an attribute of the elements of financial statements, but the unit of general purchasing power is the unit of measure.

Thus, general price level-adjusted net realizable value income contains no timing errors and no measuring unit errors. It contains no timing errors. It contains no measuring unit errors because it is expressed in units of general purchasing power.

How should we evaluate the general price-level adjusted net realizable value financial statements presented in Exhibits 5.4 and 5.5? First, they are interpretable. They are based on the concept of purchasing power productive capacity maintenance. The attribute being measured is COG in both the income statements and the balance sheet statements. Second, they are relevant because they are expressed as measures of COG. Note that the COG is in the output market rather than the input market.

In summary, general price level-adjusted net realizable value financial statements contain no timing errors, contain no measuring unit errors, are interpretable, and are relevant as measures of COG in the output market. Such statements, therefore, meet all the criteria established for the comparison and evaluation of the alternative accounting models, as shown in Exhibit 5.7.

EXHIBIT 5.7 ERROR TYPE ANALYSIS

Accounting Model	Timing Error		Measuring Unit Error	Interpretation		
	Operating Profit	Holding Gains		NOD	COG	Relevance
1. Historical Cost Accounting	Yes	Yes	Yes	Yes	No	No
2. Replacement Cost Accounting	Yes	Eliminated	Yes	Yes (Income statement)	Yes (Asset figures)	Yes (Assets figures only)
3. Net Realizable Value Accounting	Eliminated	Eliminated	Yes	Yes (Income statement)	Yes (Monetary assets & liabilities)	Yes (Monetary assets & liabilities)
4. General Price-Level Adjusted Historical Cost Accounting	Yes	Yes	Eliminated	Yes	Yes	Yes
5. General Price-Level Adjusted Replacement Cost Accounting	Yes	Eliminated	Eliminated	Eliminated	Yes	Yes
6. General Price-Level Adjusted Net Realizable Value Accounting	Eliminated	Eliminated	Eliminated	Eliminated	Yes	Yes

The U.S. Solutions to Accounting for Inflation

EARLY ATTEMPTS

Long recognized as a problem in the accounting literature, the issue of accounting for changing prices has been extensively studied by the various accounting standards-setting bodies. The Committee on Accounting Procedure in 1947, 1948, and 1953[4] and the Accounting Principles Board in Opinion No. 6, *Status of Accounting Research Bulletins*, examined the problems relating to changes in the general price level without any success. These attempts were followed by the AICPA's publication of Accounting Research Study No. 6, *Reporting the Financial Effects of Price-Level Changes*, in 1963, and by APB Statement No. 3, *Financial Statements Restated for General Price-Level Changes*, in June 1969. Both recommended supplemental disclosure of general price level information, without any success. The FASB approached the price level subject at a time when inflation was a major concern in the economy. After issuing a Discussion Memorandum, *Reporting the Effects of General Price-Level Changes in Financial Statements* on February 15, 1974; an Exposure Draft, *Financial Reporting in Units of General Purchasing Power*, on December 31, 1974; a Research Report, *Field Tests of Financial Reporting in Units of General Purchasing Power*, in May 1977; a second Exposure Draft, *Financial Reporting and Changing Prices*, on December 28, 1978; and a further Exposure Draft, supplement to the 1974 proposed Statement on general purchasing power adjustments, *Constant Dollar Accounting*, on March 2, 1979, in September 1979 the FASB issued Statement No. 33, *Financial Reporting and Changing Prices*, (FAS 33) which calls for information on the effects of both general inflation and specific price changes.

FINANCIAL ACCOUNTING STANDARDS BOARD STATEMENT NO. 33

FAS 33 is truly the result of years of attempts by the diverse standards-setting bodies to develop methods of reporting the effects of inflation on earnings and assets. In its deliberations, the FASB considered a variety of accounting systems, which are grouped under the following headings:[5]

1. Measurement of inventory and property, plant, and equipment
   a. Historical cost
   b. Current reproduction cost
   c. Current replacement cost
   d. Net realizable value
   e. Net present value of expected future cash flows (value in use)
   f. Recoverable amount
   g. Current cost
   h. Value to business (current cost or lower recoverable amount)

2. Concepts of capital maintenance
   a. Financial capital maintenance
   b. Physical capital maintenance (the maintenance of operating capacity)
3. Measuring units
   a. Measurements in nominal dollars
   b. Measurements in constant dollars

The above list suggests that the FASB examined all the alternative asset-valuation and income-determination models presented in this chapter. The Board concluded, however, that supplementary information should be presented according to historical cost/constant dollar accounting and current cost accounting. More specifically, the FASB requires major companies to disclose the effects of both general inflation and specific price changes as supplementary information in their published annual reports. Major companies are those having assets of more than $1 billion (after deducting accumulated depreciation) or those whose inventories and property, plant, and equipment (before deducting accumulated depreciation) amount to more than $125 million. Specifically, major firms were required to report the following:[6]

1. Constant dollar disclosures (current year)
   a. Information on income from continuing operations for the current fiscal year on a historical cost/constant dollar basis.
   b. The purchasing power gain or loss on net monetary items for the current fiscal year.
The purchasing power gain or loss on net monetary items shall *not* be included in income from continuing operations.
2. Current cost disclosures (current year)
   An enterprise is required to disclose:
   a. Information on income from continuing operations for the current fiscal year on a current cost basis.
   b. The current cost amounts of inventory and property, plant, and equipment at the end of the current fiscal year.
   c. Increases or decreases for the current fiscal year in the current cost amounts of inventory and property, plant, and equipment, net of inflation.
The increases or decreases in current cost amounts shall *not* be included in income from continuing operations.
3. Five-year summary data
   a. Net sales and other operating revenues
   b. Historical cost/constant dollar information
      (1) Income from continuing operations
      (2) Income per common share from continuing operations
      (3) Net assets at fiscal year-end
   c. Current cost information (except for individual years in which the information was excluded from the current year disclosures)

      (1) Income from continuing operations

      (2) Income per common share from continuing operations

      (3) Net assets at fiscal year-end

      (4) Increases or decreases in the current cost amounts of inventory and property, plant, and equipment, net of inflation

   d. Other information

      (1) Purchasing power gain or loss on net monetary items

      (2) Cash dividends declared per common share

      (3) Market price per common share at fiscal year-end

4. Limitation

Whenever the recoverable amount of an asset is less than either the constant dollar value or the current cost value, the recoverable amount should be used to value the asset. "Recoverable amount" means the current value of the net cash flow expected to be realized from the use or sale of the asset.

5. Methodology

   a. The constant dollar method should use the CPI-U index.

   b. The current cost method may use internally or externally developed specific price indexes or evidence such as vendors' invoice prices or price lists to determine the current cost of an asset. The method selected should be based on availability and cost and should be applied consistently.

   c. The constant dollar amounts should be based on average-for-the-year indexes.

   d. The current costs should be based on average current costs of the period for the restatement of items required to compute operating income (cost of goods sold, depreciation, and depletion), and should be restated at end-of-period current costs net of general inflation for measuring the increases or decreases in inventory, plant, property, and equipment. This latter statement requires the use of year-end current costs restated in average-of-the-period constant dollars.

The FASB also provided the additional following information to explain the minimum disclosure requirements for constant dollar and current cost data:[7]

1. Income from continuing operations is income after applicable income taxes but excluding the results of discontinued operations, extraordinary items, and the cumulative effects of accounting changes. If none of the foregoing is present for a business enterprise, income from continuing operations is identical to net income.

2. The purchasing power gain or loss on net monetary items and the increase or decrease in current cost amounts are excluded from income from continuing operations.

3. Current cost information need not be disclosed if it is not materially different from constant dollar information. The reason for omitting current cost information must be disclosed in notes to the supplementary information.

4. Information relating to income from continuing operations may be presented either in the format of a conventional income statement or in a reconciliation

format which discloses adjustments to income from continuing operations in the historical cost/nominal dollar income statement.

5. The *average* Consumer Price Index for All Urban Consumers (CPI-U) is used by business enterprises which present only the minimum constant dollar data for a fiscal year. If an enterprise presents comprehensive financial statements on a constant dollar basis, either the *average* or the *end-of-year* CPI-U may be used.

6. An enterprise which presents only the minimum data required by FASB Statement No. 33 need not restate any financial statement amounts other than inventories, plant assets, cost of goods sold, and depreciation, depletion, and amortization expense.

7. If the historical cost/constant dollar amounts or the current cost amounts of inventories and plant assets exceed the recoverable amounts of those assets, all data required by FAS 33 must be presented on the basis of the lower recoverable amounts. *Recoverable amount for an asset expected to be sold* is its net realizable value (expected sales proceeds less costs of completion and disposal). *Recoverable amount for an asset continuing in use* is its value in use (net present value of future cash inflows, including ultimate proceeds on disposal). Thus, *value in use* is synonymous with *direct valuation*.

8. Current cost of inventories, plant assets, cost of goods sold, and depreciation, depletion, and amortization expense may be determined by one of the following methods:

   a. Indexation by using either externally or internally developed specific price indexes

   b. Direct pricing by using current invoice prices; vendors' price lists, quotations, or estimates; or standard manufacturing costs that reflect current costs.

Exhibits 5.8, 5.9, and 5.10 illustrate these requirements. Thus, FAS 33 requires two supplementary income computations, one dealing with the effects of general inflation and the other with specific price changes. Both types of information are intended to help users in their decisions on investment, lending, and other matters in the following specific ways:

1. Assessment of future cash flows. Present financial statements include measurements of expenses and assets at historical prices. When prices are changing, measurements that reflect current prices are likely to provide useful information for the assessment of future cash flows.

2. Assessment of enterprise performance. The worth of an enterprise can be increased as a result of prudent timing of asset purchases when prices are changing. That increase is one aspect of performance even though it may be distinguished from operating performance. Measurements which reflect current prices can provide a basis for assessing the extent to which past decisions on the acquisition of assets have created opportunities for earning cash flows.

3. Assessment of the erosion of operating capability. An enterprise typically must hold minimum quantities of inventory, property, plant, and equipment and other assets to maintain its ability to provide goods and services. When the prices of those assets are increasing, larger amounts of money investment are needed to

*EXHIBIT 5.8 STATEMENT OF INCOME FROM CONTINUING OPERATIONS
ADJUSTED FOR CHANGING PRICES, FOR THE YEAR ENDED DECEMBER 31,
19X6 (in thousands of average 19X5 dollars)*

	As Reported in the Primary Statements	Adjusted for General Inflation	Adjusted for Changes in Specific Prices (Current Costs)
Net sales and other operating revenues	$500,000	$500,000	$500,000
Cost of goods sold	400,000	450,000	455,000
Depreciation and amortization expense	20,000	25,000	26,000
Other operating expense	40,000	40,000	40,000
Interest expense	15,000	15,000	15,000
Provision for income taxes	20,000	20,000	20,000
	495,000	550,000	556,000
Income (loss) from continuing operations	$ 5,000	$(50,000)	$(56,000)
Gain from decline in purchasing power of net amounts owed			
Increase in specific prices (current cost) of inventories and property, plant, and equipment held during the year[a]			$ 30,000
Effect of increase in general price level			20,000
Excess of increase in specific prices over increase in the general price level			$ 10,000

[a]At December 31, 19X5, current cost of inventory was $55,000 and current cost of property, plant, and equipment, net of accumulated depreciation was $80,000.

maintain the previous levels of output. Information on the current prices of resources that are used to generate revenues can help users to assess the extent to which and the manner in which operating capability has been maintained.

4. Assessment of the erosion of general purchasing power. When general price levels are increasing, larger amounts of money are required to maintain a fixed amount of purchasing power. Investors typically are concerned with assessing whether an enterprise has maintained the purchasing power of its capital. Financial information that reflects changes in general purchasing power can help with that assessment.[8]

EXHIBIT 5.9 FIVE-YEAR COMPARISON OF SELECTED SUPPLEMENTARY
FINANCIAL DATA ADJUSTED FOR THE EFFECTS OF CHANGING PRICES (in
thousands of average 19X5 dollars)

	Years Ended December 31				
	19X1	19X2	19X3	19X4	19X5
Net sales and other operating revenues	$350,000	$400,000	$420,000	$450,000	$500,000
Historical cost information adjusted for general inflation					
Income (loss) from continuing operations				(29,000)	(20,000)
Income (loss) from continuing operations per common share				(2.0)	(2.00)
Net assets at year-end				100,000	120,000
Current cost information					
Income (loss) from continuing operations				(10,000)	(26,000)
Income (loss) from continuing operations per common share				(1.00)	(2.6)
Excess of increase in specific prices over increase in the general price level				5,000	10,000
Net asset at year-end				120,000	130,000
Gain from decline in purchasing power of net amounts owed				4,500	5,000
Cash dividends declared per common share	2.00	2.05	2.10	2.15	2.20
Market price per common share at year-end	40	30	45	40	39
Average consumer price	170.5	181.5	195.4	205.0	220.9

EXHIBIT 5.10 STATEMENT OF INCOME FROM CONTINUING OPERATIONS ADJUSTED FOR CHANGING PRICES FOR THE YEAR ENDED DECEMBER 31, 19X6 (in thousands of average 19X5 dollars)

Income from continuing operations, as reported in the income statement		$ 5,000
Adjustments to restate costs for the effect of general inflation		
Cost of goods sold	$(50,000)	
Depreciation and amortization expense	(5,000)	(55,000)
Loss from continuing opearations adjusted for general inflation		(50,000)
Adjustments to reflect the difference between general inflation and changes in specific prices (current costs)		
Cost of goods sold	(5,000)	
	(1,000)	(6,000)
Loss from continuing operations adjusted for changes in specific prices		$(56,000)
Gain from decline in purchasing power of net amounts owed		$ 5,000
Increase in specific prices (current costs) of inventories and property, plant, and equipment held during the yeara		30,000
Effect of increase in general price level		20,000
Excess of increase in specific prices over increase in the general price level		$ 10,000

aAt December 31, 19X5, current cost of inventory was $55,000 and current cost of property, plant, and equipment, net of accumulated depreciation, was $80,000.

Obviously, because it requires the presentation of both general price level and specific price level information, FAS 33 is a step forward. It falls short of a total solution, however, which would require using general price level restated current cost accounting, with general price level restated replacement cost accounting or general price level restated net realizable value accounting. Moreover, some of the specific requirements discussed in FAS 33 do not pertain to most situations.[9]

The United Kingdom Solutions to Accounting for Inflation

Various inflation accounting proposals characterize the United Kingdom's efforts to account for inflation. These proposals include Statement of Standard Accounting Practice (SSAP) No. 7, the Sandilands Report, Exposure Draft (ED) No. 18, the Hyde Report, Exposure Draft No. 24, and SSAP No. 16.[10] Each of these proposals is reviewed next.

STATEMENT OF STANDARD ACCOUNTING PRACTICE NO. 7

In November 1972, the Institute of Chartered Accountants in England and Wales (ICAEW) supported the publication of Exposure Draft No. 8,

Accounting for Changes in the Purchasing Power of Money. However, shortly before the exposure period expired, the government intervened and appointed a committee (known as the Sandilands Committee after its chairman, Sir Francis Sandilands) to work on this topic. Rather than proceed with a standard and risk alienating governmental efforts, the Accounting Standards Committee issued a provisional rather than a full standard, known as SSAP No. 7, *Accounting for Changes in the Purchasing Power of Money*, which was substantially the same as the Exposure Draft. SSAP 7 recommended basically the adoption of general price level-adjusted historical cost accounting.

THE SANDILANDS REPORT

The Sandilands Committee rejected the general price level-adjusted historical cost accounting advocated by SSAP 7 and recommended what it labeled current cost accounting (CCA). Basically, it concluded that the following developments are necessary for changes in the law of corporations: (1) the same unit of measure should be used for all users; (2) the operating profit should be disclosed separately from the holding gains and losses, and (3) the financial statements should include relevant information for assessing the liquidity of the company.

The most important recommendation of the Sandilands Report, however, was the use of the "value to the firm" as a valuation base. Under this approach, assets are valued at an amount which represents the opportunity costs to the firm, that is, the maximum loss which might be incurred if the firm is deprived of these assets. Thus, the value to the firm in most cases will be measured by the replacement cost, given that replacement cost represents the amount of cash necessary to obtain the equivalent or identical asset. If the replacement cost is greater than the net realizable value and the discounted cash flow value, the value to the firm will be (1) the discounted cash-flow if it is greater than net realizable value, given that it is preferable to use the asset rather than to sell it, and (2) the net realizable value if it is greater than the discounted cash flow, given that it is preferable to sell the asset rather than to use it.

The Sandilands Report also recommended that all holding gains and losses be excluded from current cost profit, which leads to:

1. All realized gains arising from the reevaluation of fixed assets (and stock, where applicable) should be shown in reevaluation reserves in the balance sheet.
2. Realized holding gains arising on fixed assets should similarly be included in movements in balance sheet reserves.
3. The cost of sales adjustment (where applicable) should be taken to a balance sheet "stock adjustment reserve," whether it is positive or negative.
4. Extraordinary gains should be classed as "extraordinary items," which implies that they may be included in profit for the year, provided they are shown separately and distinguished from current cost profit.

5. Operating gains should be shown "above the line" in the profit and loss account (earnings statement) as current cost profit for the year.[11]

The report recommends also that a "summary statement of total gains and losses for the year" appear immediately after the income statement. Such a summary statement may be illustrated as follows:

Current cost profit after tax (as shown in profit and loss account)			£XXX
Extraordinary items less tax			XXX
Net profit after tax and extraordinary items			£XXX
Movements in reevaluation reserve net of tax			
Stock adjustment reserve		£XXX	
Reevaluation reserves			
Gain or loss due to change in bases			
or valuation of assets		XXX	
Other gains or losses		XXX	XXX
Total gain (loss) for the year after tax			£XXX

EXPOSURE DRAFT NO. 18

Following the publication of the Sandilands Report, the accounting profession set up the Inflation Accounting Steering Group (IASG) in January 1976, whose task was to produce an Exposure Draft on current cost accounting based on the Sandilands Report. The IASG published Exposure Draft No. 18, *Current Cost Accounting*, in November 1976. Under ED 18 the financial statements would include a profit and loss account, an appropriation account, a balance sheet, a statement of the change in net equity interest after allowing for the change in the value of money, and a statement of source and application of funds. The basic principles of ED 18 were:

a. The non-monetary assets of the business should be shown in the balance sheet at their value to the business at the balance sheet date. Value to the business would normally be replacement cost but in exceptional circumstances could be the higher of net realizable value and economic value (discounted present value) if both were lower than replacement cost.

b. Revenue should be charged with the depreciation of fixed assets calculated on their value to the business, and with the cost of stock consumed valued at its replacement cost at the date of sale.

c. Reevaluation surpluses should be credited in the first instance to the appropriate account. Reevaluation surpluses would arise mainly from the reevaluation of fixed assets and from the difference between the replacement cost and historical cost of stock consumed.

d. Directors should appropriate out of reevaluation surpluses and, if necessary, out of current cost profit, an amount based on their assessment of the needs of the business including provisions for the effect of inflation on monetary items, gearing and backlog depreciation.[12]

THE HYDE GUIDELINES

The responses to ED 18 were critical. It was judged too complex, too subjective, and too rapidly introduced. The Accounting Standards Committee decided to prepare simple guidelines to supplement historical cost results. The Hyde Guidelines were published on November 4, 1977. Financial results were to be amended by the following adjustments:

a. *Depreciation* (the difference between depreciation based on the current cost of fixed assets and the depreciation charged in computing the historical cost result).
b. *Cost of Sales* (an adjustment for the difference between the current cost of stock at the date of sale and the amount charged in computing the historical cost result).
c. *Gearing:*
   i. If the total liabilities of the business exceeded its total monetary assets, so that part of its operating capacity was effectively financed by the net monetary liabilities, an adjustment should be made to reflect the extent to which the depreciation and cost of sales adjustment did not need to be provided in full from the current revenues of the business in showing the profit attributable to the shareholders.
   ii. If the total monetary assets of the business exceeded its total liabilities, an adjustment should be made to reflect the increase in net monetary assets needed to maintain its scale of operation.[13]

EXPOSURE DRAFT NO. 24

The Hyde Guidelines were found to be more acceptable to industry than the previous proposals. However, the IASG continued its work in a revised Exposure Draft on current cost accounting which would be more acceptable to all interested parties. The result was the April 1979 publication of Exposure Draft No. 24, *Current Cost Accounting*. Unlike ED 18 and Sandilands, ED 24 required only supplementary current cost accounting statements. It also united itself with the provision of a current cost accounting profit and loss account and balance sheet.

STATEMENT OF STANDARD ACCOUNTING PRACTICE NO. 16

SSAP 16 was published on March 31, 1980. It did not differ materially from ED 24. Its objective was to guide users on such matters as the financial viability of the business; return on investment; pricing policy, cost control, and distribution decisions; and gearing. It provided for current cost information to be included in annual financial statements in addition to historical cost information. Current cost information includes:

1. Current cost operating profit derived after adjusting for depreciation, cost of sales, and monetary working capital. The depreciation adjustment is the difference between the value to the business of the part of fixed assets consumed during the accounting period and the amount of depreciation charged on a historical basis. The cost-of-sales adjustment is the difference between the value to the business of stock consumed and the cost of stock charged on a historical basis. The monetary-working-capital adjustment represents the amount of additional (or reduced) finance needed for monetary working capital as a result of changes in the input prices of goods and services used and financed by the business.

2. A current cost profit (after operations) attributable to shareholders derived after making a gearing adjustment. The gearing adjustment is calculated by first expressing net borrowing as a proportion of the net operating assets using average figures for the year from the current cost balance sheets, and next multiplying the total charges or credits made to allow for the impact of the price changes on the net operating assets of the business by the proportion determined at the first step.

3. A current cost balance sheet with (a) fixed assets and inventory at net current replacement cost and (b) a capital maintenance reserve to reflect reevaluation surpluses or deficits and adjustments made to allow for the impact of price changes in arriving at current cost profit attributable to shareholders. The notes should describe the bases and methods adopted in preparing the accounts, particularly in relation to (a) the value to the business of fixed assets and the depreciation thereon, (b) the value to the business of stock and work in progress and the cost of sales adjustment, (c) the gearing adjustment, (d) the basis for translating foreign currencies and dealing with translation differences arising, (e) other material adjustments to the historical cost information, and (f) the corresponding amounts.

4. Current cost earnings per share, based on the current cost profit attributable to equity shareholders before extraordinary items.[14]

Examples of presentation of current cost accounts are shown as Exhibits 5.11, 5.12, and 5.13.

Canadian Solutions to Accounting for Inflation

The Canadian experiences with accounting for inflation are similar to the U.S. and British experiences, namely, a consideration of general price level accounting before an adoption of some form of current value accounting.

The general price level accounting phase is characterized by two developments. First, in December 1974, the Accounting Research Committee of the Canadian Institute of Chartered Accountants published an accounting guideline, *Accounting for the Effects of Changes in the General Purchasing Power of Money,* suggesting general price level accounting statements to be presented on a supplementary basis. The guideline was followed in July 1975 by the issuance of an Exposure Draft, *Accounting for Changes in the General Purchasing Power of Money,*

EXHIBIT 5.11 ABC LIMITED AND SUBSIDIARIES, GROUP CURRENT COST PROFIT AND LOSS ACCOUNT FOR THE YEAR ENDED DECEMBER 31, 19X3 (in thousands)

Turnover...	29,000
Profit before interest and taxation on the historical cost basis.	5,800
Less: Current cost operating adjustment (Note 2)...............	3,020
Current cost operating profit...................................	2,780
Gearing adjustment................................ (332)	
Interest payable less receivable.................. 400	
....	68
Current cost profit before taxation............................	2,712
Taxation...	1,460
Current cost profit attributable to shareholders................	1,252
Dividends..	860
Retained current cost profit of the year.......................	392
Current cost earnings per share................................	20.80

Statement of retained profits/reserves

Retained current cost profit of the year.......................	392
Movements on current cost reserve (Note 4).....................	4,108
Movements on other reserves....................................	NIL
....	4,500
Retained profits/reserves at the beginning of the year..........	32,160
Retained profits/reserves at the end of the year	36,660

aNotes are included as Exhibit 5.13.

presenting a detailed description of the procedures for producing general price level accounting statements.

The current value accounting phase is characterized by the issuance of a discussion paper in 1976, an Exposure Draft in 1979 and a Reexposure Draft in 1981, and, finally, a pronouncement in Section 4510 of the *CICA Handbook* titled "Reporting the Effects of Inflation," to be effective in 1983. Section 4510 of the *CICA Handbook* places primary emphasis on current cost accounting. It calls for the adoption of two capital maintenance concepts as reflected in paragraph 4510A.9, which states the following:

Consideration was given to recommending that enterprises disclose supplementary data in a format that explicitly discloses income under different concepts of capital, but constraints of simplicity and understandability led the Committee to reject this approach. Instead, it concluded that sufficient information should be presented to enable users to make an assessment of income on a current cost basis under both the operating concept of capital and under the financial concept of capital. Also, the Recommendations include specific requirements where management decides to

EXHIBIT 5.12 ABC LIMITED AND SUBSIDIARIES, SUMMARIZED GROUP-CURRENT COST BALANCE SHEET AS AT DECEMBER 31, 19X3

	£000	£000
Assets employed:		
Fixed assets (Note 3)...		39,060
Net current assets:		
Stock..	8,000	
Monetary working capital.........................	1,600	
Total working capital............................	9,600	
Proposed dividends...............................	(860)	
Other current liabilities (Net)..................	(1140)	
....		7,600
		46,660
Financed by:		
Share capital and reserves:		
Share capital....................................	6,000	
Current cost reserve (Note 4)....................	28,808	
Other reserves and retained profit..............	7,852	
....		42,660
Loan capital.......................................		4,000
....		46,660

ªNotes are included as Exhibit 5.13.

report income attributable to common shareholders on a current cost basis under either of the two capital maintenance concepts.

Like FAS 33, Section 4510 requires large publicly traded companies to provide additional information with respect to the effects of inflation on the financial statements.

The basic supplementary information to be disclosed can be found in paragraphs 4510.6 through 4510.18 as follows:

Supplementary information about the effects of changing prices should be included in the annual report that contains an enterprise's historical cost financial statements.

Supplementary information about the effects of changing prices should disclose the following items:

a. The current cost amounts of cost of goods sold and of depreciation, depletion and amortization of property, plan and equipment or the amounts of the current cost adjustments for those items;

b. Current and deferred amounts of income tax expense; and

c. Income before extraordinary items, after reflecting the above items.

Supplementary information about the effects of changing prices should also disclose at least the following items:

1. Explanatory notes:
   (see para 58 of Standard and the example in the Guidance Notes)
2. Adjustments made in deriving current cost operating profit:

	1983
	£000
Cost of sales	920
Monetary working capital	200
Working capital	1,120
Depreciation	1,900
Current cost operating adjustments	3,020

3. Fixed assets:

| | 31 December 1983 | | | 1982 |
| | Gross | Depreciation | Net | Net |
	£000	£000	£000	£000
Land and buildings	7,560	1,360	6,200	6,140
Plant and machinery	50,560	18,700	32,860	30,120
	59,120	20,060	35,060	36,260

4. Current cost reserve

	£000	£000	£000
Balance at 1 January 1983			24,700
Revaluation surpluses reflecting price changes:			
Land and buildings	400		
Plant and machinery	2,860		
Stocks and work in progress	980	4,240	
Monetary working capital adjustment		200	
Gearing adjustment		(332)	4,108
			28,808
of which: realised (see (iii) below)			4,988
unrealised			23,820
			28,808

(i) Where applicable, surpluses or deficits arising on the following should be shown as a movement on reserves:
   (a) the revaluation of investments (other than those included in current assets);
   (b) the restatement of investments in associated companies; and
   (c) consolidation differences arising on foreign currency translations.

EXHIBIT 5.13 (continued)

(ii) Where relevant, movements should be shown net of minority interest.
(iii) The realised element represents the net cumulative total of the current
      cost adjustments which have been passed through the profits and loss
      account, including the gearing adjustment.

5. Financing of net operating assets

The following is the value to the business (normally current replacement cost net
of depreciation on fixed assets) of the net operating assets at the balance sheet
date, together with the method by which they were financed:

	31 Dec. 1983 £000
Fixed assets	39,060
Worked assets	9,600
Net operating assets	48,660
Share capital and reserves	42,660
Proposed dividends	860
Total shareholders' interest	43,520
Loan capital	4,000
Other current liabilities	1,140
Net borrowing	5,140
Net operating assets	48,660

The reconciliation between balance sheet totals and net
operating assets is as follows:

Balance sheet totals	48,660
Proposed dividends	860
Other current liabilities (net)	1,140
Net operating assets	48,660

a. The amount of the changes during the reporting period in the current cost
   amounts of inventory and property, plant and equipment, identifying the
   reduction from current cost to lower recoverable amount;

b. The carrying value of
   i. inventory; and
   ii. property, plant and equipment on a current cost basis at the end of the
       reporting period, identifying the reduction from current cost to lower
       recoverable amount; and

c. Net assets after restating inventory and property, plant and equipment on a
   current cost basis at the end of the reporting period.

Other disclosure requirements follow:

Supplementary information about the effects of changing prices should disclose the
amount of the financing adjustment, separately identifying the amount that would

result if the financing adjustment were based on current cost adjustments made to income for the period. [Paragraph 4510.21]

When income attributable to common shareholders on a current cost basis under an operating capability concept of capital is disclosed, income on a current cost basis should be adjusted by dividends on non-participating preferred shares and the financing adjustment. If an enterprise decides to exclude unrealized changes in current cost from income attributable to common shareholders, the amount of the financing adjustment would be based on the current cost adjustments made to income for the period. [Paragraph 4510.22]

Supplementary information about the effects of changing prices should disclose the following items:

a. The amount of the changes during the reporting period in the current cost amounts of inventory and property, plant and equipment that is attributable to the effects of general inflation; and

b. The amount of the gain or loss in general purchasing power that results from holding net monetary items during the reporting period. [Paragraph 4510.24]

When income attributable to common shareholders on a current cost basis under a financial concept of capital measured in constant dollars is disclosed, income on a current cost basis should be adjusted by dividends on non-participating preferred shares, the amount of changes during the reporting period in the current cost amounts of inventory and property, plant and equipment and the amounts of inventory and property, plant and equipment and the amounts required to be disclosed under paragraph 4510.24. [Paragraph 4510.25]

The Netherlands' Response to Accounting for Inflation

The Dutch have been aware of current value accounting for a long time. Accounting and "business economics" (*bedrijfseconomie*) are considered to be closely related, which leads to a concern with the important notions of value and cost. The replacement value theory, known as the Limperg Theory, originates in the Netherlands. It integrates balance sheet valuation and income determination and views income as that portion of the increase in net assets of an enterprise that could be "consumed without impairing the source of income of the entity in a continuous or going concern operation." Also, following the adoption of the Act Annual Account in 1971, a joint committee from the Federation of Enterprises, the trade unions, and the Nederlands Institut van Registeraccountants (NIVRA), known as the Tripartite Study Group, recommended, among other things, the use of current value accounting.[15] No specific professional recommendation requiring the use of current value accounting was issued.[16] However, a large Dutch multinational, called N. V. Philips, has been experimenting with current value accounting for both financial and managerial accounting. Basically, the application of the replacement value theory is integrated into the accounting system of all sections of the concern at every stage. All information for management is compiled in accordance with this principle, and thus the replacement value automatically enters into all management considerations and decisions. Basically, Philips uses a current value system with some general price level adjustment for monetary items. All accounts are adjusted every year on the basis of indexes developed by the purchasing department for fixed assets, the engineering department for internally produced machines, and the building design and plant engineering department for buildings; and increases (or decreases) in their values are credited to a revaluation account in equity. The major objective is to maintain the purchasing power of the company's net worth intact. Two actions are deemed necessary to reach that objective:

a. If a change in the price of internally manufactured products is caused by an internal technological price fall *exceeding* the general technological price fall, the difference—initially changed to Revaluation Account as part of the total price difference—is transferred to the debit of the profit and loss statement.

b. In case monetary assets exceed monetary liabilities, the annual profit is charged with an amount equal to the percentage decrease in purchasing power applied to the difference. It is of great importance for profit determination in the inflationary countries.[17]

The French Response to Accounting for Inflation

The French accounting system is governed by the Accounting Plan, which codifies generally accepted accounting standards and requires compliance by all firms. The plan is based, however, on historical-cost accounting.

In May 1976 the Delmas-Marsalet Report presented the recommendations of a working group to be integrated in the Seventh National Plan. The report suggested adopting a form of general price level-adjusted historical cost accounting. This proposition was ignored in favor of a better notion of "value." This situation led to the French Finance acts of 1977 and 1978, which decreed that balance sheet items should be reevaluated as of December 31, 1976 by a coefficient of 1.4. Therefore, in 1977 and later depreciation is based on the reevaluated assets. This was a one-time reevaluation of fixed assets which was intended to reflect a *"valeur d'utilité"* or value in use and has not yet been repeated. This value in use is basically the replacement cost of an identical asset.

Given that the revised accounting plan which came into effect in 1983 does not include any proposals for accounting inflation, one may assume that the government either does not have any intention of dealing with the issue or intends to deal with it in the future on an ad hoc basis. The issue is far from forgotten, however. The executive committee of the *Ordre des Experts Comptables* published a memorandum in February 1981 in which it suggested that French firms publish supplementary information on the effects of inflation and of changes in specific prices.[18] This is basically in line with the provisions of the Fourth Directive of the European Economic Community. They give option for member states to permit or require forms of inflation accounting.

International Response to Accounting for Inflation

Various international organizations have taken positions with regard to accounting for inflation.

1. As suggested earlier, the European Economic Commission, through its Fourth Directive, gave the option to member states to experiment with forms of accounting for inflation.
2. In November 1981 the International Accounting Standards Committee (IASC) issued IAS No. 15, *Information Reflecting the Effects of Changing Prices*. IAS 15 requires disclosing, on a supplementary basis for economically significant entities, adjustments for the effects of changing prices of depreciation on fixed assets, cost of sales, and monetary items and the overall effect of the adjustments on the results for the period.
3. The UN Working Group of Experts on International Standards of Accounting and Reporting, in a 1977 report, *International Standards of Accounting and Reporting for Transnational Corporations*, calls for disclosure of accounting policies including any asset-valuation basis.

Conclusions

Eight alternative asset-valuation and income-determination models may be conceived

1. Historical cost accounting
2. Replacement cost accounting
3. Net realizable value accounting
4. Present value accounting
5. General price level-adjusted historical cost accounting
6. General price level-adjusted replacement cost accounting
7. General price level-adjusted net realizable value accounting
8. General price level-adjusted present value accounting.

In this chapter, these models have been compared and evaluated on the basis of four criteria: the avoidance of timing errors, the avoidance of measuring-unit errors, their interpretability, and their relevance as measures of command over goods.

Although conceptually preferable, the present value models were not included in our comparison and evaluation because of the subjectivity and the uncertainty surrounding their use, which makes their implementation currently impractical. Our comparison of the remaining models shows the general price level-adjusted net realizable value accounting model to be the closest to a preferred income position concept because it meets each of the criteria set forth in the chapter. Unfortunately, U.S., British, Canadian, Dutch, French, and international solutions fall short of adopting this method.

Notes

1. J. R. Hicks, *Value and Capital*, 2d. ed. (Oxford: Clarendon Press, 1946).

2. Ibid., p. 122.

3. *Inflation Accounting: Report of the Inflation Accounting Committee* (London: Her Majesty's Stationery Service, 1975), p. 35

4. Committee on Accounting Procedure, ARB No. 33, *Depreciation and High Costs* (New York: AICPA, December 1947); Committee on Accounting Procedure, letter to AICPA members affirming the recommendations of ARB 33, October 1948; and Committee on Accounting Procedure, ARB No. 43, *Restatement and Revision of Accounting Research Bulletins*, Chap. 9, Sect. A, "Depreciation and High Costs" (New York: AICPA, June 1953.)

5. Statement No. 33, *Financial Reporting and Changing Prices* (Stamford, Conn., September 1979), pars. 47-48.

6. Ibid, pars. 29, 30, 35, 51, and 52.

7. Ibid., pars. 9, 11, 12, 14, 17, 20, and 22.

8. Ibid., pars. 1-2.

9. Several FASB pronouncements dealing with specific situations have been issued subsequent to FAS 33. These include Statement No. 39, *Financial Reporting and Changing Prices: Specialized Assets— Mining and Oil and Gas*, October 1980; Statement No. 40, *Financial Reporting and Changing Prices: Specialized Assets—Timberlands and Growing Timber*, November 1980; Statement No. 41, *Financial Reporting and Changing Prices: Specialized Assets—Income-Producing Real Estate*, November 1980; and Statement No. 46, *Financial Reporting and Changing Prices: Motion Picture Films*, March 1981.

10. C. A. Westwick, "The Lessons to Be Learned from the Development of Inflation Accounting in the UK," *Accounting and Business Research* (Autumn 1980), pp. 354-73.

11. F. E. P. Sandilands, *Report of the Inflation Accounting Committee*, No. 6225 (London: Her Majesty's Stationery Office, Reg. 6225, September 1975), par. 621.

12. Westwick, "The Lessons to Be Learned," p. 363.

13. Ibid., pp. 366-67.

14. For a complete discussion of SSAP16, see "Statement of Standard Accounting Practice No. 16: Current Cost Accounting," *Accountancy* (April 1980), pp. 99-110.

15. Henle Volten, "A Response from the Netherlands," *Journal of Accountancy* (March 1978), pp. 44-45.

16. Edward Stamp, and Alister K. Mason, "Current Cost Accounting: British Panacea or Quagmire?" *Journal of Accountancy* (April 1977), p. 66.

17. "The 1973 Annual Report of N. V. Philips—The Netherlands," in the report of the AAA Committee on International Accounting, *The Accounting Review*, Supplement (1976), p. 111.

18. D. Boussard, *Comptabilité et Inflation* (Paris: Nasson, 1983), pp. 125-26.

Bibliography

Basu, S., and J. R. Hanna. *Inflation Accounting: Alternative, Implementation Issues and Some Empirical Evidence*. Hamilton, Ont.: The Society of Management Accountants, 1977.

Chambers, R. J. *Accounting, Evaluation, and Economic Behavior*. Englewood Cliffs, N. J.: Prentice-Hall, 1966.

_____. "NOD, CPG and PuPu: See How Inflation Teases!" *Journal of Accountancy* (September 1975), pp. 56-62.

Edwards, Edgar O., and Philip W. Bell. *The Theory and Measurement of Business Income*. Berkeley, Calif.: University of California Press, 1961.

Gynther, R. S. "Capital Maintenance, Price Changes, and Profit Determination," *The Accounting Review* (October 1970), pp. 712-30.

Hanna, J. R. *Accounting Income Models: An Application and Evaluation*, Special Study No. 8. Toronto: Society of Management Accountants of Canada, July 1974.

Kerr, Jean St. G. "Three Concepts of Business Income." In *An Income Approach to Accounting Theory*, ed. Sidney Davidson et al. Englewood Cliffs, N.J.: Prentice-Hall, pp. 40-48.

Louderback, J. G. "Projectability as a Criterion for Income Determination Methods," *The Accounting Review* (April 1971), pp. 298-305.

Parker, P. W., and P.M.D. Gibbs. "Accounting for Inflation—Recent Proposals and Their Effects," *Journal of the Institute of Actuaries* (December 1974), pp. 1-10.

Revsine, L., and J. J. Weygandt. "Accounting for Inflation: The Controversy," *Journal of Accounting* (October 1974), pp. 72-78.

Rosen, L. S. *Current Value Accounting and Price-Level Restatements*. Toronto: Canadian Institute of Chartered Accountants, 1972.

Rosenfield, Paul. "Accounting for Inflation: A Field Test," *Journal of Accountancy* (June 1969), pp. 45-50.

_____. "CCP Accounting: Relevance and Interpretability," *Journal of Accountancy* (August 1975), pp. 52-60.

_____. "The Confusion between General Price Level Restatement and Current Value Accounting," *Journal of Accountancy* (October 1972), pp. 63-68.

Stamp, Edward, and Alister K. Mason. "Current Cost Accounting: British Panacea or Quagmire?" *Journal of Accountancy* (April 1977), pp. 64-67.

"Statement of Standard Accounting Practice No. 16: Current Cost Accounting," *Accountancy* (April 1980), pp. 99-100.

Sterling, R. R. "Relevant Financial Reporting in an Age of Price Changes," *Journal of Accountancy* (February 1975), pp. 42-51.

_____. *Theory of Measurement of Enterprise Income*. Lawrence: University Press of Kansas, 1970.

Volten, Henle. "A Response from the Netherlands," *Journal of Accountancy* (March 1978), pp. 44-45.

Westwick, C. A. "The Lessons to Be Learned from the Development of Inflation Accounting in the UK," *Accounting and Business Research* (Autumn 1980), pp. 353-74.

Wolk, H. I. "An Illustration of Four Price Level Approaches to Income Measure-

ment." In *Accounting Education: Problems and Prospects,* ed. J. Don
    Edwards. Sarasota, Fla.: American Accounting Association, 1974, pp. 415-23.
Zeff, S. S. "Replacement Cost: Member of the Family, Welcome Guest, or Intruder,"
    The Accounting Review (October 1962), pp. 611-25.

6.

MANAGERIAL ACCOUNTING ISSUES IN INTERNATIONAL ACCOUNTING

Multinational companies are facing specific managerial accounting issues in need of solutions. While managerial accounting concepts are to a large extent the same both domestically and internationally, the realities of multinational operations have forced mutations of domestic management accounting techniques. One important change has been the emergence of the international financial management function as a direct response to the environmental complexities and the additional variables and constraints which typify the international dimension. This new function expands the traditional scope of management accounting to cover specific problems of interest to multinational companies. Some of these issues—those pertaining to the organizational design of multinational operations, the international financial management function, and planning and control—are examined in this chapter. Other issues are examined in chapters 7 (transfer pricing), 8 (foreign exchange risk management), and 9 (international taxation).

Organizational Design for Multinational Companies

The way in which multinational companies are organized has an important impact on the type of managerial control in general and management accounting techniques in particular that these companies may adopt. The two best known forms of organizational structures, centralization and decentralization, still dominate the discussion or debate on the best form of an organization a multinational company should have. It is then appropriate to start this section by an examination of these two forms of organizational structure and the criteria used to support a multinational company's choice of one of them. But because the realities of today's complex world call for a more innovative structure than a pure centralized or decentralized firm, the types of organizational patterns used by multinational companies are examined next to emphasize the idea that in the long run multinational companies will choose the form of organization which is the most efficient for operating and financial control purposes.

TYPES OF ORGANIZATIONAL DESIGN

The design of a formal organizational structure for a multinational company must contribute to attaining corporate objectives. Such design must take into account four process criteria and one design criterion:[1]

Process Criteria

The process criteria necessary in the design of a formal organizational structure include the following:

1. *Steady state efficiency* is achieved when the unit cost of output is minimized for a given level of activity. This involves analyzing such factors as economies of scale, of skills, and of overhead.
2. *Operating responsiveness* measures an organization's ability to make efficient changes in its production level in response to environmental changes. It involves inventory control and access to all information.
3. *Strategic responsiveness* measures an organization's ability to make efficient changes in the nature of its production process in response to environmental changes. It involves a possible expense for technological and market-related changes.
4. *Structural responsiveness* measures a firm's ability to design and implement new structures when the first three criteria cannot be met.

Each of these criteria should be applied toward the evaluation of an organizational design's potential success in meeting the objectives of the firm.

Structural Design

The criteria just described can be met by at least two possible types of organizational designs: the centralized functional form and the decentralized divisional form.[2] The centralized functional form consists primarily of a departmentalization by function. In a manufacturing firm, such functions include production, finance, sales, accounting, personnel, purchasing, research and development, and so forth. Such a design is justifiable in terms of steady efficiency by allowing for economies of scale, of overhead, and of skills. It results, however, in relatively low strategic and structural responsiveness.

The decentralized divisional form consists primarily of a series of organizational units, or divisions, responsible for a specific product market under the direction of a manager having strategic and operating decision prerogatives. This form achieves steady-state efficiency and operating responsiveness, because departmentalization by function is used within each division. This design is justifiable mainly in terms of strategic and structural responsiveness. Since World War II, the decentralized divisional form has become most frequent in large firms. It is accomplished most often through departmentalization by either location (geographical diversification) or product.

DECENTRALIZATION THROUGH DIVISIONALIZATION

The Nature of Decentralization

The diversification of the types of activities of many business entities has led to the realization that centralized control and coordinating mechanisms at corporate headquarters are not always in the best interests of the firm as a whole. A brief look at some types of organizational growth will show the necessity and main reasons for decentralizing the decision-making process.

The first type of organizational growth arises through the creation of new product lines. A second type arises from *vertical mergers* and consolidations in which firms involved in different stages of production of the same product are combined. As a result, the newly merged corporation achieves greater control over its production, purchasing, and distribution processes. Examples of this growth type can be found in the automotive and petroleum industries. Another type of growth, the *horizontal merger*, involves the merger of firms in the same line of business. This eliminates duplicate facilities and allows the establishment of auxiliary divisions which provide commonly needed goods or services to other subunits in the organization. The last major growth type is *conglomeration*, where firms of unrelated lines of business are combined. Interdependencies among the subunits are usually minimal. Practical factors, including lower taxes, lower transportation costs, and the increased security of belonging to a large organization, lead to the creation of conglomerates.

These types of organizational growth require the creation of decentralized organizational structures. Ideally, management will choose the degree of decentralization which will achieve corporate goals. Decentralization should not be confused with divisionalization, which is a major organization device for decentralization, although it does not indicate to what degree. Decentralizational is essentially the freedom to make decisions.

Benefits and Costs of Decentralization

Numerous arguments have been advanced in the literature in support of decentralization:

1. The modern, integrated, multiple-product firm will function best if it is made into a miniature of the competitive free-enterprise system.[3]
2. Divisional managers may be more motivated, resulting in better decisions and greater efficiency. Solomons summarizes the benefits as follows:

First, decentralized decision making is likely to result in better decisions because the people who make them are closer to the scene of action and have a smaller area of responsibility to worry about. Second, greater efficiency results from the sense the divisional managers have that they are running "their" businesses. In motivating these managers, divisional profit plays an important part. Third, giving a person responsibility for running a division is perhaps the best way of providing preparation for a top management role at the corporate level.[4]

3. The division manager is in a better position to process information concerning resource allocation.[5]

4. The division manager is in a better position to process and transmit information in general. This advantage is reflected in the following two early observations:

   Given realistic limits on human planning capacity, *the decentralized system will work better than the centralized.*[6]

   > [Decentralization] is advantageous in economizing on the transmission of information. In particular, the detailed technical knowledge of the process need not be transmitted to a central office but can be retained in the department. We may regard it as close to an impossibility for individuals in close contact with the productive process to transmit their information in all its details to another office. This proposition, long recognized in practice, is the basis of the management literature on the questions of centralization and decentralization.[7]

5. The division manager's nearness to the marketplace provides relevant information regarding changes in the prices of output and input.[8]

6. Size and diversity of modern corporations and the promotion of morale (because of the decision-making autonomy of managers) support the concept of decentralization.[9]

7. Decentralization represents a response to two major sources of uncertainty for a complex organization: its technology and its environment.

The costs associated with dencentralization are also important:

1. Incongruence between the divisional goal and the corporate goal can result.

2. Decentralization can lead to dysfunctional decision making and, consequently, to *suboptimization* (that is, a decision that increases current divisional profit but limits the company profit as a whole).

3. Higher interdependence between the divisions will make every decision beneficial to one unit and harmful to another (and perhaps to the organization as a whole).

It can be concluded that decentralization is likely to be most beneficial and least costly when the organizational units are fairly independent.

ORGANIZATIONAL STRUCTURES OF MULTINATIONAL ENTERPRISES

The previous discussion focuses on two types of organizational structures: the centralized and decentralized forms. There is, however, no consensus about the best form for multinational corporations. What has been noted in practice are various experimentations in general and five basic patterns of organization in particular. The five basic patterns are:

1. Functionally organized—with foreign operations integrated into the functional units (Tate Chemicals Limited, India; Innocenti, Italy)

2. Functionally organized—with foreign operations assembled into one separate overall international unit (AKU, Netherlands; Volkswagen, Germany)

3. Product organization—with foreign operations integrated into product divisions or groups (Imperial Chemicals Limited, U.K.; Fiat, Italy)

4. Product organization—with foreign operations reporting directly to top management or assembled as a separate international unit (Erricson Telephone, Sweden; Dunlap Rubber Co., UK)

5. Regional organization—with foreign and domestic operations grouping into components under regional heads (Singer, USA; Standard Oil Company, US).[10]

What seems to be taking place is a search for a form of organizational structure most efficient for operating and financial control purposes. A rise of centralized and decentralized activities has appeared more recently as a way of meeting the different objectives of the various functions and goals of multinational companies. For example, centralization in production and logistics is easier with the afvent of international computer-linked communications systems. Similarly, centralized purchasing or "common sourcing" may make it easier to obtain purchaser quantity discounts, greater bargaining power for supplies, benefits from price differentials, and other economies of scale.[11] Naturally, the right mix of centralized and decentralized activities differs from one multinational company to another because of different industries and environments. There seem to be, however, common factors in the search for the mix:

1. The major decisions affecting the entire system which previously may well have been made locally, now tend to be made centrally in a coordinated fashion. For example, foreign affiliates typically now have decreased discretion over reinvestment of their earnings—headquarters, aware of all competing alternatives, allocates resources in a balanced fashion for the global system.

2. Local managers retain considerable authority in largely local matters and in other matters where it is necessary to maintain flexibility and immediacy of response at the operating levels.

3. Financial control systems are changing from the emphasis on profits under the profit center concept to control via budgets and budget variances; additionally other evaluation techniques are increasingly used supplementally. These new control systems are designed to permit *control* centrally even though a great deal of *authority* is left at the local level.

4. New systems for centralized coordination and for cooperative management are emerging. That is, a levy of new central coordination techniques, many

requiring extensive interaction with and cooperation from local managers, is emerging. As examples, Operations Research techniques (particularly simulation and network analysis) are used for coordination; formal, frequent, and lengthy meetings of managers from around the world are reaching new heights of sophistication as a coordination technique; top management policy guidelines have been refined for extensive use as a means to guide local managers in decision-making in situations important for global coordination but too complex to permit promulgation of rigid decision rules; and behind each of these new developments, the accounting and management information system must be refined, altered and expanded to accommodate information flows resulting from the use of the new techniques.[12]

The International Financial Management Function

Whatever the organizational structure chosen by the multinational corporation, the management approaches in general and managerial accounting in particular are not any more a purely domestic operation but have taken a complex and international orientation. In managerial accounting the issues of cost accounting and product costing may be the same both domestically and internationally. However, in the areas of managerial planning and control, international challenges have required an expansion and redefinition of the managerial accounting functions. The international challenges facing the managerial accounting function include dealing with environmental differences, multiple currencies, variations in inflation trends, interest rates and tax burdens, restrictions on fund remittances across national borders, political and foreign exchange risks, and the availability and costs of capital, to name only a few. The new managerial function has emerged as a direct response to such environmental complexities. It is generally known as the international financial function—a new specialization consisting of the coordinated management of all aspects of international accounting and financial operations.

The following reasons may be cited for having an international financial function and an international financial executive:

- Aggressive overseas expansion increases the burden of capital investment analysis and requires the judgment of a mature executive familiar with the risks peculiar to foreign operations.
- Foreign transactions, such as hedging, currency swaps and arbitrage require special skills.
- Rapid environmental changes abroad necessitate quick financial action and call for the experience of a financial executive who can foresee such changes and recommend appropriate action.
- Greater use of locally borrowed funds and the issuance abroad of debentures and other debt instruments place great demand on executive time and require extensive traveling.

- Negotiations with governments and foreign financial institutions make it necessary to assign responsibility to a full-time international financial executive experienced in such matters.

- U.S. Government restrictions on capital outflow and the newly instituted reporting requirements have greatly increased the financial workload. [13]

In fact, the international financial function involves managing exchange risk, managing the impact of inflation, a cash-management function, external financial sourcing and investment planning, international financial reporting, international taxation, transfer pricing, performance evaluation, international planning, and informational control systems.

With three exceptions, all these issues are treated in this chapter and Chapter 8. The exceptions are international reporting (treated in Chapters 2-4), transfer pricing (treated in Chapter 7), and international taxation (treated in Chapter 9).

The issues treated in this chapter relate to the emergence of the international financial management function and planning and control for multinational operations. It is important to note that the new international financial manager needs to be versed in all the international aspects of multinational operations, namely, the workings of the international monetary system, the foreign exchange markets, the international legal and tax systems, and the cultural, social, and political systems, and needs to be supported by an effective global intelligence system which keeps such information current.

Planning for Multinational Operations

FROM PLANNING TO BUDGETING

Planning is an effective mechanism to counter both the fire fighting and tunnel vision management styles. It allows the organization to define its relationship with the environment and is "a method of guiding managers so that their decisions and actions are set to the future of the organization in a consistent and rational manner, and in a way desired by top management."[14] Planning has also been defined as "a process which begins with objectives; defines strategies, policies and detailed plans to achieve them; which establishes an organization to implement decisions; and feedback to introduce a new planning cycle."[15]

These definitions describe planning as the process of collecting information on objectives and making decisions on the best way to achieve them. Planning is vital to an organization's future success. Thune and House analyzed the planning function in 36 similar firms in six industries. They concluded that those firms which rely on a formal planning department were more successful than those which rely on informal planning, and those firms which rely on a formal planning department perform more successfully after the system is instituted than previously.[16] Planning prepares firms to operate in a dynamic world and to adapt to the ensuing changes in technology, financing, resource availability, economic conditions, and so forth. Because of the benefits of planning, it is not surprising that most firms of all sizes and industries rely on some type of formal planning system.[17]

A decision systems framework distinguishes between planning and budgeting. Planning—or, precisely, strategic planning—takes place at the strategic planning level and principally involves elaboration of organizational goals and the strategies necessary to accomplish them. Planning reflects the organization's desire to face the future in a rational manner by providing a general guide to managerial decision making. In general, strategic planning is subdivided into two activities—business planning and diversification planning—which are defined as follows:

Business planning is the process of determining the scope of organizational activities that will be undertaken toward the satisfaction of a broad consumer need, of deciding on the objectives of the organization in its defined area of operations, and of evaluating the effectiveness with which varying magnitudes of resources may be committed toward achieving those objectives.

Diversification planning is the process of deciding on the objectives of a corporation, including the determination of which and how many lines of business to engage in, of acquiring the resources needed to attain those objectives, and of allocating resources among the different businesses in a manner intended to achieve those objectives.[18]

The strategic planning process is followed by a management control process whose purpose is to ensure that the long-term plans emerging from business and diversification planning are implemented over the years. The management control process, therefore, is a communication and interaction process for the implementation of strategic plans, and its success rests on budgeting. Budgeting, then, is the most conspicuous evidence of the planning process. The budget, the formal means by which the planning process takes shape, ties together the diverse activities of the firm which are related to specific goals and specifies the means for their realization. Vatter defines budgets as follows:

Budgets state formally—in terms of expected transactions—the decisions of all levels of management about the resources to be acquired, how they are to be used, and what ought to result. Budgets put the details of management plans for operations in money units, so that the results may be projected into expected financial statements.[19]

In short, planning precedes budgeting; budgets are quantitative, and mostly monetary, short-term expressions of plans.

BUDGETING PROCEDURES FOR MULTINATIONAL OPERATIONS

The budgeting procedures and the construction of a master budget for a multinational company may be supervised by a budget committee, which may include members representing the firm's divisions. A budget director, generally the controller or the chief financial officer, serves as head of the budget committee. Although they may differ from one organization to another, the budgeting procedures are likely to resemble the following:

1. Top management develops the overall goals of the organization and includes them in the firm's strategic plan.

2. Keeping in mind the overall organizational goals, the budget committee determines the basic economic forecasts outlining the future progress of the company and communicates these long-term forecasts to the divisions.

3. Each division determines its operating budgets in line with the overall goals and basic economic forecasts outlined for the company. These operating budgets then are communicated to the budget committee. It is important to note here that the following emphasis in multinational companies is shifting toward a dual role given that the divisional plans not only are for local operational use but are also vital to the parent company for coordination of the entire planning system. Two consequences have been noted as follows:

> As a consequence headquarters is likely to participate much more deeply than would otherwise be the case in the development of local plans—in initially helping to establish local goals and to formulate the general framework of the local plans, since all local plans must be integrated into an articulated whole. Additionally, local managers are likely to interact in the planning process with each other a great deal in cooperating to formulate their own plans so they fit in a balanced global plan. Often this is accomplished by frequent meetings of managers.[20]

4. The budget committee reviews and coordinates the budgets and either asks for revisions or approves the submitted budgets. When all the submitted budgets are approved, the budget committee puts the master budget in final form, which is then communicated to the various divisions to serve as a guide for action and control. The budgets making up the master budget, accompanied by their subsidiary schedules, include the following:
   a. Operating Budget
      i. Sales budget
      ii. Production budget
         (a) Production budget as changes in inventory levels budget
         (b) Material usage and purchases budget
         (c) Direct-labor budget
         (d) Overhead budget
      iii. Cost of goods sold budget
      iv. Budgeted income statement
   b. Financial Budget
      i. Cash budget
      ii. Budgeted balance sheet
      iii. Budgeted statement of changes in the financial position.

Performance Evaluation for Multinational Operations

Performance evaluation for multinational operations has been found to depend upon the type of attitude taken by the corporate management's multinational business policies and upon a pattern of control which has been labeled *waxing and waning*.[21]

Maximizing the type of attitude taken by top management toward multinational business policies, Perlmutter used three classifications: ethnocentric (home-country oriented); polycentric (host-country oriented), and geocentric (world oriented).[22] As a result, performance evaluation in a centralized ethnocentric company will be tightly controlled by the parent company while in a decentralized polycentric or geocentric company it will be less controlled by the parent company.

Waxing and waning was noticed by Robbins and Stobaugh, who found that the performance evaluation function for multinational operations depended mainly on the degree of foreign experience which the firm had and the size of the firm's foreign operations.[23] In fact, they noticed three phases of the evolutionary process of performance evaluation. In the first phase, given the small scale of foreign operations and the lack of foreign experience, relatively little control is exercised by the parent company and each subsidiary is practically left on its own to improve its performance with the possible result of suboptimization. Needless to say, the performance evaluation systems of the firm in general are far from being coordinated. In the second phase, as the foreign operations expand and top management gains more foreign experience, top management starts getting closer control in foreign operations. The result is a strong and coordinated performance evaluation system dominated by the parent company. In the third phase, the scale of operations is so large and complex that the control exercised by headquarters begins to diminish in favor of a more decentralized performance evaluation system. Headquarters keeps a hand in the situation, however, by formulating guidelines for the foreign subsidiaries to follow.

COST CENTERS, PROFIT CENTERS, INVESTMENT CENTERS, AND RESPONSIBILITY ACCOUNTING

Performance evaluation for multinational operations as well as for domestic operations consists of making sure that segments of the firm are being held responsible for items under their control, which is exactly the essence of responsibility accounting. In other words, responsibility accounting is a technique used within the total informational system of an organization, domestic or multinational, for classifying and reporting in accordance with managerial responsibilities. It is based on a system for reporting revenue and cost information to the manager responsible for the revenue-causing or cost-incurring functions. Such an accounting system is a reporting system designed to control expenditures by directly relating the reporting of controllable expenditures to the individuals in the organization who are responsible for their control.[24]

Central to responsibility accounting is the assignment of responsibility and authority—first, in conformity with the relationships defined by the organizational structure and, second, for each activity in terms of expenses, income, capital expenditures, asset investment, and other criteria. Under this accounting system, information on the results of each activity is reported on the basis of where the results were incurred and who has responsibility for them. Examples of the making of and the performance reports generated by a responsibility accounting system are shown as Exhibit 6.1. To design a responsibility accounting system, management may have to rely on the formal organizational system, charts, and manual to identify responsibility centers and determine the decisions and resources controlled by each center. Those spheres or responsibility centers, varying in complexity of control, structure, and purpose, include cost centers, profit centers, and investment centers.

A cost center is the smallest segment of activity or area of responsibility for which costs can be accumulated. A subsidiary of a multinational operation can be a cost center. Responsibility is restricted to cost. For planning purposes, the budget estimates are cost estimates; for control purposes, performance evaluation is guided by a cost variance equal to the difference between the actual and budgeted costs for a given period. The

EXHIBIT 6.1 A. RESPONSIBILITY ACCOUNTING SYSTEM

A. XYZ Company: Simplified Organizational Chart

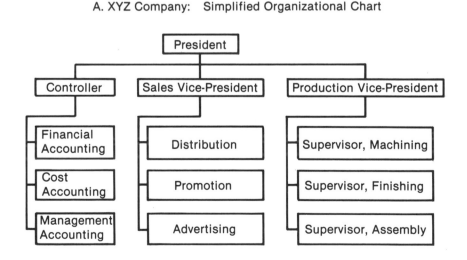

EXHIBIT 6.1 (continued)

B. Responsibility Accounting Monthly Reports for the Assembly Supervisor, the Production Vice-President, and the President for the XYZ Company

President's Performance Report

	Amount		Variance Favorable (Unfavorable)	
	This Month	Year to Date	This Month	Year to Date
President's Office	$400,000	$ 870,000	$ 26,000	$ 52,000
Controller	200,000	610,000	(12,000)	11,000
Production Vice-President →	150,000	445,000	16,000	2,000
Sales Vice-President	100,000	390,000	4,000	13,000
Total Controllable Costs	$850,000	$2,315,000	$ 34,000	$ 78,000

Production Vice-President's Performance Report

	Amount		Variance Favorable (Unfavorable)	
Machining Department	$ 40,000	$ 115,000	$ (4,150)	$(13,120)
Finishing Department	60,000	185,000	20,630	27,280
Assembly Department →	50,000	245,000	(480)	(12,160)
Total Controllable Costs →	$150,000	$ 545,000	$ 16,000	$ 2,000

Assembly Supervisor's Performance Report

	Amount		Variance Favorable (Unfavorable)	
Direct Material	$ 20,000	$ 72,000	$ 1,800	$ (210)
Direct Labor	10,000	36,000	400	(2,975)
Manufacturing Overhead	20,000	47,000	(1,720)	(8,975)
Total Controllable Costs →	$ 50,000	$ 155,000	$ 480	$(12,160)

method of evaluating the performance of a cost center can result in dysfunctional behavior. For example, a cost center manager may feel that to ensure a budgeted amount in successive years similar to that of the present, the present budget allowances should be spent. The manager may be inclined to authorize unnecessary expenditures at the end of the year to ensure that "nothing is left in the budget." To minimize or prevent such a situation, a company should identify and assign costs so managers of subsidiaries are motivated to act in a way beneficial to the firm.

A profit center is a segment of activity or area of responsibility for which both revenues and costs are accumulated. The manager has responsibility for both revenues and expenses. For planning purposes, the budget estimates are both revenue and cost estimates; for control purposes, performance evaluation is guided by both a revenue variance and a cost variance. In short, the objective function of a profit center's manager is to maximize the center's controllable profit. The determination of this profit may require allocating the income statement items of a company as a whole to the various segments of the company. To facilitate such allocation and emphasize cost behavioral patterns, a contribution approach may be used. Exhibit 6.2 illustrates the contribution approach to segment performance. This approach differentiates between the allocation of items which vary with the activity level and those which do not.

An investment center is a segment of activity or area held responsible for both profits and investment. For planning purposes, the budget estimate is a measure of the rate of *return on investment* (ROI) estimate; for control purposes, performance evaluation is guided by an ROI variance. In short, the objective function of an investment center is to maximize the center's ROI. The merits of the ROI measure and the possible problems associated with such a measure are illustrated later in the chapter. It is important to note that although the profit center and investment center concepts are vital to the implementation of decentralization, they can be also used in firms with centralization. In other words, both concepts lead essentially to a divisionalized firm, but not necessarily to a decentralized firm. Basically, as noted earlier in the chapter, decentralization implies the relative freedom to make decisions. Multinational operations can be evaluated using an ROI, a residual income, or a comparison of performance relative to a budget.[25] Each of these methods is examined next.

THE RATE OF RETURN ON INVESTMENT

Rather than using absolute-dollar profits as a test of divisional profit, most financial control systems emphasize the use of a relationship of profit to invested capital. This relationship is usually expressed by the ROI. E. I. du Pont de Nemours and Company is generally credited with the development of the ROI concept. Sloan evaluated the principle of ROI as follows:

> I am not going to say that the rate of return is a magic word for every occasion in business. There are times when you have to spend money just to stay in business, regardless of the visible rate of return. Competition is the final price determinant and competitive prices may result in profits which force you to accept a rate of return less than you hoped for, or for that matter to accept temporary losses. And, in times of inflation, the rate-of-return concept comes up against the problem of assets undervalued in terms of replacement. Nevertheless, no other financial principle with which I am acquainted serves better than rate of return as an objective aid to business management.[26]

The ROI is found simply by dividing the net income by the amount of investment. It relates the profit to invested capital, both of which are

EXHIBIT 6.2 THE CONTRIBUTION APPROACH TO SEGMENT PERFORMANCE

| | Company as a Whole | Region | | Division | | | |
		Region A	Region B	Division I	Division II	Division III	Division IV
1. Net Sales	$100,000	$60,000	$40,000	$24,000	$36,000	$8,000	$32,000
2. Variable Manufacturing Cost of Sales	60,000	36,000	24,000	14,400	21,600	4,800	19,200
3. Manufacturing Contribution Margin	$ 40,000	$24,000	$16,000	$ 9,600	$14,400	$3,200	$12,800
4. Variable Selling and Administrative Costs	10,000	6,000	4,000	2,400	3,600	1,000	3,000
5. Contribution Margin	$ 30,000	$18,000	$12,000	$ 7,200	$10,800	$2,200	$ 9,800
6. Fixed Costs Controllable by Segment Managers	10,000	6,000	4,000	3,000	3,000	1,000	3,000
7. Contribution Controllable by Segment Managers	$ 20,000	$12,000	$ 8,000	$ 4,200	$ 7,800	$1,200	6,800
8. Fixed Costs Controllable by Others	6,000	3,600	2,400	1,600	1,600	400	2,000
9. Contribution by Segments	$ 14,000	$ 8,400	$ 5,600	$ 2,200	$ 6,200	$ 800	$ 4,800
10. Unallocated Costs	6,000	—	—	—	—	—	—
11. Income before Income Taxes	$ 8,000						

important areas of management responsibility. The rationale lies in the belief that there is an optimal investment level in each asset, leading to an optimal profit level. The ROI is the product of two components: profit margin and investment turnover. The profit margin equals net income divided by sales and indicates the segment's ability to transform sales into profit. The investment turnover equals sales divided by invested capital. Thus, the ROI can be expressed as follows:

$$\text{ROI} = \frac{\text{Net income}}{\text{Invested capital}} = \frac{\text{Sales}}{\text{Invested capital}} \times \frac{\text{Net income}}{\text{Sales}}$$

This formula shows that the ROI can be increased by an increase in either the profit margin or the investment turnover, and it can be decreased by a decrease in either the profit margin or the investment turnover.

To illustrate, assume that a division desires to achieve a 25 percent return on invested capital. The present performance of the division is as follows:

$$\frac{\text{Sales}}{\text{Invested capital}} \times \frac{\text{Net Income}}{\text{Sales}} = \text{ROI,}$$

$$\text{or} \quad \frac{\$200}{\$100} \times \frac{\$20}{\$200} = 20\%.$$

Two alternatives are possible to improve the ROI up to 25 percent:

1. A $5 decrease in expenses would increase net income to $25 such that

$$\text{ROI} = \frac{\$200}{\$100} \times \frac{\$25}{\$200} = 25\%.$$

2. A $20 decrease in inventories would decrease invested capital to $80 such that

$$\text{ROI} = \frac{\$200}{\$80} \times \frac{\$20}{\$200} = 25\%.$$

These are not the only alternatives. Exhibit 6.3 shows the factors which can affect the final outcome. The advantages of using the ROI to measure divisional performance include the following: First, the ROI is a composite measuring tool combining both net income and investment features. It is useful for a comparison among the divisions of a given firm as well as for a comparison of divisional performance with that of companies in similar industries. Next, use of the ROI encourages an effective use of resources and could serve as a corporate budgeting tool and aid in making short- and long-range plans. Finally, use of the ROI may have a positive behavioral effect on managers by creating a competitive spirit and by motivating

EXHIBIT 6.3 RELATIONSHIP OF FACTORS INFLUENCING THE RATE
OF RETURN ON INVESTMENT

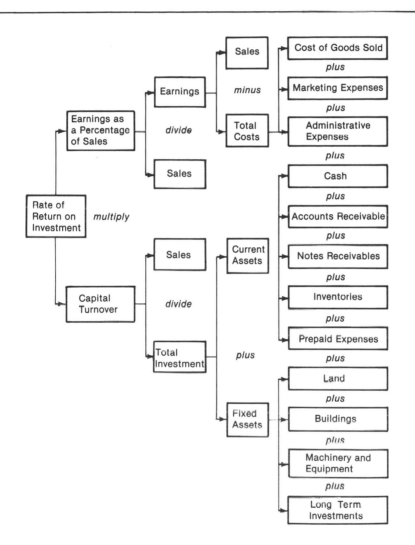

increases in efficiency, effectiveness, and congruency with corporate goals.
In fact, the three major empirical studies of performance evaluation systems
of multinationals done in the past 10 years by Robbins and Stobaugh,[27]
McInnes[28] and Morsacito[29] indicate that multinationals rely on ROI as the
major or even the only measure of performance.

Although the ROI may qualify as a good management tool, some potential problems must be recognized. The net income figure used in calculating the ROI may require certain adjustments that do not conform with generally accepted accounting principles. Exhibit 6.4 illustrates the format and content of a divisional income statement. Distinctions are made between sales to outside customers and sales to other divisions, between controllable and uncontrollable costs, and between variable and fixed costs. This format allows the possibility of distinguishing between the performance of the manager and the performance of the division. Two rates of return can be computed—the controllable ROI and the net ROI—as follows:

Controllable ROI = Controllable income ÷ Controllable capital investment.

Net ROI = Net income after taxes ÷ Total capital investment.

Another problem with the ROI is that the investment figure used in calculating the ROI may lead to an "unrealistic" ROI. Hence, the most obvious figure is the net book value of assets, which is the original cost minus depreciation to date. Such a measure has inherent weaknesses. For example, it enables divisions with old assets to earn a higher rate of return than divisions with newer assets, given the low book value resulting from greater depreciation charges.

Several solutions can overcome this limitation of the ROI method. For one, gross book value can be used. However, this approach still enables a divisional manager to increase the ROI by scrapping nonprofitable assets that may be detrimental to the company. Second, four nonhistorical cost valuation methods can be used: the economic or capitalized value, the replacement cost, the net realizable value, and the general price level-adjusted historical cost. The first three methods approximate the current value, whereas the last merely adjusts historical cost. The replacement cost represents the amount of cash or other consideration that would be required to obtain the same asset or its equation. The net realizable value represents the amount of cash for which an asset can be sold. The capitalized value refers to the present value of net cash flows expected to be received from the asset. The three current values are relevant to different types of decisions. For example, a disposal, continuance, or expansion program would entail the following alternatives:

		Alternatives	
	Disposal (Sell)	Continuance (Hold)	Expansion (Buy)
Decisions	Capitalized value versus Net realizable value	Capitalized value versus Net realizable value	Capitalized value versus Replacement cost

*EXHIBIT 6.4 FORMAT AND CONTENT OF A DIVISIONAL
INCOME STATEMENT (in thousands)*

Revenues 1200
   External sales 500
   Internal sales (transfer price equal to market value) 600
   Internal sales (transfer price different from market value) 100

Minus

Variables costs 500
   Variable cost of goods sold 200
   Variable selling and administrative divisional expenses 300
Total contribution margin 700

Add (Deduct)

Fixed costs allocated to other divisions for transfers
   made at other than market value 50

Deduct

   Controllable discretionary and committed fixed costs 20

Equals

Controllable operating income 630

Deduct

   Uncontrollable fixed costs 30
Operating income before taxes 600
Income taxes 50
Net income (after taxes) 550

Although the capitalized value appears to be dominant, it is a subjective value based on the present value of expected cash flows. Replacement cost and net realizable value may be more available and may constitute a better alternative to historical cost. Third, using an increasing-charge depreciation (annuity depreciation), the sinking fund depreciation, can lead to a lower income related to a smaller investment base. Sinking-fund depreciation is based on the financial concept that depreciation represents the return on investment. Suppose a company is considering buying an asset with a two-year life and no salvage value. If the cost of the asset is estimated to be

$8,680 and the yearly cash flow to be $5,000, the ROI using a discounted cash flow method can be obtained by solving the following equation for r:

$$\$8,680 = \sum_{i=1}^{2} \frac{\$5,000}{(1+r)^i}$$
$$r = 10\%$$

Given the knowledge of the ROI, sinking-fund depreciation assumes a capital-recovery factor. Exhibit 6.5 presents the results of sinking-fund depreciation, showing each cash payment to be equal to interest on investment plus principal. Exhibit 6.6 shows the superiority of sinking-fund depreciation with the income statement and the ROI computations using either constant, increasing, or decreasing depreciation. The sinking-fund depreciation method results in a stable, constant ROI figure compared with the fluctuating results obtained by the straight-line and accelerated methods. Therefore, sinking-fund depreciation is preferred by many companies for measuring divisional profitability.

An appropriate allocation of assets to divisions makes the ROI more meaningful and contributes to goal congruence. Such allocation differs from one company to another, given that some companies elect to centralize certain activities and decentralize others. For instance, in most decentralized companies the home office centralizes cash management, billing, or receivable collections.

EXHIBIT 6.5 EXAMPLE OF SINKING-FUND DEPRECIATION

YEAR	INITIAL INVESTMENT (a)	CASH EARNINGS (b)	RETURN OF 10% (c = 10% × a)	DEPRECIATION (d = b = c)	UNRECOVERED INVESTMENT (e = a − d)
0					$8,680
1	$8,680	$5.000	$868.0	$4,132.0	$4,548
2	4,548	5,000	454.8	4,545.2	2.8*

*Due to rounding.

As a general rule, the basis of allocation of assets among divisions should be controllability. That is, the amount of assets controllable by any given segment in its managerial activities should be the amount allocated to that segment in the computation of the rate of return on divisional investment. To summarize, the ROI limitations can be corrected if the investment base is at current value net of depreciation and if a sinking-fund depreciation method is used.

EXHIBIT 6.6 DEPRECIATION METHODS AND RATE-OF-RETURN COMPUTATIONS

METHODS OF DEPRECIATION

	Straight-Line		Accelerated Depreciation		Sinking-Fund Depreciation	
Year	1	2	1	2	1	2
Cash-earnings	$5,000	$5,000	$5,000	$5,000	$5,000	$5,000.0
Depreciation	4,340a	4,340a	5,786b	2,893b	4,132c	4,545.2c
Net income	$ 660	$ 660	$ (786)	$2,107	$ 868	$ 454.8
Investment base	$8,680	$4,340	$8,680	$2,894	$8,680	$4,548.0
Rate of return on investment	7.6%	15.2%	−9%	72%	10%	10%

a$8,680 ÷ 2 = $4,340.
b$8,680 × ⅔ = $5,786; $8680 × ⅓ = $2,983.
cSee Exhibit 6.5 for results.

RESIDUAL INCOME

Developed in the 1950s by General Electric Company, the concept of "residual income" to measure divisional performance is defined operationally as divisional income in excess of a prescribed interest on investment. This concept directs the manager toward the maximization of income above a charge for assets used. The interest rate used corresponds conceptually to the firm's cost of capital. For example, if a divisional income was $50,000 for a budgeted investment of $200,000 and a cost of capital of 10 percent, the residual income would be computed as follows:

Divisional net income	$50,000
Minus Imputed interest at 10 percent of assets	20,000
Equals Residual income	_____
	$30,000

There are two advantages to the residual income method for divisional performance evaluation: First, the method enables the division to continue to expand as long as it meets the cost of capital requirement. For the previous example, the cost of capital was 10 percent, whereas the ROI was 25 percent ($50,000 ÷ $200,000). In other words, using the ROI of 25 percent as an investment criterion would eliminate projects whose returns might exceed the cost of capital and, consequently, would eliminate projects acceptable from the point of view of the corporation as a whole. Second, the method requires setting a rate-of-return target for every type of asset, regardless of the division's profitability. The end result is a yardstick for comparisons between divisions. However, the adequate determination of the cost of capital or the rate of return of individual assets is a possible problem.

PERFORMANCE RELATIVE TO A BUDGET

Centralization/Decentralization Dilemma

The control process of firms with foreign operations may be exercised as for domestic operations by a comparison between the actual profit performance and a budgeted profit performance based on forecasted sales and expenses. Unlike the domestic operations and because the basic operating budget of the subsidiary must be expressed in the parent currency for intercountry comparability, the future course of exchange rates and the choice of exchange rates in the control process have a definite impact on the performance evaluation of subsidiaries. Given this impact of the choice of exchange rates on performance evaluation, the first decision may be to decide who should set these exchange rates in the budgeting and control process. If, as suggested by various normative models,[30] these exchange rates are set centrally, it may create negative behavioral patterns in subsidiaries where operating managers may feel that their performances are being influenced by exchange-risk policies over which they have no control. A more practical and behaviorally sound solution is to give the subsidiaries' operating managers responsibility for financial decisions in general and for setting foreign exchange rates in particular. If this decentralized solution is chosen, the problem becomes to control any attempt by the operating managers to "suboptimize," that is, choosing policies that may not be optimal from a corporate point of view as a result of an overreaction to exchange risks. This dilemma may be solved by determining the apropriate exchange rate for use in the budgeting and control process. A good solution is provided by the Lessard-Lorange Model, which will be examined next.[31]

The Lessard-Lorange Model

The model examines nine theoretical possible combinations of exchange rates in the control process. These combinations are the result of using three possible rates for determining the budget and for trading performance relative to budget. These rates are the actual (spot) rate (the initial rate) at the time the actual budget is created, the projected rate at that time for the end of the period, and the ending rate obtained by continuously updating it as exchange rates change. The nine combinations obtained are shown as Exhibit 6.7.

EXHIBIT 6.7 POSSIBLE COMBINATIONS OF EXCHANGE RATES IN THE CONTROL PROCESS

Rates Used to Determine Budget	Rates Used to Track Performance Relative to Budget		
	Actual Time of Budget	Projected at Time of Budget	Actual at End of Period
Actual Time of Budget	A-1,	A-2	A_3
Projected at time of Budget	P-1	P-2	P_3
Actual at end of period (through updating)	E-1	E-2	E_3

SOURCE: Donald R. Lessard, and Peter Lorange, "Current Changes and Management Control: Resolving the Centralization/Decentralization Dilemma," *The Accounting Review* (July 1977), p. 630. Reprinted with permission.

Of the nine combinations, four are shaded out because they appear to be undesirable or illogical combinations. The remaining five combinations — A-1, A-3, P-2, P-3, and E-3—are then analyzed to determine the appropriate exchange rate to use in the budgeting and control process. To show the differences among the five combinations and determine the appropriate exchange rate, let us use the following income statement which may result from a project considered a foreign subsidiary:

Sales	FC120,000
Cost of sales	30,000
Operating expenses	3,000
Operating income	FC87,000

Let us also assume that the subsidiary has exposed assets of FC60,000, an initial exchange rate at the time of budget setting of FC20 = $1; there are two equally likely possibilities for the dollar value of the foreign currency in the next period—a 50 percent chance that it will remain the same (FC20 = $1) and a 50 percent chance that it will move to FC30 = $1. Thus, the projected exchange rate is FC25 = $1. Based on this example, the acceptable five combinations of budget and performance measurement are shown as Exhibit 6.8. Let us examine each combination.

Combination A-1: Budget at Initial; Track at Initial

It is assumed here that there will be no exchange-rate changes and no need to forecast them, or include them in the budget and control process. As a result, the project appears profitable.

Combination P-2: Budget at Projected; Track at Projected

This approach requires a projection of exchange rates. The profitability of the project changes from $4,350 in combination A-1 to $2,880, showing that it rests on the accurate forecast of exchange-rate changes by the corporate treasurer. However, given the zero variance, the operating manager is freed of the responsibility of forecasting the exchange-rate changes.

Combination E-3: Budget at Ending; Track at Ending

As in combination A-1 or P-2, this combination allows the operating manager to ignore the effect of both anticipated and unanticipated fluctuations in exchange rates. Notice again the zero variance. Again the profitability of the project appears, however, to rest on the treasurer's forecast of future exchange rates.

Combination A-3: Budget at Initial; Track at Ending

Unlike the previous combinations, this combination makes the operating manager responsible for the foreign exchange risk. The profitability of the project depends on the ending rate. The variance is zero if the ending rate remains the same as the initial rate. It is equal to a loss of $980 if it changes to local currency 30 = $1. This combination is perceived to be the worst of all possible worlds. Lessard and Lorange explain as follows:

In the budgeting stage, no account will be taken of possible exchange fluctuations, yet their full impact will be attributed to the manager at the tracking state. The harmful effects of such a system can be expected to include "padding" of budgets or decentralized hedging actions by managers to reduce exchange risks which are likely to loom very large from their narrower local perspective.[32]

Combination P-3: Budget at Projected; Track at Ending

This combination also makes the operating manager responsible for the foreign exchange risk. The profitability is either significantly above the budget when the ending rate is FC20 = $1 (positive variance of $1,470) or

EXHIBIT 6.8 EFFECTS OF PERFORMANCE FROM POSSIBLE COMBINATIONS OF EXCHANGE RATE IN BUDGETING

A-1

	Budget at initial (FC20=$1)	Track at initial (FC20=$1)
Sales	$6,000	$6,000
Cost of Sales	1,500	1,500
Operating Expenses	150	150
Loss on Expired Assets	0	0
Operating Income (loss)	$4,350	$4,350
Variance from Budget		0

A₃ Track at ending rate

	Budget at initial (FC20=$1)	Track at ending rate (FC20=$1)	(FC30=$1)
Sales	$6,000	$6,000	$4,000
Cost of Sales	1,500	1,500	1,000
Operating Expenses	150	150	100
Loss on Expired Assets	0	0	1,000
Operating Income (loss)	$4,350	$4,350	$1,900
Variance from Budget		0	-$2,450

P-2

	Budget at projected (FC25=$1)	Track at projected (FC25=$1)
Sales	$4,800	$4,800
Cost of Sales	1,200	1,200
Operating Expenses	120	120
Loss on Expired Assets	600	600
Operating Income (loss)	$2,880	$2,880
Variance from Budget		0

A₃ Track at ending rate

	Budget at projected (FC25=$1)	Track at ending rate (FC20=$1)	(FC30=$1)
Sales	$4,800	$6,000	$4,000
Cost of Sales	1,200	1,500	1,000
Operating Expenses	120	150	100
Loss on Expired Assets	600	0	1,000
Operating Income (loss)	$2,880	$4,350	$1,900
Variance from Budget	0	$1,470	-$ 980

E₃

	Budget at ending (FC20=$1)	Track at ending (FC30=$1)	Budget at ending (FC30=$1)	Track at ending (FC30=$1)
Sales	$6,000	$6,000	$4,000	$4,000
Cost of Sales	1,500	1,500	1,000	1,000
Operating Expenses	150	150	100	100
Loss on Expired Assets	0	0	1,000	1,000
Operating Income (loss)	$4,350	$4,350	$1,900	$1,900
Variance from Budget		0		0

Loss on exposed assets: Beginning exposed exposed assets = FC60,000 ÷ 20 = $3,000.

a. When ending rate is FC25=$1, ending exposed assets = FC60,000 ÷ 25 = $2,400. Loss = $600.

b. When ending rate is FC30 = $1, ending exposed assets = FC60,000 ÷ 30 = $2,000. Loss = $1,000.

under the budget when the ending rate is FC30 = $1 (negative variance of −$980). This combination may be attractive in cases where operating plans should and can be changed in response to exchange-rate fluctuations.

Appropriate Combination

Lessard and Lorange favor combination P-2, which incorporates the projected exchange rates in both the budgeting and the control processes. These rates are viewed as "internal forward rates" since their use is analogous to the treasurer's acting as a banker and "buying forward" receipts in foreign currencies at a guaranteed rate. As a result, combination P-2 excludes unplanned exchange fluctuations but acknowledges expected fluctuations at the budgeting stage and appears as the dominant combination. Management controls criteria used to support the choice of internal forward exchange rates as the basis for decision making and performance evaluation are goal congruence and fairness. As stated by Lessard and Lorange:

Goal-congruence is restored because a corporate-wide point of view has been brought to bear on the currency exchange rate, eliminating decisions taken on the basis of the expectations and risk-preferences of local managers who necessarily have a narrower horizon on the currency risk problem than the corporate headquarters. Fairness is restored, at least in regard to the exchange rate fluctuations, by the establishment of a standard under which the local decision maker gets no blame or credit for currency fluctuations outside of the division manager's control.[33]

Conclusions

Multinational companies are facing specific managerial accounting issues in need of solutions. The issues examined in this chapter include organizational design, the international financial management function, planning, and control and performance evaluation. With respect to organizational design, experimentation may be required for each company to determine its appropriate risk of centralized and decentralized functions and to dictate the type of information system needed. With respect to planning and budgeting, interaction is needed between headquarters and its decision to achieve some form of goal congruence and eliminate the need for suboptimization. Finally, with respect to performance evaluation, experimentation may be needed to close the system most likely to lead to a coordinated functioning of the whole company.

Notes

1. H. I. Ansoff and R. G. Brandenburg, "A Language for Organizational Design: Parts 1 and 2," *Management Science* 17 (1971), pp. 705-31.
2. Ansoff and Brandenburg considered two other possible designs, namely, the

adaptive design and the innovative design. However, these designs are more applicable to program and project development than to a corporate firm.

3. Joel Dean, "Decentralization and Intracompany Pricing," *Harvard Business Review* (July-August 1955), pp. 65-74.

4. David Solomons, "Divisional Reports," in *Handbook of Cost Accounting*, ed. S. Davidson and R. L. Weil (New York: McGraw-Hill, 1978), pp. 44-49.

5. Nicholas Dopuch and D. F. Drake, "Accounting Implications of a Mathematical Programming Approach to the Transfer Price Problem," *Journal of Accounting Research* (Spring 1964), pp. 10-21.

6. J. G. March and H. A. Simon, *Organizations* (New York: Wiley, 1958).

7. K. J. Arrow, "Optimization, Decentralization, and Internal Pricing in Business Firms," in *Contributions to Scientific Management* (Los Angeles, Calif.: 1959), pp. 9-18.

8. Joshua Ronen and George McKinney III, "Transfer Pricing for Divisional Autonomy," *Journal of Accounting Research* (Spring 1970), pp. 99-112.

9. J. T. Godfrey, "Short Run Planning in a Decentralized Firm," *Accounting Review* (April 1971), pp. 286-97.

10. H. Stieglitz, *Organization Structures of International Companies, Studies in Personnel Policy* No. 198 (New York: National Industrial Conference Board, 1965), p. 5.

11. Committee on International Accounting, "Report of the Committee on International Accounting," *The Accounting Review*, Supplement (1973), p. 135.

12. Ibid, p. 136.

13. Irene W. Meister, *Managing the International Finance Function* (New York: National Industrial Conference Board, 1970), p. 15.

14. W. David Ewing, *The Practice of Planning* (New York: Harper & Row, 1968).

15. G. A. Steiner, *Top Management Planning* (New York: Macmillan, 1969).

16. Stanley Thune and Robert House, "Where Long-Range Planning Pays Off," *Business Horizons* (October 1970), pp. 81-87.

17. J. Bacon, *Planning and Forecasting in the Smaller Company* (New York: The Conference Board, 1971). In a study of 93 companies, each with 2,000 or fewer employees, Bacon found that only four do not plan at all.

18. N. Robert Anthony, J. Dearden, and R. F. Vancil, *Management Control Systems: Text Cases and Readings* (Homewood, Ill.: Irwin, 1972), p. 466.

19. W. J. Vatter, *Operating Budgets* (Belmont, Calif.: Wadsworth Publishing, 1969), pp. 15-16.

20. Committee on International Accounting, "Report of the Committee on International Accounting," p. 156.

21. Jeffrey S. Arpan and Lee H. Radebaugh, *International Accounting and Multinational Enterprises* (Boston: Warren, Gorham and Lamont, 1981), p. 312.

22. Howard Perlmutter, "The Tortuous Evolution of the Multinational Corporation," *Columbia Journal of World Business* 4 (January-February 1969), pp. 9-18.

23. S. Robbins and R. Stobaugh, *Money in the Multinational Enterprise: a Study in Financial Policy* (New York: Basic Books, 1973).

24. John A. Higgins, "Responsibility Accounting," *Arthur Andersen Chronicle* (April 1952), p. 1.

25. An extreme result of performance evaluation of subsidiaries is known as

"trimming deadwood," whereby a conglomerate rids itself of an unwanted subsidiary by selling it to another company or to the division's managers.

26. Alfred P. Sloan, Jr., *My Years with General Motors* (Garden City, N.Y.; Doubleday, 1964), p. 140.

27. Sidney N. Robbins and Robert B. Stobaugh, "The Bent Measuring Stick for Foreign Subsidiaries," *Harvard Business Review* (September-October 1973), pp. 80-85.

28. J. M. McInnes, "Financial Control Systems for Multinational Operations: An Empirical Investigation," *Journal of International Business Studies* 2 (Fall 1971), pp. 11-28.

29. Helen Morsacito, "An Investigation of the Interaction of Financial Statement Translation and Multinational Enterprise Performance Evaluation," Ph.D. diss., Pennsylvania State University, 1978, and *Currency Translation and Performance Evaluation in Multinationals* (Ann Arbor, Mich.: UMI Research Press, 1980).

30. T. Horst, "The Theory of Multinational Firms: Optimal Behavior under Different Tariffs and Tax Rates," *Journal of Political Economy* (September-October, 1971), pp. 1059-72; B. A. Lieataer, *Financial Management of Foreign Exchange: An Operational Technique to Reduce Risk* (Cambridge: MIT Press, 1970); and D. P. Rutenberg, "Maneuvering Liquid Assets in a Multinational Company: Formulation and Deterministic Solution Procedures," *Management Science* (June 1970), pp. 671-84.

31. Donald R. Lessard and Peter Lorange, "Currency Changes and Management Control: Resolving the Centralization/Decentralization Dilemma," *The Accounting Review* (July 1977), pp. 628-37.

32. Ibid. pp. 633-34.

33. Ibid. p. 634.

Bibliography

Bursk, Edward C., John Dearden, David F. Hawkins and Victor M. Longstreet. *Financial Control of Multinational Operations* (New York: Financial Executives Research Foundation, 1971).

Business International. "Evaluating Foreign Operations: The Appropriate Rates for Comparing Results with Budgets," *Business International Money Report* (May 20, 1977), pp. 153-54.

Choi, Frederick D. S. "Multinational Challenges for Management Accountants," *Management Accounting* (October 1976), pp. 45-48, 54.

Committee on International Accounting. "Report of the Committee on International Accounting," *The Accounting Review*, Supplement (1973), pp. 120-35.

Diamond, Michael A., and Helen G. Morsicato. "An Approach to 'Environmentaliz-ing' MNE Performance Evaluation Systems," *International Journal of Accounting Education and Research* 16 (Fall 1980), pp. 247-66.

Gernon, Helen Morsicato. "Internal Performance Evaluation of the Foreign Opera-tions of the Multinational Corporation." In *Multinational Accounting: A Research Framework for the Eighties*, ed. Frederick D. S. Choi (Ann Arbor, Mich.: UMI Research Press, 1981), pp. 123-37.

Farag, Shawki M. "The Problem of Performance Evaluation in International Accounting," *The International Journal of Accounting Education and Research* (Fall 1974), pp. 45-54.

Lessard, Donald R., and Peter Lorange. "Currency Changes and Management Control: Resolving the Centralization/Decentralization Dilemma," *The Accounting Review* (July 1977), pp. 628-37.

McInnes, J. M. "Financial Control Systems for Multinational Operations: An Empirical Investigation" *Journal of International Business Studies* 2 (Fall 1971), pp. 11-28.

Mauriel, John J. "Evaluation and Control of Overseas Operations," *Management Accounting* (March 1969), pp. 35-41.

Meister, Irene W. *Managing the International Finance Function* (New York: National Industrial Conference Board, 1970).

Perlmutter, Howard. "The Tortuous Evolution of the Multinational Corporation," *Columbia Journal of World Business* 4 (January-February 1969), pp. 9-18.

Robbins, Sidney M., and Robert B. Stobaugh. "The Bent Measuring Stick for Foreign Subsidiaries," *Harvard Business Review* (September-October 1973), pp. 80-88.

_____. "Multinational Companies: Growth of the Financial Function," *Financial Executive* (July 1973).

Shapiro, Alan C. "Evaluation and Control of Foreign Operations," *The International Journal of Accounting Education and Research* (Fall 1978), pp. 83-104.

Stieglitz, H. *Organizational Structures of International Companies*. Studies in Personnel Policy No. 198 (New York: National Industrial Conference Board, 1965).

Tse, Paul S. "Evaluating Performance in Multinationals, "*Management Accounting* (June 1979), pp. 21-25.

7.

TRANSFER PRICING FOR MULTINATIONAL OPERATIONS

Introduction

Transactions are the basis of all financial accounting. The value of these transactions is generally and objectively measurable if they take place between independent entities. A great number of transactions take place between parent companies and their local or foreign subsidiaries. The exchanges of goods or services, in these cases, are not based on an arm's-length bargaining process. A transfer price has to be determined for the valuation of these transactions between parent companies and their subsidiaries and among subsidiaries. Various considerations may enter into the determination of these transfer prices. The accounting literature which emphasizes the need for an efficient working of the decentralized multinational company will emphasize setting a transfer price based on managerial control considerations. The realities of the practical world may make it more beneficial to have other considerations in setting transfer prices internationally. Accordingly, this chapter examines the transfer pricing problem of multinational companies from a managerial control point of view and from other, more practical points of view.

Transfer Pricing from a Managerial Point of View

Transfer pricing is a major issue confronting decentralized multinational organizations which expect division managers to operate their divisions as semi-autonomous businesses. These organizations face the problem of what price to charge for goods and services sold by one organizational unit to another in the same company. This situation prevails within vertically integrated organizations, where transactions often occur between the company's profit centers. When goods and services are transferred between divisions, the revenue of the supplying unit becomes the cost of the purchasing unit. These intracompany charges ultimately will be reflected in the profit and loss statements of the respective divisions. Since divisional performance is evaluated by a profit-based criterion such as ROI or residual income, the profit center managers will attempt to maximize their own centers' profits. A conflict occurs when improved divisional performance is achieved at the expense of overall company profits.

In theory, to optimize an organization's profits the transfer price should be selected so it motivates and guides managers to choose their inputs and outputs in coordination with the other subunits. Ideally, any intracompany pricing method should be consistent with the goals of maximizing both company and divisional profits: Transfer pricing should insure goal congruence between units.

Because of the potential conflicts which can arise in transfer price determination, three primary objectives can be used to establish a proper transfer price. The first is to assist top management in evaluating and guiding divisional performance by providing adequate information on division revenues and expenses. The second is to help the division manager in running the division. The third objective is to ensure divisional autonomy and allow each profit center to act as an independent agent.

In theory, the design of a transfer pricing scheme ultimately must point each division manager toward top management's goals. The scheme must reward divisional external economies and prevent and penalize diseconomies. Furthermore, a firm's transfer pricing divisions must acknowledge domestic and foreign legal and tax requirements, as well as antitrust and financial reporting constraints.

Developing a set of transfer pricing rules which can integrate the complex dimensions of an organization, ensure divisional autonomy, and at the same time achieve overall corporate goals is a very difficult task. Consequently, a transfer pricing system must be developed with an awareness of these difficulties. The main positive characteristics of a transfer pricing system include ensuring goal congruence, being fair to all concerned parties, and minimizing conflicts between divisions. Various transfer pricing methods are used in practice. The most common are market price, negotiated price, actual cost, standard cost, marginal or variable cost, target profit, and dual transfer price.

MARKET PRICE

A market-based transfer price is the price at which the producing division would sell the product externally. In other words, the producing division charges the same price to other divisions as it would charge to outside customers in open market transactions. The market price has the advantage of providing an objective measure of value for goods or services exchanged, and it may result in the best information for use in performance evaluation of the profit centers. A transfer pricing system based on market price requires a competitive intermediate market, minimal interdependencies of the profit centers, and the availability of dependable market quotations.

There are, however, some drawbacks to using a transfer pricing based on market price. First, in today's regulated international economy, perfectly competitive markets are very rare. In an imperfect market, one seller or buyer, by itself, can affect the market price, rendering it inapplicable as an effective transfer price. Second, even if the intermediate market is perfect, there is no guarantee that the market price is a product strictly comparable in terms of grade quality and other relevant characteristics.[1] Third, an arm's-length market price is never fully applicable to a transfer transaction given the presence of savings to one of the divisions which gains benefits from integration. And if this is the case, "which profit center is to be awarded the benefits of the synergy?"[2] Fourth, a situation may arise in which the market price is a distress price. Should the transfer price be the distress price or should it be a long-run average, or "normal," market price? Both prices are defensible. On one hand, the use of a distress price may lead managers of the supplying division to dispose of productive facilities to positively effect the short-run ROI. However, this may reduce the activities of the buying division, which would be disadvantageous to the company as a whole. On the other hand, the use of the long-run average market price may penalize the buying division by forcing it to buy at a price higher than the market price. If the objective is to preserve the spirit of decentralization and if safeguards exist to prevent the supplying division from disposing of productive facilities, the distress price should be chosen. Finally, there may be a problem if the goods or services transferred do not have a ready market price.

In spite of these limitations, the market price is considered the most effective transfer price because it insures divisional autonomy, it provides a good performance indication for use in performance evaluation, and it creates a climate conducive to goal congruence.

NEGOTIATED PRICE

A negotiated transfer price is the price set after bargaining between the buying and selling divisions. This system requires that these divisions deal with one another in the same way that they deal with external suppliers and buyers. Thus, one basic requirement for the success of the bargaining process is the freedom of the divisions not only to bargain with one another but also to deal with external markets if unsatisfied with internal offers. This freedom will avoid the bilateral monopoly which exists when the divisions are allowed to deal with only themselves. In fact, the negotiated transfer price system works best when an intermediate market exists for the product or service transferred, providing the divisions with objective and reliable information for successful negotiations.

The literature contains several recommendations for the use of negotiated prices.[3] Writers maintain that prices negotiated in arm's-length bargaining by division managers help accomplish goal congruence. They view these prices as compatible with profit decentralization, ensuring the division managers' freedom of action and increasing their accountability for profits. A survey conducted by R. K. Mautz indicates that about 24 percent of the participating diversified companies revealed negotiation as the basis for setting transfer prices between divisions.[4]

The negotiated transfer price system also may have a negative behavioral impact when personality conflicts arise between the bargainers; succeeding in the negotiation may become a more important goal than the company's profitability. Another drawback of this system is that it can be time-consuming. Division managers may lose an overall company perspective and direct their efforts toward improving their division's profit performance. In their attempts to obtain the best possible price, managers may find themselves in very lengthy arguments.

When these conflicts arise, a transfer price should be set arbitrarily by a central decision of top management. This arbitrary, or imposed, price is the price felt to serve the overall company interests. Needless to say, the arbitrary price contradicts the spirit of decentralization, given a possible loss of divisional autonomy. Some authors in the accounting literature have fundamental objections to negotiation. Cyert and March viewed the organization as a coalition of interests and suggested that negotiation and renegotiation of transfer pricing can be expected to create conflict among the subunits constituting the coalition.[5] Dopuch and Drake have suggested that the negotiated price implies an evaluation of the power to negotiate rather than an evaluation of performance itself.[6]

ACTUAL COST

A transfer price based on actual cost is a price based on the historical full cost of the product or service exchanged. It has the obvious advantage of being measurable, verifiable, and readily available. When the actual costs are accepted for the determination of transfer prices, the problem remains of motivating the selling division to sell internally at a price other than the market price. One way of motivating the selling division is to set the transfer price at full actual cost plus some markup as a way of approximating the market price. The resulting synthetic market price may be better than the actual market price when the product existing in the intermediate market differs in terms of quality, grade, and other relevant characteristics from the product transferred.

The full-cost-plus or synthetic market price has been found to be the most popular approach under the following conditions: an absence of competitive prices, the presence of an interest in saving the cost of negotiating prices, and the presence of a need to implement a policy of pricing the final product.[7] There are several limitations inherent in the implementation of a transfer pricing model based on actual cost. First, a transfer price based on actual cost is actually based on absorption cost in the sense that it includes all direct and indirect expenses (variable and allocated joint and fixed costs). As a result, this type of transfer price may transfer the inefficiencies of the selling division to the buying division, making it unwise to use divisional profit for divisional performance evaluation. Second, a transfer price based on actual cost may lessen the selling division's incentive to control costs. Third, Shubik notes that cost-plus pricing of transfer goods can impede the search for technological progress by the manufacturing division.[8] Finally, Milburn notes that the cost-based methods contain the following areas of measurement ambiguity:

- It is unclear whether cost-based transfer values should include the costs of waste or inefficiency; any attempt to separate "normal" or "efficient" from "abnormal" or "inefficient" must leave a range of choice.

- To date, financial accounting theory has not demonstrated convincingly whether, or under what circumstances, cost-based transfers should be defined as full cost or incremental cost, or as something in between.

- There will almost always be common cost allocation ambiguities whenever two or more products are manufactured using the same facility.

- In all but incremental cost-based transfer pricing, there will be some allocation of fixed costs, and these allocations must be arbitrary.

- Some profit margin on cost (or a nil profit margin) must be specified and it is likely that a range of reasonable possibilities will exist.

- Finally, "cost" might be defined in terms of replacement cost, or on an opportunity cost basis.[9]

Various writers advocate the use of cost-plus methods. For example, Gordon's proposal was recommended for the decentralized management of a socialist economy.[10] There are, however, several limitations inherent in the implementation of a transfer pricing model based on actual cost. First, a transfer price based on actual cost is actually based on absorption cost in the sense that it includes all direct and indirect expenses (variable and allocated joint and fixed costs). As a result, this type of transfer price may transfer the inefficiencies of the selling division to the buying division, making it unwise to use divisional profit for divisional performance evaluation. Second, a transfer price based on actual cost may lessen the selling division's incentive to control costs.

STANDARD COST

We have seen that a transfer price based on actual cost can reinforce the inefficiencies of the selling division and lessen its motivation to control costs. A transfer pricing based on standard costs can correct for these problems. It reflects a normative position by expressing what costs should be under certain circumstances. As a result, a transfer price based on standard cost eliminates the inefficiencies of the selling division; when compared with actual cost, it may create an incentive to control costs. Accordingly, Vending proposed a "three-part transfer price" including the following three distinct categories: standard variable manufacturing cost, a lump-sum representing a portion of traceable budgeted fixed costs, and a charge for the use of capital employed.[11]

MARGINAL OR VARIABLE COST

A company using a transfer price based on either the full actual cost or the full standard cost may face at least two situations. First, the full actual cost and the full standard cost may be higher than the market price. Second, the full actual cost and the full standard cost include both direct and indirect costs (variable and fixed). The indirect costs can result from arbitrary allocation procedures. The fixed costs can be committed costs that are incurred whether the selling division operates at full or at less-than-full capacity. Thus, the buying division may feel that either the indirect costs or the fixed costs should not be included in the determination of the transfer price. When this situation arises, it may be more motivating and important to maintain the spirit of decentralization and resort to a transfer price based on partial cost, which charges only a *portion* of the full actual cost or, preferably, full standard cost. Conceptually, this partial cost includes values between full cost and zero cost and refers to either the *marginal* or the *variable* cost.

The marginal cost is the incremental cost of producing additional units. In general, the buying division will be willing to buy as long as the marginal revenue is superior to the marginal cost. Although conceptually appealing, a transfer price based on marginal cost requires available information on all production levels. Because such figures are not always available, a surrogate for the marginal cost may have to be used—the variable cost.

The variable cost or the variable cost plus a lump sum can be used either as a surrogate for marginal cost or as a way of encouraging the use of some facilities' services. First, the variable cost can be used when marginal cost cannot easily be computed because of the absence of adequate information. Second, using the variable cost can encourage divisions to use the services of facilities with excess capacity until it becomes more profitable or advantageous to the selling division to switch to a full cost (actual or standard).

Various writers have proposed an alternative to the marginal cost, which is the opportunity cost approach.[12] This method is judged as ideal because it satisfies both situations of availability of market price and absence of market price. If the market price is available, it is used and represents also the opportunity cost of not selling to outsiders. If the market price is not available, the transfer price should be the opportunity cost of diverting the resources of the selling division in manufacturing or acquiring the product rather than manufacturing or acquiring another product which has an outside market.

DUAL PRICE

From the preceding discussion of transfer pricing alternatives it can be seen that the best motivating transfer price for the selling division is the market price, and the most acceptable price for the buying division is the variable cost.

One way of meeting both of these optimal situations is to use a dual transfer price rather than a single transfer price. The dual price system allows the selling division to sell at either a real or a synthetic market price, hence creating a profit and motivating the selling division to sell. This system allows the buying division to buy inside the company at variable cost, which prevents the selling division from having excess capacity when the buying division buys outside at market prices equal to or lower than the variable cost. In short, the dual price system motivates both the buying and selling divisions to operate in the best interests of the company as a whole. One drawback of this system is the possibility that the divisions may no longer be motivated to control costs. Another drawback may be the negative impact on the organizational atmosphere. Hence, Horngren warned that "the looseness of dual pricing may gradually induce unwelcome attitudes and practices."[13]

Variations of dual pricing were proposed by Greer, Edwards and Roemmich, and Drebin.[14] The proposal by Drebin, for example, suggests that the buying division be charged with marginal cost whereas the selling division should be credited for selling price minus profit and cost of completion.[15] Those proposals were advocating different transfer prices for the selling and buying divisions. Other proposals called for the selection of transfer prices depending largely upon the use of transfer pricing information. For example, Bierman suggested market price for measuring performance evaluation and marginal (variable cost) or differential cost for relevant decision making in areas such as "make or buy," pricing, capital budgeting, and so on.[16] One may also add full cost as ideal for financial reporting according to generally accepted accounting principles.

TRANSFER PRICING SYSTEMS ILLUSTRATED

To illustrate the transfer pricing systems, assume the Picur Company has two divisions (X and Y). For one of the company's products, Division X produces a major subassembly, and Division Y incorporates this subassembly into a final product. In the open market, similar subassemblies can be purchased at $150 each. Division Y currently buys the total output of Division X and wants to increase purchases by 500 units. The following are some recent cost data for Division X:

SUBASSEMBLY	STANDARD COST	ACTUAL COST
Direct material	$ 50	$ 60
Direct labor	20	25
Variable manufacturing overhead	15	15
Fixed manufacturing overhead	15	20
	$100	$120

1. Using the current market price, Division X would transfer the parts at $150 each:
   500 units × $150 = $75,000.

2. Assume Divisions X and Y agree after lengthy negotiations that the outside market price includes $10 of selling and advertising expenses. The negotiated price would be $140 ($150 − $10) each:
   500 units × $140 = $70,000.

3. Assume Divisions X and Y cannot agree on the amount of selling and administrative expenses and that top management has set an arbitrary dictated price of $130 per unit:
   500 units × $130 = $65,000.

4. Using the full actual cost, Division X would transfer the parts at $120 each:
   500 units × $120 = $60,000.

5. Using the full standard cost, Division X would transfer the parts at $100 each:
   500 units × $100 = $50,000.

6. Assume Division X is already operating at full capacity, and to produce the additional 500 units it must incur additional standard fixed costs of $5 per unit. The marginal cost of production per unit is computed as follows:

Direct material	$ 500
Direct labor	20
Variable manufacturing overhead	15
Fixed manufacturing overhead ($15 + $5)	20
	$105

   500 units × $105 = $52,500.

7. Using the actual variable cost, Division X would transfer the parts at $100 each:
   500 units × $100 = $50,000.

8. Using a dual price system, Division X can be given credit for the market price of $150, and Division Y is charged at the variable cost of $100. Assuming that the variable cost of Y is $30 per unit, the profit of the division will be as follows:

DIVISION X	
Sales to division Y at $150	$ 75,000
Variable costs at $100	50,000
Contribution margin	$ 25,000

DIVISION Y	
Sales of finished product at $200 (assumed)	$100,000
Variable costs	
Division X at $100	50,000
Division Y at $30	15,000
Contribution margin	$ 35,000

Note that the profit of the company as a whole is less than the sum of the divisional profits. Some eliminations must be made before total company profit can be determined. The total profit of the company is actually only $35,000 ($200 unit selling price of the final product − $130 total unit variable cost incurred in both Divisions X and Y = $70 contribution margin per unit; $70 contribution margin per unit × 500 units = $35,000 total contribution margin). The $25,000 additional contribution reflected in the income statement of Division X is due to Division X to allow it to sell at market price; this in fact constitutes a corporate subsidy to motivate Division X to sell to Division Y.

Other Considerations in Setting Transfer Prices Internationally

The previous sections have investigated the setting of a transfer price from a managerial control point of view, or basically using internal considerations. Three criteria were used for the setting of transfer prices: goal congruence, divisional autonomy, and performance evaluation.

There are, however, other "external" conditions which may exert influences in establishing procedures and policies for a firm's transfer pricing mechanism. In fact, in a book written on behalf of the European Centre for Study and Information on Multinational Corporations, *transfer price* is said to have acquired a bad meaning because it "evokes the idea of systematic manipulation of prices in order to reduce profits artificially, cause losses, avoid taxes or duties."[17] This fact contrasts sharply with the concept that transfer prices provide the intracompany charging mechanism necessary for management control of decentralized organizations. That is, they may conflict with goal congruence, divisional autonomy, and performance evaluation. The conflict arises from the need to "manipulate" transfer prices in order to meet this new internal consideration. The resulting situation may be summarized as the parent company's dictating what the transfer price should be. Needless to say, the complexities may transform the selling price problem into a nightmare. As noted by Fantl:

The first hurdle involves personal relations with foreign management: it is easier to explain the need for arbitrary pricing to a domestic executive and to discount its effects in evaluating its performance. The foreign manager starts from a basis of suspicion of the motives of the U.S. parent. Any system that would make him feel unappreciated or misunderstood can undermine the success of the foreign venture. For internal measurement purposes, transfer pricing becomes much more crucial than in domestic relations.[18]

In short, transfer price manipulation for considerations other than managerial control may carry a penalty because goal congruence, incentive, and autonomy between the parent and its subsidiaries are destroyed.

TAX CONSIDERATIONS IN THE UNITED STATES

One goal of multinational corporations, most often mentioned, is the maximization of global after-tax profits. This is accomplished by minimizing the global income tax liability. Other things being the same, profits are increased by setting high transfer prices to take out profits from subsidiaries located in high-tax countries and low transfer prices to move profits to subsidiaries domiciled in low-tax countries. This arbitrary shifting of profits purely for tax avoidance is being challenged by most governments in the developing and developed countries through their enacting appropriate legislations. In the United States, the main legislation restricting the internal pricing policies of multinational corporations is contained within the 1954 Internal Revenue Code, Section 482, and the 1977 Regulation 861. Both are examined next.

Intercorporate Transfer Pricing: Section 482

In any case of two or more organizations, trades, or businesses (whether or not incorporated, whether or not organized in the United States, and whether or not affiliated) owned or controlled directly or indirectly by the same interests, the Secretary or his delegate may distribute, apportion or allocate gross income, deductions, credits, or allowances between or among such organizations, trades, or businesses, if he determines that such distribution, appointment, or allocation is necessary in order to prevent evasion of taxes or to clearly reflect the income of such organizations, trades or businesses.[19]

The purpose of Section 482 is "to place a controlled taxpayer on a tax parity with an uncontrollable taxpayer by determining according to the standards of an uncontrolled taxpayer, the true taxable income from the property and business of a controlled taxpayer."[20] Basically, the IRS is allowed to disallow an existing transfer pricing system and reallocate income to reflect the "true taxable income." The true taxable income is described as the income resulting if each member were acting "at arm's length" with the others. Detailed regulations were issued under the section which are based on the principle that transactions between related parties should take place on an arm's-length basis. These regulations set forth three pricing methods to be used in determining the arm's-length price, namely, in order of perference, the comparable uncontrolled price method, namely, in price method, and the cost-plus method. The comparable uncontrolled price method determines the transfer price as the basis of "uncontrolled sales" made to buyers which are not part of the same controlled group. Guidelines for what constitutes a "comparable uncontrolled price" are provided in the regulations as follows:

Uncontrolled sales are considered comparable to controlled sales if the physical property and circumstances involved in the uncontrolled sales are identical to the physical property and circumstances involved in the controlled sales, or if such properties and circumstances are so nearly identical that any differences either have no effect on price, or such differences can be reflected by a reasonable number of adjustments to the price of uncontrolled sales. . . . Some of the differences which may affect the price of property are differences in the quality of the product, terms of sale, intangible property associated with the sale, time of sales, and the level of the market and the geographic market in which the sale takes place.[21]

If there are no comparable uncontrolled sales, the regulations prescribed the use of the resale price method. It is applicable when the buyer does not add significant value to the product, that is, is simply a distributor. In such a case the transfer price is equal to the resale price to unrelated parties less an appropriate markup, plus or minus certain adjustments. The cost-plus method is prescribed in those situations where both the comparable uncontrolled price and the resale price methods are not applicable. The cost-plus price is equal to full cost (actual or standard) plus an appropriate profit percentage similar to that earned by the division or other companies in similar transactions with unrelated parties. Besides these three methods, the regulations prescribe the use of "some appropriate method" of pricing if it is comparable to the pricing which would be charged to an unrelated party.

Allocation of Expenses: Section 861

While Section 482 is intended to allocate the proper taxable income to the parent at arm's length, Section 861 is intended to allocate corporate expenses to the foreign source income. Basically, it allocates and apportions all of a firm's expenses, losses, and other deductions to specific sources of income (sales, royalties, dividends) and then apportions the expenses between domestic and foreign source income.

IMPORT/EXPORT DUTIES CONSIDERATIONS

The desire to reduce import/export duties is another consideration in the setting of transfer prices. Plasschaert notes: "Underinvoicing imports in the host country obviously reduces the import duty bill. The saving thus obtainable may be sizeable in developing countries, in which import duties are quite high. One may add, however, that the duties on raw materials and on intermediates imported are typically much lower than those on final products."[22] It seems, however, that many companies no longer consider import/export duties as an important determinant of transfer pricing. On one hand, governments are taking action to limit and contain the practice of underinvoicing imports. On the other hand, various countries are beginning to assess customs duties on equivalent market prices rather than on the invoice amount. In short, the manipulation of transfer prices to reduce import/export duties may appear to be irrelevant and useless.[23]

EXCHANGE RATE CONSIDERATIONS

Exchange rate fluctuations may cause problems in the performance evaluation of divisions. To eliminate differences in profit evaluation due to exchange rate fluctuations, Malstrom proposed a dollar-indexing formula used by Honeywell. It goes as follows:

$$NTP = OTP \times \frac{CER}{PER}$$

where
NTP = New transfer price
OTP = Old transfer price
CER = Current exchange rate
PER = Planned exchange rate.[24]

To illustrate the application of this formula, let us assume that a subsidiary in Country X sells goods to another subsidiary in Country Y. The two subsidiaries use a transfer price system based on U.S. dollars. The subsidiary in Country X produced 2,000 units to be sold to the subsidiary in Country Y for FC20,000 at a transfer price of $5 per unit. At the time of the sale the planned exchange rate was $1 = FC8 (where FC is the currency of Country X). The financial performance for the subsidiary in Country X may be expressed as follows:

	$	RATE	FC
Sales	$10,000	$1 = FC8	FC 80,000
Costs	2,500	$0.125 = FC1	FC 20,000
Profit	$ 7,500		FC 60,000
% of sales	75%		75%

Let us now assume that as a result of a devaluation in the U.S. dollar, the exchange rate is $1 = FC4; the financial performance without any adjustment to the transfer price will be as follows:

	$	RATE	FC
Sales	$10,000	$1 = FC4	FC 40,000
Costs	5,000	$0.85 = FC1	FC 20,000
Profit	$ 5,000		FC 20,000
% of sales	50%		50%

It appears that the profit performance is distorted and the performance evaluation is destroyed. To correct the situation the transfer price should be adjusted as follows:

$$NTP = \$5 \times \frac{.25}{.125} = \$10$$

Now, the profit performance after the devaluation may be expressed as follows:

	$	RATE	FC
Sales	$20,000	$1 = FC4	FC 80,000
Costs	5,000	$0.25 = FC1	FC 20,000
Profit	$15,000		FC 60,000
% of sales	75%		75%

It appears that the adjustment of the transfer price has eliminated differences in profit evaluation due to exchange rate fluctuations. This dollar indexing as adopted by Honeywell's control systems has had the following benefits: "By implementing this procedure Honeywell was able to eliminate distorted performance measurement of subsidiary locations, and allow the dollar transfer price of each product to accurately reflect its economic cost to the total corporation."[25]

CULTURAL AND NATIONAL CONSIDERATIONS

A study by Arpan on non-U.S. transfer pricing systems found distinguishable national differences in the number of variables considered in transfer pricing determination, in the relative importance given these variables, and in preference to transfer pricing systems.[26] With respect to the relative importance of the variables in transfer pricing determination, the main findings are: "The degree of competition and differences in income tax rates emerge as the two most important variables, with custom duties, export subsidies and tax credits, exchange controls, inflation and changes in exchange rates receiving varying degrees of mentioned importance."[27] With respect to the national preferences to transfer pricing systems, the main findings are:

The French prefer non-market-oriented systems because they can thus minimize world tax payments. The English also prefer a cost orientation, but their goal is to achieve their target return on investment rates. The Italians use market-oriented systems to maximize corporate income in Italy, which is equivalent to minimizing their tax liability. Canadians also employ market-oriented systems, but essentially because of specific government regulations and a desire to maintain good relations with other governments. The Scandinavian firms view good relations with other governments as paramount, and consequently they are the biggest supporters and users of market-oriented systems. The Germans are the least concerned about transfer pricing, do not seem to prefer any given orientation, and do not exhibit any dominant pattern.[28]

Besides these national and cultural differences, governments tend to differ in their reactions to transfer pricing systems. Most of them try to exert influence on the transfer price indirectly through income taxes and import/export duties. And if they feel that transfer prices are being manipulated to escape the income tax and customs duties constraints, some governments do not hesitate to dictate what is a fair transfer price. These interventions by governments, where transfer prices became the results of external pressures rather than internal considerations, were viewed by many multinational companies as a restraint to corporate goals.[29]

However, in their relations with multinationals, governments are beginning to view transfer pricing as one of many potentially negotiable elements, with the view that resources belong first and foremost to the trading nations themselves. A case for this view of the role of government is made as follows:

Nations have varying powers to influence transfer prices, exercised through income tax, customs and/or other government agencies, each agency operating under common direction consistent with agreed upon national goals. Fundamental to an effective transfer price bargaining position is acceptance of responsibility for (1) systematically monitoring these transactions where they affect national interests, and (2) acquiring sufficient accounting and economic expertise to be able to evaluate international companies transfer pricing positions.[30]

This role is accomplished in the United States through IRS Section 482. In Canada, the government established the Foreign Investment Review

Agency to negotiate new international company investments. Most other countries have adopted some form of similar legislation.

There are various other considerations which may motivate multinationals to overprice (overinvoice) or underprice (underinvoice) transfers between subsidiaries or between subsidiaries and the parent company. First, overpricing would yield benefits to the multinational corporations in the following cases:

1. The multinational corporation may attach an excessive value to *assets-in-kind* it had contributed to the subsidiary. Such overpricing may not be always welcome in the developing countries. As noted by Plasschaert: "The complaint that the physical or intangible assets, thus transferred, are capitalized at an excessive price, is widespread in developing countries. Such overpricing also widens the base against which depreciation allowances can be charged for tax purposes."[31]

2. It may overprice the transfers to the subsidiaries toward achieving a higher price for the final products in those situations where there may be some form of price or wage freeze or control.

3. It may overprice to reduce the profits of the subsidiary and nullify claims for higher wages by local unions.

4. It may overprice to escape charges of antidumping practices.

5. It may overprice in order to repatriate profit and sometimes capital in those situations where some constraints are being imposed on profit and capital repatriations, or where some threat of expropriation without adequate compensation is perceived. By charging a high transfer price, the visible profits in the host country are low and funds are repatriated through payment of intercompany balances. Needless to say, the local authorities are aware of such practices and may be on the lookout. An interesting observation is made by Fantl:

> But even in lesser-developed countries, officials are not so naive as to let these subterfuges pass if they are too blatant. After all, many of these officials have graduated from prestigious American business schools. In many cases, for example, import tariffs are charged not on the listed transfer price but on the current market price for the product.[32]

Second, underpricing would yield benefits to the multinational company in the following cases:

1. The multinational may underprice to avoid antimonopoly indictments.

2. It may underprice to provide support to the subsidiary. As noted by Plasschaert: "This in-house favor is more likely when the subsidiary is still in an infant stage, and on its own, has not yet achieved the credit standing with the local financial community, needed to obtain working capital or other funds, without the guarantee of the parent company."[33]

3. It may underprice as a way of achieving "predatory pricing" aimed at driving competitors out of the local market, and at enlarging the subsidiary's market share.

International Tax Legislation on Transfer Pricing

Tax legislation may be needed to prohibit or control the use of most tax-avoidance schemes associated with transfer pricing. Some of these schemes include a potential shift of income to countries with lower tax rates, repatriation of profits in a transfer price rather than a dividend (which would be subject to withholding tax), reduction of customs and sales in a low transfer pricing to and from foreign affiliates.[34] The issue is very important to any government. In effect, the incorrect pricing of goods or services exported from and imported to a given country would result in a material loss of tax revenue. Some of the legislations used in the industrialized world are presented next.

THE OECD

In 1979, the OECD's Committee on Fiscal Affairs issued *Transfer Pricing and Multinational Enterprises* with the objective to set out, as far as possible, the considerations to be taken into account and to describe, where possible, generally agreed-upon practices in determining transfer prices for tax purposes. The OECD recommendations are the same as those prescribed under Internal Revenue Code Section 488, namely, the comparable uncontrolled price method, the resale price method, the cost-plus method, and any other method found to be acceptable.

CANADA

Tax legislation of transfer pricing in Canada is found in Subsections 69(1), 69(2), and 69(3) of the Canadian Income Tax Act. They read as follows:

69(1) Except as expressly otherwise provided in this act
    (a) where a taxpayer has acquired anything from a person with whom he was not dealing at arm's length at an amount in excess of the fair market value thereof at the time he acquired it, he shall be deemed to have acquired it at that fair market value;
    (b) where a taxpayer has disposed of anything
      (i) to a person with whom he was not dealing at arm's length for no proceeds or for proceeds less than the fair market value at the time he so disposed of it, or
      (ii) to any person by way of gift inter vivos, he shall be deemed to have received proceeds of disposition therefore equal to that fair market value; and

(c) where a taxpayer has acquired property by way of gift, bequest or inheritance, he shall be deemed to have acquired the property at its fair market value at the time he acquired it.

69(2) Where a taxpayer carrying on business in Canada has not paid or agreed to pay, to a non-resident person with whom he was not dealing at arm's length as to price, rental, royalty, or other payment for, or for the use of or reproduction of any property, or as consideration for the carriage of goods or passengers or for other services, an amount greater than the amount (in this subsection referred to as "the reasonable amount") that would have been reasonable in the circumstances if the nonresident person and the taxpayer had been dealing at arm's length, the reasonable amount shall, for the purpose of computing the taxpayer's income from the business, be deemed to have been the amount that was paid or is payable therefore.

69(3) Where a nonresident person had paid, or agreed to pay, to a taxpayer carrying on business in Canada with whom he was not dealing at arm's length as price, rental, royalty or other payment for or for the use or reproduction of any property, or as consideration for the carriage of goods or passengers or for other services, an amount less than the amount (in this subsection referred to as "the reasonable amount") that would have been reasonable in the circumstances if the non-resident person and the taxpayer had been dealing at arm's length, the reasonable amount shall, for the purpose of computing the taxpayer's income from the business, be deemed to have been the amount that was paid or is payable therefore.

Subsection 69(1) was enacted to protect Canada against a loss of revenue resulting from income shifting at the domestic level, while Subsections 69(2) and 69(3) were enacted for the same purpose at the international level. While Subsection 69(1) uses "fair market value" as the criteria to be used in non-arm's-length transactions, Subsections 69(2) and 65(9) use "a reasonable in the circumstances" concept in setting non-arm's-length prices. Naturally, questions arise as to what is meant by these two concepts. Are they similar or is there a distinction? Unfortunately, the act has no definitions or guidelines. Interpretation or a decision of the court remains the solution. The situation, as with IRS Section 482, is confusing and may lead to arbitrary, capricious, or unreasonable decisions. Witness the following remark by Hogg:

Although other cases unrelated to transfer pricing have tried to define fair market value, no concrete definition for income tax purposes has yet been developed. Judicial evaluation of the evidence presented was the overriding concern in these cases. Canadian management, therefore, will find little legislative or judicial help in finding guideposts in the pricing of non-arm's length transactions.[35]

It is easy to criticize the tax authorities. However, it is a fact that the transfer pricing review process must be a complex, time-consuming, and difficult one. Revenue Canada has developed three review approaches to deal with the transfer pricing problem: the large file program, the industry-wide evaluation approach, and the simultaneous audit (joint audits).[36] The large file program involves auditing the large Canadian companies on a national basis as opposed to a piecemeal approach by various district offices. The industry-wide evaluation approach involves focusing on a major industry and thus guarantees consistency in the application of the tax provisions within that industry. The simultaneous audit involves a joint audit with the tax authorities of another country to audit multinational corporations operating in both countries.

OTHER INDUSTRIALIZED NATONS

Tax legislation of transfer pricing in Germany is found under Section 1 of the Aussenteuergesetz (1968 West German Tax Code, as amended by the 1980 Income Tax Act). It specifies that an arm's-length price must be charged between related parties in an international transaction where available; if not, a cost-plus method is to be used.

Tax legislation of transfer pricing in the United Kingdom is found under Section 485 of the United Kingdom Income and Corporation Taxes Act of 1970. It specifies that when property is sold at less than fair market value or bought at more than fair market value, and one of the entities controls the other or both are under the control of a third entity, the Inland Revenue may use the arm's-length price. However, no guidelines are provided for the determination of such price, hence joining IRS Section 482 and Canadian Sections 69(1), 69(2), and 69(3) in making transfer pricing more of an act than the practice of sound business judgment.

Reporting Financial Information by Segment

Multinational corporations, as well as domestic multiproduct corporations, can provide either the total combined performance of the corporation and its subsidiaries or detailed segment information. Because of its so-called usefulness, segment information is preferred and is the subject of mandated disclosure in several countries. In what follows, the U.S., Canadian, international, and other positions on reporting information by segment are presented.

THE U.S. POSITION

The U.S. position on reporting financial information by segment is expressed in FASB Statement No. 14, *Financial Reporting for Segments of a Business Enterprise.* It requires public companies whose securities are publicly traded or which are required to file financial statements with the SEC to include *disaggregated* information about operations in various industries, foreign operations, export sales, and sales to major customers.

Domestic Operations

The first requirement of FAS 14 is to determine which industry segment may or may not be reported separately. The procedures may be outlined as follows: First, the company should identify sources of revenue (by product or service rendered) on a worldwide basis for the entity. Second, it should group related products or services into industry segments. Basically, the following factors may be used in determining whether products and services are related or unrelated.

1. The nature of the product. Related products and services have similar purposes or end uses.

2. *The nature of the production process.* Sharing of common or interchangeable productive techniques may suggest that products or services are related.

3. *Markets and marketing methods.* Related products and services may be sold in similar geographic areas and to similar types of customers.

Third, the company should determine the reporting segments on the basis of the following tests: The first test, known as the *revenue test,* requires that the segment revenue be 10 percent or more of the combined revenue (sales to unaffiliated customers and intersegment sales or transfers) of all the enterprise's industry segments. Segment revenue is calculated as follows:

$$SR = S + IS + INTO + INTR$$

where SR = segment revenue
   S = sales to unaffiliated customers
   IS = intersegment sales and transfers
INTO = Interest income from sources outside the firm
INTR = Interest income from intersegment notes receivables.

The second test, known as the *profitability test,* requires that the absolute of the segments operating profit or loss be 10 percent or more of the greater, in absolute amount, of: (1) the combined operating profits of all industry segments that did not incur an operating loss or (2) the combined operating losses of all industry segments which did incur an operating loss. The third test, if the segment fails both preceding tests, is the *asset test.* It requires that the identifiable assets of the segments be 10 percent or more of the combined identifiable assets of all industry segments. The fourth test, whether the segment has or has not met any of the previous tests, is the *interperiod comparability test.* It requires that the segment be reported separately if management feels such a treatment is needed to achieve interperiod comparability. The fifth test, assuming the segment has met any of the three major tests and the interperiod comparability test, is the *test of dominance.* It requires that the segment *not* be reported separately if it can be classified as dominant. A dominant segment should represent 90 percent or more of the combined revenues, operating profits or losses, *and* identifiable assets. The final test is the *explanation test*. It determines whether a substantial portion of an enterprise's operations is explained by its segment information. The combined total of the revenue from reportable segments must be 75 percent or more of all revenue from sales to unaffiliated customers. If the combined revenues do not meet this test, additional segments must be added until the test is met.

Once the reportable segment has finally been identified after the application of all these tests, the following information is to be disclosed.

1. Revenue information for each reportable segment including (a) sales to unaffiliated customers and (b) intersegment sales or transfers and, if this accounting basis is changed, the nature of the change and its impact on segment operating profit or loss

2. Profitability information including (a) operating profits or losses for each segment and (b) the nature of the change, if any, in the method of allocating operating expenses between segments and the impact of such change on segment operating profit or loss

3. Identifiable assets information

4. Other related disclosures including (a) the aggregate amount of depreciation, depletion, and amortization expense for each reportable segment, (b) the amount of each reportable segment's capital expenditures, (c) whether the firm has an investment carried on the equity method, or an unconsolidated investee whose operations are vertically integrated with a reportable segment, and the geographical area of operations of the investee, and (d) the effect of a change in accounting principle on the operating profit of a reportable segment.

Foreign Operations

FAS 14 requires separate disclosure of domestic and foreign activities. Foreign operating activities are those revenue-generating activities that are located outside the enterprise's home country and are generating revenue either from sales to unaffiliated customers or from intra-enterprise sales or transfers between geographic areas. Two tests may be used to determine if foreign operations are to be reported separately: (1) Revenue from sales to unaffiliated customers must be 10 percent or more of consolidated revenue as reported in the firm's income statement, (2) identifiable assets of the firm's foreign operations are 10 percent or more of consolidated total assets as reported in the firm's balance sheet. After a foreign operation has been determined to be reportable, it must be added to foreign operations in the same geographic area. A geographic area is considered significant if its revenues from sales to unaffiliated customers or its identifiable assets are 10 percent or more of related consolidated amounts.

Other Requirements

The FASB amended certain FAS 14 provisions by issuing Statements No. 18, *Financial Reporting for Segments of a Business Enterprise—Interim Financial Statements* (November 1977), No. 21, *Suspension of the Reporting Earnings per Share and Segment Information by Nonpublic Enterprises* (April 1978), No. 24, *Reporting Segment Information in Statements That Are Presented in Another Enterprise's Financial Report* (December 1978), and No. 30, *Disclosure of Information about Major Customers* (August 1979). These Statements made the following changes to FAS 14.

1. In FAS 18, the requirement contained in FAS 14 that segmented information be included in the interim financial statements was dropped.

2. In FAS 21, the requirements for companies which do not sell their securities in public markets were dropped.

3. In FAS 24, the FASB eliminated the requirement to disclose segment information in the separate financial statements of: (a) the parent company or affiliated companies which have been consolidated or combined in other financial reports, (b) certain foreign investee companies, and (c) investee companies accounted for by the cost or equity method if that segment is not significant in relation to the consolidated or combined financial statements.

4. In FAS 30, the FASB changed a requirement of FAS 14 which required disclosure if 10 percent or more of the firm's revenue was derived from sales to domestic governmental units in the aggregate or to foreign governments in the aggregate. This statement requires disclosure only when 10 percent or more of the revenues of the enterprise are derived from the federal government, a state government, a local government, or a foreign government.

THE CANADIAN POSITION

The Canadian position on reporting financial information by segment is expressed in Section 1700 of the *CICA Handbook*. The requirements of the section are in general similar to the provisions of FAS 14. The only exception relates to the required disclosure of information about major customers of the enterprise. The exposure draft of Section 1700 required this information, but it was deleted from the final version.

INTERNATIONAL POSITIONS

In August 1981 the International Accounting Standards Committee issued IAS 14, *Reporting Financial Information by Segment*. It suggests basically the following disclosures for each reported industry and geographic segment: (1) sales or other operating revenues, distinguishing between revenue derived from customers outside the enterprise and revenue derived from other segments; (2) segment results; (3) segment assets employed, expressed either in monetary amounts or as percentages of the consolidated totals; and (4) the basis of intersegment pricing. The reportable segments are referred to as economically significant entities, defined as those subsidiaries whose levels of revenues, profits, assets, or employment are significant in the countries in which their major operations are conducted.

In the United Kingdom, disclosure of segment sales and profits is made in Directors' reports. One of the provisions of the Fourth Directive of the European Economic Community requires *turnover* only to be analyzed by activity and geographic segment. In Australia there is no requirement to disclose segment information except disclosure of the extent to which each corporation in a group contributes to consolidated profit or loss.

"Carve Out" and "Push Down" Accounting

Recently, many multinational corporations have attempted to raise capital by publicly selling stock in their subsidiaries. To make the offerings attractive, some of these companies do not show the true cost of the unit. The true cost of the business is likely to be hidden because companies put subsidiary expenses on the books of the parent company. The bottom line for the parent is the same because its profits and losses include those of the subsidiaries. However, the subsidiaries' profits look better than they really are, which allows the parent company to sell the subsidiaries' stock at a much higher price than it is really worth. To stop this practice of overstating the profits of subsidiaries by understating their costs, in 1984 the SEC initiated two new rules: "carve out" accounting and "push down" accounting.

Under "carve out" accounting the SEC requires that subsidiaries selling stock must subtract all their selling, general, administrative, interest, and tax expenses from their earnings as reported in the stock offering prospectus. Under "push down" accounting, the subsidiary's books must reflect the goodwill generated when the parent company bought the subsidiary, rather than being taken as an expense on the parent's book. In other words, the new rule transfers (pushes down) the goodwill to the subsidiary.

Conclusions

Transfer pricing is of utmost importance to the management of a multinational corporation given that successful pricing in a competitive environment is a key element in achieving business profit. The cost accounting literature puts a clear emphasis on managerial control in setting transfer prices. As a result, the criteria used for setting transfer prices are mainly (1) to assist top management in evaluating and guiding divisional performance, (2) to help the division manager in running the division, and (3) to ensure divisional autonomy. But the realities of running a complex divisionalized multinational company impose other external considerations in setting transfer prices internationally, which conflict with the managerial control considerations. These external considerations include, among others, tax, import/export duties, exchange risk, cultural and national factors, and other considerations. They require transfer pricing manipulations whose costs may likely outweigh the benefits received.

Notes

1. *Setting Intercorporate Pricing Policies* (New York: Business International, 1973), p. 12.

2. Bruce D. Henderson, and John Dearden, "New System for Divisional Control," *Harvard Business Review* (September/October 1966), pp. 144-60.

3. Joel Dean, "Decentralization and Intracompany Pricing," *Harvard Business Review* (July-August 1955), pp. 65-74; David H. Li, "Interdivisional Transfer Planning," *Management Accounting* (June 1965), pp. 51-54; Timothy P. Haidinger, "Negotiate for Profits," *Management Accounting* (December 1970), pp. 23-24; James M. Fremgen, "Transfer Pricing and Management Goals," *Management Accounting* (December 1970), pp. 25-31; and H. James Shaub, "Transfer Pricing in a Decentralized Organization," *Management Accounting* (April 1978), pp. 33-36, 42.

4. R. K. Mautz, *Financial Reporting by Diversified Companies* (New York: Financial Executives Research Foundation, 1968), p. 36.

5. R. Cyert and J. March, *A Behavioral Theory of the Firm* (Englewood Cliffs, N.J.: Prentice-Hall, 1963), p. 276.

6. Nicholas Dopuch and D.F. Drake, "Accounting Implications of a Mathematical Programming Approach to the Transfer Price Problem," *Journal of Accounting Research* (Spring 1964), p, 13.

7. National Association of Accountants, Research Report No. 30, *Accounting for Intra-Company Transfers* (New York, 1954), pp. 31-36.

8. Martin Shubik, "Incentives, Decentralized Control: The Assignment of Joint Costs and Internal Pricing," in *Management Controls: New Directions in Basic Research*, ed. C. P. Bonini, R. K. Jaedicke, and H. M. Wagner (New York: McGraw-Hill, 1964), pp. 221-22.

9. J. Alex Milburn, "International Transfer Transactions: What Price?" *CA Magazine* (December 1976), pp. 23-24.

10. Myron J.Gordon, "A Method for Pricing for a Socialist Economy," *The Accounting Review* 45 (July 1970), pp. 427-43.

11. R. E. Vending, "A Three-Part Transfer Price," *Management Accounting* 55 (September 1973), pp. 33-36.

12. M. Onsi, "A Transfer Pricing System Based on Opportunity Cost," *The Accounting Review* 45 (July 1970), pp. 535-43; Gary L. Holstrum, and E. H. Sauls, "The Opportunity Cost Transfer Price," *Management Accounting* 54 (May 1973), pp. 29-33.

13. C. H. Horngren, *Cost Accounting: A Managerial Emphasis* (Englewood Cliffs, N.J.: Prentice Hall, 1977), pp. 673-92.

14. H. C. Greer, "Divisional Profit Calculation: Notes on the 'Transfer Rate' Problem," *NAA Bulletin* 43 (July 1962), pp. 5-12; J. D. Edwards, and R. A. Roemmick, "Transfer Pricing: The Wrong Tool for Performance Evaluation," *Cost and Management* 50 (January-February 1976), pp. 35-37; A. R. Drebin, "A Proposal for Dual Pricing of Intracompany Transfers," *NAA Bulletin* 40 (February 1959), pp. 51-55.

15. Drebin, "A Proposal for Dual Pricing," p. 54.

16. H. Bierman, Jr., "Pricing Intercompany Transfer," *The Accounting Review* 34 (July 1959), pp. 429-32.

17. Sylvain R. F. Plasschaert, *Transfer Pricing and Multinational Corporations: An Overview of Concepts, Mechanisms and Regulations* (New York: Praeger Publishers, 1979), p. 1.

18. Irving L. Fantl, "Transfer Pricing—Tread Carefully," *The CPA Journal* 44 (December 1974), p. 44.

19. U.S. Internal Revenue Code (1954), Section 482.

20. Ibid., Section 482-1(b)(L).

21. Ibid., Section 482-1(e)(2)(ii).

22. Sylvain R. F. Plasschaert, "The Multiple Motivations for Transfer Pricing Modulations in Multinational Enterprises and Governmental Counter-Measures: An Attempt at Clarification," *Management International Review* 21, 1 (1981), p. 52.

23. Jeffrey S. Arpan, *International Intracorporate Pricing, Non-American Systems and Views* (London: Praeger Publishers, 1971).

24. Duane Malstrom, "Accommodating Exchange Rate Fluctuations in Intercompany Pricing and Invoicing," *Management Accounting* 59 (September 1977), pp. 24-28.

25. Ibid, p. 28.

26. Jeffrey S. Arpan, "International Intracorporate Pricing: Non-American Systems and Views," *Journal of International Business Studies* 3 (Spring 1972), pp. 1-8.

27. Ibid, p. 9.

28. Arpan, *International Intracorporate Pricing*, p. 105.

29. James Green and Michael G. Duerr, *Intercompany Transactions in the Multinational Firm* (New York: National Industrial Conference Board, 1970).

30. Milburn, "International Transfer Transactions," p. 26.

31. Plasschaert, "The Multiple Motivations for Transfer Pricing Modulations," p. 54.

32. Fantl, "Transfer Pricing," p. 44.

33. Plasschaert, "The Multiple Motivations for Transfer Pricing Modulations," p. 55.

34. Pricing subsidies as an alternative means of financing overseas operations, and the use of transfer pricing to thwart exchange controls and to circumvent profit or price controls in the host country, are some nontax issues.

35. Roy D. Hogg, "A Canadian Tax Overview of Transfer Pricing," *CA Magazine* (December 1983), p. 59.

36. Ibid, p. 60.

Bibliography

Arpan, Jeffrey S. *International Intracorporate Pricing: Non-American Systems and Views* (London: Praeger Publishers, 1971).

_____. "International Intracorporate Pricing: Non-American Systems and Views," *Journal of International Business Studies* 3 (Spring 1972), pp. 1-18.

_____. "Transfer Pricing in Multinational Financial Management," *The Financial Review* 2 (1972), pp. 141-55.

Burns, Jane O. "Transfer Pricing Decisions in U.S. Multinational Corporations," *Journal of International Business Studies* 11 (Fall 1980), pp. 23-39.

Burns, Jane O., and Ronald S. Ross. "Establishing International Transfer Pricing Standards for Tax Audits of Multinational Enterprises," *The International Journal of Accounting Education and Research* 17 (Fall 1981), pp. 161-80.

Business Internal Corporation. *Setting Intercorporate Pricing Policies* (New York: BIC, 1973).

Coburn, David L., Joseph K. Ellis III, and Duane R. Milano. "Dilemmas in MNC Transfer Pricing," *Management Accounting* 63 (November 1981), pp. 53-58.

Cowen, Scott S. "Multinational Transfer Pricing." *Management Accounting* 60 (January 1979), pp. 17-22.

Elam, Rick, and Hamid Henaidy. "Transfer Pricing for the Multinational Corporation," *The International Journal of Accounting Education and Research* 16 (Spring 1981), pp. 49-65.

Fantl, Irving. "Transfer Pricing—Tread Careful," *The CPA Journal* 44 (December 1974), pp. 42-26.

Fowler, D. J. "Transfer Prices and Profit Maximization in Multinational Operations," *Journal of International Business Studies* 9 (Winter 1978), pp. 9-26.

Greene, James, and Michael G. Duerr. *Intercompany Transactions in the Multinational Firm* (New York: National Industrial Conference Board, 1970).

Kaye, Rodney. "Transfer Pricing," *The Accountant* 182 (April 10, 1980), pp. 536-38.

Kim, S. H. "Financial Motives of U.S. Corporate Investment Abroad," *California Management Review* (Summer 1976), pp. 60-65.

Kim, Seung H., and Stephen W. Miller. "Constituents of the International Transfer Pricing Decision." *Columbia Journal of World Business* 14 (Spring 1979), pp. 69-77.

Lamp, Walter. "The Multinational Whipping Boy." *Financial Executive* 44 (December 1976), pp. 44-47.

Lauter, G.P. "Sociological, Cultural and Legal Factors Impending Decentralization of Authority in Developing Countries," *Academy of Management Journal* (September 1969).

McDaniel, Paul R., and Hugh J. Ault. *Introduction to United States International Taxation* (Seventer, The Netherlands: Kluwer, 1981).

Malstrom, Duane. "Accommodating Exchange Rate Fluctuations in Intercompany Pricing and Invoicing," *Management Accounting* 59 (September 1977), pp. 24-28.

Merville, Larry J., and J. William Petty. "Transfer Pricing for the Multinational Firm," *The Accounting Review* 53 (October 1978), pp. 935-51.

Milburn, J. Alex. "International Transfer Transactions: What Price?" *CA Magazine* (December 1976), pp. 22-27.

Nagy, Richard J. "Transfer Price Accounting for MNC's" *Management Accounting* 59 (January 1978), pp. 34-38.

Petty, J. William, and Ernest W. Walker. "Optimal Transfer Pricing for the Multinational Firm," *Financial Management* 1 (Winter 1972), pp. 74-78.

Plasschaert, Sylvain. *Transfer Pricing and Multinational Corporations: An Overview of Concepts, Mechanisms and Regulations* (Farnborough: Saxon House—ECSIM, 1979).

Plasschaert, Sylvain R. F. "The Multiple Motivations for Transfer Pricing Modulations in Multinational Enterprises and Governmental Counter-Measures: An Attempt at Clarification," *Management International Review* 21, (1981), pp. 49-63.

Sharav, Itzhak. "Transfer Pricing—Diversity of Goals and Practices," *Journal of Accountancy* 137 (April 1974), pp. 56-62.

Shulman, J. S. "When the Price Is Wrong-By Design," *Columbia Journal of World Business* (May-June 1967), pp. 69-76.

Shulman, James S. "The Tax Environment of Multinational Firms," *The Tax Executive* (April 1967), pp. 173-87.

Stewart, J. C. "Multinational Companies and Transfer Pricing," *Journal of Business Finance & Accounting* 4 (Autumn 1977), pp. 353-71.

Tang, Roger Y. W. "Canadian Transfer Pricing Practices," *CA Magazine* 113 (March 1980), pp. 32-38.

———. *Transfer Pricing Practices in the United States and Japan* (New York: Praeger Publishers, 1979).

Tang, Roger Y. W., C. K. Walter, and Robert H. Raymond. "Transfer Pricing—Japanese vs. American Style," *Management Accounting* 60 (January 1979), pp. 12-16.

Tang, Roger Y. W., and K. H. Chan. "Environmental Variables of International Transfer Pricing: A Japan-United States Comparison," *Abacus* 15 (June 1979), pp. 3-12.

Wu, Frederick H., and Douglas Sharp. "An Empirical Study of Transfer Pricing Practices," *The International Journal of Accounting Education and Research* 14 (Spring 1979), pp. 71-100.

8.

FOREIGN EXCHANGE AND POLITICAL RISK MANAGEMENT

Multinational operations face a variety of risks. Two of the most challenging are foreign exchange and political risks. Foreign exchange risk affects a firm's cash flows as a result of currency fluctuations. Political risk threatens the multinational operation's existence itself. A case may be made for management accountants involved in multinational operations to attempt to deal with foreign exchange and political risks. Therefore, this chapter covers the issues and solutions related to the management of foreign exchange and political risks.

Managing Foreign Exchange Risk

Changes in foreign exchange rates create one of the most complex uncertanties faced by multinational firms. These changes create a risk to these firms known as foreign exchange risk—a risk that affects firms' cash flows as a result of currency fluctuations. It can also affect contractual cash flows arising from debt payable or receivable or noncontractual cash flows which are usually associated with expected revenues and expenses.

Is there a case for corporate management of foreign exchange risk? Six arguments may be used that oppose hedging at the level of the firm because either foreign exchange risk does not exist or, if it exists, it does not need to be hedged: the purchasing power parity, the capital asset-pricing model, the Modigliani-Miller Theorem, the concept of self-insurance and the efficient market hypothesis, the hedging of consumption bundle, and the uncertainty of forward rates and spot rates. Each of these arguments may be used against corporate management of foreign exchange risk. However, the same arguments may also be used to argue *for* corporate management of foreign exchange risk as summarized in Exhibit 8.1. Basically, because real-world imperfections for real goods and services as well as financial assets do exist, firms can be subject to exchange risk, and corporate management of foreign

Against	For
1. *Purchasing Power Parity Theorem:* PPP implies offsetting changes in price levels and exchange rates; hence, there is no exposure to exchange risk.	1. Deviations from PPP have been well documented: the shorter the time horizon, the greater the deviations. Even if PPP holds with respect to an index of tradeable goods, a particular firm may still be exposed to exchange risk, since the relative price of its inputs and outputs may change.
2. *Capital Asset Pricing Model (CAPM):* According to CAPM, what matters is only one systematic risk; it does not matter whether exchange risk is managed separately in foreign exchange markets, or passed along to the capital market.	2. When default risk is important, hedging can reduce default risk and add to the debt capacity of the firm.
3. *Modigliani-Miller (MM) Theorem:* According to MM, what the firm does, an investor can do; hence, there is no need for corporate management of exchange risk.	3. There are several obstacles to individuals in coping better with exchange risk. A firm is in a position to obtain a low-cost hedge; also information on the firm's exposure is not symmetrically distributed between shareholders and managers.
4. *The Concept of Self-Insurance:* The forward market is a fair bet and does not provide bargains. The foreign exchange gains and losses average out over a period. *The Efficient Market Hypothesis:* Since the foreign exchange markets are efficient, forward contracts are priced properly	4. This concept implies maximizing expected value without regard to variance, and thus assumes risk neutrality. However, economic agents are usually risk averse. The objective of hedging is not to earn excess returns, but to achieve a desired pattern of risk and return.

EXHIBIT 8.1 (continued)

Against	For
and there are no excess returns from hedging.	
5. *Hedging of Consumption Bundle:* A firm's exchange-related gains and losses may be useful to hedge the consumption bundles of its shareholders.	5. As the consumption bundle is investor-specific, its management is better left to the shareholder. Firms should hedge exchange risk and the shareholder should hedge consumption bundle risk.
6. *The Uncertainty of Forward Rates and Spot Rates:* Since future forward rates are as uncertain as future spot rates, hedging is of dubious value.	6. Hedging makes available exact information regarding anticipated cash flows; such information can be useful for activities for which the planning and action horizon is the same as the maturity of the forward contract.

SOURCE: Gunter Dufey and S. L. Srivinivasulu, "The Case for Corporate Management of Foreign Exchange Risk," *Financial Management* (Winter 1983), p. 55. Reprinted with permission.

exchange may be supported.[1] These market imperfections may include incomplete securities markets, positive transactions and information costs, the dead-weight costs of financial distress, and agency cost considerations.

Assuming then that the foreign exchange market is far from being perfect, the first step in managing foreign exchange risk would be to attempt to forecast the foreign exchange rate under a floating exchange exposure. The third step is to suggest ways to manage the foreign exchange risk.

FORECASTING FOREIGN EXCHANGE RISK UNDER A FREELY FLOATING SYSTEM

Under a freely floating system characterized by the absence of any governmental interference, the procedure would be to develop a formal forecasting model based on diagnostic variables derived from established economic theories. In fact, four theories have been proposed as a basis for determining the diagnostic variables which may influence exchange rates under either a floating or pegged system: the Theory of Purchasing Power Parity, the Fisher Effect, the International Fisher Effect, the Theory of Interest-Rate Parity, and the Forward Rate as an Unbiased Predictor of the Future Spot Rate.

The Theory of Purchasing Power Parity

The theory of purchasing power parity holds that the rate of change in the spot exchange rate is equal to the difference between the inflation rates in the home country and the foreign country.[2] In other words, any difference in the rates of inflation between two countries tends to be offset in the long run by an equal and opposite change in the spot exchange rate. Basically,

$$S = \mu - \mu'$$

where

S = rate of change in the spot exchange rate in percentage terms
μ = domestic inflation rate in percentage terms
μ' = foreign inflation rate in percentage terms.

Therefore, a 6 percent higher inflation rate in Canada will be offset by a 6 percent depreciation in the spot exchange rate of Canadian dollars for U.S. dollars. Empirical results seem to show that this theory may hold over the long run.[3]

The Fisher Effect

The Fisher effect holds that the nominal interest rate in a country is equal to the required real interest rate plus the expected rate of inflation. For two countries it would mean the following relationships:

Home interest rate $= i = r + \mu$ (a)
Foreign interest rate $= i' - r' + \mu$ (b)

Substracting equation (b) from equation (a) gives

$$i - i' = (r - r') + (\mu - \mu')$$ (c)

Assuming that real rates of returns should tend toward equality between two countries, the Fisher effect holds then that nominal interest rates will vary by the difference in the expected rates of inflation, and

$$i - i' = \mu - \mu'.$$

Therefore, if nominal interest rates in Canada and in the U.S. on one-year maturities were respectively 16 percent and 10 percent, it would be consistent with the differences in inflation rates where these rates were respectively 13 percent in Canada and 7 percent in the U.S.

The International Fisher Effect

The international Fisher effect holds that the rate of change in the spot exchange rate is equal to the difference between the interest rates in the home country and the foreign country. In other words, any difference in the interest rates between two countries tends to be offset by an equal but opposite change in the spot exchange rate. Basically,

$$\frac{E(S) - S}{S} \times \frac{12}{n} \times 100 = i - i'$$

where

S = The spot exchange rate (expressed in the number of home currency units for each unit of foreign currency)

$E(S)$ = the expected future spot exchange rate n months from now

i = nominal interest rate in the home country

i' = number of months in the forecasting firms.[4]

Therefore, the Canadian dollar will depreciate by 6 percent relative to the U.S. dollar if the interest rates were respectively 16 percent in Canada and 10 percent in the U.S. Basically, the Canadian dollar will depreciate by 6 percent to be consistent with a 6 percent higher interest rate. Empirical evidence seems to support this theory for the short run.[5]

The Theory of Interest Rate Parity

The theory of interest rate parity holds that the difference in nominal interest rates between two countries should be equal but opposite in sign to the forward exchange rate discount or premium. Basically,

$$\frac{F - S}{S} \times \frac{12}{n} \times 100 = i - i'$$

where

F = forward exchange rate for contracts due in n months

S = spot exchange rate

i = nominal interest rate in the home country

i' = nominal interest rate in the foreign country

n = number of months in the forecasting firms.

Therefore, a 6 percent interest rate in Canada will be offset by a 6 percent discount on the Canadian dollar for delivery in one year.

The interest rate parity results from the use of interest arbitrage. It may be illustrated as follows:

An interest arbitrager may either get an investment yield of $1 + i$ from a deposit in home currency or $\frac{F}{S}(1 + i')$ from a deposit in foreign currency because the arbitrager has to convert the home currency using the spot exchange rate S, receives a yield of $\frac{(1 + i')}{s}$, and has to stay covered by buying home currencies at the forward rate F. If the return in the foreign units is high, more funds will move in, resulting in a reduction in i', an increase in S, and a decrease in F. Therefore, according to the interest rate parity hypothesis, the following relationship will hold:

$$\frac{F}{S}(1 + i') = 1 + i.$$

Dividing by $(1 + i')$ and subtracting one from both sides will yeild

$$\frac{F - S}{S} = \frac{i - i'}{1 + i'} \cong i - i'.$$

The Forward Rate as an Unbiased Predictor of the Future Spot Rate

Assuming an efficient foreign exchange market, it may be advanced that the forward rate acts as an unbiased predictor of the future spot rate.[6] In other words, a 6 percent one-year forward premium on the Canadian dollar acts as an unbiased predictor that the Canadian dollar will appreciate by 6 percent over the next year.

The foreign exchange market has not conclusively been proven efficient. While Poole[7] and Dooley and Shafer[8] found evidence for the Price Dynamics view of exchange rate behavior, Rogalski and Vinso,[9] Giddy and Dufey,[10] Logue and Sweeny,[11] and finally Kohlhagen provided evidence supporting the efficient market hypothesis for international money and foreign exchange markets.[12]

FORECASTING A FOREIGN EXCHANGE RATE UNDER A MANAGED OR
FIXED EXCHANGE RATE SYSTEM

Besides the theories just presented, the forecasting process under a managed or fixed exchange rate system will need to examine the politics of devaluation and all possible economic and social indicators which may signal a change in the exchange rate. Eiteman and Stonehill identify the following variables as the possible indicators of pressure which could be placed on the troubled exchange rate: the balance-of-payments deficit, different national rates of inflation, growth in the money supply, lack of synchronization of national business cycles, a decline in international monetary reserves, increased spread between official and "free" rates of exchange, governmental policies which treat symptoms rather than causes, and excessive government spending.[13] Jacque developed a four-step procedure for forecasting pegged yet adjustable exchange rates.[14] These steps are:

Step 1: To assess balance-of-payments outlook by using certain macroeconomic indicators as a warning system. The indicators include the rate of depletion or growth in international reserves, covering import spending by export earnings for the case of stabilized exchange rates, the consumer price index, the growth in the money supply, and the degree of diversification of exports.

Step 2: To measure the magnitude of required adjustments which may bring the balance of payments into equilibrium by measuring the pressures the market forces are exercising upon the prevailing exchange rates. This step may result in a determination of the magnitude of the possible devaluation or revaluation.

Step 3: To time the adjustment policies by an examination of the central bank's foreign exchange reserves.

Step 4: To predict the type of adjustment policies—either a parity change (devaluation or revaluation) or inflationary or deflationary policies, coupled with exchange controls and extensive international borrowings.

FOREIGN EXCHANGE EXPOSURE

It has already been stated that changes in exchange rates subject the multinational firm to important risks. Measuring the exposure of such a firm to the risk of losses from changes in exchange rates is an important input in deciding how to manage such risk. Therefore, the measurement of foreign exchange exposure needs to be examined. Traditionally, foreign exchange exposure has been defined around one of the combinations of the concepts of *transaction exposure, translation exposure,* and *economic exposure.* Each of these concepts is examined next.

Transaction Exposure

A transaction exposure arises whenever a firm has a receivable, a payable, a revenue, an expense, or a forward contract denominated in other than its *functional* currency, which is usually the local currency or the currency in which the firm does most of its business. The result of a transaction exposure is a transaction exchange gain or loss.

If the firm is committed to a receivable denominated in a foreign currency the transaction exchange gain or loss would be:

Transaction exchange gain or loss = Dollar worth of accounts receivable when actual payments are made — dollar worth of accounts receivable when export transaction was initiated.

If the firm is committed to a liability denominated in a foreign currency the transaction exchange gain or loss would be:

Transaction exchange gain or loss = Dollar worth of liability when payment comes due − dollar worth of liabilities when first incurred.

The recognition of transaction exposure in the U.S. is governed by FASB Statement No. 52. Basically, the foreign currency transaction is recognized at the exchange rate prevailing at the date of the transaction, then reevaluated at each subsequent balance sheet date until it is settled.

Translation Exposure

A translation exposure results from the necessity of periodically consolidating or aggregating parents' and subsidiaries' financial statements. To do so, the subsidiaries' financial statements have to be translated into the parent's currency before being consolidated with the parent's financial statements. Translation exposure results from the possibility that a change in exchange rates will create an exchange gain or loss and therefore depends on the translation method and the exchange rate used for the translation of individual items in the balance sheet and income statement. Basically, the accounting or translation exposure may be stated as follows:

Translation exposure = Foreign assets minus foreign liabilities translated at the current exchange rate.

Under the current-rate method, all accounts are translated at the exchange rate prevailing at the time of consolidation. In such case, the translation exposure is equal to the net worth of the subsidiary as expressed in the local currency.

Under the current/noncurrent method, current assets and liabilities are translated at the current exchange rate while noncurrent assets and liabilities are translated at historical rates. In such a case, the translation exposure is equal to the difference between current assets and current liabilities, that is the working capital.

Under the monetary/nonmonetary method, monetary assets and liabilities are translated at the current rate while nonmonetary assets and liabilities are translated at historical rates. In such a case, the translation exposure is equal to the difference between the monetary assets and monetary liabilities.

Under the temporal method, assets and liabilities are translated in a manner that retains their original measurement bases. Basically, cash, receivables, and payables are translated at the current rate. Assets carried at historical costs are translated at the historical rate while assets carried at current costs are translated at the current rate. The method advocated by FAS 8 deviates a little from the temporal method because foreign currency-denominated long-term debt must be translated at the current rate. In such a case, the translation exposure may be expressed as follows:

Translation exposure (using the temporal method) = (Cash + accounts receivables) − (accounts payable + long-term debt) denominated in currencies other than the functional currency.

Economic Exposure

Economic exposure results from the possibility that a firm's economic value will change as a result of an exchange rate change. Basically, it means that economic exposure to exchange rate change is the present value of assets minus liabilities which change in value with exchange rate change. Operationally, it is the change in the net present value of expected future after-tax flows as a result of an exchange rate change. Needless to say, economic exposure is considerably more important to the multinational firm than translation or transaction exposures. It is more difficult to detect, given that it depends on the estimation procedures used to forecast future cash flows. It does not result, however, from the idiosyncrasies of the accounting process but from economic analysis and planning. As such it requires from management an integrated planning process involving strategies in finance, marketing, production, and so forth. That planning has to start at the strategic rather than the management or operational level to be preventive rather than reactive. Puchon states the case as follows:

A proper strategic planning framework that gives full recognition of the financial and operating implications of inflation and foreign exchange can provide senior management greater effectiveness in managing economic exposure in the long run. It might require the integration of operating and financial responsibilities from the policy-making level down to the implementation and performance evaluation levels.[15]

FOREIGN EXCHANGE RISK MANAGEMENT

Given the impact of foreign exchange risk on the financial statements and value of the firm, a comprehensive exposure management program is necessary, with well-defined policies and procedures with respect to exposure management. Besides an overall policy, the firm must define the maximum allowable level of exchange risk it is prepared to face. The overall policy must be to maximize long-term stockholder wealth, which necessitates reacting to economic exposure, or to maximize short-term earnings for shares, which necessitates reacting to transaction and translation exposures. Either goal requires a different exchange risk management.

Reacting to Economic Exposure

As stated earlier, reacting to economic exposure requires strategic planning in the functional areas of marketing, finance, and production.

Marketing strategies may involve careful planning of pricing, product promotion, and distribution to be implemented in the event of exchange rate changes. Production strategies may involve securing alternative sources and plants to be used for changes in production techniques and locations in the event of exchange rate changes. Similarly, financial strategies may involve securing alternative lines of credit in various countries to be used in the event of exchange rate changes.

Reacting to Translation and Transaction Exposure

Reacting to translation and transaction exposure rests on using the following protective measures:

1. *Forward Exchange Contracts*: One way of minimizing translation and transaction exposures is to use a forward exchange market hedge, or to supply a "forward edge." It consists of buying or selling a currency to meet a future transaction or to hedge a balance sheet position. It is basically a present agreement in an exchange rate for a foreign exchange transaction which is to take place at a future date. As an example, suppose a U.S. firm holds a foreign currency-denominated receivable which matures in six months. To hedge its long position, the firm may sell the foreign currency forward, matching the amount and maturity date of the forward contract with the amount and maturity date of the receivable. In other words, a U.S. exporter who expects to receive 800 million French francs in four months from a French customer, but thinks those francs will be worth less than they are today, would be protected against the weakening franc by arranging to sell 200 million francs four months from now to a bank at a set price. That price might be less than the current value of francs but more than what the exporter figures francs will be going for in four months.[16] By locking the exchange rate, the company not only protects profit but also helps in planning, budgeting, and pricing.

2. *Borrowing and Lending*: Another way of minimizing translation and transaction exposure is to use foreign currency credits, such as foreign bank loans, overdrafts, and lines of credit to finance repayables in foreign currency. A further way is to borrow in a local currency in anticipation of a devaluation and to convert the proceeds into a strong currency. Finally, the firm may borrow in a local currency and use the proceeds to buy commodities from that country before their prices increase as a result of devaluation. This action is known as a "commodity hedge."

   Three obstacles may arise against the use of borrowing and lending. First, some countries limit the amount of local money foreigners may borrow. Second, companies may end up holding too much foreign currency. They end up scrambling to convert their local currency deposits and receivables into more usable bond currency—such as pounds, dollars, and marks—and then repatriate the cash to the U.S. Third, some countries may become inclined to impose stricter controls on lending by their banks at home and through their foreign subsidiaries. One such proposal was made in February 1984 by the West German Finance Ministry to limit a bank's credit exposure to any single borrower to 50 percent of the bank's equity, down from the current 75 percent.[17] In fact, the proposal would extend Germany's banking rules to foreign subsidiaries, especially in Luxemburg where regulations specify only that a bank's lending cannot exceed 33 times its equity, and which may have encouraged Luxemburg subsidiaries of German banks to exceed the lending norms applying at home.

3. *Balance Sheet Hedge*: One way of minimizing translation exposure is to try to reach a "monetary balance" where exposed assets are equal to exposed liabilities. This may be achieved by early declaration of dividends, prepayment of debts in foreign currencies and settlement of other liabilities denominated in strong currencies.

4. *Currency Options*: Currency options allow multinational companies to buy or sell a fixed amount of currency at a prearranged price within a set time, from a few days to a couple of years. The option buyer can choose the exchange rate he/she wants to guarantee, as well as the length of the contract. In essence, currency options act as an insurance policy for corporate treasurers. It lets them gain on rate savings and guard against loss. In other words, it lets them take advantage of the agreed on exchange rate or not, depending on what happens to the currency value. This is drastically different from the hedging in the forward market where they are committed to buying or selling a currency at a given rate. Given the wide savings in foreign exchange markets, when currency values can change as much as 4 percent in a single day, currency options will remain an attractive mechanism to encourage risks.

5. *Hedging against Fluctuating Interest Rates*: Corporate treasurers have started to hedge against fluctuating interest rates as much as they have been doing against currency shifts. While some are still using the regulated financial-futures markets in Chicago and London, others are going off-market through London banks. The off-market futures' hedging is simpler and more flexible than the regulated markets. As an example, a corporate treasurer who has to borrow $3 million 3 months from now to finance inventory buildup would want to lock in low current interest rates. To do so he finds a bank willing to give him an acceptable rate. When the time comes to borrow, if interest rates have risen, the bank will pay the company any difference in the interest rates; if, on the other hand, interest rates have fallen, the company will pay the bank the difference. Basically, under the regulated financial-futures market the hedger pays a little every day, while under the off-market he pays all of it at the end of the transaction. Most banks participating in such a hedge feel that they are offering a simpler way to hedge than futures markets.

6. *Leading and Lagging*: Leading and lagging, as a way of reducing exposure, consist of speeding up collections on lagging payments in payables denominated in foreign currency. It is sometimes known as an "operating hedge." The basic idea is that when the firm expects a currency to appreciate, it speeds up payments of imports and debts, and slows the collection of export receipts. When it expects a currency to depreciate, it reverses the tactic, slowing import payments and accelerating collections.

7. *Gold Hedge*: The shortage of foreign currencies in the developing countries means that overseas subsidiaries of multinational companies may end up loaded with weak currencies like Brazilian cruzeiros and Mexican pesos. For example, in 1983 a growing number of U.S. multinationals bought gold on the Brazilian

market to protect their corporate assets against the country's runaway inflation of 107 percent and almost weekly devaluations. In the past, the companies had bought government-indexed bonds to provide insurance against devaluation and inflation. A loss of confidence in these dollar-pegged government bonds led to the move to gold.[18]

8. *Swaps*: A firm may use swaps to reduce foreign exchange exposure. They are essentially a set of parallel transactions in opposite directions. In other words, a swap is an agreement between two entities to exchange one currency for another now and provides dates on which to give back the original amount swapped. Types of swaps include forward swaps, "back-to-back" or "parallel" loans, "currency swaps," and "credit swaps."

A back-to-back or parallel-loan is an agreement between firms to borrow each other's currency for a period of time and to return the borrowed currencies at a given time in the future. Without at any time going through the foreign "exchange" market. For example, a British firm in the United Kingdom lends a given amount in sterling to a French affiliate in the United Kingdom while the French parent of a subsidiary in France or in another country lends an equal amount in French francs or in any other currency to the British firm's affiliate in France or in any other country.

A currency swap is similar to a back-to-back loan except that it does not appear in any of the firms' balance sheets and does not involve any interest.

A credit swap involves the exchange of currency between a firm and a bank in the foreign country to be reversed at a later date.

Managing Political Risk

Because of the political risk elements in most international operations and investments there is a strong need for a systematic evaluation of political risks, "involving their identification, their likely incidence, and their specific consequences for company operations."[19] Accordingly, in what follows, the nature of political risk, the ways of forecasting it, and the accounting role in managing political risk are examined.

NATURE OF POLITICAL RISK

Political risk is not necessarily limited to unfavorable conditions encountered by multinationals in most developing countries. It can easily be encountered in industrialized countries including the U.S. In general, it refers to the potential economic losses resulting from some forms of most government influences which may either limit the multinational activities of a firm or eliminate (through takeover, for example) these same activities. Various operational definitions of political risks have been proposed. Robock and Simmonds maintain that political risk in international business exists "(1) when discontinuities occur in the business environment, (2) when they are difficult to anticipate, and (3) when they result from political change."[20]

They also make a distinction between macropolitical risks when politically motivated environmental changes affect all foreign firms and micropolitical risks when the changes affect only selected foreign firms or industries or foreign firms with specific characteristics. Greene defines political risk as "that uncertainty stemming from unanticipated and unexpected acts of governments or other organizations which may cause loss to the business firm."[21] Basically, political risk is manifest through a climate of uncertainty dominated by a probable loss to the business enterprise. It may arise from different sources. Root notes that a wide spectrum of political risks may be generated "by the attitudes, policies and overt behavior of those governments and other local power centers such as rival political parties, labor unions, and nationalistic groups."[22] A study prepared for the Financial Executives Research Foundation identifies instead the following 12 political risk factors: radical change in government composition or policy, expropriation, nationalization, attitude of opposition groups, probability of opposition-group takeover, attitude toward foreign investment, quality of government management, ownership requirements, anti-private-sector influence, labor instability, relationship with the company's home government, and relationship with neighboring countries.[23] Political risk may lead to various possible outcomes, namely, expropriation/ nationalization, compulsory local equity participation, operational restrictions, discrimination, price controls, blockage of remittances, and breach of government contracts. Given the negative impacts of the outcomes of political risk on foreign operations, especially in the extreme cases where a government takes over a business activity through confiscation and expropriation, there is a strong need to be able to forecast political risk.

HOW TO FORECAST POLITICAL RISKS

It would not be surprising to learn that various proposals have been made about how to forecast political risks. Robock and Simmonds suggest an evaluation of the vulnerability of a company to political risk by an analysis of its operations, with the following questions in mind:

1. Are periodic external inputs of new technology required?
2. Will the project be competing strongly with local nationals who are in, or trying to enter, the same field?
3. Is the operation dependent on natural resources, particularly minerals or oil?
4. Does the investment put pressure on balance of payments?
5. Does the enterprise have a strong monopoly position in the local market?
6. Is the product socially essential and acceptable?[24]

Stobaugh noticed that a number of U.S.-based multinational enterprises had developed scales to rate countries on the basis of their investment climates.[25] An *Argus Capital Market Report* offered for country risk analysis a laundry list of economic indicators to "educate the decision-maker and force him to think in terms of the relevant economic fundaments."[26] These indicators are monetary base, domestic base, foreign reserves, purchasing power parity index, currency/deposit ratio, consumer prices as a percentage change, balance of payments—goods and services as a percentage of GNP, balance of payments—goods and services as a percentage of foreign reserves, percentage change exports/percentage change imports, exports as a percentage of GNP, imports as a percentage of GNP, foreign factor income payments as a percentage of GNP, average tax rate, government deficit as a percentage of GNP, government expenditures, real GNP as a percentage change, and real per capita GNP as a percentage change.

More recently, Rummel and Heenan have provided a four-way classification of attempts to forecast political interference: "grand tours," "old hands," Delphi techniques, and quantitative methods.[27] A grand tour involves a visit of the potential host country by an executive or a team of people for an inspection tour and a report later to the home office. Superficiality and overdose of selective information have marred the grand tour technique.

The old hands technique involves acquiring area expertise from seasoned educators, diplomats, journalists, or business persons. Evidently too much implicit faith is put in the judgment of these so-called experts.

The Delphi techniques may be used to survey a knowledgeable group. First, selective elements influencing the political climate are chosen. Next, experts are asked to rank these factors toward the development of an overall measure or index of political risk. Finally, countries are ranked on the basis of the index. As stated by Rummel and Heenan, the "strength of the Delphi technique rests on the posing of relevant questions. When they are defective, the entire structure crumbles."[28]

The quantitative methods technique involves developing elaborate models using multivariate analysis to either explain and describe underlying relationships affecting a nation-state or predict future political events. Two such political risk models using this technique may be identified in the literature and are examined next.

THE KNUDSEN "ECOLOGICAL APPROACH"

Harald Knudsen's model involves gathering socioeconomic data depicting the "ecological structures" or investment climate of a particular foreign environment, to be used to predict political behavior in general and the national propensity to expropriate in particular.[29] The model, which is depicted graphically as Exhibit 8.2, maintains that the national propensity

EXHIBIT 8.2 THE NATIONAL PROPENSITY TO EXPROPRIATE MODEL

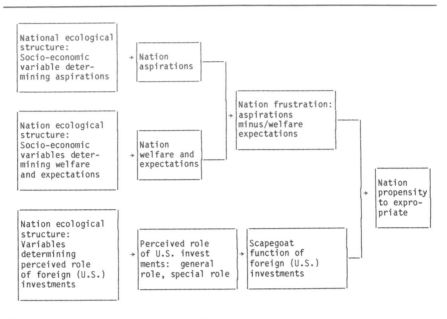

Note: Double line denotes measurable entities.

SOURCE: Harald Knudsen, "Explaining the National Propensity to Expropriate: An Ecological Approach." *Journal of International Business Studies,* Spring 1974, p. 54.

Reprinted with Permission.

to expropriate may be explained by "a nation frustration" factor and "scapegoat function of foreign investments." Basically, if the level of national frustration is high and at the same time the level of foreign investment presence is also high, these foreign investments become a scapegoat leading to a high propensity to expropriate.

The variables in the model are defined as follows: The level of frustration is expected to be the difference between the level of aspirations and the level of welfare and expectations. Also, the scapegoat of foreign investment is determined by the perceived general and special role of foreign investment.

The variables are measured as follows: First, national aspirations may be measured by six proxy variables, namely, degree of urbanization, literacy rate, number of newspapers, number of radios, degree of labor unionization, and the national endowment of national resources. Second, the welfare of people may be measured by six proxy variables, namely, infant survival rate, caloric consumption, number of doctors per population size, number of hospital beds per population size, percentage of housing with piped water supply, and per capita gross national product. Third, national expectations may be measured by the percentage change in per capita gross national product and the percentage of gross national product being invested. These are surrogate measures of the underlying factors in Knudsen's model. The model's reliability may be improved by a search for more relevant measures by subjecting a bigger selection of these surrogate measures to factor analysis. Such an analysis used in a conformatory way may reduce their number to only the salient measures. Needless to say, more research, especially in the management accounting field, may be needed to improve and test Knudsen's model or similar "components-based" models of predicting political risk.

THE HAENDEL-WEST-MEADOW "POLITICAL SYSTEM STABILITY INDEX"

Another components approach to the forecasting of political risk was provided by Haendel, West, and Meadow in an empirical, indicator-based measure of political system stability—a Political System Stability Index (PSSI)—in 65 developing countries.[30] The PSSI is depicted graphically as Exhibit 8.3. It is composed of three equally weighted indexes: the Socioeconomic Index, the Governmental Process Index, and the Societal Conflict Index which is itself derived from three sub-subindexes on public unrest, internal violence, and coercion potential. All these indexes are derived from 15 indirect measures of the political system's stability and adaptability. Basically, the higher the PSSI score the greater the stability of the political system. The index was based on data from the 1961-1966 period. There is a need to test the validity of the index with more recent data before using the index as a forecasting tool. In any case the model demonstrates again the feasibility of a components approach to the study of political risk. As stated by Haendel: "The Political System Stability Index (PSSI) derives its importance from the role the political system plays in establishing power relationship and norms for resolving conflicts in society. It assumes that the degree of political stability in a country may indicate the society's capacity to cope with new demands."[31]

COPING WITH POLITICAL RISK

Forecasting political risk is not enough; the problem is how to cope and live with it or to minimize it. Various techniques have been proposed for minimizing political risk. Eiteman and Stonehill suggest the following three categories of techniques for dealing with political risk:

1. Negotiating the environment prior to investment by including concession agreements, adaptation to host-country goals, planned investment, and investment guarantees.

EXHIBIT 8.3 FORMATION OF POLITICAL SYSTEM STABILITY INDEX (PSSI)

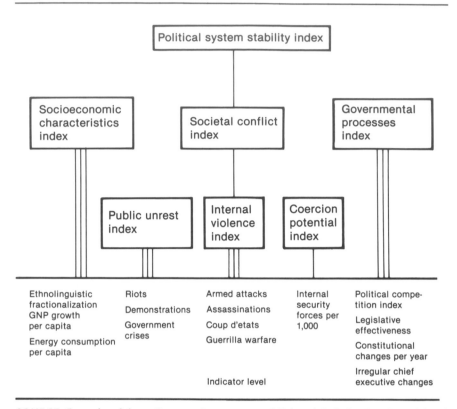

SOURCE: Reproduced from *Overseas Investment and Political Risk*, by Dan Haendel and Gerald T. West, with Robert G. Meadow, FPRI Monograph Series Number 21, 1975, p. 64, with permission of the Foreign Policy Research Institute, Philadelphia.

Exhibit 8.3 Continued

Component Indicators Of The Haendel-West-Meadow
Political System Stability Index

I. Socioeconomic Characteristics Index

    A. Ethnolinguistic Fractionalization: The Atlas Narodov Mira index, based on a country's ethnic and linguistic heterogeneity, is used. (Source: Charles Taylor and Michael Hudson, World Handbook of Political and Social Indicators, second edition. New Haven: Yale University Press 1972.

    B. Percentage growth in per capita gross national product. This measure indicates a developing nation's ability to satisfy the economic demands of its citizenry as well as the ability of the political system to provide a political climate favorable to economic expansion. (Source: Taylor and Hudson)

Exhibit 8.3 Continued

C. Percentage growth in per capita energy consumption. This measure indicates a developing nation's ability to satisfy the economic demands of its citizenry and serves as a predictor of the future since growth often leads to additional growth. (Source: Taylor and Hudson)

II. Societal Conflict Index

A. Public Unrest Index. These three indicators reflect public dissatisfaction and thus provide an estimate of the pressure for change in the political system. This index was given half of the weight of the following two indexes.

1. Number of demonstrations. A demonstration is a peaceful gathering of at least 100 people for the primary purpose of displaying opposition to government policies or authority. Source: Arthur Banks, Cross-Polity Time-Series Data, Cambridge, Massachusetts: MIT Press, 1971.

2. Number of riots. A riot is a demonstration involving the use of force and resulting in material damage or bloodshed. (Source: Taylor and Hudson)

3. Number of government crises. A government crisis is a rapidly developing situation that threatens to bring about the immediate downfall of the government. (Source: Banks)

B. Internal Violence Index. The four indicators for this index reflect opposition to the means by which conflicting values are resolved within a society, rather than just opposition to some particular policy. Typically the product of deep-seated grievances, they are useful indicators of future internal violence.

1. Number of armed attacks. An armed attack is an act of violent political conflict carried out by an organized group to destroy the power exercised by another organized group. (Source: Taylor and Hudson)

2. Number of assassinations. An assassination is the politically motivated murder of a high government official or politician. (Source: Banks)

3. Number of coup d'etats. A coup d'etat is an attempt by officers of the armed forces or police or by members of the ruling elite to overthrow the central government by force or threat of force. (Source: Banks)

4. Number of guerrilla warfare incidents. Such an incident is activity by bands of citizens or irregular forces aimed at overthrow of the existing government. (Source: Banks)

C. Coercion Potential Index. This index measures the capability of the political system to punish certain forms of behavior and to reinforce others. It also indicates the government's perception of the magnitude of the internal threat it faces.

1. Number of internal security forces per thousand persons of the working-age population. The size of this force reflects calculations of the number needed to maintain order. (Source: not indicated)

Exhibit 8.3 Continued

III. Governmental Processes Index

A. Political Competition Index. The index is derived from variables
    that measure the competitiveness of the nominating process, the
    presence of legislative coalitions, legislative effectiveness, and
    the degree of party legitimacy. (Source and explanation of scoring:
    Banks, p. xxii)

B. Legislative Effectiveness. Effectiveness was coded as follows:
    (Source: Banks)

    1. No legislature: 0 points
    2. "Rubber stamp" legislature: 1 point
    3. Executive power outweighs legislative: 2 points
    4. Legislature has significant autonomy: 3 points

C. Number of Constitutional Changes per Year. Frequent changes
    indicate lack of fundamental agreement on the political "rules of
    the game." (Source: Banks)

D. Number of Irregular Executive Changes. A change refers to the
    national executive's office outside of the conventional legal or
    customary procedure. (Source: Taylor and Hudson)

Source: Except for these items credited to Taylor and Hudson and to Banks,
the source for this exhibit is Dan Haendel and Gerald T. West, with Robert G.
Meadow, Overseas Investment and Political Risk, Philadelphia: Foreign Policy
Research Institute, Monograph Series Number 21. 1975. (Published in
association with Lexington Books, D. C. Heath.)
Reprinted with Permission.

2. Implementing specific operating strategies after the investment decision in production, logistics, marketing, finance, organization, and personnel. For example,
   local zoning, a safe location of facilities, and control of transportation and of
   patents and processes are examples of operating strategies in production and
   logistics which may reduce the likelihood of political interference or
   expropriation.

3. Resorting to specific compensation strategies after expropriation, which include
   rational negotiation, application of power tactics to bargaining, legal remedies,
   use of the International Centre for Settlement of Investment Disputes, and
   management, surrenders in the interest of seeking salvage.[32]

Haendel classifies, appropriately, the traditional tools of risk management
into five general categories:

1 . Avoidance, where the risk manager may recommend not investing or
    diversifying, or else imposing a ceiling on the exposure a firm allows a country.

2. Transfer, where the risk manager may recommend including local individuals as
   either investors or managers.

3. Diversification and loss prevention, where the risk manager may recommend diversifying in order to reduce the reliance on a production facility or natural resource supply in one given country.

4. Insurance, where the risk manager may recommend that the firm secure insurance against political risk as a way of shielding the firm's assets from unexpected losses. This may even include self-insurance in the form of a separate fund.

5. Retention, where the risk manager may recommend that not all political risks can be avoided, transferred, diversified, or insured against. In such a case the firm should include political risk analysis in its decision-making process.[33]

The question remains to know what the multinationals actually do to cope with political risk. A study prepared for the Financial Executives Research Foundation surveyed multinationals and found a number of techniques which could be used both prior to the investment and when operating overseas.[34] The techniques found to be most useful by the participant firm in their preinvestment negotiations with local governments were using local nationals, securing prior agreements on the remittance of funds or other fees and on control of the company, and looking into joint ventures with local businesses. The techniques found to be most useful by the participant firms once the investment has been made and the firms committed were maximizing the use of local debt and local funding, adapting to changing governmental priorities, sourcing locally to stimulate the economy and to reduce dependence on imports, and increasing exports. Besides those techniques the respondent firms admitted to insuring against the losses which may be caused by expropriation/confiscation, nationalization, foreign exchange inconvertibility, war, revolution or insurrection damages, kidnapping and ransom, long-term currency losses, and even inflation. The insurances were provided by the Overseas Private Investment Corporation (OPIC), a credit insurance program administered by the Export/Import Bank of the U.S. (Eximbank) jointly with the Foreign Credit Insurance Association (FCIA), and private political risk insurance organizations like the American International Group (AIG) and Lloyds of London.

Conclusions

Two of the most important risks facing multinational firms are foreign exchange and political risks. This chapter first makes a case for the management of foreign and political risk and second examines some of the issues and solutions proposed in practice and in the relevant literature.

Notes

1. Gunter Dufey and S. L. Srinivasulu, "The Case for Corporate Management of Foreign Exchange Risk," *Financial Management* (Winter 1983), p. 51.

2. The theory of purchasing power parity was introduced by the economist

Gustave Cassel to explain the exchange-rate parities under a floating-rate system.

3. Lawrence H. Officer, "The Purchasing-Power-Parity Theory of Exchange Rates: A Review Article," *IMF Staff Papers* (March 1976), pp. 1-60.

4. This algebraic expression is only an approximation. The actual expression should be $\dfrac{E(S-S)}{S} \times \dfrac{12}{n} \times 100 = \dfrac{i-i'}{i-i'}$.

5. Ian H. Giddy, "Exchange Risk: Whose View?" *Financial Management* 6, (Summer 1977), p. 24.

6. A foreign exchange market in which rates of exchange always fully reflect all available information is said to be efficient.

7. William Poole, "Speculative Prices As Random Walks: An Analysis of Ten Time Series of Flexible Exchange Rates," *Southern Economic Journal* (April 1967), pp. 468-78.

8. Michael P. Dooley, and Jeffrey R. Shafer, "Analysis of Short Run Exchange Rate Behavior: March 1973 to September 1975," *International Finance Discussion Papers* (New York: Federal Reserve System, 1975).

9. Richard J. Rogalski, and Joseph D. Vinso, "Price Level Variations As Predictors of Flexible Exchange Rates," *Journal of International Business Studies* (Spring/Summer 1977), pp. 71-82.

10. Ian H. Giddy, and Gunter Dufey, "The Random Behavior of Flexible Exchange Rate: Implications for Forecasting," *Journal of International Business Studies* (Spring 1975), pp. 1-32.

11. Dennis E. Logue and Richard James Sweeny, "White Noise in Imperfect Markets: The Case of the Franc-Dollar Exchange Rate," *The Journal of Finance* (June 1977), pp. 761-68.

12. Steven W. Kohlhagen, "The Performance of the Foreign Exchange Markets: 1971-1974," *Journal of International Business Studies* (Fall 1975), pp. 33-39.

13. David K. Eiteman and Arthur I. Stonehill, *Multinational Business Finance* (Reading, Mass.: Addison-Wesley, 1979), p. 67.

14. Laurent L. Jacque, *Management of Foreign Exchange Risk* (Lexington, Mass.: Lexington Books, D. C. Heath Company, 1978), p. 99.

15. Gilles Puchon, "Defining and Measuring Currency Exposure," in *International Finance Handbook*, ed. Abraham N. George and Ian H. Giddy (New York: John Wiley and Sons, 1983), Vol. 2, No. 7, p. 7.

16. The exporter, in effect, buys insurance to lock in a dollar-franc exchange rate in four months.

17. This may be an effort to prevent severe exposures, such as the one which caused the near collapse of Schroeder, Nuenchmeyer, Hengst and Company in 1983 when it overextended itself on loans to IBH Holding AG, which eventually was forced into bankruptcy proceedings.

18. Gold, in fact, presents much less political risk and yields a better return than the government-indexed bonds. Moreover, gold has a tax advantage over bonds because it can be carried as an unrealized gain until resale, while revenues derived from bonds are immediately taxable.

19. Franklin R. Root, "U.S. Business Abroad and the Political Risks," *MSU Business Topics* (Winter 1968).

20. Stephan H. Robock and Kenneth Simmonds, *International Business and Multinational Enterprises* (Homewood, Ill.: Richard D. Irwin, 1973), p. 356.

21. Fred Greene, "The Management of Political Risk," *Best's Review* (July 1974), p. 15.

22. Root, "U.S. Business Abroad," p. 73.

23. Charles M. Newman, II and I. James Czechowicz, *International Risk Management* (Morristown, N.J.: FERF, 1983), pp. 15-16.

24. Robock and Simmonds, *International Business and Multinational Enterprises*, p. 371.

25. Robert Stobaugh, Jr., "How to Analyze Foreign Investment Climates," *Harvard Business Review* (September-October 1969), pp. 101-2.

26. "A Primer on Country Risk," *Argus Capital Market Report* (June 4, 1975).

27. R. J. Rummel and David A. Heenan, "How Multinationals Analyze Political Risk," *Harvard Business Review* (January-February 1978), pp. 67-76.

28. Ibid., p. 70.

29. Harald Knudsen, "Explaining the National Propensity to Expropriate: An Ecological Approach," *Journal of International Business Studies* (Spring 1974), pp. 51-71.

30. Dan Haendel and Gerald T. West, with Robert G. Meadow, *Overseas Investment and Political Risk* Monograph Series No. 21 (Philadelphia: Foreign Policy Research Institute, 1957).

31. Dan Haendel, *Foreign Investments and the Management of Political Risk* (Boulder, Colo.: Westview Press, 1979), pp. 106-7.

32. Eiteman and Stonehill, *Multinational Business Finance*, pp. 203-23.

33. Haendel, *Foreign Investments*, pp. 139-46.

34. Newman, and Czechowicz, *International Risk Management*, p. 81.

Bibliography

FINANCIAL RISK MANAGEMENT

Abdel-Malek, Talaat. "Managing Exchange Risks under Floating Rates: The Canadian Experience," *Columbia Journal of World Business* 11 (Fall 1976), pp. 41-52.

Adler, Michael, and Bernard Dumas. "The Exposure of Long-Term Foreign Currency Bonds," *Journal of Financial and Quantitative Analysis* 15 (November 1980), pp. 973-94.

Ankrom, Robert K. "Top-Level Approach to the Foreign Exchange Problem," *Harvard Business Review* 52 (July-August 1974), pp. 79-90.

Barnett, John S. "Corporate Foreign Exposure Strategy Formulations," *Columbia Journal of World Business* 11 (Winter 1976), pp. 87-97.

Batt, W.F.J. "Reducing Your Currency Risk," *Accountancy* 85 (August 1974), pp. 60-62.

Bhushan, Bhuwan. "Effects of Inflation and Currency Fluctuation," *Management Accounting* 56 (July 1974), pp. 17-19.

Booth, G. Geoffrey, Fred R. Kaen, and Peter E. Koveos. "Currency Interdependence in Foreign Exchange Markets," *The Financial Review* 15 (Fall 1980), pp. 36-44.

Bowers, David A. "A Warning Note on Empirical Research Using Foreign Exchange Rates," *Journal of Financial and Quantitative Analysis* 12 (June 1977), pp. 315-19.

Bradford, Samuel R. "Foreign Exchange Exposure," *Accountancy* 86 (September 1975), pp. 74-78.

_____. "Managing Foreign Exchange," *Accountancy* 86 (March 1975), pp. 80-84.

Bradman, E. A. "Accounting for Foreign Exchange: Some Difficulties of Banks," *The Accountant* 174 (January 1, 1976), pp. 6-8.

Calderon-Rossell, Jorge R. "Covering Foreign Exchange Risks of Single Transactions: A Framework for Analysis," *Financial Management* 8 (Autumn 1979), pp. 78-85.

Callier, Philippe. "Speculation and the Forward Foreign Exchange Rate: A Note," *The Journal of Finance* 35 (March 1980), pp. 173-76.

Cornell, Bradford. "Inflation, Relative Price Changes, and Exchange Risk," *Financial Management* 9 (Autumn 1980), pp. 30-34.

Dufey, Gunter. "Corporate Finance and Exchange Rate Variations," *Financial Management* 1 (Summer 1972), pp. 51-58.

Dufey, Gunter, and Rolf Mirus. "Forecasting Foreign Exchange Rates: A Pedagogical Note," *Columbia Journal of World Business* 16 (Summer 1981), pp. 53-61.

Eaker, Mark R. "Covering Foreign Exchange Risks: Comment," *Financial Management* 9 (Winter 1980), pp. 64-65.

_____. "Denomination Decisions for Multinational Transactions," *Financial Management* 9 (Autumn 1980), pp. 23-29.

Eun, Choel S. "Global Purchasing Power View of Exchange Risk," *Journal of Financial and Quantitative Analysis* 16 (December 1981), pp. 639-50.

Evans, Thomas G. "Some Concerns about Exposure after the FASB's Statement No. 8," *Financial Executive* 44 (November 1976), pp. 28-31.

Everett, Robert M., Abraham M. George, and Aryeh Blumberg. "Appraising Currency Strengths and Weaknesses: An Operational Model for Calculating Parity Exchange Rates," *Journal of International Business Studies* 11 (Fall 1980), pp. 80-91.

Ferchat, Robert. "Managing Foreign Exchange Risk," *CA Magazine* 114 (January 1981), pp. 26-28.

Feskoe, Gaffney. "Reducing Currency Risks in a Volatile Foreign Exchange Market," *Management Accounting* 62 (September 1980), pp. 19-24.

Fletcher, John W. "Managing Foreign Exchange Risk," *The Australian Accountant* 50 (August 1980), pp. 450-55.

Folks, William R., Jr. "Decision Analysis For Exchange Risk Management," *Financial Management* 1 (Winter 1972), pp. 101-12.

_____. "The Optimal Level of Forward Exchange Transactions," *Journal of Financial and Quantitative Analysis* 8 (January 1973), pp. 105-10.

Folks, William R., Jr., and Stanley R. Stansell. "The Use of Discriminant Analysis in Forecasting," *Journal of International Business Studies* 6 (Spring 1975), pp. 33-50.

Fotheringham, K. B. "The Foreign Currency Hedge Market in Australia," *The Australian Accountant* 49 (December 1979), pp. 780-85.

Franck, Peter, and Allan Young. "Stock Price Reaction of Multinational Firms to Exchange Realignments," *Financial Management* 1 (Winter 1972), pp. 66-73.

Frey, Karen M. "Management of Foreign Exchange Risk with Forward Contracts," *Management Accounting* 58 (March 1977), pp. 45-48.

Friedman, Daniel. "Makin's MARP: A Comment," *The Journal of Finance* 36 (June 1981), pp. 739-42.

Giddy, Ian H. "Exchange Risk: Whose View?" *Financial Management* 6 (Summer 1977), pp. 23-33.

Goodman, Stephen H. "Foreign Exchange-Rate Forecasting Techniques: Implications for Business and Policy," *The Journal of Finance* 34 (May 1979), pp. 415-27.

Gull, Don S. "Composite Foreign Exchange Risk," *Columbia Journal of World Business* 10 (Fall 1975), pp. 51-69.

Gupta, Sanjeer. "A Note on the Efficiency of Black Markets in Foreign Currencies," *The Journal of Finance* 36 (June 1981), pp. 705-10.

Heckerman, Donald. "The Exchange Risks of Foreign Operations," *The Journal of Business* 45 (January 1972), pp. 41-48.

Hilley, John L., Carl R. Beidleman, and James A. Greenleaf. "Does Covered Interest Arbitrage Dominate in Foreign Exchange Markets?" *Columbia Journal of World Business* 14 (Winter 1979), pp. 99-107.

Hollis, Martha. "A Decentralized Foreign Exchange Risk Model," *Management International Review* 20, 3 (1980), pp. 53-60.

Hoyt, Newton H. "The Management of Currency Exchange Risk by the Singer Company," *Financial Management* 1 (Spring 1972), pp. 13-20.

Imai, Yutaka. "Exchange Rate Risk Protection in International Business," *Journal of Financial and Quantitative Analysis* 10 (September 1975), pp. 447-56.

Jacque, Laurent L. "Why Hedgers Are Not Speculators," *Columbia Journal of World Business* 14 (Winter 1979), pp. 108-16.

Kahnamouyipour, Heydar. "Foreign Exchange: Hedge, Speculation, or Swap?" *Accountancy* 91 (October 1980), pp. 52-55.

_____. "Foreign Exchange Exposure Analysis," *Accountancy* 90 (January 1979), pp. 81-84.

Kettell, Brian. "Foreign Exchange Exposure," *Accountancy* 89 (March 1978), pp. 83-89.

Kim, Seung H., and Paul J. Kuzdrall. "The Simulation of Financing Strategy under Fluctuating Exchange Rate Conditions," *The International Journal of Accounting Education and Research* 12 (Spring 1977), pp. 93-108.

Kohlhagen, Steven W. "A Model of Optimal Foreign Exchange Hedging without Exchange Rate Projections," *Journal of International Business Studies* 9 (Fall 1978), pp. 9-19.

_____. "Reducing Foreign Exchange Risks," *Columbia Journal of World Business* 13 (Spring 1978), pp. 33-38.

Lasusa, Peter R. "Accounting for Hedged Transactions," *The CPA Journal* 48 (June 1978), pp. 17-24.

Lieberman, Gail. "A Systems Approach to Foreign Exchange Risk Management," *Financial Executive* 46 (December 1978), pp. 14-19.

Logue, Dennis E., and George S. Oldfield. "Managing Foreign Assets When Foreign Exchange Markets Are Efficient," *Financial Management* 6 (Summer 1977), pp. 16-22.

Makin, John H. "Portfolio Theory and the Problem of Foreign Exchange Risk," *The Journal of Finance* 33 (May 1978), pp. 517-34.

_____. "Portfolio Theory and the Problem of Foreign Exchange Risk: Reply," *The Journal of Finance* 36 (June 1981), pp. 743-46.

McEnally, Richard W., and Michael L. Rice. "Hedging Possibilities in the Flotation of Debt Securities," *Financial Management* 8 (Winter 1979), pp. 12-18.

Mathur, Ike. "Attitudes of Financial Executives toward Foreign Exchange Issues," *Financial Executive* 48 (October 1980), pp. 22-26.

Murenbeeld, Martin. "Economic Factors for Forecasting Foreign Exchange Rate Changes," *Columbia Journal of World Business* 10 (Summer 1975), pp. 81-95.

Naidu, G. N., and Tai S. Shin. "Effectiveness of Currency Futures Market in Hedging Foreign Exchange Risk," *Management International Review* 21, 4 (1981), pp. 5-16.

Neukomm, Hans U. "Risk and Error Minimization in Foreign Exchange Trading," *Columbia Journal of World Business*, 10 (Winter 1975), pp. 77-85.

Oldfield, George S., and Richard J. Messina. "Forward Exchange Price Determination in Continuous Time," *Journal of Financial and Quantitative Analysis* 12 (September 1977), pp. 473-79.

Olstein, R. A., and T. L. O'glove. "Devaluation and Multinational Reporting," *Financial Analysts Journal* 29 (September/October 1973), pp. 65-69.

Parker, Mark R. "The Numeraire Problem and Foreign Exchange Risk," *The Journal of Finance* 36 (May 1981), pp. 419-26, 440-42.

Parkinson, J., and D. P. Walker. "Taxation and Foreign Exchange Management," *Managerial Finance* 4, 2 (1978), pp. 189-97.

Reiss, John. "Currency Risk: The Disappearing Profits Trick," *Accountancy* 91 (March 1980), pp. 105-6.

Robichek, Alexander A., and Mark R. Eaker. "Foreign Exchange Hedging and the Capital Asset Pricing Model," *The Journal of Finance* 33 (June 1978), pp. 1011-18.

Rodriguez, Rita M. "Corporate Exchange Risk Management: Theme and Aberration," *The Journal of Finance* 36 (May 1981), pp. 427-38, 442-44.

_____. "Management of Foreign Exchange Risk in the U.S. Multinationals," *Journal of Financial and Quantitative Analysis* 9 (November 1974), pp. 849-57.

_____. "Management of Foreign Exchange Risk in the U.S. Multinationals,' *Sloan Management Review* 19 (Spring 1978), pp. 31-50.

_____. "Measuring Multinationals' Exchange Risk," *Financial Analysts Journal* 35 (November/December 1978), pp. 49-56.

Rogalski, Richard J., and Joseph D. Vinso. "Empirical Properties of Foreign Exchange Rates," *Journal of International Business Studies* 9 (Fall 1978), pp. 69-79.

Rossitch, Eugene, and Jack M. Meckler. "Foreign Currency Exposure Control," *Management Accounting* 55 (July 1973), pp. 29-37.

Rueschhoff, Norlin G. "U.S. Dollar Based Financial Reporting of Canadian Multinational Corporations," *The International Journal of Accounting Education and Research* 8 (Spring 1973), pp. 103-9.

Schwab, Bernhard, and Peter Lusztig. "Apportioning Foreign Exchange Risk through the Use of Third Currencies: Some Questions on Efficiency," *Financial Management* 7 (Autumn 1978), pp. 25-30.

Serfass, William D., Jr. "You Can't Outguess the Foreign Exchange Market," *Harvard Business Review* 54 (March-April 1976), pp. 134-37.

Shapiro, Alan C. "Defining Exchange Risk," *The Journal of Business* 50 (January 1977), pp. 37-39.

————. "Exchange Rate Changes, Inflation, and the Value of the Multinational Corporation," *The Journal of Finance* 30 (May 1975), pp. 485-502.

Shapiro, Alan C., and David P. Rutenberg. "Managing Exchange Risks in a Floating World," *Financial Management* 5 (Summer 1976), pp. 48-58.

Sherwin, James T. "Foreign Exchange Exposure Management," *Financial Executive* 47 (May 1979), pp. 18-23.

Soenen, Luc. "Foreign Exchange Exposure Management," *Management International Review* 19, 2 (1979), pp. 31-38.

Srinivasulu, S. L. "Strategic Response to Foreign Exchange Risks," *Columbia Journal of World Business* 16 (Spring 1981), pp. 13-23.

Stanley, Marjorie, and Stanley Block. "Portfolio Diversification of Foreign Exchange Risk: An Empirical Study," *Management International Review* 20, 1 (1980), pp. 83-92.

Stokes, Houston H., and Hugh Neuburger. "Interest Arbitrage, Forward Speculation and the Determination of the Forward Exchange Rate," *Columbia Journal of World Business* 14 (Winter 1979), pp. 86-98.

Stockton, K. J. "Currency Hedging and Related Problems," *The Australian Accountant* 49 (January-February 1979), pp. 33-35.

Teck, Alan. "Control Your Exposure to Foreign Exchange," *Harvard Business Review* 52 (January-February 1974), pp. 66-75.

Upson, Roger B. "Random Walk and Forward Exchange Rates: A Spectral Analysis," *Journal of Financial and Quantitative Analysis* 7 (September 1972), pp. 1897-1905.

Walton, Horace C. "Foreign Currency—To Hedge or Not to Hedge," *Financial Executive* 42 (April 1974), pp. 48-55.

Wentz, Rolf-Christian. "Towards a General Foreign Exchange Risk Consciousness," *Columbia Journal of World Business* 14 (Winter 1979), pp. 127-35.

Wihlborg, Clas. "Economics of Exposure Management of Foreign Subsidiaries of MNC," *Journal of International Business Studies* 11 (Winter 1980), pp. 9-18.

POLITICAL RISK MANAGEMENT

Bradley, David G. "Managing against Expropriation," *Harvard Business Review* 55 (July-August 1977), pp. 75-83.

Brewer, Thomas L. "Political Risk Assessment for Foreign Direct Investment Decisions: Better Methods for Better Results," *Columbia Journal of World Business* 16 (Spring 1981), pp. 5-12.

Choi, Frederick D. S. "Political Risk—An Accounting Challenge," *Management Accounting* 60 (June 1979), pp. 17-20.

Jones, Randall J. "A Model for Predicting Expropriation in Latin America Applied to Jamaica," *Columbia Journal of World Business* 15 (Spring 1980), pp. 74-80.

Kobrin, Stephen J. "When Does Political Instability Result in Increased Investment Risk?" *Columbia Journal of World Business* 13 (Fall 1978), pp. 113-22.

McCosker, Joseph S. "Accounting Valuations in Nationalization Settlements," *Journal of International Business Studies* 4 (Fall 1973), pp. 15-29.

Micallef, Joseph. "Political Risk Assessment," *Columbia Journal of World Business* 16 (Summer 1981), pp. 47-52.

Rummel, R. J., and David A. Heenan. "How Multinationals Analyze Political Risk," *Harvard Business Review* 56 (January-February 1978), pp. 67-76.

Shapiro, Alan C. "Managing Political Risk: A Policy Approach," *Columbia Journal of World Business* 16 (Fall 1981), pp. 63-70.

Van Agtmael, Antoine W. "How Business Has Dealt with Political Risk," *Financial Executive* 44 (January 1976), pp. 26-31.

9.

CAPITAL BUDGETING FOR THE MULTINATIONAL CORPORATION

Capital budgeting involves a current outlay or series of outlays of cash resources in return for anticipated benefits to be received beyond one year in the future. The capital budgeting decision has three distinguishing characteristics: anticipated cash benefits, a time lag between the initial capital investment and the realization of the benefits, and a degree of risk associated with the realization of the benefits. Ideally, a firm with a profit-maximization motive will seek an investment that will generate large benefits in a short period and with a minimum of risk. However, investments with potentially large benefits generally are possible only with high risk and may require more time than investments with lower benefits.

Given these less-than-ideal relationships between the dimensions of a capital budgeting decision, managements would desire a trade-off between these elements in making a capital budgeting decision that will meet their objectives. Although firms may choose various objective functions, the most useful for evaluating capital budgeting decisions is the stockholders' wealth maximization model (SWMM).[1] Despite the fact that it represents a normative model, the SWMM provides a generally acceptable and meaningful criterion for the evaluation of capital budgeting proposals: maximization of owners' wealth. There are many similarities between capital budgeting for the multinational corporation and capital budgeting for domestic companies. There are, however, specific problems which may complicate capital budgeting for the multinational corporation. This section examines the similarities of and the problems encountered by multinational corporations in analyzing the financial benefits and costs of a potential investment.

Administering Capital Budgeting

Although the administrative process of capital budgeting differs from one firm to another, it involves five basic steps. First is the planning, or origination and specification, of capital investments. Because capital investments are considered essential to a firm's profitable long-run growth, managers constantly search for new methods, processes, plants, and products.[2] Second is the evaluation of the proposed capital investments. Firms differ in their routines for processing capital budgets, but most evaluate and approve the projects at various managerial levels. For example, a request for capital investment made by the production department may be examined, evaluated,and approved by the plant managers, the vice-president for operations, and a capital budget committee or department which may submit recommendations to the president. The president, after adding recommendations, may submit the project to the board of directors. The routine is often complemented and simplified by a uniform policy and procedures manual presenting in detail the firm's capital budgeting philosophy and techniques.

The third step in capital budgeting is decision making based on the results of the evaluation process. Some decisions are made at a high level, such as the board of directors (if they are large projects), or at a lower level if they are small or medium-sized projects. The fourth step is control. The firm includes each of the accepted projects in the capital budget and appropriates funds. Control is periodically exercised over the expenditures made for the project. If the appropriated funds are insufficient, a budgetary review can be initiated to examine and approve the estimated overrun. The control step can be extended to include a continuous evaluation process to incorporate current information and check the validity of the original predictions. Last is the postaudit. This involves a comparison of the actual cash flows of a capital investment with those planned and included in the capital budget.

Determining the Project Cash Flows

There are material differences between the project cash flows and the cash flows back to the parent firm because of various constraints such as tax regulations and exchange controls to name only a few. One opinion on project cash flows states that "to the extent that the corporation views itself as a true multinational, the effects of restrictions on repatriation may not be severe."[3] If this position is adopted, then all the elements of return on overseas investment must be considered project cash flows. P. O. Gaddis provided the following list of elements of projected return from an overseas industrial investment:

1. All income, operating and nonoperating, from the overseas operating unit, based on its demonstrated capacity to supply existing markets with its present management and excluding any impact of the merger of resources with those of the investing company

2. Additional operating income of the overseas unit resulting from the merger of its own capabilities with those of the investing corporation

3. Additional income from increased export sales resulting from the proposed investment action, including (a) additional export income at each U.S. operating unit which manufactures products related to those which will be produced overseas, and (b) additional earnings from new export activity at the overseas operating unit resulting from its increased capabilities to sell beyond the boundaries of its traditional national markets

4. Additional income from increased licensing opportunities shown both in the books of the affected U.S. units and the books of the overseas unit

5. Additional income from importing technology, product design, or hardware from the overseas operating unit to U.S. operating units

6. Income presently accruing from the investment but seriously and genuinely threatened by economic, political, or social change in an overseas region.[4]

A second position, derived from economic theory, is that the value of a project is determined by the net present value of future cash flows back to the investor. Therefore, the project cash flows should include only those cash flows which are or can be repatriated, "since only accessible funds can be used to pay dividends and interest, amortize the firm's debt, and be reinvested."[5] In spite of the strong theoretical argument in favor of analyzing foreign projects from the viewpoint of the parent, empirical evidence from surveys of multinationals shows that firms are using project flows and rates of return as well as parent flows and rates of return.[6] In fact, a more recent survey shows that multinationals were almost evenly split among those that looked at cash flow solely from the parent's perspective, solely from the subsidiaries' perspective, and from both perspectives.[7] Those who viewed cash flow from the point of view of the subsidiary felt that the subsidiaries were separate businesses and should be viewed as such. Those who took the parent's view argued that the investment was ultimately made from the parent company's stockholders. Finally, those who adopted both perspectives considered it the safest approach because it provides two ways of making a final decision. One of the respondent treasurers put it as follows:

The project must first be evaluated on its chances of success locally. It must be profitable from the subsidiary's point of view. Then you step back and look at it from the parent's point of view. What cash flows are available to be remitted or otherwise used in another country? What's going to come back to the parent is the real issue. The project has to meet both tests to be acceptable.[8]

Capital Budgeting Techniques

The project-evaluation phase consists of evaluating the attractiveness of the investment proposals. Managers first choose the project-evaluation methods best suited to the capital budgeting decision. The most common are the discounted cash flow (DCF) methods, internal rate of return (IRR) method, net present value (NPV) method, profitability index (PI), the payback method, and the accounting rate of return (ARR) method.

DISCOUNTED CASH FLOW METHODS

The DCF methods consider the time value of money in the evaluation of capital budgeting proposals. A dollar received now is worth more than a dollar received in the future; a dollar in the hand today can be invested to earn a return. Hence, to understand the DCF methods, it is necessary to grasp the time value concepts.

The DCF methods focus on cash flows generated over the life of a project rather than on the accounting income. These methods involve discounting the cash flow of a project to its present value using an appropriate discount rate. There are two basic discounted cash flow methods: the internal rate of return (or time-adjusted rate of return) method and the net present value method.

INTERNAL RATE OF RETURN METHOD

The IRR is the interest rate which equates the present value of an investment's cash flows and the cost of the investment. The IRR equation is

$$\sum_{t=0}^{n} \frac{C_t}{(1 + r)^t} = 0$$

where

C_t = Cash flow for period t, whether it be a net inflow or a net outflow, including the initial investment at $t = 0$

n = Investment life, that is, the last period in which a cash flow is expected

r = IRR as the discount rate which equates the present value of cash flow (C_t) with zero.

If the initial cash outlay or cost occurs at a time 0, the IRR equation becomes

$$\sum_{t=1}^{n} \frac{C_t}{(1 + r)^t} - C_0 = 0$$

Solving for r is on a trial-and-error basis; the procedures differ depending on whether the cash flows are uniform or nonuniform.

Uniform Cash Flows

To illustrate, assume a project considered by the Camelli Corporation requires a cash outlay of $39,100 and has an expected after-tax annual net cash savings of $10,000 for six years and no salvage value. Find the interest rate (r) that equates the present value of future annual cash flows of $10,000 and the initial outlay of $39,100 at time 0. Experimenting with two discount rates, 12 and 14 percent, you find:

DISCOUNT RATE	DISCOUNT FACTOR	CASH FLOW	PRESENT VALUE OF STREAM
12%	4.1110	$10,000	$41,110
14%	3.8890	$10,000	$38,890

Thus, the IRR that equates the present value of the stream of annual savings and $39,100 is between 12 and 14 percent. This rate can be found by interpolating between 12 and 14 percent:

12%	$41,110 (too large)
14	38,890 (too small)
2%	$ 2,220

$$\frac{\$41,110 - \$39,100}{\$2,220} = 0.905$$

IRR $= 12\% + (0.905 + 2\%) = 13.81\%$.

A trial-and-error process determines that 13.81 percent is the IRR which equates the present value of the stream of savings and the cost of the investment. This indicates that the investment will yield a return of 13.81 percent per year in addition to recovering the original cost of $39,100. Exhibit 9.1 depicts the amortization schedule of the investment: The six-year cash savings of $10,000 recovers the original investment plus an annual return of 13.81 percent on the investment.

The computation of the IRR does not determine if the project is to be accepted or rejected. To do so, the IRR generally is compared with a required rate of return. For example, if the IRR exceeds the required rate of return, the project is acceptable. The required rate of return, also known as a cutoff rate or hurdle rate, is the firm's cost of capital (the cost of acquiring funds). Passing the test does not mean the project will be funded, as funds may be rationed.

EXHIBIT 9.1 AMORTIZATION SCHEDULE: PROOF FOR THE INTERNAL
RATE OF RETURN

YEAR	UNRECORDED INVESTMENT AT BEGINNING OF YEAR	ANNUAL CASH SAVINGS	13.81% RETURN OR INTEREST[a]	COST RECOVERY[b]	UNRECORDED INVESTMENT AT END OF YEAR[c]
1	$39,100.00	$10,000	$5,399.71	$4,600.29	$34,499.71
2	34,499.71	10,000	4,764,41	5,235.59	29,264.12
3	29,264.12	10,000	4,041.38	5,958.62	23,305.50
4	23,305.50	10,000	3,218.49	6,781.51	16,523.99
5	16,523.99	10,000	2,281.96	7,718.04	8,805.95
6	8,805.95	10,000	1,216.10	8,783.90	22.05[d]

[a]Return = Unrecorded investment × 13.81%.
[b]Cost recovery = Annual cash savings — Return.
[c]Unrecorded investment at the end of the year = Unrecorded investment at the beginning of the year — Cost recovery.
[d]Rounding error.

Nonuniform Cash Flows

The following example illustrates a project yielding cash flows which are not equal for all the periods of the project's life. We assume the machine considered by the Camelli Corporation costs $39,100 and yields the following cash savings:

YEAR	CASH SAVINGS
1	$20,000
2	14,000
3	10,000
4	6,000
5	5,000
6	4,000

Solving for the IRR which equates the present value of these savings and the cost of the investment also requires trial and error. First, experimenting with an interest rate of 16 percent, we find:

YEAR	DISCOUNT FACTOR	× CASH SAVINGS	= PRESENT VALUE OF CASH SAVINGS
1	0.862	$20,000	$17,240
2	0.743	14,000	10,240
3	0.641	10,000	6,410
4	0.552	6,000	3,312
5	0.476	5,000	2,380
6	0.410	4,000	1,640
Present value of cash savings			$41,384
Present value of cash outflow (cost of the machine)			39,100
Difference			$ 2,284

Given that the present value of cash savings is $2,284 higher than the present value of the cash outflow, the IRR must be higher than 16 percent. Second, experimenting with an interest rate of 20 percent, we find:

YEAR	DISCOUNT FACTOR	× CASH SAVINGS	= PRESENT VALUE OF CASH SAVINGS
1	0.833	$20,000	$16,660
2	0.694	14,000	9,716
3	0.579	10,000	5,790
4	0.482	6,000	2,892
5	0.402	5,000	2,010
6	0.335	4,000	1,340
Present value of cash savings			$38,408
Present value of cash outflow (cost of the machine)			39,100
Difference (NPV)			$ (692)

Given that the present value of cash savings is $692 lower than the present value of the cash outflow, the IRR must be between 16 and 20 percent, but closer to 20 percent. Third, experimenting with 19 percent we obtain:

YEAR	DISCOUNT FACTOR	× CASH SAVINGS	= PRESENT VALUE OF CASH SAVINGS
1	0.840	$20,000	$16,800
2	0.706	14,000	9,884
3	0.593	10,000	5,930
4	0.499	6,000	2,994
5	0.419	5,000	2,095
6	0.352	4,000	1,480
Present value of cash savings			$39,111
Present value of cash outflow (cost of the machine)			39,100
Difference			$ 11

Given that the present value of cash savings is only $11 higher than the cost of the machine, the IRR is approximately 19 percent.

NET PRESENT VALUE METHOD

The NPV method compares the cost of an investment with the present value of the future cash flows of the investment at a selected rate of return, or hurdle rate. The NPV of an investment is:

$$\text{NPV} = \sum_{t=0}^{n} \frac{C_t}{(1 + r)^t} = C_0$$

where
$$C_t = \text{Project cash flows}$$
$$r = \text{Selected hurdle rate}$$
$$n = \text{Project life}$$
$$C_0 = \text{Cost of the investment.}$$

If the NPV is greater than or equal to zero, the project is deemed acceptable, but it may not be funded if there is rationing. The required rate of return, or hurdle rate, is usually the cost of capital. The NPV procedure differs depending upon whether the cash flows are uniform or nonuniform.

Uniform Cash Flows

To illustrate the NPV method, let us return to the Camelli Corporation example in which a new machine costing $39,100 would yield an annual cash savings of $10,000 for the six years of its life. Assuming a cost of capital of 10 percent, the NPV of the project can be stated as follows:

$$\text{NPV} = \sum_{t=1}^{6} \frac{\$10,000}{(1 + 0.10)^6} - \$39,100.$$

The appropriate discount factor for the Camelli Corporation is 4.355. Thus, the NPV is computed: NPV = ($10,000 × 4.355) − $39,100 = $4.450. Given that the NPV is greater than zero, the Camelli Corporation should accept the new machine proposal. The positive NPV indicates that the Camelli Corporation will earn a higher rate of return on its investment than its cost of capital.

Different NPVs result from different hurdle rates. For example:

NPV at an 8% required rate = ($10,000 × 4.623) − $39,100 = $7,130
NPV at a 14% required rate = ($10,000 × 3.889) − $39,100 = $(210).

Thus, given a stream of uniform cash flows, the higher the hurdle rate, the less attractive any investment proposal becomes.

The NPV method rests on two assumptions: (1) The cash flows are *certain* (this applies also to the IRR), and (2) the original investment can be viewed as either borrowed or loaned by the Camelli Corporation at the hurdle rate.

Thus, if the Camelli Corporation borrows $39,100 from the bank at 10 percent and uses the cash flows generated to repay the loan, it will obtain the same return as if it had invested $4,450 at the same rate.

Nonuniform Cash Flows

The following example illustrates a project yielding cash flows which are not equal for all periods of the project's life. Assume again that the machine considered by the Camelli Corporation yields annual cash savings of $20,000, $14,000, $10,000, $6,000, $5,000, and $4,000 for the six years, respectively, and the cost of capital is 10 percent. The computation of the NPV follows:

YEAR	DISCOUNT FACTOR ×	CASH SAVINGS =	PRESENT VALUE OF CASH SAVINGS
1	0.909	$20,000	$18,180
2	0.826	14,000	11,564
3	0.753	10,000	7,530
4	0.683	6,000	4,098
5	0.621	5,000	3,105
6	0.564	4,000	2,256
Present value of cash savings			$46,733
Present value of cash outflow (cost of the machine)			39,100
Difference (NPV)			$7,633

The NPV method is easier to apply than the IRR method with nonuniform cash flows because it does not require iterative numerical methods.

PROFITABILITY INDEX

The PI, or benefit/cost ratio, is another form of the NPV method. It is generally expressed as:

$$PI = \frac{\text{Present value of cash inflows}}{\text{Present value of cash outflows}}.$$

For the Camelli Corporation example with uniform cash flows, the PI would be:

$$PI = \frac{\$43,550}{\$39,100} = 1.114.$$

For the Camelli Corporation example with nonuniform cash flows, the PI would be:

$$PI = \frac{\$46,733}{\$39,100} = 1.195.$$

The decision rule when evaluating different projects is to choose the project with the highest PI.

The NPV and the PI result in the same acceptance or rejection decision for any given project. However, the NPV and the PI can give different rankings for mutually exclusive projects. In such a case, the NPV method is the preferred method; it expresses the absolute profitability of a project whereas the PI expresses the relative profitability.

PAYBACK METHOD

The payback method, also called the payout method, is simply the number of years before the initial cash outlay of a project is fully recovered by its future cash inflows. For example, assume a firm is considering purchasing at $15,000 a delivery truck expected to save $5,000 per year in shipping expenses for four years. The payback formula is:

$$\text{Payback} = \frac{\text{Initial cost of the project}}{\text{Annual net cash flows}}$$

$$= \frac{\$15,000}{\$\ 5,000}$$

$$= 3 \text{ years.}$$

In other words, the cost of the delivery truck will be recovered in three years. If the payback period calculated is less than an acceptable maximum payback period, the firm should accept the truck proposal.

For projects with nonuniform cash flows the procedure is slightly different. For example, assume the yearly cash savings are $4,000 in year 1, $5,000 in year 2, $3,000 in year 3, $3,000 in year 4, and $6,000 in year 5. It takes up to year 4 to recover a cumulative cash savings equal to the initial cost of the truck. Therefore, the payback period is four years.

An extension of the payback method is the bailout method, which takes into account both the cash savings and the salvage value needed to recover the initial cost of a project. Going back to the first example of the $15,000 truck with an expected savings of $5,000 per year in shipping expenses, assume also that the salvage value is estimated to be $8,000 at the end of year 1 and $5,000 at the end of year 2. The cash savings and salvage value of the truck for the next two years, then, are as follows:

YEAR	CASH SAVINGS	SALVAGE VALUE	CUMULATIVE CASH SAVINGS AND SALVAGE VALUE
1	$5,000	$8,000	$13,000 = $5,000 + $8,000
2	$5,000	$5,000	$15,000 = $5,000 + $5,000 + $5,000

Thus, at the end of year 2, the total of the cumulative cash savings and the salvage value is equal to the initial cost of the truck. The bailout period is two years.

Businesses commonly use the payback method to provide a quick ranking of capital projects. Some of its features, including both advantages and disadvantages, follow.

1. It is easy to calculate and provide a quick answer to the question. How many years will it take before the initial cash outlay is completely recovered?

2. The payback method does not take into account the time value of money. The annual cash flows are given the same weight from one year to another. While the first feature can be interpreted as one of the strengths of the method, this feature is definitely a weakness.

3. The payback method ignores both the cash flows occurring after the payback period and the project's total physical life plan.

4. The payback period can be used to compute the payback reciprocal, which is equal to the IRR of the project, provided the project's expected cash flows are constant and are anticipated to continue indefinitely. Although projects rarely, if ever, have a perpetual life, a rule of thumb states that the payback reciprocal yields a reasonable approximation of the IRR. The formula for the payback reciprocal is:

$$\text{Payback reciprocal} = \frac{\text{Payback period}}{r}$$

ACCOUNTING RATE OF RETURN

The ARR method is a capital budgeting evalution technique which uses the ratio of the average annual profit after taxes to the investment of the project. The ARR formula based on initial investmentis:

$$\text{ARR} = \frac{\text{Annual revenue from the project} - \text{Annual expenses of the project}}{\text{Initial investment}}$$

The ARR formula based on average investment is:

$$\text{ARR} = \frac{\text{Annual revenue from the project} - \text{Annual expenses of the project}}{\text{Average investment}}$$

These computed ARR values are compared with a cutoff rate before an acceptance or rejection decision is made. For example, assume the Saxon Company is contemplating the purchase of a new machine costing $20,000 and having a five-year useful life and no salvage value. The new machine is expected to generate annual operating revenues of $7,000 and annual expenses of $5,000. The ARR can be computed as follows:

$$\text{ARR based on initial investment} = \frac{\$7,000 - \$5,000}{\$20,000} = 10\%$$

$$\text{ARR based on average investment} = \frac{\$7,000 - \$5,000}{\left(\dfrac{\$200,000 + 0}{2}\right)} = 20\%.$$

The ARR, then, depends on the choice of an initial or average investment base. Using an average investment base leads to substantially higher rates of return. This can be corrected, however, by choosing a higher required cutoff ARR.

The principal strength of the ARR may be its simplicity. It can be computed easily from the accounting records. Since this same characteristic can be perceived as a weakness, the ARR relies on accounting income rather than cash flows. It fails to take into account the timing of cash flows and the time value of money.

COST OF CAPITAL FOR THE MULTINATIONAL FIRM

In both the internal rate of return method and the net present value method a cost of capital, or "hurdle rate," is needed. Basically, the two rules of thumb are either:

1. The internal rate of return must be superior to the hurdle rate for a project to be acceptable.

2. The present value, obtained by discontinuing the cash flows at the bundle rate, must be positive for a project to be acceptable.

For a multinational corporation, the overall cost of capital is the sum of the costs of each financing source, weighted by the proportion of that financing source in the firm's total capital structure. The weighted average cost of capital is, therefore:

$$K = \frac{E}{V} k_e + \frac{D}{V} k_d (1 - t)$$

where

> K = Weighted average cost of capital
> K_d = Cost of debt
> K_e = Cost of equity
> t = Tax rate
> D = Value of the firm's debt
> E = Value of the firm's equity
> U = D+E = Total value of the firm.[9]

Problems Encountered by Multinationals

Besides the problem of choosing between parent and project flows and rates of return, multinationals' capital budgeting analyses are complicated by problems related to foreign tax regulations, political and economic risks, expropriation, blocked funds, and inflation. Each of these problems is examined next.

FOREIGN TAX REGULATIONS

Because only after-tax cash flows are relevant, the amount of foreign income taxes must be determined before conducting the capital budgeting analyses. The subject of international taxation is rather complex and is covered in Chapter 11. Not only cash flows are treated after tax, but also the project cost of capital must be adjusted to reflect the impact of taxes.[10]

POLITICAL AND ECONOMIC RISKS

As suggested in Chapter 8, multinational companies face the risks created by political, exchange, and economic changes. Chapter 8 covers some of the techniques used to manage political and economic risks. In a capital budgeting context various ways may be used to account for political risks. One is to adjust each year's cash flows by the cost of an exchange-risk adjustment.[11] Other ways include shortening the minimum payback period, raising the discount rate or required rate of return without adjusting cash flows, adjusting cash flows without adjusting the discount rate, and adjusting cash flows and raising the discount rate.[12] A consensus seems to exist, however, to suggest that multinationals should use either the risk-adjusted discount rate or the certainty-equivalent approach to adjust proper estimates for political risk.[13]

Risk-Adjusted Discount Rate Method

One of the techniques for incorporating risk in the evaluation process is the risk-adjusted discount rate, which involves manipulating the discount rate applied to the cash flows to reflect the amount of risk inherent in a project. The higher the risk associated with a project, the higher the discount rate applied to the cash flows. If a given project is perceived to be twice as risky as most projects acceptable to the firm and the cost of capital is 12 percent, then the correct risk-adjusted discount rate is 24 percent.

Certainty-Equivalent Method

Another technique for incorporating risk in the evaluation process is the certainty-equivalent method, which involves adjusting the future cash flows so a project can be evaluated on a riskless basis. The adjustment is formulated as follows:

$$NPV = \sum_{t=0}^{n} \frac{\alpha_t \, CF_t}{(1 + R_F)^t} - I_0$$

where

α_t = Risk coefficient applied to the cash flow of period t (CF_t)
I_0 = Initial cost of the project
R_F = Risk-free rate.

As this formula shows, the method multiplies the future cash flows by certainty equivalents to obtain a riskless cash flow. Note also that the discount rate used is R_F, which is a risk-free rate of interest.

To illustrate the certainty-equivalent method, assume an investment with the following characteristics:

I_0 = Initial cost   = \$30,000
CF_1 = Cash flow, year 1   = \$10,000
CF_2 = Cash flow, year 2   = \$20,000
CF_3 = Cash flow, year 3   = \$30,000
α_1 = Certainty equivalent, year 1 = 0.9
α_2 = Certainty equivalent, year 2 = 0.8
α_3 = Certainty equivalent, year 3 = 0.6.

The NPV of the investment using a risk-free discount rate of 6 percent is computed as follows:

PERIOD	CASH FLOW (CF$_t$)	RISK COEFFICIENT (α_t)	CERTAINTY EQUIVALENT	RISK-FREE RATE (R$_F$)	PRESENT VALUE
1	$10,000	0.9	$ 9,000	0.943	$ 8,487
2	20,000	0.8	16,000	0.890	14,240
3	30,000	0.6	18,000	0.840	15,120
Present Value of Cash Flows					$37,847
Initial Investment					30,000
Net Present Value					$ 7,847

Since the NPV is positive, the investment should be considered acceptable. The main advantage of the certainty equivalent method is that it allows the assignment of a different risk factor to each cash flow, given that risk can concentrate in one or more periods.

The certainty-equivalent method and the risk-adjusted discount rate method are comparable methods of evaluating risk. To produce similar ranking, the following equation must hold:

$$\frac{\alpha_t \, CF_t}{(1 + R_F)^t} = \frac{CF_t}{(1 + R_A)^t}$$

where

α_t — Risk coefficient used in the certainty-equivalent method
R_F = Risk-free discount rate
R_A — Discount rate used in the risk-adjusted discount rate method
CF_t = Future cash flow

Solving for α_t yields:

$$\alpha_t = \frac{(1 + R_F)^t}{(1 + R_A)^t}$$

Given that R_A and R_F are constant and $R_A > R_F$, then α_t decreases over time, which means that risk increases over time. To illustrate, assume that in the previous example $R_A = 15$ percent. Then

$$\alpha_1 = \frac{(1 + R_F)^1}{(1 + R_A)^1} = \frac{(1 + 0.06)^1}{(1 + 0.15)^1} = 0.921.$$

$$\alpha_2 = \frac{(1 + R_F)^2}{(1 + R_A)^2} = \frac{(1 + 0.06)^2}{(1 + 0.15)^2} = 0.848.$$

$$\alpha_3 = \frac{(1 + R_F)^3}{(1 + R_A)^3} = \frac{(1 + 0.06)^3}{(1 + 0.15)^3} = 0.783.$$

In many cases this assumption of increasing risk may not be realistic.

EXPROPRIATION

As presented in Chapter 8, multinational companies sometimes face the extreme result of political risk—expropriation. One way to account for expropriation is to charge a premium for political risk insurance to each year's cash flow whether such insurance is actually purchased or not. Another way, suggested by Shapiro, is to examine the impact of expropriation on the project's present value to the parent.[14] As a result, the old and new present values will equal:

$$\text{Old present value} = -C_0 + \sum_{t=1}^{n} \frac{X_t}{(1 + k)^t}$$

$$\text{New present value} = C_0 + \sum_{t=1}^{h-1} \frac{X_t}{(1 + k)^t} + \frac{G_h}{(1 + k)^h}$$

where

C_0 = Initial investment outlay
X_t = Parent's expected after-tax dollar cash flow from the project in year t
n = Life of the project
k = Project cost of capital
h = Year in which expropriation takes place
G_h = Expected value of the net compensation provided.

The compensation (G_h) is supposed to come from one of the following sources: direct compensation paid to the firm by the local government; indirect compensation such as other business contracts to the firm expropriated (an example would be the management contracts received by oil companies after the Venezuelan government nationalized their properties); payment received from political insurance; tax deductions received after the parent declares the expropriation as an extraordinary loss; and a reduction in the amount of capital that must be repaid by the project equal to the unamortized portion of any local borrowing.[15]

BLOCKED FUNDS

Multinationals sometimes face the situation where funds are blocked for various reasons including forms of exchange controls. Again, Shapiro suggests raising the present value expression to include the impact of locked funds on the project's cash flows.[16] As a result, the old and the new present values will equal:

$$\text{Old present value} = -C_0 + \sum_{t=1}^{n} \frac{X_t}{(1 + k)^t}$$

$$\text{New present value} = -C_0 + \sum_{t=1}^{j-1} \frac{X_t}{(1 + K)^t} + \sum_{t=j}^{n} \frac{Y_t}{(1 + k)^t} + (1 \quad \alpha_j) \sum_{t=j}^{n} \frac{X_t - Y_t}{(1 + k)^t}$$

$$+ \alpha_j \sum_{t=j}^{n} \frac{(X_t - Y_t)(1 + r)^{n-t}}{(1 + k)^n}$$

where the symbols C_0, X_t, n, and k are as in the formulas used for expropriation. The new symbols are:

j = Year in which funds become blocked
n = Year in which exchange controls are removed
α_j = probability of exchange controls in year j and 0 in other years
Y_t = Number of dollars which can be repatriated when exchange costs do exist.

INFLATION

With the high rates of inflation experienced by most countries, it is advisable to consider the rate of inflation explicitly in developing cash flows forecasts. The correct analysis can be done in either of two ways: using a money discount rate to discount money cash flows or using a real discount rate to discount real cash flows.

Conclusions

Capital budgeting for multinational operations relies on the same evaluation technique as for domestic operations. There are, however, specific problems encountered by multinationals. These problems are, mainly, foreign tax regulations, political and economic risks, expropriations, blocked funds, inflation, the determination of the project cash flows, and the determination of the cost of capital. These issues and their corresponding solutions have been examined in this chapter.

Notes

1. Ahmed Belkaoui, *Conceptual Foundations of Management Accounting* (Reading, Mass.: Addison-Wesley, 1980), pp. 58-60.

2. These projects usually come from various sources, including the following: new products or markets, and the expansion of existing products or markets; research and development; replacement of fixed assets; and other investments to reduce costs; improve the quality of the product; improve morale; or comply with government orders, labor agreements, insurance policy terms, and so forth.

3. Rita M. Rodriguez and E. Eugene Carter, *International Financial Management* (Englewood Cliffs, N.J.: Prentice Hall, 1979), p. 34.

4. Paul O. Gaddis, "Analyzing Overseas Investments," *Harvard Business Review* (May/June 1966), p. 119.

5. A. C. Shapiro, "Capital Budgeting and Long-Term Financing," *Financial Management* (Spring 1978), p. 8.

6. Vinod B. Bavishi, "Capital Budgeting Practices of Multinationals," *Management Accounting* (August 1981), pp. 32-35.

7. Charles M. Newman II and I. James Czechowicz, *International Risk Management* (Morristown, N.J.: FERF, 1983), p. 88.

8. Ibid., p. 89.

9. The weighted average cost of capital concept can be extended to include debt denominated in foreign currencies, debt issued by foreign subsidiaries, retained earnings of foreign subsidiaries, and so forth.

10. W. N. Ness, Jr., "U.S. Corporate Income Taxation and the Dividend Remittance Policy of Multinational Corporations," *Journal of International Business Studies* (Spring 1975), p. 67.

11. Arthur Stonehill and Leonard Nathanson, "Capital Budgeting Techniques and the Multinational Corporation," *California Management Review* (Summer 1968), p. 49.

12. Newman and Czechowicz, *International Risk Management*, p. 93.

13. In fact, both methods may be also used in accounting for the following risks: (1) the *dollar price risk*, associated with a decline in the number of dollars used to acquire a financial asset; (2) the *purchasing power risk*, associated with a decline in the purchasing power of the monetary unit; (3) the *interest rate risk*, associated with changes in the interest rate and which affects market values of many types of securities; (4) the *business risk*, associated with the operational cash flows of a firm; (5) the *financial risk*, associated with financial leverage; (6) the *systematic* or *market risk*, associated with the common stock of a particular industry, and (7) the *unsystematic risk*, associated with a particular company.

14. Alan C. Shapiro, "Capital Budgeting for the Multinational Corporation," *Financial Management* (Spring 1978), p. 10.

15. If the firm could predict the probability of expropriation, P_h, in year h, using any of the models presented in Chapter 8, then the present value would equal

$$-C_0 + \sum_{t=1}^{h-1} \frac{X_t}{(1+k)^t} + (1-P_h) \sum_{t=h}^{n} \frac{X_t}{(1+h)^t} + P_h \frac{G_h}{(1+k)^h}$$

where term $(1 - P_h) \sum_{t=h}^{n} \dfrac{X_t}{(1 + k)^t}$ reflects the fact that
there is no expropriation in period h.

16. Shapiro, Alan C., "Capital Budgeting for the Multinational Corporation".
p. 11.

Bibliography

Aharoni, Y. *The Foreign Investment Decision Process* (Boston: Harvard Graduate School of Business Administration, Division of Research, 1966).

Baker, J. C., and L. J. Beardsley. "Capital Budgeting by U.S. Multinational Companies," *The Financial Review* 2 (1972), pp. 115-21.

Baker, James C., and Lawrence J. Beardsley. "Multinational Companies Use of Risk Evaluation and Profit Measurement for Capital Budgeting Decisions," *Journal of Business Finance* (Spring 1973), pp. 38-43.

Bardsley, R. G. "Managing International Financial Transactions," *The International Journal of Accounting Education and Research* (Fall 1977), pp. 67 76.

Bavishi, Vinod B. "Capital Budgeting Practices at Multinationals," *Management Accounting* (August 1981), pp. 32-35.

Bennett, J. W. "Capital Expenditure Evaluation in a Multinational Business," *The Australian Accountant* 51 (November 1981), pp. 673-75.

Gaddis, Paul O. "Analyzing Overseas Investments," *Harvard Business Review* (May/June 1966), pp. 115-22.

Kim, Suk H., and T. Crick. "How Non-U.S. MNCs Practice Capital Budgeting," *Management Accounting* (January 1984), pp. 28-31.

Lessard, Donald R. "Evaluating International Projects: An Adjusted Present Value Approach." In *International Financial Management: Theory and Application*, ed. Donald R. Lessard (Boston: Warren, Gorham & Lamont, 1979), pp. 577-92.

Mehta, Dileep R. "Capital Budgeting Procedures for a Multinational." In *Management of Multinationals*, ed. P. Sethi and R. Holton (New York: Free Press, 1974), pp. 271-91.

Oblak, David J., and Roy J. Helm, Jr. "Survey and Analysis of Capital Bugeting Methods Used by Multinationals," *Financial Management* (Winter 1980), pp. 37-41.

Piper, James R. "How U.S. Firms Evaluate Foreign Investment Opportunities," *MSU Business Topics* (Summer 1971), pp. 11-20.

Polk, Judd, Irene W. Meister, and Lawrence A. Veit. *U.S. Production Abroad and the Balance of Payments* (New York: The Conference Board, 1966).

Rodriguez, Rita M., and E. Eugene Carter. *International Financial Management* (Englewood Cliffs, N.J.: Prentice Hall, 1979), chaps. 10 and 11.

Shapiro, Alan C. "Capital Budgeting for the Multinational Corporation," *Financial Management* (Spring 1978), pp. 7-16.

Shapiro, Alan C., and Arthur I. Stonehill. "Capital Budgeting with Segmented Capital Markets." Working paper, University of Pennsylvania, 1976.

Stobaugh, Robert B., Jr. "How to Analyze Foreign Investment Climates," *Harvard Business Review* (September/October 1969), pp. 100-108.

Stonehill, Arthur, and Leonard Nathanson. "Capital Budgeting and the Multinational Corporation," *California Management Review* (Summer 1968), pp. 39-54.

Weston, J. Fred, and Bart W. Sorge. *Guide to International Financial Management* (New York: McGraw-Hill, 1977), chap. 15.

Zenoff, David, and Jack Zwick. *International Financial Management* (Englewood Cliffs, N.J.: Prentice-Hall, 1969), chap. 5.

10.

INTERNATIONAL TAXATION ISSUES IN INTERNATIONAL ACCOUNTING

Everybody knows about death and taxes. That applies also to multinational corporations. International taxation is a complex array of changing rules which have become either a mystery or an annoyance to most national executives. In either case international taxation creates real problems to these executives. These problems:

stem from the fact that he [the international executive] must be a combination of an administrator, tax attorney, tax accountant, computer expert, and a human being. He must work within the framework of a society he had very little to do with creating. The complications and intricacies of the U.S. tax laws are monumental. In addition, he is faced with sophisticated tax treaties superimposed over U.S. law which frequently negate its clear implication. The pyramid of levels of tax law priorities is further compounded by the invariable differences in local tax laws which continually exert their influence in eroding the "bottom line" of international business. The dilemma is further enlarged by the fact that international U.S. law and foreign tax laws are in a continual flux of change.[1]

In view of these problems the international executive needs to understand some of the common themes underlying international taxation before engaging in any sensible tax planning. These themes include various tax philosophies, types of taxes, systems of tax administration, tax treaties, and tax havens. All these issues are examined in this chapter before an examination of the source of the relevant features of United States international taxation.

Taxation Philosophies

Taxation of business does vary from one country to another. Not only are tax rates different, but opinions differ as to definitions of taxable income and types of taxes to be used.[2] This situation is due mainly to international differences in taxation philosophies. These differences center mainly on the worldwide versus territorial assertions of taxation. According to the *territorial approach*, each country has the right to tax income earned inside its borders. Countries adopting such philosophy include Hong Kong, Panama, Switzerland, Argentina, Venezuela, and many Central American and Caribbean lands.

According to the *worldwide approach*, each country can claim the right to tax income arising outside its border, if that income is received by a corporation domiciled, incorporated, or with its center of control within the country.[3] Needless to say, the worldwide approach leads to double taxation. Fortunately, most countries adhering to the worldwide approach grant some form of relief from double taxation by taxing foreign subsidiary earnings only when they are sent home to the parent company. This is known as the *deferral principle*. The only exceptions are a U.S. law ("Subpart F") and "Foreign Personal Holding Company" income which are taxed even though not repatriated.

Central to the idea of granting some form of relief from double taxation is the notion of tax neutrality. Tax neutrality is considered an appropriate goal in forming transnational tax policy. It means that tax aspects should have no effect on investment decisions. Different views of tax neutrality exist and there is no agreement as to which is best. These views are *capital-export neutrality*, which is achieved when a firm pays the same total tax on foreign profits as on domestic profits; *capital-import neutrality*, which is achieved when all firms, domestic or foreign, operating in the same industry in a given country pay the same total corporate tax on earnings; and *national neutrality*, which assumes that the total country returns of capital are shared by that country's government in the forms of taxes and that local investors remain the same whether the capital is located at home or abroad.

Besides these different views of tax neutrality, countries differ in their attempts to achieve tax neutrality. In particular, they differ in their treatment of the tax-deferral privilege, foreign tax credits, provisions in tax treaties, and the treatment of intracompany transactions.[4]

Types of Taxes

Multinational companies face a variety of taxes besides corporate income taxes. These taxes include turnover, value-added, border, net-worth, and withholding taxes.

Corporate Income Taxes

The corporate income tax is the most widely used type of tax in the world. The United States relies heavily on this tax as a major source of government revenue. In fact, the ordinary business income of a corporation in the U.S. is subject to tax at the following rates:

TAXABLE INCOME	RATE (in percentages)
Up to $25,000	15 percent
$25,001 to $ 50,000	18 percent
$50,001 to $ 75,000	30 percent
$75,001 to $100,000	40 percent
Over $100,000	46 percent

The national rates in the other major industrial countries are 50 percent in France, 52 percent in the U.K., 56 percent in Germany, 40 percent in Japan, 46 percent in Canada, 40 percent in Sweden, 35 percent in Taiwan, 33 percent in Korea, 35 percent in the Philippines, 33 percent in Argentina, 15 percent in Chile, 33 percent in Spain, 17 percent in Hong Kong, and less than 10 percent in Switzerland. Some countries have also important local income taxes. This includes Germany with a rate of 10-18 percent, Japan with a rate of 12-13 percent, Sweden with a rate of 26-31 percent, and Switzerland with a rate of 5-40 percent. The rates are even greater in some of the developing countries which depend exclusively on corporate income taxes as sources of government revenues, and lower in some of the developing countries which are anxious to encourage direct investment, foreign or local.

TURNOVER TAXES

Turnover taxes are indirect taxes which may be assessed at one or more stages in the production processes, including sales. Therefore, they can be assessed when production is completed, when the products are wholesaled, when the products are retailed, or even at all of these stages. This tax obviously creates a premise for firms to integrate vertically in order to reduce payments, whether or not this integration is determinable from an economic or social point of view.

VALUE-ADDED TAX

One effective way of eliminating this premise for firms to integrate vertically in order to reduce payments under a turnover tax is to use instead a value-added tax. First introduced in France in the 1950s, the value-added tax (VAT) (or TVA-Taxe sur la Valeur Ajoutée) is also levied at each stage of the production process, but only on the value added at that specific stage. Each firm invoices the VAT separately and passes it on until it is eventually paid by the final consumer. Basically every producer and distributor gets a VAT rebate except the consumer. All the members of the European Economic Committee use VAT but at different rates. Other countries using VAT include Austria, Norway, Sweden, Argentina, Brazil, Chile, and Mexico. Typical rates include Ecuador at 4 percent, Mexico at 10 percent,

Korea at 13 percent, Brazil at 13-15 percent, Sweden at 17 percent, Norway at 6 percent, United Kingdom at 15 percent, West Germany at 11-13 percent, Denmark at 22 percent, France at 17.6 percent, and Peru at 22 percent. VAT has been praised since its adoption. It encourages export by allowing a rebate on exports and levy on import activity, in this case as a border tax. It avoids all the accounting adjustments required under a corporate income tax system, forcing the unprofitable firms to face the realities of the marketplace and reallocating scarce economic resources in a more optimal way. Finally, it may be used selectively to reach some industrial objectives better.

OTHER TAXES

Other taxes include border, net-worth, and withholding taxes. Border taxes are the most prevalent form of international taxes. They are used mainly to make domestic goods more competitive with imports. In most developing countries, they provide a great proportion of government revenues.

Net-worth taxes are assessed on the undistributed earnings of a firm as a way of encouraging firms to source finances for investment projects externally.

Withholding or remittance taxes are assessed on dividends, interest, and royalties. They range from a high of 30 percent in Australia to as low as 10 percent in Korea. Nationally these taxes could be modified by tax treaties between the countries concerned.

Systems of Tax Administration

In addition to differences in the types of taxes and taxation philosophies, countries differ in terms of systems of tax administration. There are basically three international systems of tax administration: the classical or separate corporate tax system, the partial integration system, and the fully integrated or assimilated system.

THE CLASSICAL OR SEPARATE CORPORATE TAX SYSTEM

This system, used by the United States, does not make any distinction between the taxation of retained and distributed earnings. Basically, it bases both the incomes of corporations and the dividends paid to shareholders separately. Needless to say, this system leads to double taxation.

THE PARTIAL INTEGRATION SYSTEM

This system consists of two possible subsystems: the split-rate system and the imputation or tax credit system. Under the split-rate system, retained profits are taxed at a higher rate than the distributed profits. Countries using this method include Germany, Japan, and Norway.

Under the imputation or tax credit system, the retained and distributed profits are based at the same rate, but the shareholders receive a credit for the part of the tax paid or deemed paid by the corporation. Countries using this method include the United Kingdom, Italy, and France.

THE FULLY INTEGRATED OR ASSIMILATED SYSTEM

Under such a system no double taxation with or without credit is accepted. Proposals for fully integrated systems have been made in Canada, the United States, and Germany. Only Greece does not levy corporate tax on distributed profits.

Tax Treaties

To create a favorable climate to foreign trade and foreign investment, and to avoid or relieve double taxation of profits, countries sign bilateral or multilateral agreements known as tax treaties. These treaties basically define in general the way joint income should be allocated between national taxing jurisdictions and are intended, in particular, to limit taxation by the source country.

The most important provision of these treaties focuses on the term *permanent establishment*. In the various U.S. treaties, "permanent establishment may take the form of an office or other fixed place of business or a resident agent of the taxpayer with authority to enter in contractual relationships on who fills orders from a stock of goods located in the foreign country."[5] Besides these two principles, the treaty generally enumerates the types of activities which will or will not constitute a permanent establishment.

Besides the concept of permanent establishment, most treaties have provisions limiting the amount of withholding tax on various items, such as interest, dividends, and royalties.

TYPES OF TREATIES

Basically, three types of treaties have emerged: First, in 1977 the U.S. published a Model Income Tax Treaty to be used as a basis for its future treaty negotiations. This treaty includes articles on the general scope, the taxes covered, the residence, the permanent establishment, the income from real property (immovable property), business profits, shipping and air transport, associated enterprises, dividends, interest, royalties, gains, independent personal services, dependent personal services, limitations on benefits, artists and athletes, pensions, annuities, alimony and child support, government service, students and trainees, other income, capital, relief from double taxation, nondiscrimination, mutual-agreement procedures, exchange of information and administrative assistance, diplomatic agents and consular officers, entry into force, and termination.

Second, in 1963 the Organization for Economic Cooperation and Development (OECD) had proposed a model treaty for the elimination of double taxation. The OECD treaty has in fact greatly influenced the U.S. model. Detailed differences between the two focus on either the permanent establishment article or the dividend withholding article. While the Treasury model requires 24 months before a building site is considered a permanent establishment, the OECD model requires only 12 months. Similarly, while the Treasury model requires only 10 percent of the voting stock to qualify for the 5 percent limitation on withholding, the OECD model requires 25 percent of the capital. Other significant differences between the two models include differences in personal scope, taxes covered, interest, investments in holding company, and relief from double taxation.

Third, the United Nations has also proposed a Draft Model Double Taxation Convention between Developed and Developing Countries. In fact, when it comes to developing countries, "tax sparing" and "investment credit" are the major inducements or concessions sought from the developed countries. Tax-sparing provisions exist when the developing country offers some form of tax reduction or "tax holiday" to attract foreign investment. Unfortunately, the U.S. Senate refuses tax-sparing provisions. U.S. arguments used against tax sparing include:

1. Tax sparing is inequitable in that those investing capital in the United States must pay a full tax whereas those investing in a "tax sparing" country are taxed neither by the foreign government nor the United States on the income spared.

2. Tax sparing is "capricious" in that the benefit depends on the nominal rate of tax in the less developed country. A country which does not have a tax holiday may need the foreign investment more than another which does.

3. Tax sparing encourages repatriation of earnings. If a tax incentive such as a tax holiday without tax sparing is used by the foreign country in which a subsidiary is operating, a United States tax will be payable on remitting the earnings to the United States parent. A tax sparing provision removes this restraint on the remittance of earnings.

4. Tax sparing encourages less developed countries to compete against each other in offering tax incentives. This is undesirable as it lessens the revenue.[6]

Unlike tax sparing, investment credit provisions were found acceptable by the U.S. Senate as a way of making inducement to developing countries. These provisions allow a certain percentage of a qualified investment as a credit against U.S. tax. Needless to say, more work needs to be done to find formulas acceptable to both developing and developed countries. The OECD model is now the norm rather than the exception. For example, the new Canada-Germany treaty went into effect September 23, 1983. It replaces the 1956 treaty and is patterned on the OECD model. However, when it comes to developing countries, some, like China, prefer to follow the UN model.

TREATY SHOPPING

One noticeable difference between the U.S. and the OECD models is that the U.S. has included some form of Article 16 in all its treaties. Article 16 has always required that a corporation have some degree of local ownership if it is to get treaty benefit. In fact, Article 16 of the latest version of the model treaty provides generally that corporations resident in a treaty country do not get its treaty benefits unless (1) at least 75 percent of its shares are owned directly or indirectly by individuals resident in the country or the U.S. and (2) the corporation's income is not used substantially, directly or indirectly, to meet liabilities to residents of a country other than the U.S. or the other treaty partner. The idea behind Article 16 is to discourage what is known as treaty shopping which is, basically, the use of tax treaty by the resident of a third country in his or her tax planning. It is accomplished by forming a corporation in a country, generally a tax haven, which has a treaty with the target country. The U.S. Treasury view is that tax treaties are to protect tax revenues and are not intended to benefit residents of third countries. In general, the Treasury gives the following reasons that Article 16 is needed:

- Treaty shopping is causing loss of revenue and encourages tax avoidance.
- Treaty shopping lets residents of non-treaty companies get treaty benefits, so these countries see little need to grant U.S. residents concessions via a tax treaty with the U.S.
- U.S. internal law is violated; for example, interest witholding is eliminated unlawfully when treaties are invoked by third country residents.[7]

The OECD model treaty is not exactly silent in treaty shopping. In fact, the OECD commission is looking into treaty abuse. The U.S., however, decided to go it alone.

Tax Havens

Most non-U.S. multinational corporations have subsidiaries which act as tax havens for corporate funds awaiting a decision on reinvestment or repatriation. The U.S. Revenue Act of 1962 has made it more difficult for U.S. multinational corporations to use tax havens. Basically, a tax haven may be defined as "a place where foreigners may receive income or own assets without paying buyer rates of taxes upon them."[8] In fact, tax havens can be classified in various categories:

1. Traditional tax havens with virtually no taxes at all, such as the Bahamas, Bermuda, and the Cayman Islands
2. Tax havens which impose a relatively low rate, such as the British Virgin Islands and Jersey
3. Tax havens which tax income from domestic sources but exempt all income from foreign sources, such as Hong Kong, Liberia, and Panama
4. Tax havens which allow special privileges, such as Brazil, Luxembourg, and the Netherlands.[9]

The popularity of tax havens decreased in the U.S. when the Revenue Act of 1962 added Subpart F in order to tax concurrently the sham transactions of a controlled foreign corporation (CFC). However, despite increased U.S. crackdowns the use of Caribbean tax havens has continued to increase. It is reasonable to assume that a great deal of activity designed to violate the tax and other laws of the U.S. still takes place in the Caribbean Basin havens. Revenue-loss estimates cannot be calculated because of difficulties in obtaining data.

Tax havens depend on inconsistencies in U.S. tax laws and, therefore, can be wiped out overnight. For example, because U.S. companies can raise capital from overseas more cheaply if they have an Antilles address, about 2,500 of them set up "subsidiaries" on the islands. Though they usually aren't much more than a mail box, these subsidiaries have issued $40 billion of corporate bonds to overseas investors. European corporations with U.S. tax exposure also have found that Antilles financing units can save them money. U.S. corporations have set up units on the islands because bonds issued from those units are tax-free to overseas investors. That makes the bonds a cheaper source of capital than U.S. issued bonds which are not tax free. Not only do U.S. companies benefit through their access to cheaper capital, in addition, the parent corporations can credit any tax to the Antilles against its IRS bill. All these advantages to the Antilles can be wiped out because a 1984 U.S. law permits U.S. companies as well as the government to directly offer tax-free bonds to overseas investors. This will eliminate the need to circumvent the IRS by issuing bonds through the Netherlands Antilles. Such a law was passed in 1984 unsettling a former Caribbean tax haven. The law is acting as a carrot for foreign investors. It eliminated the 30 percent withholding taxes that foreigners have been paying on interest from American securities. In addition, to attract individual foreigners to invest in treasury bonds without having to supply their names and addresses when investing, the Treasury Department announced in August of 1984 that it will issue a new type of security available only to foreigners. Overseas buyers of the new bonds would not have to disclose their names to the U.S. Government. Needless to say this would provide another way for some American investors to dodge taxes by buying the new bonds from a foreign dealer.

U.S. International Taxation

The U.S. international taxation system has as its basic principles:

1. Equal taxation of U.S. taxpayers having the same amount of income regardless of its origins.
2. Tax neutrality as to making decisions whether they invest at home or abroad.

As a result of these principles, the U.S. adopted the general principle of taxing foreign income only when it has been realized by the taxpayer. In fact, the deferral of tax on the earnings of foreign corporations until realized is a basic well-established principle of corporate law. Another result of these principles are the attempts to alleviate international double taxation on foreign-source income derived by U.S. citizens. One mechanism used is the foreign tax credit which, with other relevant issues, is examined next.

FOREIGN TAX CREDIT

The foreign tax credit is used to provide relief from double taxation. Basically, a credit is available for taxes paid directly by a U.S. corporation to a foreign government or deemed to have been paid by it. U.S. foreign tax credit is shown in the following example:

Earnings before tax	$600,000
Foreign income tax paid (assuming 50%)	300,000
Earnings after foreign tax	300,000
Dividends paid to U.S. corporation	$200,000
Foreign withholding tax at 20%	40,000
Net dividends received by the U.S. parent	$160,000
Computation of tax credit:	
Direct credit for withholding tax	$ 22,500
Deemed direct credit·	

$$\frac{\text{Dividend}}{\text{Earnings after foreign tax}} \times \text{Foreign tax}$$

$\dfrac{200,000}{300,000} \times 300,000$	$200,000
Total credit	$222,500

The U.S., however, generally limits the amount of foreign tax creditable in any one year. The overall limitation is computed as follows:

$$\text{Overall limitation} = \frac{\text{Foreign source income}}{\text{Total world income}} \times \text{U.S. tax liability,}$$

where the foreign source income is computed as dividend received plus the deemed direct credit. In tax jargon, this way of computing the foreign source income is known as "grossing up the dividend."

Using the same example as above, let us assume that the U.S. corporation's total world income is $2,000,000 and that its U.S. tax liability before credit is $1,000,000. The overall limitation may then be computed as follows:

$$\text{Overall limitation} = \frac{(\$2000,000 + \$200,000)}{\$2,000,000} \times \$1,000,000 = \$200,000$$

This means that the U.S. corporation can claim only $200,000 as a foreign tax credit. The excess credit of $22,500 ($222,500 − $200,000) may be carried back two years and forward five years as long as the foreign tax credit remains within the limitations in the recomputed carryover years.

Countries differ on the need for foreign tax credit, on how to compute it, and on what kind and amount of limitations to place on the total amount claimed. Belgium, Germany, and France do not ban foreign branch income and therefore do not allow a foreign tax credit. Belgium, France, and the Netherlands do not tax foreign subsidiary dividends and therefore do not allow a deemed foreign tax credit. Belgium, France, Germany, Italy, and the United Kingdom use a per-country limitation on allowable foreign tax credits. Japan and the Netherlands have a limitation similar to that of the U.S.

DOMESTIC INTERNATIONAL SALES CORPORATION

In reaction to concern over the level of U.S. exports, the Revenue Act of 1971 introduced the Domestic International Sales Corporation (DISC) provisions providing a tax subsidy for U.S. companies to conduct their export sales through domestic subsidiaries. Under these rules the earnings of a DISC, a U.S. corporation organized to export goods and services, are taxable only to its shareholders (or the parent company) when actually or constructively distributed to them. Basically, no more than 42.5 percent of the DISC's earnings are subject to a tax deferral. Therefore, at least 57.5 percent of the DISC's earnings are deemed distributed and taxed as a dividend currently to its shareholders whether or not actually distributed.[10] Payment of the deferred tax could be postponed indefinitely.

To qualify as a DISC a nonmanufacturing domestic U.S. corporation must meet the following 3 requirements:

1. *The gross-receipts test*: At least 95 percent of its gross receipts must be composed of "qualified export receipts," that is, those derived from export sales or lease transactions and certain export-related activities usually undertaken on behalf of a related corporation.
2. *The export-assets test*: At least 95 percent of the total assets of the DISC must consist of "qualified export assets," that is, property used in export-related activities.
3. *The capitalization requirement*: A DISC must have a nominal capitalization of at least $2,500 and one class of stock.

One of the types of assets included in the "qualified export assets" is the "producer's loans," which are loans (subject to certain restrictions) made to U.S. producers of export property, including the parent company. This allows a U.S. parent to receive a loan from its DISC and thus be able to use the tax-deferred funds without losing the benefit of the deferral. One limitation on the use of this devise is that the amount loaned may not exceed the amount of the borrower's assets considered to be related to its export sales and provided that the amount loaned to any borrower in a particular year does not exceed the annual increase of the borrower's investment in such assets.

Taxable income of the DISC is based on a transfer price between the parent and DISC such as to allow a DISC taxable income not exceeding the greater of 4 percent of the qualified export receipts on the sale of the DISC plus 10 percent of the DISC's export promotional expenses, or 50 percent of the contributed taxable income of the DISC and its supplier plus 10 percent of the DISC's export promotional expenses, or taxable income computed on the basis of Section 482 rules. (See Chapter 7.) The DISC provisions have not been overwhelmingly acclaimed. Not surprisingly, a GATT panel in 1976 found that it violated the GATT provisions on export subsidies. Its impact on exports has not been empirically proven.[11] In fact, the Senate Finance Committee summed up the general feelings about DISC provisions as follows:

The committee has examined the DISC provisions at great length and has concluded that the legislation has had a beneficial impact on U.S. exports. Since 1971, when DISC was enacted, exports have increased from $43 billion to $107 billion for 1975. It is clear that much of the increase has resulted from the devaluation of the dollar which has taken place since that period. Nonetheless, the committee concluded that a significant portion of the increase in exports which has taken place resulted from the DISC legislation. This increase in exports, the committee concluded, provides jobs for U.S. workers and helps the U.S. balance of payments.

However, the committee also recognized that questions have been raised as to the revenue cost of the DISC program. In 1975, the program is expected to cost nearly

$1.3 billion and in 1976 the amount is estimated to be $1.4 billion. Furthermore, the committee believes that the DISC legislation is made less efficient because the benefits apply to all exports of a company, regardless of whether or not a company's products would be sold in similar amounts without export initiative and regardless of whether or not the company is increasing or decreasing its exports.

Given these considerations, the committee concluded that the DISC program could become more efficient and less costly while still providing the same incentive for increased exports and jobs by generating DISC benefits only to the extent that a company increases its exports or a base period amount.[12]

THE FOREIGN SALES CORPORATION

Technically under the GATT agreement, the DISC is an illegal trade subsidy. It violates Article XVI:4 of the agreement. To remove the DISC as a contentious issue and to avoid further disputes over retaliation, the United States introduced in March 1983 a DISC replacement proposal intended to defuse the illegal trade subsidy issue and still provide tax incentives to U.S. exporters. Passed as a bill, the proposal provides that a portion of the export income of an eligible foreign sales corporation (FSC) will be exempt from Federal income tax. It also allows a domestic corporation a 100 percent dividends-received deduction for dividends distributed from the FSC out of earnings attributable to certain foreign trade income. To qualify as an FSC, a foreign corporation must satisfy the following requirements. The FSC shall have 1) at least one foreign director, 2) a foreign home office, 3) separate billing and material ordering functions, 4) the accounting records must be kept at the home office and 5) formal agency and procurement contracts must be drawn up between the FTC and its parent (to eliminate arbitrary pricing). Basically, the FSC must have a foreign presence, have economic substance, and have the activities that relate to the export income performed by the FSC outside the U.S. Customs territory.

The foreign trade income to be exempt from Federal income tax is defined as the gross income of a FSC attributable to foreign trading gross receipts. The general foreign trading gross receipts mean the gross receipts of a FSC which are attributable to the exports of certain goods and services. These include (1) the sale of export property, (2) the lease or rental of export property, (3) services related and subsidiary to the sale or lease of export property, (4) engineering and architectural services, and (5) export management services.

The FSC has already been criticized as more favorable to the large firms. Basically, a company setting up a DISC, at home and on paper, used to get a tax break for increasing its exports; a FSC would provide tax breaks even without any increase in exports, and even a decline in sales could justify the benefits. However, these benefits will go only to those firms with actual facilities abroad which happens to be the case for the multinational corporations. Most small exporting firms cannot afford to maintain a corporate "presence" abroad in the form of an office, a director, records, and actual sales-related activities, all intended to satisfy GATT requirements. The unfairness to the small exporter may be easily illustrated by the following example of a small Ohio manufacturer that regularly exports through a large Chicago wholesaler exporter. With DISC the Ohio manufacturer was able to get the full tax benefits based on its foreign profits. Under the FSC rules, the Chicago wholesaler would get all the tax benefits and may have no reason to pass some of it on to the small Ohio manufacturer. To correct for this situation the FSC bill provides that a small company keep its DISC as before, but must pay interest on all DISC-deferred taxes at the Treasury bill rates. Needless, to say, it wipes out the DISC benefit to the small manufacturer.

American companies that want to take advantage of the FSC breaks would have to shop for an overseas office to meet legal requirements. In effect, to qualify as an FSC the operation must incorporate in a U.S. possession, except for Puerto Rico, or in a country that has a treaty with the U.S. calling for an exchange of tax related information. Most industrial nations have such treaties with the U.S., but the tax laws require that each agreement be certified with the Treasury Department before the country can be designated a legal location for an FSC. The second important consideration is whether the host country will grant tax breaks to the FSC. That makes most U.S. possessions ideal places for setting FSCs. One wonders whether those islands have the necessary communications, financial, computer and related systems to handle business.

UNITARY TAXATION

The question is whether an individual state should be allowed to impose income taxes on foreign-source income. Proponents of the unitary-tax method answer the question positively. What is the unitary tax and why has it stirred up so much controversy? The concept of unitary taxation is relatively simple: Corporations are perceived as a single worldwide unit, and they are taxed on the proportion of the total operation that is located within the state. A unitary formula, previously devised to measure the income of a functionally related enterprise which operated in several states, is used to compute the state corporate tax. Previously, state tax was tabulated by taking state sales, payroll, and property and averaging them in relation to national figures for the same categories. Now worldwide sales, payroll, and property are used. Basically, the state calculates the tax by multiplying the percentage of business a company does in the state by its worldwide income, which supposedly will give the state more revenues than when it was using only national income. California has been using the unitary-tax method for the last 45 years.

Needless to say, the unitary-tax method is not popular with most multinational corporations. Various arguments are used by critics of the method. The first argument is that since the state unitary method has no provision for credits for foreign tax paid, the worldwide unitary method leads to international double taxation. A second is that since it is the federal government and not the states which conducts the nation's foreign relations, any state action which interferes with internal commerce threatens the federal uniformity ordained by the Founding Fathers.[13] A third is related to legitimacy of a state's levying taxes on business conducted in another country. What allows a state to consider any sale made outside its borders as a state sale if it is in another state or country? To be more critical, how can a state claim it has the right to tax profits that a Mexican company with a Californian subsidiary makes on a sale in Canada?[14]

TAXATION OF FOREIGN CORPORATIONS CONTROLLED BY U.S. FIRMS

As stated earlier, the deferral principle allows income from a foreign branch to be deferred from U.S. taxation until it is received as a dividend or as a liquidation distribution. This principle was questioned, however, and 1962 legislation attempted to distinguish between "legitimate" deferral of U.S. taxation in foreign operations and deferral resulting from a manipulation of U.S. tax rules. The decision was to curtail deferral through the so-called Subpart F provisions for foreign operations. Basically, the decision calls for excluding from the deferral principle a certain class of income (Subpart F income) of a certain type of corporation (controlled foreign corporation—CFC).

A CFC is a foreign corporation of which more than 50 percent of the total combined voting power of all classes of stock entitled to vote is owned directly, indirectly, or constructively by U.S. shareholders on any given day during the taxable year of such foreign corporations. A U.S. shareholder for tax purposes is one owning 10 percent or more of the voting power.

Subpart F income includes income from the issuance of the U.S. risks; certain international-boycott-related income; certain illegal bribes, kick-backs, or other payments to government officials, employees, or agents; and foreign-based company income. The foreign-based company income includes the following elements:

1. Foreign personal holding company income, which includes passive income such as interest, dividends, rents, royalties, and so on
2. Foreign-based company sales income, which includes income derived from the purchase and sale of personal property to a related party if the property is manufactured and sold for use in the CFC's country of incorporation
3. Foreign-based company services income, which includes income derived from the performance of services outside the CFC's country of incorporation for or on behalf of a related person

4. Foreign-based company shipping income, which includes income derived from the use of aircrafts or vessels in foreign commerce, outside the CFC's country of incorporation

5. Foreign-based company oil-related income, which includes foreign oil-related income of a company which is a large oil producer for the taxable year.[15]

Conclusions

As the chapter shows, international taxation is a complex array of rules and conventions. To minimize and avoid unnecessary taxes, multinational corporations will have to try to achieve an orderly and systematic approach to tax planning. Some firms have adopted the following procedures:

1. Explicit statement of the objectives of tax planning in international operations

2. Assigning definite responsibilities, at both headquarters and the subsidiaries, for various aspects of the planning

3. Acquiring a thorough knowledge of the variables in international taxation, preferably in an information-gathering system designed to routinely generate the necessary information

4. Determining what decisions and operating procedures are affected by tax considerations and how they are affected, and dissemination of this information to the decision makers

5. Defining the procedures which will ensure the interaction of the tax planners with the decision makers

6. Evaluating the impact of the tax considerations on international operating and investment decisions and on operating procedures.[16]

Such elaborate tax-planning systems may be the first step toward a comprehensive approach to international taxation.

Notes

1. Richard H. Kalish and John P. Casey, "The Dilemma of the International Tax Executive," *Columbia Journal of World Business* (Summer 1975), p. 67.

2. Carl S. Shoup, "Taxation of Multinational Corporations," *The Impact of Multinational Corporations on Development and on International Relations*, UN Publications, Sales No. E.74II.A.6, (New York, October 1974), pp. 3-36.

3. Frederick K. Howard, "Overview of International Taxation," *Columbia Journal of World Business* 10 (Summer 1975), pp. 8-9.

4. The differences in the treatment of intracompany transactions is presented in Chapter 7.

5. Paul R. McDaniel and High J. Ault, *Introduction to United States International Taxation* (September, The Netherlands, Kluwer, 1981), p. 171.

6. Vance N. Kirby and Williard H. Pedricks, *The Study of Federal Tax Law, Transnational Transactions, 1983-1984* (Chicago: Commerce Clearing House, 1983), p. 228.

7. Nick Hammer, "Tax Treaty Developments," *Price Waterhouse International Tax Review* (January/February 1984), p. 7.

8. Milka Casanegra de Jantscher, "Tax Havens Explained," *Finance and Development* (March 1976), p. 31.

9. Jean Doncet and Kenneth J. Good, "What Makes a Good Tax Haven?" *Banker* (May 1973), p. 493.

10. Given that the dividends are taxed on the parent company at the effective rate of 46 percent, the federal income tax rate on the total earnings of a DISC may be as little as 26.45 percent (46 percent × 57.5 percent), resulting in a maximum savings of $.1955 on the dollar.

11. Jane Offett Burns, *The Domestic International Sales Corporation: An Empirical Investigation*, Ph.D. diss., Pennsylvania State University, 1976.

12. U.S. Cong., 94th Congress, 2d sess., Senate Finance Committee Report on H.R. 10612, Rep. No. 94-938, p. 291.

13. This point was not, however, supported in court. In December 1983, the Supreme Court refused to consider an appeal by Shell Petroleum, supported by the 10 member nations of the European Economic Community, that California's unitary method violates a commercial treaty between the U.S. and the Netherlands.

14. After five months of lobbying state governments in 1984, Japanese companies are beginning to make good on their threat to invest only in those U.S. states that prohibit unitary taxes. For example, on August 6, 1984, Japan's Kyocera Corporation, the world's leading manufacturer of ceramic packages for integrated circuits, blamed the unitary tax for its decision to build a new $30 million plant in Washington state rather than to expand its San Diego facility.

15. Naturally, one would expect some companies to resort to drastic actions to avoid Subpart F, which forces repatriation of profits. One good example is the action taken in January 1983 by a U.S. $4.8 billion company, McDermott Inc., to move to Panama. McDermott claimed at that time that if it were to run its business the way it would like in the next five years, it would have to pay some $220 millions in taxes in Subpart F income. The move to Panama would make that income untaxable. Moreover, McDermott claimed that it could now move capital or assets around from subsidiary to subsidiary or even make too much in investment income from any foreign holding without being forced into Subpart F to repatriate these profits.

16. George M. Scott, *An Introduction to Financial Control and Reporting in Multinational Enterprises* (Austin: The University of Texas at Austin, Bureau of Business Research, 1973), p. 56.

Bibliography

Arthur, Robert J. "Obtaining Tax Data from Foreign Affiliates," *The International Tax Journal* 4 (October 1977), pp. 596-652.

Bartlett, R. T. "The Taxation of Overseas Earnings," *The Accountant* (January 26, 1978), pp. 103-6.

Bawly, Dan. "The Multinational Company," *Accountancy* 84 (December 1973), pp. 80-86.

_____. "The Multinational Company—II," *Accountancy* 85 (January 1974), pp. 69-71.

Berg, Robert. "The Effect of the New UK/US Double Tax Treaty," *Accountancy* 88 (November 1977), pp. 70-71.

Binkowski, Edward. "Tax Consequences of Creeping Expropriation," *The International Tax Journal* 7 (December 1980), pp. 117-26.

Brantner, Paul F. "Taxation and the Multinational Firm," *Management Accounting* 55 (October 1973), pp. 11-16.

Briner, Ernst K. "International Tax Management," *Management Accounting* 54 (February 1973), pp. 47-50.

Broke, Adam. "How Are Foreign Earnings Taxed?" *Accountancy* 87 (May 1976), pp. 68-70.

Burns, Jane O. "DISC Accounting: An Empirical Investigation," *The International Tax Journal* 4 (April 1978), pp. 882-91.

_____. "Exports and the Tax Reform Act of 1976," *The International Tax Journal* 4 (February 1978), pp. 810-23.

_____. "How IRS Applies the Intercompany Pricing Rules of Section 482: A Corporate Survey," *The Journal of Taxation* 52 (May 1980), pp. 308-14.

_____. "Taxation Policies for Plant and Equipment in Industrial Nations," *The Tax Executive* 34 (October 1981), pp. 1-10.

Calhoun, Donald A. "The Foreign Tax Credit," *Management Accounting* 57 (September 1975), pp. 41-42, 53.

Calitri, Joseph C. "The Challenge of Burke-Hartke," *Financial Executive* 40 (June 1972), pp. 36-39.

Carmichael, Keith. "Tax on Foreign Earnings," *Accountancy* 85 (October 1974), pp. 84-86.

_____. "Tax on Foreign Earnings," *Accountancy* 88 (June 1977), pp. 46-52.

Chan, K. H., and Herbert L. Jensen. "Tax Accounting for Capital Assets—The U.S. vs. Canada," *CA Magazine* 112 (December 1979), pp. 36-41.

Choate, Alan G., and Michael L. Moore. "Bribes and Boycotts under the Tax Reform Act of 1976," *The International Tax Journal* 4 (December 1977), pp. 736-44.

Chown, John. "Towards Tax Unifications," *Accountancy* 83 (June 1972), pp. 23-25.

Christie, Andrew J. "The UK/Norway Double Tax Treaty," *The Accountant's Magazine* 83 (December 1979), pp. 514-15.

Cretton, Colin, and Alan Reid. "A Practitioner's Guide to the UK/US Double Tax Treaty (Part 1)," *Accountancy* 91 (June 1980), pp. 101-2.

_____. "A Practitioner's Guide to the UK/US Double Tax Treaty (Part 2)," *Accountancy* 91 (August 1980), pp. 52-53.

_____. "A Practitioner's Guide to the UK/US Double Tax Treaty (Part 3)," *Accountancy* 91 (October 1980), pp. 97-98.

Davis, Michael. "The Tax Haven Company—Dispelling the Myths," *Accountancy* 87 (February 1976), pp. 46-48.

Deakin, E. "Country by Country Aspects of VAT," *Accountancy* 83 (February 1972), pp. 76-79.

Delap, Richard L. "Apportionment of Expenses to DISC Income," *The International Tax Journal* 5 (February 1979), pp. 214-26.

Dilley, Steven. "Allocation and Apportionment under Reg. 1.861.8," *The CPA Journal* 50 (December 1980), pp. 33-38.

Dreier, Ronald. "U.S. Income Tax Treaties," *Columbia Journal of World Business* 10 (Summer 1975), pp. 21-28.

Feinschreiber, Robert. "Allocation and Apportionment of Miscellaneous Deductions," *the Internatiional Tax Journal* 4 (October 1977), pp. 653-68.

_____. "Allocation and Apportionment of Research Expense," *The International Tax Journal* 4 (April 1978), pp. 902-24.

_____. "Analysis of the Allocation and Apportionment Examples," *The International Tax Journal* 4 (August 1978), pp. 1027-70.

_____. "Analysis of the Allocation and Apportionment Examples—Part II," *International Tax Journal* 5 (October 1978), pp. 45-72.

_____. "Apportioning Interest Expense to the U.S. Branch of a Foreign Corporation," *The International Tax Journal* 7 (October 1980), pp. 51-75.

_____. "Consolidated Foreign Tax Credit: Analysis of the ITT Case," *The International Tax Journal* 6 (April 1980), pp. 302-6.

_____. "DISC: A New Export Tax Incentive," *Financial Executive* 40 (April 1972), pp. 66-70.

_____. "Earnings and Profits Translation of Specific Items," *The International Tax Journal* 5 (April 1979), pp. 334-46.

_____. "FBC Sales Income and Its Exclusions," *The International Tax Journal* 5 (February 1979), pp. 231-50.

_____. "The Foreign Tax Credit under Siege," *Financial Executive* 47 (October 1979), pp. 56-63.

_____. "How to Double DISC Benefits through FISC and Grouping," *The International Tax Journal* 6 (June 1980), pp. 367-72.

_____. "The Impact of Arrow Fastener on DISC Operations," *The International Tax Journal* 7 (August 1981), pp. 413-27.

_____. "Intercompany Pricing after DuPont," *The International Tax Journal* 6 (February 1980), pp. 222-29.

_____. "Interest-Free International Loans," *The International Tax Journal* 5 (June 1979), pp. 394-409.

_____. "New Deductions for Overseas Americans," *The International Tax Journal* 5 (December 1978), pp. 93-108.

_____. "New Strategies for Increasing DISC Benefits," *Financial Executives* 44 (August 1976), pp. 32-37.

_____. "Tax Benefits for Domestic International Sales Corporations (DISCs)—How to Qualify," *The CPA Journal* 42 (February 1972), pp. 131-38.

_____. "Tax Benefits for Domestic International Sales Corporations (DISCs)—Pricing, Profits, and Dividends," *The CPA Journal* 42 (March 1972), pp. 221-24.

_____. "Treaty Provisions for Allocating and Apportioning Deductions," *The International Tax Journal* 4 (June 1978), pp. 995-1006.

Feinschreiber, Robert, and Caryl Nackenson. "Obtaining Interest and Royalties from Foreign Subsidiaries: The Impact of Xerox v. Maryland," *The International Tax Journal* 7 (October 1980), pp. 5-13.

Finney, Malcolm J. "Taxation and International Financing," *The Accountant* 178 (June 29, 1978), pp. 882-84.

Gaskins, J. Peter. "Taxation of Foreign Source Income," *Financial Analysts Journal* 29 (September/October 1973), pp. 55-64.

Green, Alex. "The New UK/Canada Tax Treaty," *Accountancy* 90 (August 1979), pp. 83-86.

Green, Jeffrey. "Foreign Source Income and Dutch Corporate Taxation," *The Accountant* 176 (June 22, 1977), pp. 635-36.

Green, William H. "Analysis of the New ITT Case," *The International Tax Journal* 7 (August 1981), pp. 466-73.

_____. "Analysis of the 1977 DISC Report," *The International Tax Journal* 4 (October 1977), pp. 579-95.

_____. "Analysis of the 1981 Treasury Report on DISC," *The International Tax Journal* 7 (June 1981), pp. 333-52.

_____. "Planning DISC Operations in the '80's" *The International Tax Journal* 6 (June 1980), pp. 373-89.

Hammer, Richard. "Financial Planning to Avoid Tax Problems," *The International Journal of Accounting Education and Research* 7 (Spring 1972), pp. 23-24.

Harless, Donald S. "Recent Rulings Affect Allocation and Apportionment," *The International Tax Journal* 7 (August 1981), pp. 461-65.

Heinz, Peter Danser. "Mathematical Strategies for the Foreign Tax Credit Limitation," *The International Tax Journal* 7 (August 1981), pp. 454-60.

Howard, Frederick. "Overview of International Taxation," *Columbia Journal of World Business* 10 (Summer 1975), pp. 5-11.

Hughes, Anthony. "Tax Concessions Ahead in UK/India Treaty," *Accountancy* 92 (November 1981), pp. 148-50.

Ioannides, J. D. "Invest in Cyprus: Taxation and Other Incentives," *The Accountant* 179 (July 20, 1978), pp. 70-71.

James, George F. "MNCs and the Foreign Tax Credit," *Columbia Journal of World Business* 9 (Winter 1974), pp. 61-66.

Kolmin, Frank W., and Christopher W. Nobes. "The Accumulated Earnings Tax: An Anglo-American Comparison," *The International Tax Journal* 5 (June 1979), pp. 410-19.

Lagae, Jean-Pierre, and Patrick Kelley. "Tax Aspects of American Investment in Belgium," *The International Tax Journal* 5 (October 1978), pp. 23-34.

Lamp, Walter. "US-UK Tax Treaty Proposal: New Look at Dividends," *Financial Executive* 44 (March 1976), pp. 14-25.

Lillie, Jane. "A New Strategy for Recognizing Exchange Gains and Losses," *The International Tax Journal* 4 (August 1978), pp. 1071-80.

McDermott, John E., and Martin Oliver. "The Effect of Foreign Source Capital Losses on the Foreign Tax Credit," *The International Tax Journal* 4 (December 1977), pp. 679-87.

Morgan, John R., and Colin Robinson. "The Comparative Effects of the UK and Norwegian Oil Taxation Systems on Profitability and Government Revenue," *Accounting and Business Research* 7 (Winter 1976), pp. 2-16.

Ness, Walter L. "U.S. Corporate Income Taxation and the Dividend Remission Policy of Multinational Corporations," *Journal of International Business Studies* 6 (Spring 1975), pp. 67-78.

Newman, Barry, and Jeffrey Kadet. "United States Taxation of Foreign Flag Shipping," *Columbia Journal of World Business* 12 (Spring 1977), pp. 103-11.

Nobes, C. W. "Imputation System of Corporation Tax within the EEC," *Accounting and Business Research* 10 (Spring 1980), pp. 221-31.

Nobes, C. W. "Corporation Tax: Toward EEC Harmonization," *Accountancy* 90 (January 1979), pp. 52-55.

Nordhauser, Susan L., and John L. Kramer. "Repeal of the Deferral Privilege for Earnings from Direct Foreign Investments: An Analysis," *The Accounting Review* 56 (January 1981), pp. 54-69.

O'Connor, Walter F., and Samuel M. Russo. "Tax Consequences of the Currency Float," *Financial Executive* 43 (January 1975), pp. 48-53.

Oliver, David. "How Not to Lose Out on the UK/US Tax Treaty," *Accountancy* 91 (July 1980), pp. 80-81.

Peckron, Harold S. "Tax Consequences of Currency Futures after Hoover," *The International Tax Journal* 6 (February 1980), pp. 165-77.

Perlstein, Pinkus. "International Tax Planning," *Accountancy* 87 (December 1976), pp. 69-70.

Radler, Albert J. "International Capital Markets and Taxation," *Management International Review* 13, 6 (1973), pp. 65-74.

Raskhin, Michael D. "The Branch Rule and the Subpart F Exclusion," *The International Tax Journal* 4 (June 1978), pp. 980-94.

Ravenscroft, Donald R. "Foreign Investment, Exchange Rates, Taxable Income and Real Values," *Columbia Journal of World Business* 10 (Summer 1975), pp. 50-61.

———. "Translating Foreign Currency under U.S. Tax Law," *Financial Executive* 42 (September 1974), pp. 58-69.

Romito, Edwin L. "Amending the DISC Return," *The International Tax Journal* 7 (April 1981), pp. 300-308.

Ryan, Edward D. "International Tax Problems and the Financial Officer," *Management Accounting* 57 (October 1975), pp. 49-58.

Sale, J. Timothy, and Karen B. Carroll. "Tax Planning Tools for the Multinational Corporation," *Management Accounting* 60 (June 1979), pp. 37-41.

Schlag, Rene C. "Accounting for Taxes of Foreign Subsidiaries—A Simplified Approach," *Management Accounting* 61 (December 1979), pp. 15-19.

Schmitz, Marvin N. "Taxation of Foreign Exchange Gains and Losses." *Management Accounting* 57 (July 1976), pp. 49-51.

Schwartz, Bill. "Partial Income Tax Allocation and Deferred Taxation: An International Accounting Issue," *Management International Review* 20; 4 (1980), pp. 74-82.

Seghers, Paul D. "Intercompany Pricing—Tax Audits," *The International Tax Journal* 5 (August 1979), pp. 437-41.

Shagam, Jerome, and Kenneth G. Kolmin. "Temporary Regulations Resolve Some Problems for U.S. Persons Working Abroad," *The International Tax Journal* 5 (June 1979), pp. 363-93.

Simms, Charles A. "Summarizing the Foreign Earned Income Tax Act of 1978," *Management Accounting* 61 (August 1979), pp. 32-36.

Simon, Stuart H. "Depreciation Proposal Would Impair Foreign Tax Credit," *The International Tax Journal* 7 (June 1981), pp. 353-56.

Smith, C. W. Davidson. "The New United States Double Taxation Agreement," *The Accountant's Magazine* 80 (March 1976), pp. 96-97.

Stitt, Carl. "The UK as a Tax Haven," *The Accountant* 182 (March 20, 1980), pp. 436-38.

Stobaugh, Robert B. "More Taxes on Multinationals," *Financial Executive* 42 (April 1974), pp. 12-17.

Symonds, Edward. "Still Hotter Rivalry under New Tax Treaty," *The Accountant* 1982 (April 10, 1980), pp. 542-43.

Tomsett, Eric. "Double Taxation: The New Treaty between UK and the Netherlands," *Accountancy* 92 (July 1981), pp. 88-90.

Van Valkenburg, Marilyn. "Foreign Income and the Internal Revenue Code," *Management Accounting* 55 (June 1974), pp. 18-22.

Wainman, David. "Currency Fluctuation: Accounting and Taxation Implications," *The Accountant* 174 (August 19, 1976), pp. 211-12.

Yost, George J. "Establishing Intercompany Pricing Comparables after U.S. Steel," *The International Tax Journal* 6 (June 1980), pp. 360-66.

_____. "Impact of the Debt-Equity Regulations on International Operations," *The International Tax Journal* 7 (February 1981), pp. 217-28.

_____. "Unwritten International Loans," *The International Tax Journal* 7 (April 1981), pp. 253-61.

APPENDIX 10.1

EXAMPLES OF TAX TREATIES

As mentioned earlier in the chapter, the two main tax treaty models used are the OECD model and U.S. model. In 1977 the OECD committee on Fiscal Affairs issued its final model treaty which amplified and changed the text of certain treaty articles. Countries unable to agree with the text of a particular provision of the model treaty so indicate by *reservations*. Countries unable to agree with the interpretation of a treaty article given in the commentaries use *observations* to indicate the way in which they will apply the particular provision.

In June 1981, the Treasury issued a draft of a proposed new U.S. model income tax treaty.

The texts of both models, the 1977 OECD model and the June 1981 U.S. Model Income Tax Treaty follow:

ORGANIZATION FOR ECONOMIC CO-OPERATION AND DEVELOPMENT DRAFT CONVENTION FOR THE AVOIDANCE OF DOUBLE TAXATION WITH RESPECT TO TAXES ON ESTATES AND INHERITANCES

TITLE OF THE CONVENTION

Convention between (State A) and (State B) for the avoidance of double taxation with respect to taxes on estates and inheritances

PREAMBLE

Note: The preamble of the Convention shall be drafted in accordance with the constitutional procedure of both Contracting States.

CHAPTER I

SCOPE OF THE CONVENTION

Article 1

Estates Covered

This Convention shall apply to estates of deceased persons whose domicile at their death was in one or both of the Contracting States.

Article 2

Taxes Covered

1. This Convention shall apply to taxes on estates and inheritances imposed on behalf of each Contracting State or of its political sub-divisions or local authorities, irrespective of the manner in which they are levied.

2. There shall be regarded as taxes on estates and inheritances all taxes imposed on the occasion of death in the form of tax on the corpus of the estate, of tax on inheritances, of transfer duties, or of taxes on donations *mortis causa.*

3. The existing taxes to which the Convention shall apply are, in particular:

    (*a*) in the case of (State A): ....

    (*b*) in the case of (State B): ....

4. The Convention shall also apply to any taxes on estates and inheritances which are subsequently imposed in addition to, or in place of the existing taxes. At the end of each year, the competent authorities of the Contracting States shall notify to each other any changes which have been made in their respective taxation laws.

CHAPTER II

DEFINITIONS

Article 3

General Definitions

1. In this Convention:

    (*a*) the terms "a Contracting State" and "the other Contracting State" mean (State A) or (State B), as the context requires;

    (*b*) the term "competent authority" means:

        1. in (State A) ....

        2. in (State B) ....

2. As regards the application of the Convention by a Contracting State, any term not otherwise defined shall, unless the context otherwise requires, have the meaning which it has under the laws of that Contracting State relating to the taxes which are the subject of the Convention.

Source: Reproduced with the permission of the Organisation for Economic Co-operation and Development, Paris.

Article 4
Fiscal Domicile

1. For the purposes of this Convention, the question whether a person at his death was domiciled in a Contracting State shall be determined according to the law of that State.

2. Where by reason of the provisions of paragraph 1 a person was domiciled in both Contracting States, then this case shall be determined in accordance with the following rules:

(a) He shall be deemed to have been domiciled in the Contracting State in which he had a permanent home available to him. If he had a permanent home available to him in both Contracting States, the domicile shall be deemed to be in the Contracting State with which his personal and economic relations were closest (centre of vital interests);

(b) If the Contracting State in which he had his centre of vital interests cannot be determined, or if he had not a permanent home available to him in either Contracting State, the domicile shall be deemed to be in the Contracting State in which he had an habitual abode;

(c) If he had an habitual abode in both Contracting States or in neither of them, the domicile shall be deemed to be in the Contracting State of which he was a national;

(d) If he was a national of both Contracting States or of neither of them, the competent authorities of the Contracting States shall settle the question by mutual agreement.

CHAPTER III
TAXING RULES

Article 5
Immovable Property

1. Immovable property may be taxed in the Contracting State in which such property is situated.

2. The term "immovable property" shall be defined in accordance with the law of the Contracting State in which the property in question is situated. The term shall in any case include property accessory to immovable property, livestock and equipment used in agriculture and forestry, rights to which the provisions of general law respecting landed property apply, usufruct of immovable property and rights to variable or fixed payments as consideration for the working of, or the right to work, mineral deposits, sources and other natural resources; ships, boats and aircraft shall not be regarded as immovable property.

3. The provisions of paragraphs 1 and 2 shall also apply to immovable property of an enterprise and to immovable property used for the performance of professional services or other independent activities of a similar character.

Article 6
Business Property of a Permanent Establishment and Assets Pertaining to a Fixed Base Used for the Performance of Professional Services

1. Except for assets referred to in Articles 5 and 7, assets forming part of the business property of a permanent establishment of an enterprise may be taxed in the Contracting State in which the permanent establishment is situated.

2. The term "permanent establishment" means a fixed place of business in which the business of the enterprise is wholly or partly carried on.

3. The term "permanent establishment" shall include especially:

(a) a place of management;

(b) a branch;

(c) an office;

(d) a factory;

(e) a workshop;

(f) a mine, quarry or other place of extraction of natural resources;

(g) a building site or construction or assembly project which exists for more than twelve months.

4. The term "permanent establishment" shall not be deemed to include:

(a) the use of facilities solely for the purpose of storage, display or delivery of goods or merchandise belonging to the enterprise;

(b) the maintenance of a stock of goods or merchandise belonging to the enterprise solely for the purpose of storage, display or delivery;

(c) the maintenance of a stock of goods or merchandise belonging to the enterprise solely for the purpose of processing by another enterprise;

(d) the maintenance of a fixed place of business solely for the purpose of purchasing goods or merchandise, or for collecting information, for the enterprise;

(e) the maintenance of a fixed place of business solely for the purpose of advertising, for the supply of information, for scientific research or for similar activities which have a preparatory or auxiliary character, for the enterprise.

5. A person acting in a Contracting State on behalf of an enterprise of the other Contracting State—other than an agent of an independent status to whom paragraph 6 applies—shall be deemed to be a permanent establishment in the first-mentioned State if he has, and habitually exercises in that State, an authority to conclude contracts in the name of the enterprise, unless his activities are limited to the purchase of goods or merchandise for the enterprise.

6. An enterprise of a Contracting State shall not be deemed to have a permanent establishment in the other Contracting State merely because it carries on business in that other State through a broker, general commission agent or any other agent of an independent status, where such persons are acting in the ordinary course of their business.

7. Except for assets described in Article 5, assets pertaining to a fixed base used for the performance of professional services or other independent activities of a similar character may be taxed in the Contracting State in which the fixed base is situated.

Article 7

Ships, Boats and Aircraft

1. Ships and aircraft operated in international traffic and boats engaged in inland waterways transport, and movable property pertaining to the operation of such ships, aircraft and boats, may be taxed in the Contracting State in which the place of effective management of the enterprise is situated.

Article 8

Property Not Expressly Mentioned

1. Property other than property referred to in Articles 5, 6 and 7 shall be taxable only in the Contracting State in which the deceased was domiciled at his death.

Article 9

Deduction of Debts

1. Debts especially secured on any property referred to in Article 5 shall be deducted from the value of that property. Debts, not being especially secured on any property referred to in Article 5, which are represented by the acquisition, conversion, repair or upkeep of any such property, shall be deducted from the value of that property.

2. Subject to paragraph 1, debts pertaining to a permanent establishment of an enterprise or to a fixed base used for the performance of professional services or other independent activities of a similar character, and debts pertaining to any business of shipping, inland waterways transport or air transport, shall be deducted from the value of property referred to in Article 6 or Article 7, as the case may be.

3. Other debts shall be deducted from the value of property to which Article 8 applies.

4. If a debt exceeds the value of the property from which it is deductible in a Contracting State, according to paragraphs 1, 2 and 3, the excess shall be deducted from the value of any other property taxable in that State.

5. Any excess still remaining after the deductions referred to in the preceding paragraphs shall be deducted from the value of the property liable to tax in the other Contracting State.

CHAPTER IV

METHODS FOR ELIMINATION OF DOUBLE TAXATION

Article 10A

Exemption Method

1. The Contracting State in which the deceased was domiciled at his death shall exempt from tax any property which, in accordance with the provisions of this Convention, may be taxed in the other Contracting State but may, in calculating tax on any property which it remains entitled to tax, apply the rate of tax which would have been applicable if the exempted property had not been so exempted.

Article 10B

Credit Method

1. The Contracting State in which the deceased was domiciled at his death shall deduct from the tax calculated according to its law an amount equal to the tax paid in the other Contracting State on property which, in accordance with the provisions of this Convention, may be taxed in the other State.

2. The deduction shall not, however, exceed that part of the tax, as computed before the deduction is given, which is appropriate to the property which may be taxed in the other Contracting State.

CHAPTER V

SPECIAL PROVISIONS

Article 11

Non-Discrimination

1. The nationals of a Contracting State shall not be subjected in the other Contracting State to any taxation or any requirement connected therewith which is other or more burdensome than the taxation and connected requirements to which nationals of that other State in the same circumstances are or may be subjected.

2. The term "nationals" means:

(a) all individuals possessing the nationality of a Contracting State;

(b) all legal persons, partnerships and associations deriving their status as such from the law in force in a Contracting State.

3. Stateless persons shall not be subjected in a Contracting State to any taxation or any requirement connected therewith which is other or more burdensome than the taxation and connected requirements to which nationals of that State in the same circumstances are or may be subjected.

4. The taxation on a permanent establishment which an enterprise of a Contracting State has in the other Contracting State shall not be less favourably levied in that other State than the taxation levied on enterprises of that other State carrying on the same activities.

This provision shall not be construed as obliging a Contracting State to grant to residents of the other Contracting State any personal allowances, reliefs and reductions for taxation purposes on account of civil status or family responsibilities which it grants to its own residents.

5. Enterprises of a Contracting State, the capital of which is wholly or partly owned or controlled, directly or indirectly, by one or more residents of the other Contracting State, shall not be subjected in the first-mentioned Contracting State to any taxation or any requirement connected therewith which is other or more burdensome than the taxation and connected requirements to which other similar enterprises of that first-mentioned State are or may be subjected.

6. In this Article the term "taxation" means taxes of every kind and description.

Article 12

Mutual Agreement Procedure

1. Any person who considers that the actions of one or both of the Contracting States result or will result for him in taxation not in accordance with this Convention may, notwithstanding the remedies provided by the national laws of those States, present his case to the competent authority of either State.

2. The competent authority shall endeavour, if the objection appears to it to be justified and if it is not itself able to arrive at an appropriate solution, to resolve the case by mutual agreement with the competent authority of the other Contracting State, with a view to the avoidance of taxation not in accordance with the Convention.

3. The competent authorities of the Contracting States shall endeavour to resolve by mutual agreement any difficulties or doubts arising as to the interpretation or application of the Convention. They may also consult together for the elimination of double taxation in cases not provided for in the Convention.

4. The competent authorities of the Contracting States may communicate with each other directly for the purpose of reaching an agreement in the sense of the preceding paragraphs. When it seems advisable in order to reach agreement to have an oral exchange of opinions, such exchange may take place through a Commission consisting of representatives of the competent authorities of the Contracting States.

Article 13
Exchange of Information

1. The competent authorities of the Contracting States shall exchange such information as is necessary for the carrying out of this Convention and of the domestic laws of the Contracting States concerning taxes covered by this Convention insofar as the taxation thereunder is in accordance with this Convention. Any information so exchanged shall be treated as secret and shall not be disclosed to any persons or authorities other than those concerned with the assessment or collection of the taxes which are the subject of the Convention.

2. In no case shall the provisions of paragraph 1 be construed so as to impose on one of the Contracting States the obligation:

(a) to carry out administrative measures at variance with the laws or the administrative practice of that or of the other Contracting State;

(b) to supply particulars which are not obtainable under the laws or in the normal course of the administration of that or of the other Contracting State;

(c) to supply information which would disclose any trade, business, industrial, commercial or professional secret or trade process, or information the disclosure of which would be contrary to public policy (ordre public).

Article 14
Diplomatic and Consular Officials

Nothing in this Convention shall affect the fiscal privileges of diplomatic or consular officials under the general rules of international law or under the provisions of special agreements.

Article 15
Territorial Extension

1. This Convention may be extended, either in its entirety or with any necessary modifications, [to any part of the territory of (State A) or of (State B) which is specifically excluded from the application of the Convention or] to any State or territory for whose international relations (State A) or (State B) is responsible, which imposes taxes substantially similar in character to those to which the Convention applies. Any such extension shall take effect from such date and subject to such modifications and conditions, including conditions as to termination, as may be specified and agreed between the Contracting States in notes to be exchanged through diplomatic channels or in any other manner in accordance with their constitutional procedures.

2. Unless otherwise agreed by both Contracting States, the denunciation of the Convention by one of them under Article 17 shall terminate, in the manner provided for in that Article, the application of the Convention [to any part of the territory of (State A) or of (State B) or] to any State or territory to which it has been extended under this Article.

NOTE: The words between brackets are of relevance when, by special provision, a part of the territory of a Contracting State is excluded from the application of the Convention.

CHAPTER VI
FINAL PROVISIONS

Article 16
Entry Into Force

1. This Convention shall be ratified and the instruments of ratification shall be exchanged at .... as soon as possible.

2. The Convention shall enter into force on the day on which the instruments of ratification are exchanged and its provisions shall have effect in relation to estates of persons dying on or after that day.

Article 17
Termination

This Convention shall remain in force until denounced by one of the Contracting States. Either Contracting State may denounce the Convention, through diplomatic channels, with effect from the end of any calendar year not earlier than the year .... by giving at least six months notice of termination. In such an event, the Convention will not apply to estates of persons who died after the expiry of the calendar year with respect to the end of which the Convention has been denounced.

Terminal Clause

NOTE: The terminal clause concerning the signing shall be drafted in accordance with the constitutional procedure of both Contracting States.

ORGANIZATION FOR ECONOMIC CO-OPERATION AND DEVELOPMENT MODEL CONVENTION FOR THE AVOIDANCE OF DOUBLE TAXATION WITH RESPECT TO TAXES ON INCOME AND CAPITAL

SUMMARY OF THE CONVENTION

TITLE AND PREAMBLE

Chapter I

Scope of the convention

Art. 1   Personal scope
Art. 2   Taxes covered

Chapter II

Definitions

Art. 3   General definitions
Art. 4   Resident
Art. 5   Permanent establishment

Chapter III

Taxation of income

Art. 6   Income from immovable property
Art. 7   Business profits
Art. 8   Shipping, inland waterways transport and air transport
Art. 9   Associated enterprises
Art. 10   Dividends
Art. 11   Interest
Art. 12   Royalties
Art. 13   Capital gains
Art. 14   Independent personal services
Art. 15   Dependent personal services
Art. 16   Directors' fees
Art. 17   Artistes and athletes
Art. 18   Pensions
Art. 19   Government service
Art. 20   Students
Art. 21   Other income

Chapter IV

Taxation of Capital

Art. 22   Capital

Chapter V

Methods for elimination of double taxation

Art. 23A   Exemption method
Art. 23B   Credit method

Chapter VI

Special provisions

Art. 24   Non-discrimination
Art. 25   Mutual agreement procedure
Art. 26   Exchange of information
Art. 27   Diplomatic agents and consular officers
Art. 28   Territorial extension

Chapter VII

Final provisions

Art. 29   Entry into force
Art. 30   Termination

TITLE

Convention between (State A) and (State B) for the avoidance of double taxation with respect to taxes on income and on capital

Reproduced with the permission of the organization for Economic Co-operation and Development.

PREAMBLE

Note: The Preamble of the Convention shall be drafted in accordance with the constitutional procedure of both Contracting States.

CHAPTER I

SCOPE OF THE CONVENTION

Article 1

Personal Scope

This Convention shall apply to persons who are residents of one or both of the Contracting States.

Article 2

Taxes Covered

1. This Convention shall apply to taxes on income and on capital imposed on behalf of a Contracting State or of its political subdivisions or local authorities, irrespective of the manner in which they are levied.

2. There shall be regarded as taxes on income and on capital all taxes imposed on total income, on total capital, or on elements of income or of capital, including taxes on gains from the alienation of movable or immovable property, taxes on the total amounts of wages or salaries paid by enterprises, as well as taxes on capital appreciation.

3. The existing taxes to which the Convention shall apply are in particular:

(a) (in State A): . . . .

(b) (in State B): . . . .

4. The Convention shall apply also to any identical or substantially similar taxes which are imposed after the date of signature of the Convention in addition to, or in place of, the existing taxes. At the end of each year, the competent authorities of the Contracting States shall notify each other of changes which have been made in their respective taxation laws.

CHAPTER II

DEFINITIONS

Article 3

General Definitions

1. For the purposes of this Convention, unless the context otherwise requires:

(a) the term "person" includes an individual, a company and any other body of persons;

(b) the term "company" means any body corporate or any entity which is treated as a body corporate for tax purposes;

(c) the terms "enterprise of a Contracting State" and "enterprise of the other Contracting State" mean respectively an enterprise carried on by a resident of a Contracting State and an enterprise carried on by a resident of the other Contracting State;

(d) the term "international traffic" means any transport by a ship or aircraft operated by an enterprise which has its place of effective management in a Contracting State, except when the ship or aircraft is operated solely between places in the other Contracting State;

(e) the term "competent authority" means:

(i) (in State A): . . . .

(ii) (in State B): . . . .

2. As regards the application of the Convention by a Contracting State any term not defined therein shall, unless the context otherwise requires, have the meaning which it has under the law of that State concerning the taxes to which the Convention applies.

Article 4
Resident

1. For the purposes of this Convention, the term "resident of a Contracting State" means any person who, under the laws of that State, is liable to tax therein by reason of his domicile, residence, place of management or any other criterion of a similar nature. But this term does not include any person who is liable to tax in that State in respect only of income from sources in that State or capital situated therein.

2. Where by reason of the provisions of paragraph 1 an individual is a resident of both Contracting States, then his status shall be determined as follows:

(a) he shall be deemed to be a resident of the State in which he has a permanent home available to him; if he has a permanent home available to him in both States, he shall be deemed to be a resident of the State with which his personal and economic relations are closer (centre of vital interests);

(b) if the State in which he has his centre of vital interests cannot be determined, or if he has not a permanent home avilable to him in either State, he shall be deemed to be a resident of the State in which he has an habitual abode;

(c) if he has an habitual abode in both States or in neither of them, he shall be deemed to be a resident of the State of which he is a national;

(d) if he is a national of both States or of neither of them, the competent authorities of the Contracting States shall settle the question by mutual agreement.

3. Where by reason of the provisions of paragraph 1 a person other than an individual is a resident of both Contracting States, then it shall be deemed to be a resident of the State in which its place of effective management is situated.

Article 5
Permanent Establishment

1. For the purposes of this Convention, the term "permanent establishment" means a fixed place of business through which the business of an enterprise is wholly or partly carried on.

2. The term "permanent establishment" includes especially:

(a) a place of management;

(b) a branch;

(c) an office;

(d) a factory;

(e) a workshop; and

(f) a mine, an oil or gas well, a quarry or any other place of extraction of natural resources.

3. A building site or construction or installation project constitutes a permanent establishment only if it lasts more than twelve months.

4. Notwithstanding the preceding provisions of this Article, the term "permanent establishment" shall be deemed not to include:

(a) the use of facilities solely for the purpose of storage, display or delivery of goods or merchandise belonging to the enterprise;

(b) the maintenance of a stock of goods or merchandise belonging to the enterprise solely for the purpose of storage, display or delivery;

(c) the maintenance of a stock of goods or merchandise belonging to the enterprise solely for the purpose of processing by another enterprise;

(d) the maintenance of a fixed place of business solely for the purpose of purchasing goods or merchandise or of collecting information, for the enterprise;

(e) the maintenance of a fixed place of business solely for the purpose of carrying on, for the enterprise, any other activity of a preparatory or auxiliary character;

(f) the maintenance of a fixed place of business solely for any combination of activities mentioned in sub-paragraphs (a) to (e), provided that the overall activity of the fixed place of business resulting from this combination is of a preparatory or auxiliary character.

5. Notwithstanding the provisions of paragraphs 1 and 2, where a person—other than an agent of an independent status to whom paragraph 6 applies—is acting on behalf of an enterprise and has, and habitually exercises, in a Contracting State an authority to conclude contracts in the name of the enterprise, that enterprise shall be deemed to

have a permanent establishment in that State in respect of any activities which that person undertakes for the enterprise, unless the activities of such person are limited to those mentioned in paragraph 4 which, if exercised through a fixed place of business, would not make this fixed place of business a permanent establishment under the provisions of that paragraph:

6. An enterprise shall not be deemed to have a permanent establishment in a Contracting State merely because it carries on business in that State through a broker, general commission agent or any other agent of an independent status, provided that such persons are acting in the ordinary course of their business.

7. The fact that a company which is a resident of a Contracting State controls or is controlled by a company which is a resident of the other Contracting State, or which carries on business in that other State (whether through a permanent establishment or otherwise), shall not of itself constitute either company a permanent establishment of the other.

CHAPTER III

TAXATION OF INCOME

Article 6

Income from Immovable Property

1. Income derived by a resident of a Contracting State from immovable property (including income from agriculture or forestry) situated in the other Contracting State may be taxed in that other State.

2. The term "immovable property" shall have the meaning which it has under the law of the Contracting State in which the property in question is situated. The term shall in any case include property accessory to immovable property, livestock and equipment used in agriculture and forestry, rights to which the provisions of general law respecting landed property apply, usufruct of immovable porperty and rights to variable or fixed payments as consideration for the working of, or the right to work, mineral deposits, sources and other natural resources; ships, boats and aircraft shall not be regarded as immovable property.

3. The provisions of paragraph 1 shall apply to income derived from the direct use, letting, or use in any other form of immovable property.

4. The provisions of paragraphs 1 and 3 shall also apply to the income from immovable property of an enterprise and to income from immovable property used for the performance of independent personal services.

Article 7

Business Profits

1. The profits of an enterprise of a Contracting State shall be taxable only in that State unless the enterprise carries on business in the other Contracting State through a permanent establishment situated therein. If the enterprise carries on business as aforesaid, the profits of the enterprise may be taxed in the other State but only so much of them as is attributable to that permanent establishment.

2. Subject to the provisions of paragraph 3, where an enterprise of a Contracting State carries on business in the other Contracting State through a permanent establishment situated therein, there shall in each Contracting State be attributed to that permanent establishment the profits which it might be expected to make if it were a distinct and separate enterprise engaged in the same or similar activities under the same or similar conditions and dealing wholly independently with the enterprise of which it is a permanent establishment.

3. In determining the profits of a permanent establishment, there shall be allowed as deductions expenses which are incurred for the purposes of the permanent establishment, including executive and general administrative expenses so incurred, whether in the State in which the permanent establishment is situated or elsewhere.

4. Insofar as it has been customary in a Contracting State to determine the profits to be attributed to a permanent establishment on the basis of an apportionment of the total profits of the enterprise to its various parts, nothing in paragraph 2 shall preclude that Contracting State from determining the profits to be taxed by such an apportionment as may be customary; the method of apportionment adopted shall, however, be such that the result shall be in accordance with the principles contained in this Article

5. No profits shall be attributed to a permanent establishment by reason of the mere purchase by that permanent establishment of goods or merchandise for the enterprise.

6. For the purposes of the preceding paragraphs, the profits to be attributed to the permanent establishment shall be determined by the same method year by year unless there is good and sufficient reason to the contrary.

7. Where profits include items of income which are dealt with separately in other Articles of this Convention, then the provisions of those Articles shall not be affected by the provisions of this Article.

Article 8

Shipping, Inland Waterways Transport and Air Transport

1. Profits from the operation of ships or aircraft in international traffic shall be taxable only in the Contracting State in which the place of effective management of the enterprise is situated.

2. Profits from the operation of boats engaged in inland waterways transport shall be taxable only in the Contracting State in which the place of effective management of the enterprise is situated.

3. If the place of effective management of a shipping enterprise or of an inland waterways transport enterprise is aboard a ship or boat, then it shall be deemed to be situated in the Contracting State in which the home harbour of the ship or boat is situated, or, if there is no such home harbour, in the Contracting State of which the operator of the ship or boat is a resident.

4. The provisions of paragraph 1 shall also apply to profits from the participation in a pool, a joint business or an international operating agency.

Article 9

Associated Enterprises

1. Where

(a) an enterprise of a Contracting State participates directly or indirectly in the management, control or capital of an enterprise of the other Contracting State, or

(b) the same persons participate directly or indirectly in the management, control or capital of an enterprise of a Contracting State and an enterprise of the other Contracting State,

and in either case conditions are made or imposed between the two enterprises in their commercial or financial relations which differ from those which would be made between independent enterprises, then any profits which would, but for those conditions, have accrued to one of the enterprises, but, by reason of those conditions, have not so accrued, may be included in the profits of that enterprise and taxed accordingly.

2. Where a Contracting State includes in the profits of an enterprise of that State— and taxes accordingly—profits on which an enterprise of the other Contracting State has been charged to tax in that other State and the profits so included are profits which would have accrued to the enterprise of the first-mentioned State if the conditions made between the two enterprises had been those which would have been made between independent enterprises, then that other State shall make an appropriate adjustment to the amount of the tax charged therein on those profits. In determining such adjustment, due regard shall be had to the other provisions of this Convention and the competent authorities of the Contracting States shall if necessary consult each other.

Article 10

Dividends

1. Dividends paid by a company which is a resident of a Contracting State to a resident of the other Contracting State may be taxed in that other State.

2. However, such dividends may also be taxed in the Contracting State of which the company paying the dividends is a resident and according to the laws of that State, but if the recipient is the beneficial owner of the dividends the tax so charged shall not exceed:

(a) 5 per cent of the gross amount of the dividends if the beneficial owner is a company (other than a partnership) which holds directly at least 25 per cent of the capital of the company paying the dividends;

(b) 15 per cent of the gross amount of the dividends in all other cases.

The competent authorities of the Contracting States shall by mutual agreement settle the mode of application of these limitations.

This paragraph shall not affect the taxation of the company in respect of the profits out of which the dividends are paid.

3. The term "dividends" as used in this Article means income from shares, "jouissance" shares or "jouissance" rights, mining shares, founders' shares or other rights, not being debt-claims, participating in profits, as well as income from other corporate rights which is subjected to the same taxation treatment as income from shares by the laws of the State of which the company making the distribution is a resident.

4. The provisions of paragraphs 1 and 2 shall not apply if the beneficial owner of the dividends, being a resident of a Contracting State, carries on business in the other Contracting State of which the company paying the dividends is a resident, through a permanent establishment situated therein, or performs in that other State independent personal services from a fixed base situated therein, and the holding in respect of which the dividends are paid is effectively connected with such permanent establishment or fixed base. In such case the provisions of Article 7 or Article 14, as the case may be, shall apply.

5. Where a company which is a resident of a Contracting State derives profits or income from the other Contracting State, that other State may not impose any tax on the dividends paid by the company, except insofar as such dividends are paid to a resident of that other State or insofar as the holding in respect of which the dividends are paid is effectively connected with a permanent establishment or a fixed base situated in that other State, nor subject the company's undistributed profits to a tax on the company's undistributed profits, even if the dividends paid or the undistributed profits consist wholly or partly of profits or income arising in such other State.

Article 11

Interest

1. Interest arising in a Contracting State and paid to a resident of the other Contracting State may be taxed in that other State.

2. However, such interest may also be taxed in the Contracting State in which it arises and according to the laws of that State, but if the recipient is the beneficial owner of the interest the tax so charged shall not exceed 10 per cent of the gross amount of the interest. The competent authorities of the Contracting States shall by mutual agreement settle the mode of application of this limitation.

3. The term "interest" as used in this Article means income from debt-claims of every kind, whether or not secured by mortgage and whether or not carrying a right to participate in the debtor's profits, and in particular, income from government securities and income from bonds or debentures, including premiums and prizes attaching to such securities, bonds or debentures. Penalty charges for late payment shall not be regarded as interest for the purpose of this Article.

4. The provisions of paragraphs 1 and 2 shall not apply if the beneficial owner of the interest, being a resident of a Contracting State, carries on business in the other Contracting State in which the interest arises, through a permanent establishment situated therein, or performs in that other State independent personal services from a fixed base situated therein, and the debt-claim in respect of which the interest is paid is effectively connected with such permanent establishment or fixed base. In such case the provisions of Article 7 or Article 14, as the case may be, shall apply.

5. Interest shall be deemed to arise in a Contracting State when the payer is that State itself, a political subdivision, a local authority or a resident of that State. Where, however, the person paying the interest, whether he is a resident of a Contracting State or not, has in a Contracting State a permanent establishment or a fixed base in connection with which the indebtedness on which the interest is paid was incurred, and such interest is borne by such permanent establishment or fixed base, then such interest shall be deemed to arise in the State in which the permanent establishment or fixed base is situated.

6. Where, by reason of a special relationship between the payer and the beneficial owner or between both of them and some other person, the amount of the interest, having regard to the debt-claim for which it is paid, exceeds the amount which would have been agreed upon by the payer and the beneficial owner in the absence of such relationship, the provisions of this Article shall apply only to the last-mentioned amount. In such case, the excess part of the payments shall remain taxable according to the laws of each Contracting State, due regard being had to the other provisions of this Convention.

Article 12

Royalties

1. Royalties arising in a Contracting State and paid to a resident of the other Contracting State shall be taxable only in that other State if such resident is the beneficial owner of the royalties.

2. The term "royalties" as used in this Article means payments of any kind received as a consideration for the use of, or the right to use, any copyright of literary, artistic or scientific work including cinematograph films, any patent, trade mark, design or model, plan, secret formula or process, or for the use of, or the right to use, industrial, commercial, or scientific equipment, or for information concerning industrial, commercial or scientific experience.

3. The provisions of paragraph 1 shall not apply if the beneficial owner of the royalties, being a resident of a Contracting State, carries on business in the other Contracting State in which the royalties arise, through a permanent establishment situated therein, or performs in that other State independent personal services from a fixed base situated therein, and the right or property in respect of which the royalties are paid is effectively connected with such permanent establishment or fixed base. In such case the provisions of Article 7 or Article 14, as the case may be, shall apply.

4. Where, by reason of a special relationship between the payer and the beneficial owner or between both of them and some other person, the amount of the royalties, having regard to the use, right or information for which they are paid, exceeds the amount which would have been agreed upon by the payer and the beneficial owner in the absence of such relationship, the provisions of this Article shall apply only to the last-mentioned amount. In such case, the excess part of the payments shall remain taxable according to the laws of each Contracting State, due regard being had to the other provisions of this Convention.

Article 13

Capital Gains

1. Gains derived by a resident of a Contracting State from the alienation of immovable property referred to in Article 6 and situated in the other Contracting State may be taxed in that other State.

2. Gains from the alienation of movable property forming part of the business property of a permanent establishment which an enterprise of a Contracting State has in the other Contracting State or of movable property pertaining to a fixed base available to a resident of a Contracting State in the other Contracting State for the purpose of performing independent personal services, including such gains from the alienation of such a permanent establishment (alone or with the whole enterprise) or of such fixed base, may be taxed in that other State.

3. Gains from the alienation of ships or aircraft operated in international traffic, boats engaged in inland waterways transport or movable property pertaining to the operation of such ships, aircraft or boats, shall be taxable only in the Contracting State in which the place of effective management of the enterprise is situated.

4. Gains from the alienation of any property other than that referred to in paragraphs 1, 2 and 3, shall be taxable only in the Contracting State of which the alienator is a resident.

Article 14

Independent Personal Services

1. Income derived by a resident of a Contracting State in respect of professional services or other activities of an independent character shall be taxable only in that State unless he has a fixed base regularly available to him in the other Contracting State for the purpose of performing his activities. If he has such a fixed base, the income may be taxed in the other State but only so much of it as is attributable to that fixed base.

2. The term "professional services" includes especially independent scientific, literary, artistic, educational or teaching activities as well as the independent activities of physicians, lawyers, engineers, architects, dentists and accountants.

Article 15

Dependent Personal Services

1. Subject to the provisions of Articles 16, 18 and 19, salaries, wages and other similar remuneration derived by a resident of a Contracting State in respect of an employment shall be taxable only in that State unless the employment is exercised in the

other Contracting State. If the employment is so exercised, such remuneration as is derived therefrom may be taxed in that other State.

2. Notwithstanding the provisions of paragraph 1, remuneration derived by a resident of a Contracting State in respect of an employment exercised in the other Contracting State shall be taxable only in the first-mentioned State if:

(a) the recipient is present in the other State for a period or periods not exceeding in the aggregate 183 days in the fiscal year concerned, and

(b) the remuneration is paid by, or on behalf of, an employer who is not a resident of the other State, and

(c) the remuneration is not borne by a permanent establishment or a fixed base which the employer has in the other State.

3. Notwithstanding the preceding provisions of this Article, remuneration derived in respect of an employment exercised abroad a ship or aircraft operated in international traffic, or abroad a boat engaged in inland waterways transport, may be taxed in the Contracting State in which the place of effective management of the enterprise is situated.

Article 16
Directors' Fees

Directors' fees and other similar payments derived by a resident of a Contracting State in his capacity as a member of the board of directors of a company which is a resident of the other Contracting State may be taxed in that other State.

Article 17
Artistes and Athletes

1. Notwithstanding the provisions of Articles 14 and 15, income derived by a resident of a Contracting State as an entertainer, such as a theatre, motion picture, radio or television artiste, or a musician, or as an athlete, from his personal activities as such exercised in the other Contracting State, may be taxed in that other State.

2. Where income in respect of personal activities exercised by an entertainer or an athlete in his capacity as such accrues not to the entertainer or athlete himself but to another person, that income may, notwithstanding the provisions of Articles 7, 14 and 15, be taxed in the Contracting State in which the activities of the entertainer or athlete are exercised.

Article 18
Pensions

Subject to the provisions of paragraph 2 of Article 19, pensions and other similar remuneration paid to a resident of a Contracting State in consideration of past employment shall be taxable only in that State.

Article 19
Government Service

1. (a) Remuneration, other than a pension, paid by a Contracting State or a political subdivision or a local authority thereof to an individual in respect of services rendered to that State or subdivision or authority shall be taxable only in that State.

(b) However, such remuneration shall be taxable only in the other Contracting State if the services are rendered in that State and the individual is a resident of that State who:

(i) is a national of that State; or

(ii) did not become a resident of that State solely for the purpose of rendering the services.

2. (a) Any pension paid by, or out of funds created by, a Contracting State or a political subdivision or a local authority thereof to an individual in respect of services rendered to that State or subdivision or authority shall be taxable only in that State.

(b) However, such pension shall be taxable only in the other Contracting State if the individual is a resident of, and a national of, that State.

3. The provisions of Articles 15, 16 and 18 shall apply to remuneration and pensions in respect of services rendered in connection with a business carried on by a Contracting State or a political subdivision or a local authority thereof.

Article 20

Students

Payments which a student or business apprentice who is or was immediately before visiting a Contracting State a resident of the other Contracting State and who is present in the first-mentioned State solely for the purpose of his education or training receives for the purpose of his maintenance, education or training shall not be taxed in that State, provided that such payments arise from sources outside that State.

Article 21

Other Income

1. Items of income of a resident of a Contracting State, wherever arising, not dealt with in the foregoing Articles of this Convention shall be taxable only in that State.

2. The provisions of paragraph 1 shall not apply to income, other than income from immovable property as defined in paragraph 2 of Article 6, if the recipient of such income, being a resident of a Contracting State, carries on business in the other Contracting State through a permanent establishment situated therein, or performs in that other State independent personal services from a fixed base situated therein, and the right or property in respect of which the income is paid is effectively connected with such permanent establishment or fixed base. In such case the provisions of Article 7 or Article 14, as the case may be, shall apply.

CHAPTER IV

TAXATION OF CAPITAL

Article 22

Capital

1. Capital represented by immovable property referred to in Article 6, owned by a resident of a Contracting State and situated in the other Contracting State, may be taxed in that other State.

2. Capital represented by movable property forming part of the business property of a permanent establishment which an enterprise of a Contracting State has in the other Contracting State or by movable property pertaining to a fixed base available to a resident of a Contracting State in the other Contracting State for the purpose of performing independent personal services, may be taxed in that other State.

3. Capital represented by ships and aircraft operated in international traffic and by boats engaged in inland waterways transport, and by movable property pertaining to the operation of such ships, aircraft and boats, shall be taxable only in the Contracting State in which the place of effective management of the enterprise is situated.

4. All other elements of capital of a resident of a Contracting State shall be taxable only in that State.

CHAPTER V

METHODS FOR ELIMINATION OF DOUBLE TAXATION

Article 23A

Exemption Method

1. Where a resident of a Contracting State derives income or owns capital which, in accordance with the provisions of this Convention, may be taxed in the other Contracting State, the first-mentioned State shall, subject to the provisions of paragraphs 2 and 3, exempt such income or capital from tax.

2. Where a resident of a Contracting State derives items of income which, in accordance with the provisions of Articles 10 and 11, may be taxed in the other Contracting State, the first-mentioned State shall allow as a deduction from the tax on the income of that resident an amount equal to the tax paid in that other State. Such deduction shall not, however, exceed that part of the tax, as computed before the deduction is given, which is attributable to such items of income derived from that other State.

3. Where in accordance with any provision of the Convention income derived or capital owned by a resident of a Contracting State is exempt from tax in that State, such State may nevertheless, in calculating the amount of tax on the remaining income or capital of such resident, take into account the exempted income or capital.

Article 23B
Credit Method

·1. Where a resident of a Contracting State derives income or owns capital which, in accordance with the provisions of this Convention, may be taxed in the other Contracting State, the first-mentioned State shall allow:

(a) as a deduction from the tax on the income of that resident, an amount equal to the income tax paid in that other State;

(b) as a deduction from the tax on the capital of that resident, an amount equal to the capital tax paid in that other State.

Such deduction in either case shall not, however, exceed that part of the income tax or capital tax, as computed before the deduction is given, which is attributable, as the case may be, to the income or the capital which may be taxed in that other State.

2. Where in accordance with any provision of the Convention income derived or capital owned by a resident of a Contracting State is exempt from tax in that State, such State may nevertheless, in calculating the amount of tax on the remaining income or capital of such resident, take into account the exempted income or capital.

CHAPTER VI

SPECIAL PROVISIONS

Article 24
Non-discrimination

1. Nationals of a Contracting State shall not be subjected in the other Contracting State to any taxation or any requirement connected therewith, which is other or more burdensome than the taxation and connected requirements to which nationals of that other State in the same circumstances are or may be subjected. This provision shall, notwithstanding the provisions of Article 1, also apply to persons who are not residents of one or both of the Contracting States.

2. The term "nationals" means:

(a) all individuals possessing the nationality of a Contracting State;

(b) all legal persons, partnerships and associations deriving their status as such from the laws in force in a Contracting State.

3. Stateless persons who are residents of a Contracting State shall not be subjected in either Contracting State to any taxation or any requirement connected therewith, which is other or more burdensome than the taxation and connected requirements to which nationals of the State concerned in the same circumstances are or may be subjected.

4. The taxation on a permanent establishment which an enterprise of a Contracting State has in the other Contracting State shall not be less favourably levied in that other State than the taxation levied on enterprises of that other State carrying on the same activities. This provision shall not be construed as obliging a Contracting State to grant to residents of the other Contracting State any personal allowances, reliefs and reductions for taxation purposes on account of civil status or family responsibilities which it grants to its own residents.

5. Except where the provisions of paragraph 1 of Article 9, paragraph 6 of Article 11, or paragraph 4 of Article 12, apply, interest, royalties and other disbursements paid by an enterprise of a Contracting State to a resident of the other Contracting State shall, for the purpose of determining the taxable profits of such enterprise, be deductible under the same conditions as if they had been paid to a resident of the first-mentioned State. Similarly, any debts of an enterprise of a Contracting State to a resident of the other Contracting State shall, for the purpose of determining the taxable capital of such enterprise, be deductible under the same conditions as if they had been contracted to a resident of the first-mentioned State.

6. Enterprises of a Contracting State, the capital of which is wholly or partly owned or controlled, directly or indirectly, by one or more residents of the other Contracting State, shall not be subjected in the first-mentioned State to any taxation or any requirement connected therewith which is other or more burdensome than the taxation and connected requirements to which other similar enterprises of the first-mentioned State are or may be subjected.

7. The provisions of this Article shall, notwithstanding the provisions of Article 2, apply to taxes of every kind and description.

Article 25
Mutual Agreement Procedure

1. Where a person considers that the actions of one or both of the Contracting States result or will result for him in taxation not in accordance with the provisions of this Convention, he may, irrespective of the remedies provided by the domestic law of those States, present his case to the competent authority of the Contracting State of which he is a resident or, if his case comes under paragraph 1 of Article 24, to that of the Contracting State of which he is a national. The case must be presented within three years from the first notification of the action resulting in taxation not in accordance with the provisions of the Convention.

2. The competent authority shall endeavour, if the objection appears to it to be justified and if it is not itself able to arrive at a satisfactory solution, to resolve the case by mutual agreement with the competent authority of the other Contracting State, with a view to the avoidance of taxation which is not in accordance with the Convention. Any agreement reached shall be implemented notwithstanding any time limits in the domestic law of the Contracting States.

3. The competent authorities of the Contracting States shall endeavour to resolve by mutual agreement any difficulties or doubts arising as to the interpretation or application of the Convention. They may also consult together for the elimination of double taxation in cases not provided for in the Convention.

4. The competent authorities of the Contracting States may communicate with each other directly for the purpose of reaching an agreement in the sense of the preceding paragraphs. When it seems advisable in order to reach agreement to have an oral exchange of opinions, such exchange may take place through a Commission consisting of representatives of the competent authorities of the Contracting States.

Article 26
Exchange of Information

1. The competent authorities of the Contracting States shall exchange such information as is necessary for carrying out the provisions of this Convention or of the domestic laws of the Contracting States concerning taxes covered by the Convention insofar as the taxation thereunder is not contrary to the Convention. The exchange of information is not restricted by Article 1. Any information received by a Contracting State shall be treated as secret in the same manner as information obtained under the domestic laws of that State and shall be disclosed only to persons or authorities (including courts and administrative bodies) involved in the assessment or collection of, the enforcement or prosecution in respect of, or the determination of appeals in relation to, the taxes covered by the Convention. Such persons or authorities shall use the information only for such purposes. They may disclose the information in public court proceedings or in judicial decisions.

2. In no case shall the provisions of paragraph 1 be construed so as to impose on a Contracting State the obligation:

   (a) to carry out administrative measures at variance with the laws and administrative practice of that or of the other Contracting State;

   (b) to supply information which is not obtainable under the laws or in the normal course of the administration of that or of the other Contracting State;

   (c) to supply information which would disclose any trade, business, industrial, commercial or professional secret or trade process, or information, the disclosure of which would be contrary to public policy (ordre public).

Article 27
Diplomatic Agents and Consular Officers

Nothing in this Convention shall affect the fiscal privileges of diplomatic agents or consular officers under the general rules of international law or under the provisions of special agreements.

Article 28
Territorial Extension

1. This Convention may be extended, either in its entirety or with any necessary modifications [to any part of the territory of (State A) or of (State B) which is specifically excluded from the application of the Convention or], to any State or territory for whose international relations (State A) or (State B) is responsible, which imposes taxes substantially similar in character to those to which the Convention applies. Any such exten-

sion shall take effect from such date and subject to such modifications and conditions, including conditions as to termination, as may be specified and agreed between the Contracting States in notes to be exchanged through diplomatic channels or in any other manner in accordance with their constitutional procedures.

2. Unless otherwise agreed by both Contracting States, the termination of the Convention by one of them under Article 30 shall also terminate, in the manner provided for in that Article, the application of the Convention [to any part of the territory of (State A) or of (State B) or] to any State or territory to which it has been extended under this Article.

Note: The words between brackets are of relevance when, by special provision, a part of the territory of a Contracting State is excluded from the application of the Convention.

CHAPTER VII

FINAL PROVISIONS

Article 29

Entry into Force

1. This Convention shall be ratified and the instruments of ratification shall be exchanged at .... as soon as possible.

2. The Convention shall enter into force upon the exchange of instruments of ratification and its provisions shall have effect:

    (*a*) (in State A): ....

    (*b*) (in State B): ....

Article 30

Termination

This Convention shall remain in force until terminated by a Contracting State. Either Contracting State may terminate the Convention, through diplomatic channels, by giving notice of termination at least six months before the end of any calendar year after the year .... In such event, the Convention shall cease to have effect:

    (*a*) (in State A): ....

    (*b*) (in State B): ....

Terminal Clause

Note: The terminal clause concerning the signing shall be drafted in accordance with the constitutional procedure of both Contracting States.

MODEL OF _____, 1981

CONVENTION BETWEEN THE UNITED STATES OF AMERICA AND _____ FOR THE AVOIDANCE OF DOUBLE TAXATION AND THE PREVENTION OF FISCAL EVASION WITH RESPECT TO TAXES ON INCOME AND CAPITAL

The United States of America and _____, desiring to conclude a convention for the avoidance of double taxation and the prevention of fiscal evasion with respect to taxes on income and capital, have agreed as follows:

Article 1

GENERAL SCOPE

1. This Convention shall apply to persons who are residents of one or both of the Contracting States, except as otherwise provided in the Convention.

2. The Convention shall not restrict in any manner any exclusion, exemption, deduction, credit, or other allowance now or hereafter accorded

    a) by the laws of either Contracting State; or

    b) by any other agreement between the Contracting States.

3. Notwithstanding any provision of the Convention except paragraph 4, a Contracting State may tax its residents (as determined under Article 4 (Residence)), and by reason of citizenship may tax its citizens, as if the Convention had not come into effect. For this purpose, the term "citizen" shall include a former citizen whose loss of citizenship had as one of its principal purposes the avoidance of income tax, but only for a period of 10 years following such loss.

4. The provisions of paragraph 3 shall not affect

    a) the benefits conferred by a Contracting State under paragraph 2 of Article 9 (Associated Enterprises), under paragraphs 1 b) and 4 of Article 18 (Pensions, Annuities, Alimony, and Child Support), and under Articles 23 (Relief From Double Taxation), 24 (Non-Discrimination), and 25 (Mutual Agreement Procedure); and

b) the benefits conferred by a Contracting State under Articles 19 (Government Service), 20 (Students and Trainees), and 27 (Diplomatic Agents and Consular Officers), upon individuals who are neither citizens of, nor have immigrant status in, that State.

Article 2

TAXES COVERED

1. The existing taxes to which this Convention shall apply are

a) in the United States: the Federal income taxes imposed by the Internal Revenue Code (but excluding the accumulated earnings tax, the personal holding company tax, and social security taxes), and the excise taxes imposed on insurance premiums paid to foreign insurers and with respect to private foundations. The Convention shall, however, apply to the excise taxes imposed on insurance premiums paid to foreign insurers only to the extent that the risks covered by such premiums are not reinsured with a person not entitled to the benefits of this or any other convention which applies to these taxes;

b) in _____: _____

_____.

2. The Convention shall apply also to any identical or substantially similar taxes which are imposed after the date of signature of the Convention in addition to, or in place of, the existing taxes. The competent authorities of the Contracting State shall notify each other of any significant changes which have been made in their respective taxation laws and of any official published material concerning the application of the Convention, including explanations, regulations, rulings, or judicial decisions.

Article 3

GENERAL DEFINITIONS

1. For the purposes of this Convention, unless the context otherwise requires

a) the term "person" includes an individual, an estate, a trust, a partnership, a company, and any other body of persons;

b) the term "company" means any body corporate or any entity which is treated as a body corporate for tax purposes;

c) the terms "enterprise of a Contracting State" and "enterprise of the other Contracting State" mean respectively an enterprise carried on by a resident of a Contracting State and an enterprise carried on by a resident of the other Contracting State;

d) the term "international traffic" means any transport by a ship or aircraft, except when such transport is solely between places in the other Contracting State;

e) the term "competent authority" means

(i) in the United States: the Secretary of the Treasury or his delegate; and

(ii) in _____: _____

_____;

f) the term "United States" means the United States of America, but does not include Puerto Rico, the Virgin Islands, Guam, or any other United States possession or territory;

g) the term _____ means _____.

2. As regards the application of the Convention by a Contracting State any term not defined therein shall, unless the context otherwise requires or the competent authorities agree to a common meaning pursuant to the provisions of Article 25 (Mutual Agreement Procedure), have the meaning which it has under the laws of the State concerning the taxes to which the Convention applies.

Article 4
RESIDENCE

1. For the purposes of this Convention, the term "resident of a Contracting State" means any person who, under the laws of that State, is liable to tax therein by reason of his domicile, residence, citizenship, place of management, place of incorporation, or any other criterion of a similar nature, provided, however, that

a) this term does not include any person who is liable to tax in that State in respect only of income from sources in that State or capital situated therein; and

b) in the case of income derived or paid by a partnership, estate, or trust, this term applies only to the extent that the income derived by such partnership, estate, or trust is subject to tax in that State as the income of a resident, either in its hands or in the hands of its partners or beneficiaries.

2. Where by reason of the provisions of paragraph 1, an individual is a resident of both Contracting States, then his status shall be determined as follows:

a) he shall be deemed to be a resident of the State in which he has a permanent home available to him: if he has a permanent home available to him in both States, he shall be deemed to be a resident of the State with which his personal and economic relations are closer (center of vital interests);

b) if the State in which he has his center of vital interests cannot be determined, or if he does not have a permanent home available to him in either State, he shall be deemed to be a resident of the State in which he has an habitual abode;

c) if he has an habitual abode in both States or in neither of them, he shall be deemed to be a resident of the State of which he is a national;

d) if he is a national of both States or of neither of them, the competent authorities of the Contracting States shall settle the question by mutual agreement.

3. Where by reason of the provisions of paragraph 1 a company is a resident of both Contracting States, then if it is created under the laws of a Contracting State or a political subdivision thereof, it shall be deemed to be a resident of that State.

4. Where by reason of the provisions of paragraph 1 a person other than an individual or a company is a resident of both Contracting States, the competent authorities of the Contracting States shall settle the question by mutual agreement and determine the mode of application of the Convention to such person.

Article 5
PERMANENT ESTABLISHMENT

1. For the purposes of this Convention, the term "permanent establishment" means a fixed place of business through which the business of an enterprise is wholly or partly carried on.

2. The term "permanent establishment" includes especially

a) a place of management;

b) a branch;

c) an office;

d) a factory;

e) a workshop; and

f) a mine, an oil or gas well, a quarry, or any other place of extraction of natural resources.

3. A building site or construction or installation project, or an installation or drilling rig or ship used for the exploration or exploitation of natural resources, constitutes a permanent establishment only if it lasts more than twelve months.

4. Notwithstanding the preceding provisions of this Article, the term "permanent establishment" shall be deemed not to include

a) the use of facilities solely for the purpose of storage, display, or delivery of goods or merchandise belonging to the enterprise;

b) the maintenance of a stock of goods or merchandise belonging to the enterprise solely for the purpose of storage, display, or delivery;

c) the maintenance of a stock of goods or merchandise belonging to the enterprise solely for the purpose of processing by another enterprise;

d) the maintenance of a fixed place of business solely for the purpose of purchasing goods or merchandise, or of collecting information, for the enterprise;

e) the maintenance of a fixed place of business solely for the purpose of carrying on, for the enterprise, any other activity of a preparatory or auxiliary character;

.f) the maintenance of a fixed place of business solely for any combination of the activities mentioned in subparagraphs a) to e).

5. Notwithstanding the provisions of paragraphs 1 and 2, where a person—other than an agent of an independent status to whom paragraph 6 applies—is acting on behalf of an enterprise and has and habitually exercises in a Contracting State an authority to conclude contracts in the name of the enterprise, that enterprise shall be deemed to have a permanent establishment in that State in respect of any activities which that person undertakes for the enterprise, unless the activities of such person are limited to those mentioned in paragraph 4 which, if exercised through a fixed place of business, would not make this fixed place of business a permanent establishment under the provisions of that paragraph.

6. An enterprise shall not be deemed to have a permanent establishment in a Contracting State merely because it carries on business in that State through a broker, general commission agent, or any other agent of an independent status, provided that such persons are acting in the ordinary course of their business.

7. The fact that a company which is a resident of a Contracting State controls or is controlled by a company which is a resident of the other Contracting State, or which carries on business in that other State (whether through

a permanent establishment or otherwise), shall not of itself constitute either company a permanent establishment of the other.

Article 6

INCOME FROM REAL PROPERTY (IMMOVABLE PROPERTY)

1. Income derived by a resident of a Contracting State from real property (including income from agriculture or forestry) situated in the other Contracting State may be taxed in that other State.

2. The term "real property" shall have the meaning which it has under the law of the Contracting State in which the property in question is situated.

3. The provisions of paragraph 1 shall apply to income derived from the direct use, letting, or use in any other form of real property.

4. The provisions of paragraphs 1 and 3 shall also apply to the income from real property of an enterprise and to income from real property used for the performance of independent personal services.

5. A resident of a Contracting State who is liable to tax in the other Contracting State on income from real property situated in the other Contracting State may elect for any taxable year to compute the tax on such income on a net basis as if such income were attributable to a permanent establishment in such other State. Any such election shall be binding for the taxable year of the election and all subsequent taxable years unless the competent authorities of the Contracting States, pursuant to a request by the taxpayer made to the competent authority of the Contracting State in which the taxpayer is a resident, agree to terminate the election.

Article 7

BUSINESS PROFITS

1. The business profits of an enterprise of a Contracting State shall be taxable only in that State unless the enterprise carries on business in the other Contracting State through a permanent establishment situated therein. If the enterprise carries on business as aforesaid, the business profits of the enterprise may be taxed in the other State but only so much of them as is attributable to that permanent establishment.

2. Subject to the provisions of paragraph 3, where an enterprise of a Contracting State carries on business in the other Contracting State through a permanent establishment situated therein, there shall in each Contracting State be attributed to that permanent establishment the business profits which it might be expected to make if it were a distinct and independent enterprise engaged in the same or similar activities under the same or similar conditions.

3. In determining the business profits of a permanent establishment, there shall be allowed as deductions expenses which are incurred for the purposes of the permanent establishment, including a reasonable allocation of executive and general administrative expenses, research and development expenses, interest, and other expenses incurred for the purposes of the enterprise as a whole (or the part thereof which includes the permanent establishment), whether incurred in the State in which the permanent establishment is situated or elsewhere.

4. No business profits shall be attributed to a permanent establishment by reason of the mere purchase by that permanent establishment of goods or merchandise for the enterprise.

5. For the purposes of this Convention, the business profits to be attributed to the permanent establishment shall include only the profits derived from the assets or activities of the permanent establishment and shall be determined by the same method year by year unless there is good and sufficient reason to the contrary.

6. Where business profits include items of income which are dealt with separately in other Articles of the Convention, then the provisions of those Articles shall not be affected by the provisions of this Article.

7. For the purposes of the Convention, the term "business profits" means income derived from any trade or business, including the rental of tangible personal property and the rental or licensing of cinematographic films or films or tapes used for radio or television broadcasting.

Article 8
SHIPPING AND AIR TRANSPORT

1. Profits of an enterprise of a Contracting State from the operation of ships or aircraft in international traffic shall be taxable only in that State.

2. For the purposes of this Article, profits from the operation of ships or aircraft in international traffic include profits derived from the rental of ships or aircraft if such ships or aircraft are operated in international traffic by the lessee or if such rental profits are incidental to other profits described in paragraph 1.

3. Profits of an enterprise of a Contracting State from the use, maintenance, or rental of containers (including trailers, barges, and related equipment for the transport of containers) used in international traffic shall be taxable only in that State.

4. The provisions of paragraphs 1 and 3 shall also apply to profits from participation in a pool, a joint business, or an international operating agency.

Article 9
ASSOCIATED ENTERPRISES

1. Where

(a) an enterprise of a Contracting State participates directly or indirectly in the management, control or capital of an enterprise of the other Contracting State; or

(b) the same persons participate directly or indirectly in the management, control, or capital of an enterprise of a Contracting State and an enterprise of the other Contracting State,

and in either case conditions are made or imposed between the two enterprises in their commercial or financial relations which differ from those which would be made between independent enterprises, then any profits which, but for those conditions would have accrued to one of the enterprises, but by reason of those conditions have not so accrued, may be included in the profits of that enterprise and taxed accordingly.

2. Where a Contracting State includes in the profits of an enterprise of that State, and taxes accordingly, profits on which an enterprise of the other Contracting State has been charged to tax in that other State, and the profits so included are profits which would have accrued to the enterprise of the first-mentioned State if the conditions made between the two enterprises had been those which would have been made between independent enterprises, then that other State shall make an appropriate adjustment to the amount of the tax charged therein on those profits. In determining such adjustment, due regard shall be paid to the other provisions of this Convention and the competent authorities of the Contracting States shall if necessary consult each other.

3. The provisions of paragraph 1 shall not limit any provisions of the law of either Contracting State which permit the distribution, apportionment, or allocation of income, deductions, credits, or allowances between persons, whether or not residents of a Contracting State, owned or controlled directly or indirectly by the same interests when necessary in order to prevent evasion of taxes or clearly to reflect the income of any of such persons.

Article 10

DIVIDENDS

1. Dividends paid by a company which is a resident of a Contracting State to a resident of the other Contracting State may be taxed in that other State.

2. However, such dividends may also be taxed in the Contracting State of which the company paying the dividends is a resident, and according to the laws of that State, but if the beneficial owner of the dividends is a resident of the other Contracting State, the tax so charged shall not exceed

a) 5 percent of the gross amount of the dividends if the beneficial owner is a company which owns at least 10 percent of the voting stock of the company paying the dividends;

b) 15 percent of the gross amount of the dividends in all other cases.

This paragraph shall not affect the taxation of the company in respect of the profits out of which the dividends are paid.

3. The term "dividends" as used in this Article means income from shares or other rights, not being debt-claims, participating in profits, as well as income from other corporate rights which is subjected to the same taxation treatment as income from shares by the laws of the State of which the company making the distribution is a resident.

4. The provisions of paragraph 2 shall not apply if the beneficial owner of the dividends, being a resident of a Contracting State, carries on business in the other Contracting State, of which the company paying the dividends is a resident, through a permanent establishment situated therein, or performs in that other State independent personal services from a fixed base situated therein, and the dividends are attributable to such permanent establishment or fixed base. In such case the provisions of Article 7 (Business Profits) or Article 14 (Independent Personal Services), as the case may be, shall apply.

5. A Contracting State may not impose any tax on dividends paid by a company which is not a resident of that State, except insofar as

a) the dividends are paid to a resident of that State.

b) the dividends are attributable to a permanent establishment or a fixed base situated in that State, or

c) the dividends are paid out of profits attributable to one or more permanent establishments of such company in that State, provided that the gross income of the company attributable to such permanent establishment constituted at least 50 percent of the company's gross income from all sources.

Where subparagraph c) applies and subparagraphs a) and b) do not apply, the tax shall be subject to the limitations of paragraph 2.

Article 11
INTEREST

1. Interest derived and beneficially owned by a resident of a Contracting State shall be taxable only in that State.

2. The term "interest" as used in the Convention means income from debt-claims of every kind, whether or not secured by mortgage, and whether or not carrying a right to participate in the debtor's profits, and in particular, income from government securities, and income from bonds or debentures, including premiums or prizes attaching to such securities, bonds, or debentures. Penalty charges for late payment shall not be regarded as interest for the purposes of the Convention.

3. The provisions of paragraph 1 shall not apply if the beneficial owner of the interest, being a resident of a Contracting State, carries on business in the other Contracting State, in which the interest arises, through a permanent establishment situated therein, or performs in that other State independent personal services from a fixed base situated therein, and the interest is attributable to such permanent establishment or fixed base. In such case the provisions of Article 7 (Business Profits) or Article 14 (Independent Personal Services), as the case may be, shall apply.

4. Interest shall be deemed to arise in a Contracting State when the payer is that State itself or a political subdivision, local authority, or resident of that State. Where, however, the person paying the interest, whether he is a resident of a Contracting State or not, has in a Contracting State a permanent establishment or a fixed base in connection with which the indebtedness on which the interest is paid was incurred, and such interest is borne by such permanent establishment or fixed base, then such interest shall be deemed to arise in the State in which the permanent establishment or fixed base is situated.

5. Where, by reason of a special relationship between the payer and the beneficial owner or between both of them and some other person, the amount of the interest, having regard to the debt-claim for which it is paid, exceeds the amount which would have been agreed upon by the payer and the beneficial owner in the absence of such relationship, the provisions of this Article shall apply only to the last-mentioned amount. In such case the excess part of the payments shall remain taxable according to the laws of each Contracting State, due regard being had to the other provisions of the Convention.

6. A Contracting State may not impose any tax on interest paid by a resident of the other Contracting State, except insofar as

a) the interest is paid to a resident of the first-mentioned State;

b) the interest is attributable to permanent establishment or a fixed base situated in the first-mentioned State; or

c) the interest arises in the first-mentioned State and is not paid to a resident of the other State.

Article 12

ROYALTIES

1. Royalties derived and beneficially owned by a resident of a Contracting State shall be taxable only in that State.

2. The term "royalties" as used in this Convention means payments of any kind received as a consideration for the use of, or the right to use, any copyright of literary, artistic, or scientific work (but not including cinematographic films or films or tapes used for radio or television broadcasting), any patent, trademark, design or model, plan, secret formula or process, or other like right or property, or for information concerning industrial, commercial, or scientific experience. The term "royalties" also includes gains derived from the alienation of any such right or property which are contingent on the productivity, use, or disposition thereof.

3. The provisions of paragraph 1 shall not apply if the beneficial owner of the royalties, being a resident of a Contracting State, carries on business in the other Contracting State, in which the royalties arise, through a permanent establishment situated therein, or performs in that other State independent personal services from a fixed base situated therein, and the royalties are attributable to such permanent establishment or fixed base. In such case the provisions of Article 7 (Business Profits) or Article 14 (Independent Personal Services), as the case may be, shall apply.

4. Where, by reason of a special relationship between the payer and the beneficial owner or between both of them and some other person, the amount of the royalties, having regard to the use, right, or information for which they are paid, exceeds the amount which would have been agreed upon by the payer and the beneficial owner in the absence of such relationship, the provisions of this Article shall apply only to the last-mentioned amount. In such case the excess part of the payments shall remain taxable according to the laws of each Contracting State, due regard being had to the other provisions of the Convention.

Article 13

GAINS

1. Gains derived by a resident of a Contracting State from the alienation of real property referred to in Article 6 (Income from Real Property (Immovable Property)) and situated in the other Contracting State may be taxed in that other State.

2. Gains from the alienation of

a) shares of the stock of a company (whether or not a resident of a Contracting State) the property of which consists principally of real property situated in a Contracting State; or

b) an interest in a partnership, trust, or estate (whether or not a resident of a Contracting State) to the extent attributable to real property situated in a Contracting State may be taxed in that State. For the purposes of this paragraph, the term "real property" includes the shares of a company referred to in subparagraph a (or an interest in a partnership, trust, or estate referred to in subparagraph b).

3. Gains from the alienation of personal property which are attributable to a permanent establishment which an enterprise of a Contracting State has in the other Contracting State, or which are attributable to a fixed base available to a resident of a Contracting State in the other Contracting State for the purpose of performing independent personal services, and gains from the alienation of such a permanent establishment (alone or with the whole enterprise) or such a fixed base, may be taxed in that other State.

4. Gains derived by an enterprise of a Contracting State from the alienation of ships, aircraft, or containers operated in international traffic shall be taxable only in that State.

5. Gains described in Article 12 (Royalties) shall be taxable only in accordance with the provisions of Article 12.

6. Gains from the alienation of any property other than property referred to in paragraphs 1 through 5 shall be taxable only in the Contracting State of which the alienator is a resident.

Article 14

INDEPENDENT PERSONAL SERVICES

Income derived by an individual who is a resident of a Contracting State from the performance of personal services in an independent capacity shall be taxable only in that State, unless such services are performed in the other Contracting State and the income is attributable to a fixed base regularly available to the individual in that other State for the purpose of performing his activities.

Article 15

DEPENDENT PERSONAL SERVICES

1. Subject to the provisions of Articles 18 (Pensions, Annuities, Alimony, and Child Support) and 19 (Government Service), salaries, wages, and other similar remuneration derived by a resident of a Contracting State in respect of an employment shall be taxable only in that State unless the employment is exercised in the other Contracting State. If the employment is so exercised, such remuneration as is derived therefrom may be taxed in that other State.

2. Notwithstanding the provisions of paragraph 1, remuneration derived by a resident of a Contracting State in respect of an employment exercised in the other Contracting State shall be taxable only in the first-mentioned State if

a) the recipient is present in the other State for a period or periods not exceeding in the aggregate 183 days in the taxable year concerned;

b) the remuneration is paid by, or on behalf of, an employer who is not a resident of the other State; and

c) the remuneration is not borne by a permanent establishment or a fixed base which the employer has in the other State.

3. Notwithstanding the preceding provisions of this Article, remuneration derived by a resident of a Contracting State in respect of an employment as a member of the regular complement of a ship or aircraft operated in international traffic may be taxed only in that State.

Article 16
LIMITATION ON BENEFITS

1. A person (other than an individual) which is a resident of a Contracting State shall not be entitled under this Convention to relief from taxation in the other Contracting State unless

a) more than 75 percent of the beneficial interest in such person is owned, directly or indirectly, by one or more individual residents of the first-mentioned Contracting State; and

b) the income of such person is not used in substantial part, directly or indirectly, to meet liabilities (including liabilities for interest or royalties) to persons who are residents of a State other than a Contracting State and who are not citizens of the United States.

For the purposes of subparagraph a), a company that has substantial trading in its stock on a recognized exchange in a Contracting State is presumed to be owned by individual residents of that Contracting State.

2. Paragraph 1 shall not apply if it is determined that the acquisition or maintenance of such person and the conduct of its operations did not have as a principal purpose obtaining benefits under the Convention.

3. Any relief from tax provided by a Contracting State to a resident of the other Contracting State under the Convention shall be inapplicable to the extent that, under the law in force in that other State, the income to which the relief relates bears significantly lower tax than similar income arising within that other State derived by residents of that other State.

Article 17
ARTISTES AND ATHLETES

1. Notwithstanding the provisions of Articles 14 (Independent Personal Services) and 15 (Dependent Personal Services), income derived by a resident of a Contracting State as an entertainer, such as a theatre, motion picture, radio, or television artiste, or a musician, or as an athlete, from his personal activities as such exercised in the other Contracting State, may be taxed in that other State, except where the amount of the gross receipts derived by such entertainer or athlete, including expenses reimbursed to him or borne on his behalf, from such activities does not exceed twenty thousand United States dollars ($20,000) or its equivalent in _____ for the taxable year concerned.

2. Where income in respect of activities exercised by an entertainer or an athlete in his capacity as such accrues not to the entertainer or athlete but to another person, that income of that other person may, notwithstanding the provisions of Articles 7 (Business Profits) and 14 (Independent Personal Services), be taxed in the Contracting State in which the activities of the entertainer or athlete are exercised, unless it is established that neither the entertainer or athlete nor persons related thereto participate directly or indirectly in the profits of that other person in any manner, including the receipt

of deferred remuneration, bonuses, fees, dividends, partnership distributions, or other distributions.

Article 18
PENSIONS, ANNUITIES, ALIMONY, AND CHILD SUPPORT

1. Subject to the provisions of Article 19 (Government Service)

a) pensions and other similar remuneration derived and beneficially owned by a resident of a Contracting State in consideration of past employment shall be taxable only in that State; and

b) social security benefits and other public pensions paid by a Contracting State to a resident of the other Contracting State or a citizen of the United States shall be taxable only in the first-mentioned State.

2. Annuities derived and beneficially owned by a resident of a Contracting State shall be taxable only in that State. The term "annuities" as used in this paragraph means a stated sum paid periodically at stated times during a specified number of years, under an obligation to make the payments in return for adequate and full consideration (other than services rendered).

3. Alimony paid to a resident of a Contracting State shall be taxable only in that State. The term "alimony" as used in this paragraph means periodic payments made pursuant to a written separation agreement or a decree of divorce, separate maintenance, or compulsory support, which payments are taxable to the recipient under the laws of the State of which he is a resident.

4. Periodic payments for the support of a minor child made pursuant to a written separation agreement or a decree of divorce, separate maintenance, or compulsory support, paid by a resident of a Contracting State to a resident of the other Contracting State, shall be taxable only in the first-mentioned State.

Article 19
GOVERNMENT SERVICE

Remuneration, including a pension, paid from the public funds of a Contracting State or a political subdivision or local authority thereof to a citizen of that State in respect of services rendered in the discharge of functions of a governmental nature shall be taxable only in that State. However, the provisions of Article 14 (Independent Personal Services), Article 15 (Dependent Personal Services) or Article 17 (Artistes and Athletes), as the case may be, shall apply, and the preceding sentence shall not apply, to remuneration paid in respect of services rendered in connection with a business carried on by a Contracting State or a political subdivision or local authority thereof.

Article 20
STUDENTS AND TRAINEES

Payments received for the purpose of maintenance, education, or training by a student, apprentice, or business trainee who is or was immediately before visiting a Contracting State a resident of the other Contracting State and who is present in the first-mentioned State for the purpose of his full-time education or training shall not be taxed in that State, provided that such payments arise outside that State.

Article 21
OTHER INCOME

1. Items of income of a resident of a Contracting State, wherever arising,

not dealt with in the foregoing Articles of this Convention shall be taxable only in that State.

2. The provisions of paragraph 1 shall not apply to income, other than income from real property as defined in paragraph 2 of Article 6 (Income from Real Property (Immovable Property)), if the beneficial owner of the income, being a resident of a Contracting State, carries on business in the other Contracting State through a permanent establishment situated therein, or performs in that other State independent personal services from a fixed base situated therein, and the income is attributable to such permanent establishment or fixed base. In such case the provisions of Article 7 (Business Profits) or Article 14 (Independent Personal Services), as the case may be, shall apply.

Article 22

CAPITAL

1. Capital represented by real property referred to in Article 6 (Income from Real Property (Immovable Property)), owned by a resident of a Contracting State and situated in the other Contracting State, may be taxed in that other State.

2. Capital represented by personal property forming part of the business property of a permanent establishment which an enterprise of a Contracting State has in the other Contracting State, or by personal property pertaining to a fixed base available to a resident of a Contracting State in the other Contracting State for the purpose of performing independent personal services, may be taxed in that other State.

3. Capital represented by ships, aircraft, and containers owned by a resident of a Contracting State and operated in international traffic, and by personal property pertaining to the operation of such ships, aircraft, and containers shall be taxable only in that State.

4. All other elements of capital of a resident of a Contracting State shall be taxable only in that State.

Article 23

RELIEF FROM DOUBLE TAXATION

1. In accordance with the provisions and subject to the limitations of the law of the United States (as it may be amended from time to time without changing the general principle hereof), the United States shall allow to a resident or citizen of the United States as a credit against the United States tax on income

 a) the income tax paid to _____ by or on behalf of such citizen or resident; and

 b) in the case of a United States company owning at least 10 percent of the voting stock of a company which is a resident of _____ and from which the United States company receives dividends, the income tax paid to _____ by or on behalf of the distributing company with respect to the profits out of which the dividends are paid

For the purposes of this paragraph, the taxes referred to in paragraphs 1b) and 2 of Article 2 (Taxes Covered) shall be considered income taxes. Credits allowed solely by reason of the preceding sentence, when added to otherwise allowable credits for taxes referred to in paragraphs 1b) and 2 of Article 2, shall not in any taxable year exceed that proportion of the United States tax on income which taxable income arising in _____ bears to total taxable income.

2. In accordance with the provisions and subject to the limitations of the law of _____ (as it may be amended from time to time without amending the general principle hereof) _____ shall allow to a resident or citizen of _____ as a credit against the _____ tax on income _____

3. For the purposes of allowing relief from double taxation pursuant to this Article, income shall be deemed to arise exclusively as follows

a) income derived by a resident of a Contracting State which may be taxed in the other Contracting State in accordance with this Convention (other than solely by reason of citizenship in accordance with paragraph 2 of Article 1 (General Scope)) shall be deemed to arise in that other State;

b) income derived by a resident of a Contracting State which may not be taxed in the other Contracting State in accordance with the Convention shall be deemed to arise in the first-mentioned State.

The rules of this paragraph shall not apply in determining credits against United States tax for foreign taxes other than the taxes referred to in paragraphs 1b) and 2 of Article 2 (Taxes Covered).

Article 24

NON-DISCRIMINATION

1. Nationals of a Contracting State shall not be subjected in the other Contracting State to any taxation or any requirement connected therewith which is other or more burdensome than the taxation and connected requirements to which nationals of that other State in the same circumstances are or may be subjected. This provision shall apply to persons who are not residents of one or both of the Contracting States. However, for the purposes of United States tax, a United States national who is not a resident of the United States and a _____ national who is not a resident of the United States are not in the same circumstances.

2. For the purposes of this Convention, the term "nationals" means

a) in relation to _____, _____

_____; and

b) in relation to the United States, United States citizens.

3. The taxation on a permanent establishment which an enterprise of a Contracting State has in the other Contracting State shall not be less favorably levied in that other State than the taxation levied on enterprises of that other State carrying on the same activities. This provision shall not be construed as obliging a Contracting State to grant to residents of the other Contracting State any personal allowances, reliefs, and reductions for taxation purposes on account of civil status or family responsibilities which it grants to its own residents.

4. Except where the provisions of paragraph 1 of Article 9 (Associated Enterprises), paragraph 5 of Article 11 (Interest), or paragraph 4 of Article 12 (Royalties) apply, interest, royalties, and other disbursements paid by a resident of a Contracting State to a resident of the other Contracting State

shall, for the purposes of determining the taxable profits of the first-mentioned resident, be deductible under the same conditions as if they had been paid to a resident of the first-mentioned State. Similarly, any debts of a resident of a Contracting State to a resident of the other Contracting State shall, for the purposes of determining the taxable capital of the first-mentioned resident, be deductible under the same conditions as if they had been contracted to a resident of the first-mentioned State.

5. Enterprises of a Contracting State, the capital of which is wholly or partly owned or controlled, directly or indirectly, by one or more residents of the other Contracting State, shall not be subjected in the first-mentioned State to any taxation or any requirement connected therewith which is other or more burdensome than the taxation and connected requirements to which other similar enterprises of the first-mentioned State are or may be subjected.

6. The provisions of this Article shall, notwithstanding the provisions of Article 2 (Taxes Covered), apply to taxes of every kind and description imposed by a Contracting State or a political subdivision or local authority thereof.

Article 25

MUTUAL AGREEMENT PROCEDURE

1. Where a person considers that the actions of one or both of the Contracting States result or will result for him in taxation not in accordance with the provisions of this Convention, he may, irrespective of the remedies provided by the domestic law of those States, present his case to the competent authority of the Contracting State of which he is a resident or national.

2. The competent authority shall endeavor, if the objection appears to it to be justified and if it is not itself able to arrive at a satisfactory solution, to resolve the case by mutual agreement with the competent authority of the other Contracting State, with a view to the avoidance of taxation which is not in accordance with the Convention. Any agreement reached shall be implemented notwithstanding any time limits or other procedural limitations in the domestic law of the Contracting States.

3. The competent authorities of the Contracting States shall endeavor to resolve by mutual agreement any difficulties or doubts arising as to the interpretation or application of the Convention. In particular the competent authorities of the Contracting States may agree

a) to the same attribution of income, deductions, credits, or allowances of an enterprise of a Contracting State to its permanent establishment situated in the other Contracting State;

b) to the same allocation of income, deductions, credits, or allowances between persons;

c) to the same characterization of particular items of income;

d) to the same application of source rules with respect to particular items of income;

e) to a common meaning of a term;

f) to increases in any specific amounts referred to in the Convention to reflect economic or monetary developments; and

g) to the application of the provisions of domestic law regarding penalties, fines, and interest in a manner consistent with the purposes of the Convention.

They may also consult together for the elimination of double taxation in cases not provided for in the Convention.

4. The competent authorities of the Contracting States may communicate with each other directly for the purpose of reaching an agreement in the sense of the preceding paragraphs.

Article 26

EXCHANGE OF INFORMATION AND ADMINISTRATIVE ASSISTANCE

1. The competent authorities of the Contracting States shall exchange such information as is necessary for carrying out the provisions of this Convention or of the domestic laws of the Contracting States concerning taxes covered by the Convention insofar as the taxation thereunder is not contrary to the Convention. The exchange of information is not restricted by Article 1 (General Scope). Any information received by a Contracting State shall be treated as secret in the same manner as information obtained under the domestic laws of that State and shall be disclosed only to persons or authorities (including courts and administrative bodies) involved in the assessment, collection, or administration of, the enforcement or prosecution in respect of, or the determination of appeals in relation to, the taxes covered by the Convention. Such persons or authorities shall use the information only for such purposes. They may disclose the information in public court proceedings or in judicial decisions.

2. In no case shall the provisions of paragraph 1 be construed so as to impose on a Contracting State the obligation

a) to carry out administrative measures at variance with the laws and administrative practice of that or of the other Contracting State;

b) to supply information which is not obtainable under the laws or in the normal course of the administration of that or of the other Contracting State;

c) to supply information which would disclose any trade, business, industrial, commercial, or professional secret or trade process, or information the disclosure of which would be contrary to public policy (public order).

3. If information is requested by a Contracting State in accordance with this Article, the other Contracting State shall obtain the information to which the request relates in the same manner and to the same extent as if the tax of the first-mentioned State were the tax of that other State and were being imposed by that other State. If specifically requested by the competent authority of a Contracting State, the competent authority of the other Contracting State shall provide information under this Article in the form of depositions of witnesses and authenticated copies of unedited original documents (including books, papers, statements, records, accounts, and writings), to the same extent such depositions and documents can be obtained under the laws and administrative practices of that other State with respect to its own taxes.

4. Each of the Contracting States shall endeavor to collect on behalf of the other Contracting State such amounts as may be necessary to ensure that relief granted by the Convention from taxation imposed by that other State does not enure to the benefit of persons not entitled thereto.

5. Paragraph 4 of this Article shall not impose upon either of the Contracting States the obligation to carry out administrative measures which are of a different nature from those used in the collection of its own taxes, or which would be contrary to its sovereignty, security, or public policy.

6. For the purposes of this Article, the Convention shall apply, notwithstanding the provisions of Article 2 (Taxes Covered), to taxes of every kind imposed by a Contracting State.

Article 27

DIPLOMATIC AGENTS AND CONSULAR OFFICERS

Nothing in this Convention shall affect the fiscal privileges of diplomatic agents or consular officers under the general rules of international law or under the provisions of special agreements.

Article 28

ENTRY INTO FORCE

1. This Convention shall be subject to ratification in accordance with the applicable procedures of each Contracting State and instruments of ratification shall be exchanged at _____ as soon as possible.

2. The Convention shall enter into force upon the exchange of instruments of ratification and its provisions shall have effect

a) in respect of taxes withheld at source, for amounts paid or credited on or after the first day of the second month next following the date on which the Convention enters into force;

b) in respect of other taxes, for taxable periods beginning on or after the first day of January next following the date on which the Convention enters into force.

Article 29

TERMINATION

1. This Convention shall remain in force until terminated by a Contracting State. Either Contracting State may terminate the Convention at any time after 5 years from the date on which the Convention enters into force, provided that at least 6 months prior notice of termination has been given through diplomatic channels. In such event, the Convention shall cease to have effect

a) in respect of taxes withheld at source, for amounts paid or credited on or after the first day of January next following the expiration of the 6 months period;

b) in respect of other taxes, for taxable periods beginning on or after the first day of January next following the expiration of the 6 months period.

DONE at _____ in duplicate, in the English and _____ languages, the two texts having equal authenticity, this _____ day of _____ 19___.

FOR THE UNITED STATES OF AMERICA

FOR _____

11.

ACCOUNTING AND ECONOMIC DEVELOPMENT

The developing countries face insurmountable problems in their attempts to achieve progress in their economic development programs. Their efforts led to the rise of a new economic subdiscipline, namely, development economics to address the various problems and policies affecting economic development. These problems and policies are either domestic—such as growth, poverty and income distribution, unemployment, population growth, education, agricultural transformation and rural development—or international—such as international trade and development, foreign investment and aid, and a new international economic order. These problems and policies are examined first in this chapter.

Accounting has a crucial role too in economic development by providing the relevant information necessary to implementing the above-mentioned policies. This role is particularly important in development planning in general and project appraisal in particular. Accordingly, the role of accounting in economic development, development planning, and project appraisal are also examined.

The Meaning of Underdevelopment

Two-thirds of the world's population subsists on only 20 percent of the world's income. These people live in a shocking state of underdevelopment. It is forcefully portrayed as follows:

Underdevelopment is shocking: The squalor, disease, unnecessary deaths, and hopelessness of it all! No man understands if underdevelopment remains for him a mere statistic reflecting low income, poor housing, premature mortality and underemployment. The most empathetic observer can speak objectively about underdevelopment only after undergoing, personally or vicariously, the "shock of underdevelopment." This unique culture shock comes to one as he is initiated to the emotions which prevail in the "culture of poverty." The reverse shock is felt by those living in destitution when a new self-understanding reveals to them that their life is neither human nor inevitable. . . . the prevalent emotion of underdevelopment is a sense of personal and societal impotence in the face of disease and death, of confusion and ignorance as one gropes to understand change, of servility toward men whose decisions govern the course of events, of hopelessness before hunger and natural catastrophe. Chronic poverty is a cruel kind of hell; and one cannot understand how cruel that hell is merely by gazing upon poverty as an object.[1]

These much less fortunate people live in what is generally known as the Third World. The countries in the Third World, known as the developing countries, share some common characteristics of underdevelopment generally grouped into the following six broad categories:

1. Low levels of living
2. Low levels of productivity
3. High rates of population growth and dependency burdens
4. High and rising levels of unemployment and underemployment
5. Significant dependence on agricultural production and primary product exports
6. Dominance, dependence, and vulnerability in international relations.[2]

The combination of any number of these categories in a given country creates a state of underdevelopment. It is the result of not only economic but also social forces, not only internal but external factors, and not only national but also international origins. It calls for each of these nations to formulate appropriate strategies of growth and development at the national level and, as seen later, modification of the international economic order at the international level. The basic objective of these strategies would be to break what Myrdal referred to as the phenomenon of "circular and cumulative causation" generated by the interactions between low levels of living and low productivity.[3]

Economic Development

THE NATURE OF DEVELOPMENT ECONOMICS

The study of development economics is a relatively new and separate development in the disciplines of economics and political economy. It deals with the economic, social, and institutional tools necessary to bring changes in the levels of living of developing economies. It has been appropriately defined as follows:

Thus, development economics to a greater extent than to additional economics or even political economy is concerned with the economic and political processes necessary for affecting *rapid structural and institutional transformations of entire societies in a manner that will most efficiently bring the fruits of economic progress to the broadest segments of their populations.*

Basically, developing economics addresses the critical questions about the economies of the developing countries, questions which center on finding the best way, economically, socially and institutionally, of bringing these countries to an acceptable and decent level of living and productivity. It obviously goes beyond simple economics. In fact, there is an implicit assumption in development economics about the limited relevance of traditional theory. Myrdal states the case as follows:

Economic theorists, more than any other social scientists, have long been disposed to arrive at general propositions and then postulate them as valid for every time, place and culture. There is a tendency in contemporary economic theory to follow this path to the extreme . . . when theories and concepts designed to fit the special conditions of the Western world—and thus containing the implicit assumptions about social reality by which this fitting was accomplished are used in the study of underdeveloped countries, where they do *not* fit, the consequences are serious.[5]

THE MEANING OF DEVELOPMENT

As stated earlier, development is more than an economic process. It involves the economic, social, and institutional processes necessary to efficiently eliminate the major evils of underdevelopment: malnutrition, disease, illiteracy, slums, unemployment, and inequality. Besides the creation of self-sustained growth in per capita GNP, it involves the requisite modernization of economic, social, and political structures implicit in the achievement of GNP growth. The basic purpose and meaning of development is *depauperization*. It has been defined as follows:

Depauperization has both economic and noneconomic dimensions and stresses the removal not only of material but equally importantly of social, political and spiritual forms of deprivation. It involves not only equity but more significantly the creation of conditions conducive to continuing improvements in equity. It may require temporary sacrifices in national economic growth and involves major social, political and institutional change.[6]

Two basic schools of thought dominate the economic development literature: an early literature on the "stages-of-economic-growth" theories and a more recent literature on the "structural-internationalist" models. For one, the stages-of-economic-growth models include both Rostow's arguments that advanced countries have passed the stage of "take-off into self-sustaining growth," that the developing countries are in the "pre-conditions stage," and that take-off in the form of mobilization of domestic and foreign savings would accelerate economic growth,[7] and the Harrod-Domar growth model which simply states that the growth of national income will be directly, or positively, related to the savings ratio.[8] These theories did not work in developing countries because more savings and investment are not sufficient for economic growth. Favorable institutional and attitudinal conditions need to be present before take-off can take place. Todaro argues the case as follows:

The Marshall Plan worked for Europe because the European countries receiving aid possessed the necessary structural, institutional and attitudinal conditions (e.g., well-integrated commodity and money markets, highly developed transport facilities, well trained and educated manpower, the motivation to succeed, an efficient government bureaucracy) to convert new capital effectively into higher levels of output. The Rostow-Harrod-Domar models implicitly assume the existence of these same attitudes and arrangements in underdeveloped nations. But in many cases they are not present nor are the complementary factors such as managerial competence, skilled labor, and the ability to plan and administer a wide assortment of development projects often present in sufficient quantities.[9]

Second, the international-structuralist models view the developing countries as being dependent upon and dominated by the rich countries in addition to their institutional and structural economic problems. Two streams of thought characterize the international-structuralist models, namely, the *neo-classical dependence model* and the *false-paradigm model*. The neo-classical dependence model views the world as being dominated by rich countries (the core) at the expense of poor countries (the periphery). In addition, the policies of the core countries have an effect on the peripheral countries because of this dependency situation and most of the time are responsible for the continuing and worsening poverty of the Third World.

The effects are perceived to be negative most of the time given the developed countries' power to control world commodities to their advantages, to dominate the domestic economies of the developing countries through direct foreign investment, to affect the developing economies' trade by exporting unsuitable products, and by dumping cheap products and locking them into exporting primary products with declining revenues. These accusations are well contained in the following observation.

The very forces which are set in motion by the rapid growth of rich countries—specifically the development of even more sophisticated, costly and capital-intensive technologies, and of mortality reducing health improvements and disease controls—specifically a population explosion, rising unemployment and inability to develop their own technological capacities, which may in fact assure that they will not have the time needed for the continued maintenance of current growth rates, let alone their acceleration, so as to result in acceptable levels of development.[10]

The false-paradigm model attributes the underdevelopment of the Third World to faulty advice received from international experts sent to help the developing countries.[11] These experts resort to sophisticated models, some theoretical and more analytical, which are deemed inappropriate to resolve the practical problems of underdevelopment.

DOMESTIC PROBLEMS AND POLICIES

There are a number of critical domestic problems which are the main target of development policies in the Third World. In what follows, these problems are described and the economic policies used for their ultimate resolution are explored.

Growth, Poverty, and Income Distribution

The first problem is the problem of growth, poverty, and income distribution. In effect, one main objective of development is to eliminate poverty and income inequalities. As in some developed economies, the developing economies face the situation where only a small portion of the population constituting the rich class controls a very large share of the national income and resources, influencing henceforth the consumption and production patterns toward expensive consumer goods. These income inequalities are aggravated by high levels of "absolute poverty," which is generally measured by the number of people living below a specified minimum level of income. Absolute poverty in the world is widespread, leading World Bank economists Ahluwalia, Carter, and Chenery to conclude that

almost 40 percent of the population of the developing countries live in absolute poverty defined in terms of income levels that are insufficient to provide adequate nutrition. The bulk of the poor are in the poorer countries: in South Asia, Indonesia and sub-Saharan Africa. These countries account for two-thirds of the total (world) population and well over three-fourths of the population in poverty. The incidence of poverty is 60 percent or more in countries having the lowest level of real GNP.[12]

Development goals originally focused on maximizing rates of GNP growth and expecting a "trickle down" of the benefits of economic growth to the very poor. Failure of those policies led to a redefining of development goals toward broad-based income growth, with special emphasis on accelerating the growth of incomes of "target" poverty groups. Four policy options are generally advocated in determining a developing economy's distribution of income: (1) to alter the functional distribution of income through policies designed to change relative factor prices, (2) to modify the size distribution through progressive redistribution of asset ownership, (3) to reduce the size distribution at the upper levels through progressive income and wealth taxes, and (4) to affect distribution at the lower levels through direct transfer payments and the public provision of goods and services.[13]

Unemployment

The second problem is the problem of unemployment. Not only is a very large section of the population unemployed, but unemployment in the Third World seems to grow faster than employment, mainly due to the phenomenon of labor underutilization. Edwards distinguishes among the following forms of underutilization of labor: open unemployment; underemployment; the visibly active but underutilized as disguised underemployment, hidden unemployment, and prematurely retired; the impaired; and the unproductive.[14] All major economic models of employment determination are advocated in the literature, namely, classical, Keynesian, the output/employment macro model, the price-incentive micro model, and the two-sector labor transfer model. The classical model relies on the forces of supply and demand to set the wage rate and the level of employment. The Keynesian model relies on demand factors such as increases in government expenditures and encouragement of private investments for reducing unemployment. Both the classical and the Keynesian models are considered to be far from relevant to the developing countries. The output/employment macro model argues that the rate of national output and employment depend upon the rate of savings and investment, lending credence to the "big push" for industrialization in some developing countries. The price-incentive model maintains that the combination of labor and capital will be dictated by the relative factor prices. Cheap labor would lead to labor-intensive production processes. Finally, the two-sector labor transfer of rural-urban migration focuses on the determinants of both demand and supply. Two variations characterize the last model: the Lewis theory of development[15] and the Todaro model.[16] The Lewis model divides the economy into two sectors: (1) a traditional, rural subsistence sector characterized by zero- or low-productivity surplus labor, and (2) a growing urban industrial sector characterized by an influx of labor from the subsistence sector. The Todaro model hypothesizes that migration is due to urban-rural differences in expected rather than actual earnings. All these approaches lead to a consensus position on employment strategy. It would include the following five elements:

1. Creating an appropriate rural-urban economic balance
2. Expansion of small-scale, labor-intensive industries
3. Elimination of factor-price distortions
4. Choosing appropriate labor-intensive technologies of production
5. Noting the direct linkage between education and employment.[17]

Another way of reducing unemployment is by creating special trading zones. These zones are usually intended to attract foreign investors to produce assembly goods for export. The zones are made attractive to investors through offering inducements such as reducing taxes or offering tax holidays, relaxing tariffs and currency-exchange facilities, and allowing administrative advantages which may include a watering down of union and labor laws.[18] Some groups, however, criticize the concept of special trade zones as merely sweatshops exported by "footloose" multinational companies. For example, the International Confederation of Free Trade Unions, which is the largest organization of democratic labor unions, is concerned by the possible exploitation of workers who are often desperate for a job, and by the possible isolation of worldwide conventions on labor norms and employee protection drafted under the auspices of the UN International Labor Organization (ILO) in Geneva and ratified by most governments.

Population Growth

The third problem is the problem of ever-expanding human numbers. All positions on the population debate seem to agree that in the long run "zero population growth" is not only a necessity but an important means to a better life in the developing countries. The population growth in the developing countries is now accentuated by lower death rates due undoubtedly to the rapid improvement in health conditions. As a result, one may notice that high birth rates are generally associated with national poverty and low per capita income. The question is whether population is a real problem, and whatever the position in this question the problem is to find adequate solutions to the population growth. Two extreme positions may be explored. The first claims that population growth is not a real problem but a result of other problems such as underdevelopment, depletion of world resources, and population distribution. The solution advocated is through development programs focusing on improvements in health, nutrition, income, social justice, status of women, and other such general factors. The second position claims that population growth is a real problem requiring deliberate governmental "population policies" which may include providing family-planning services, programs and laws affecting information and education, incentives directed toward fertility behavior, and programs to alter the frequency and age of marital unions.

Advocates of the first position attribute the decline in fertility in some developing countries to their experienced economic development, industrialization, and urbanization while advocates of the second position point to the intensive population and family-planning programs in these countries for a better explanation of the declining birth rates. One way of solving the debate between both positions is to reach a consensus position based on a population program-plus-development position. Such a position was advocated by Teitelbaum as follows:

The consensus position begins with a frank recognition that population growth is not the only, or even the primary, source of poverty, disease, illiteracy, and gross inequality which now characterize the world. The ultimate solution to such problems depends on the true social and economic development of the poor countries and regions of the world. Such development cannot be "bought cheaply" through concentration on population as the major problem. Second, the consensus position recognizes that whatever the population problem may be it is not uniform throughout the world, nor can a single characterization be correctly applied to all countries or even to all developing countries. In some areas it is evident that the population is already too large for indigenous resources, while in others resources are available in abundance, and development may be served by substantial increases in population size. Third, it is recognized that many of the problems arising from population concentrations derive from patterns of distribution and rural-urban migration as well as from overall rates of population increase. Fourth, the consensus position explicitly recognizes that barring catastrophe, the population of the world and particularly of the developing countries will increase dramatically no matter what population policies are adopted; hence the world's technological and economic resources must be mobilized to assure that these sharply increased numbers can be accommodated and provided with opportunities for lives of dignity. Fifth, the consensus notes the happy convergence of most voluntary population programs with the goal of maximizing the basic human rights of each individual to determine his or her own fertility.[19]

Education

The fourth problem pertains to the need for improving the human resources of the developing countries by providing a sound education system. The general mechanism used is the formal education system, which takes place in schools, uses the traditional academic curriculum, and prepares students to join the modern economic lifestyles. There are, however, other types of education most beneficial to the developing countries, namely, *informal education* or learning by doing which "includes agricultural training, programmes, evening adult literacy classes, radio and mass media campaigns, and vocational training programmes"[20] and *education for self-reliance* or problem-posing education, which "teaches groups of people to study together and become aware of the political and economic determinants of their poverty."[71]

Given the inadequacy of formal education, various developing countries have experimented with informal education and education for self-reliance. The results are far from conclusive at this time. So the call for education reform beyond the boundaries of formal education continue to stir interest and debate in the developing countries. Education is considered to be the best determinant and hope for a better lifestyle in the developing countries. As stated by Husen, "The mood has swung from the almost euphonic conception of education as the Great Equalizer to that of education as the Great Sieve that sorts and certifies people for their (predetermined) slot in society."[22] Most calls for an education reform stress the need for a curriculum most beneficial and in accordance with the real needs of each developing country, and more relevant to the development needs.

Agricultural Transformation and Rural Development

The fifth problem pertains to the need for agricultural transformation and rural development. One of the most proven theses in economics relates to the secular decline of the agricultural population and the labor force and agriculture's share of GNP in the course of economic development coupled with a consistent rise in the share of labor in the service sector. Various explanations are given for this structural transformation.

To some, this structural transformation is simply a consequence of development—of the increase in productivity and incomes in the various sectors of an economy that entails changes in the patterns of consumer demand and the composition of output. Other writers take the position that structural transformation should be viewed not merely as a consequence of development but as a process that should be deliberately fostered by policy measures to accelerate development and to ensure that low income, pre-industrial societies will succeed in realizing their goals of achieving self-sustained economic growth.[23]

Besides this structural transformation, the performance of Third World agriculture has been relatively poor due mainly to inefficiency and low productivity. Subsistence agriculture on small plots of land and extensive cultivation characterize agriculture in most of the developing countries. These countries need to move from an objective of achieving subsistence to one of agricultural sufficiency. Three stages may be necessary: a first stage of subsistence farming characterized by risk, uncertainty, and survival; a second stage of transition to mixed and diversified farming; and a third stage of specialization and modern commercial farming. To achieve this goal, a strategy of agricultural and rural development is needed. Todaro proposes three necessary conditions for rural development—land reform, supportive policies, and integrated development objectives—which are outlined as follows:

Proposition I: *Farm structure and land-tenure patterns need to be adapted to the dual objectives of increasing food production and promoting a wider distribution of the benefits of agrarian progress. . .*

Proposition II: *The full benefits of small-scale agricultural development cannot be realized unless government support systems are created that provide the necessary incentives, economic opportunities, and access to needed inputs to enable small cultivators to expand their output and raise their productivity. . . .*

Proposition III: *Rural development, while dependent primarily on small-farmer agricultural progress, implies much more. It encompasses (a) improvements in "levels of living" including income, employment, education, health and nutrition, housing, and a variety of related social services; (b) a decreasing inequality in the distribution of rural incomes and in urban-rural imbalances on incomes and economic opportunities; and (c) the capacity of the rural sector to sustain and accelerate the pace of these improvements over time. . . .*[24]

INTERNATIONAL PROBLEMS AND POLICIES

There are a number of critical international problems which are also the main target of development policies in the Third World, In what follows, these problems are described and the economic policies used for their ultimate resolution are explored.

International Trade and Development

Development countries suffer from two main limitations in their trading with developed countries. First, their export is heavily composed of nonnumerical primary products while their imports include everything from new materials to capital goods, intermediate producer goods, and consumer products. Second, the commodity terms of trade as measured by the ratio between the price of a typical unit of exports and the price of a typical unit of imports are deteriorating. The result shows up in a continuous deficit in the current and capital accounts of their balance of payments. To solve this problem a variety of options are used: export promotion or import-substitution policies, encouragement of private foreign investment or call for public and private foreign assistance, greater use of the Special Drawing Rights of the IMF, foreign exchange controls or currency devaluation, economic integration with other developing countries in the form of customs union, free trade area, or common markets.[25] But above all, the major option is the choice of a trade strategy for development. Should it be an outward- or inward-looking policy? Outward-looking policy results from the classical trade theory and comparative cost-advantage arguments with the implication that free trade will maximize global output by allowing every country to specialize in what it does best. Streeten states that point as follows: "Outward-looking policies encourage not only free trade but also the free movement of capital, workers, enterprises and students, a welcome to the multinational enterprise, and open system of communications. If it does not imply laissez-faire, it certainly implies *laissez-passer.*"[26]

Inward-looking policy results from the belief that the developing countries should be encouraged to engage in their own style of development and not be constrained by or dependent upon foreign importation, and to learn by doing. Streeten explains this option as follows:

Inward-looking policies emphasize the need for an indigenous technology, appropriate for the factors available in the country, and for an appropriate range of products. If you restrict trade, the movement of people and communications, if you keep out the multinational enterprise, with its wrong products and wrong want-stimulation and hence its wrong technology, you will evolve your own style of development and you will be stronger, more independent, master of your own fate.[27]

In short, outward-looking is identifiable with export promotion while inward-looking is identifiable with import substitution. These two strategies, when added to the strategies of primary and secondary or manufacturing production, yield a fourfold division: primary outward-looking policies, secondary outward-looking policies, primary inward-looking policies, and secondary inward-looking policies.[28] The choice of any one of these options determines the nature of international trade of each developing country and of its impact on development.

Foreign Investment and Aid

Most developing countries tend to rely on outside financial aid to alleviate the deficits in their current account balances. This aid takes place in the form of either private foreign investment or public development assistance. Both types of aid are examined next.

Private foreign investment is playing a major role in economic development through the activities of the large multinational corporations. The nature of the role of the large multinational corporations is claimed to be either positive or negative depending upon which side of the controversy one is on. Enthoven has successfully summarized the results, both positive and negative, claimed for multinational corporations by the spokesmen for developing countries as follows:

POSITIVE EFFECTS (Benefits/Advantages): 1. Transfer of capital; 2. transfer of know-how and management; 3. balance-of-payments benefits; 4. increase in competition and lower prices; 5. increase in entrepreneurial spirit; 6. help in training and education; 7. increase in employment; 8. help in infrastructure; 9. improvement of living conditions in developing countries; 10. identification, allocation, management, and efficient use of world material and human and financial resources; 11. greater international unity and interdependency; 12. ensuring a more equal distribution of income and wealth.

NEGATIVE EFFECTS (Costs/Disadvantages): 1. Hampering of balance of payments; export of profits and interest beyond investment; 2. technology too advanced for country and too capital-intensive; 3. limited training and education; 4. input of foreign management to the neglect of local managers; 5. curbing of local enterprises; 6. enforcement of consumption functions (luxury items); 7. uneven distribution of income; 8. affecting employment; restricting transfer of know-how; 9. subordination of companies and countries to the multinational corporations, threatening the sovereignty of the nation-state; 10. hampering of the endogenous socioeconomic development of a nation; 11. disruption of social, political, and cultural patterns in the host country; 12. resentment against foreign penetration, resulting in upsetting the social balance; 13. recession resulting from inability of national industries to compete; 14. loss of national pride and nationalistic spirit.[29]

Public development assistance is as much the subject of a heated debate as private foreign investment. It is viewed by some as essential and beneficial to economic development by supplementing scarce resources and helping the developing countries to achieve more forms of self-sustaining economic growth. Others maintain that foreign aid may have retarded growth through reduced savings and worsened income inequalities.[30] They would even add that countries have strong strategic, political, and economic motivations behind their foreign-aid programs. Witness the following statement made by a former U.S. aid official:

The biggest single misconception about the foreign aid program is that we send money abroad. We don't. Foreign aid consists of American equipment, raw materials, expert services, and food—all provided for specific development projects which we ourselves review and approve. . . . Ninety-three percent of AID funds are spent directly in the United States to pay for these things. Just last year some 4,000 American firms received $1.3 billion in AID funds for products supplied as part of the foreign aid program.[31]

Obviously, a new view of private foreign investment and foreign aid is needed to relieve the "disillusionment" on the part of developing countries and "weariness" on the part of the developed countries. Some useful suggestions have been made in what is now known as the "New International Economic Order" proposal.

New International Economic Order

Faced with their bleak situation, the Third World countries began asking for a "New International Economic Order" (NIEO). In fact, the UN General Assembly, in a special session convened in April 1974 following the petroleum crisis, concluded its deliberations by committing itself

to work urgently for the establishment of a new international economic order based on equity, sovereign equality, common interest and cooperation among all states, irrespective of their economic and social systems, which shall correct inequalities and redress in existing injustices, make it possible to eliminate the widening gap between the developed and the developing countries and ensure steadily accelerating economic and social development and peace and justice for present and future generations.

Before this declaration the UN began a series of programs and targets toward achieving this NIEO. Examples include the launching of the first UN

Development Decade, the Alliance for Progress in 1961, the Yaunde Convention in 1967, and the second UN Development Decade of the 1970s. The Third World countries used their new-found political and economic leverage to demand a new structure of international economic relations and a new set of rules affecting trade, industrialization, transfer of technology, and foreign assistance. A list of the NIEO demands includes the following:

1. Attaining UN Official Development Assistance targets
2. Providing technical assistance for developing countries
3. Renegotiating the debts of developing countries
4. Undertaking special measures to assist land-locked, least-developed, and island developing countries
5. Using disarmament funds for development
6. Improving the terms and conditions of trade for developing countries: tariff and nontariff barriers, general systems of preference, duties and taxes on imports, invisible trade
7. Adopting an integrated approach to commodities: the integrated program, buffer stocks, producers' associations, indexation
8. Developing an international food program
9. Adjusting the economic policies of developed countries to facilitate expanding and diversifying the exports of developing countries
10. Improving and intensifying trade relations between countries having different social and economic systems
11. Strengthening economic and technical cooperation among developing countries
12. Reforming the international monetary system: using special drawing rights for development assistance and as the central reserve asset of the international monetary system, promoting stable rates of exchange and protection from the effects of inflation
13. Assuring adequate participation by developing countries in World Bank and IMF decision making
14. Increasing the transfer of resources through the World Bank and IMF
15. Negotiating the redeployment of industrial productive capacities to developing countries
16. Establishing mechanisms for the transfer of technology to developing countries
17. Regulating and supervising the activities of transnational enterprises and eliminating restrictive business practices
18. Improving the competitiveness of natural resources and ending their waste
19. Providing equitable access to the resources of the seabed and the ocean floor
20. Achieving a more equitable distribution of income and raising the level of employment
21. Providing health services, education, higher cultural standards, and qualification for the work force, and assuring the well-being of children and the integration of women in development

22. Assuring the economic sovereignty of states: natural resources, foreign property, choice of economic systems

23. Compensating for adverse effects on the resources of states, territories, and people of foreign occupation, alien and colonial domination, or apartheid

24. Establishing a system of consultations at global, regional, and sectoral levels with the aim of promoting industrial development

25. Restructuring the economic and social sections of the United Nations.[32]

The Role of Accounting in Economic Development

The role of accounting in economic development rests on a clear understanding of what is required to efficiently achieve and implement economic and social policies. First, accounting has to be structured in developing countries to conform to the social, political, and economic systems and institutions. Accordingly, an examination of the development of accounting in the developing countries is the first objective of this section. Second, economic development rests on development planning in general and project appraisal in particular. Both concepts are also examined in this section. Third, the role of accounting in economic development rests in its usefulness and adaptability to the environment of development planning. Standardization of accounting is suggested as the solution. Finally, the importance of accounting education to economic development is examined.

THE DEVELOPMENT OF ACCOUNTING IN THE DEVELOPING COUNTRIES

Accounting in the developing countries has for a long time been the result of the spread of western accounting which in turn resulted from colonialism, or powerful foreign investors, or through the influence of multinational companies, foreign aid, and education. Consider, for example, the following statement by Wilkinson:

The accounting principles of one country have never been "sold" to another country on the basis of convincing arguments in support of those principles. Accounting principles of one country have moved to another country when two conditions have existed:

1. The second country had no organized body of accounting principles in the first place and

2. Large amounts of capital from the first country were invested in business in the second country, with the consequent ability on the part of those investors to impose their own accounting requirements on the businesses. . . .[33]

Given this situation, the solution which seems the most obvious and acceptable to the developing countries is to accept these "foreign" techniques and accept the harmonization or internal legitimization and extension of currently dominant practices. Some developing countries have adopted this kind of strategy. Indonesia, for example, as a result of factors such as multinationals, international firms of accountants, U.S. aid, and language, is adopting American techniques to the point where university courses are biased toward American texts and courses are structured with much more emphasis upon finance and management. The resulting situation is impractical, as described in the following statement:

As a consequence of this evolution, the Indonesian profession is Dutch in its qualification structure, but the training (which is exclusively undertaken in universities) and philosophy are American. Neither, however, is in the least relevant to the needs of Indonesia, a country with no companies act, no capital market, a massive public sector, and an economic and cultural environment totally dissimilar to that of the Netherlands or of the United States.[34]

The question is, then, to determine whether the developing countries should continue in their efforts to comply with the international harmonization efforts, which some may label as merely the internal legitimization and extension of western dominant practices; or should they concentrate upon an assessment of their information needs in the private, public, and national accounting sectors and educate their accountants to produce and use that information?

Most of those familiar with the economic, cultural, political, and social conditions in the developing countries would argue that each developing country should create an accounting system appropriate to its own needs. Various arguments are used to support this position. A general argument used in support of the unique system for each developing country is that harmonization in international accounting can be achieved only when all countries have the same objectives from the accounting systems.[35]

Second, international harmonization attempts as currently dominated by Anglo-American accounting principles and practices are merely legitimizing certain values worldwide and may be harmful to the developing countries. Samuels and Oliga argue the case as follows:

The point is that most developing countries had little chance to evolve accounting systems which truly reflected the needs and circumstances of their own societies. Their existing systems are largely extensions of those in developed countries. In this light, the benefits of their being more deeply integrated into systems that predominantly suit developed countries becomes questionable. For the Third World, international harmonization may do more harm than good if it preempts the possibility of changing the old, inappropriate systems and evolving new ones which are better suited to their development needs. Furthermore, given that Anglo-American accounting principles and practices currently dominate the attempts at harmonization, the attempt becomes largely a one-sided exercise, and "international" standards essentially represent internationalization of domestic standards of dominant members of the standard-setting bodies.[36]

Third, international standards, which may result from the international harmonization of accounting, can only assist users to make decisions at an international level, which is far different from the needs of users from developing countries. Besides, the needs of users in the developing countries are not essentially restricted to financial costs and returns. These needs are more complex. As emphasized in the cost/benefit literature, the economic decisions in a developing country should be based on a knowledge of shadow prices and costs. That includes more information than those provided by accounts conforming to international standards. In most developing countries, the public sector is larger than the private sector and relies on different information requirements for economic decisions than those provided by accounting standards of the private sector. As a result, developing countries may have to supplement accounting standards for the private sector by assessing their information needs in the government and national accounting sectors and corresponding accounting standards.

The developing countries need an accounting system most uniform to their historical, political, economic, and social conditions. There are a lot of questions which need to be answered before the construction of such a system. Examples of such questions include the following:

To what extent should current costs, opportunity costs, replacement costs, social costs, benefits, and so on be taken into account? What use should be made of sensitivity analysis? Should a feasibility study be required by law for all major projects? Should this feasibility study be made subject to independent audit? If so, should this be carried by an internal auditor, a private external auditor, or a government auditor? At the max level, what are the objectives of the government and what information is necessary to devise plans for the attainment of those objectives? What rules are necessary to ensure that the private sector provides the necessary information in an easily accessible fashion? Does information need to be submitted to the government on foreign exchange transactions, investment plans, projected imports and exports, profits (if so, how defined), social costs and benefits, and such? Which accountancy system will permit this information to be collected in the most efficient and best-integrated fashion? How are the decisions of multinationals to be monitored? Should these be controlled through formal concession agreements? If so, what right of access is the government to be given to obtain information to ensure that the agreement is being adhered to? Should the government have the right to monitor investment plans and feasibility studies therefor?[37]

DEVELOPMENT PLANNING AND ACCOUNTING

Development planning is generally accepted as essential to the economic development of the developing and even some of the developed countries. The need for planning in the developing countries is accentuated by the "failure" of the market in those countries to price factors of production correctly. This argument was forcefully made in a 1965 UN Conference on Planning as follows:

It is an integrated task of planning to achieve the best possible use of scarce resources for economic development. . . . The need for using appropriate criteria for selecting projects arose because of the failure of the market mechanism to provide a proper guideline. In less-developed economies, market prices of such factors of production as labor, capital and foreign exchange deviated substantially from their social opportunity costs and were not, therefore, a correct measure of the relative scarcity or abundance of the factor in question.[38]

Besides the market-failure argument, development planning was justified for a better resource mobilization and allocation, a better development-oriented atmosphere, and as grounds for foreign aid.[39] Given this rationale for development planning, the questions become to effectively define and implement it.

Various definitions of development planning exist in the literature. Todaro refers to "a deliberate governmental attempt to coordinate economic decision making over the long run and to influence, direct, and in some cases even control the level and growth of a nation's principal economic variables (income, consumption, employment, investment, saving, exports, imports, etc.) in order to achieve a predetermined set of development objectives."[40] Enthoven speaks of "the preparatory evaluation and decision making process of a forward-looking character for an economy, in which alternatives have to be measured, weighed and outlined, and priorities for the use of resources established."[41] Both definitions point to the guidance of development by a deliberate attempt to quantify, measure, and control the level of crucial economic variables to reach an acceptable level of growth. Thus, development planning rests on a well-defined, comprehensive economic policy for reaching well-specified goals and targets and a deliberate governmental attempt to formulate and monitor the required development plans.

Three basic strategies are used for the implementation of development planning, namely, aggregate growth models based on a forecasting of macro-variables, multisector input-output models based on the inter-relationships and flows among the various industries, and project appraisal through cost/benefit analysis. These three stages are also labeled the macro, middle, and micro phases of development planning. They have been adequately described as follows:

The macrophase has to show the most desirable development in macro-economic terms, without subdivision in regions or industries. In this phase, then, only such overall figures are used as the national product and capital, the total investments, imports and exports and state expenditure. In the middle phase, the picture resulting from the macrophase is made clearer by distinguishing a number of sectors or industries and a number of regions. Finally, in the microphase, an even clearer and more detailed picture is obtained by dealing with separate projects and even smaller geographical regions, perhaps even separate rural and urban districts.[42]

Because the accounting-oriented data are most needed for the project appraisal or micro-phase, the next section deals with only that phase.[43]

PROJECT APPRAISAL IN DEVELOPMENT PLANNING

Project appraisal in development planning rests to a large extent on the use of cost/benefit analysis. It is a method used to assess the desirability of projects, when it is necessary to take both a long and a wide view of the impact of a proposed project on the general welfare of a society.[44] It calls for an enumeration and evaluation of all the relevant costs and benefits the project may generate and, second, for choosing the alternatives that maximize the present value of all benefits less costs, subject to specified constraints and given specified objectives. Cost/benefit analysis is useful when all the economic impacts of a project, side effects as well as direct effects, have to be considered. It is a favorite method of analysis by governmental agencies for assessing the desirability of particular program expenditures or policy changes. In fact, it has been formally adopted into U.S. federal government budgetary procedures under the Planning-Programming-Budgeting System (PPBS).[45] It acts as a structure of a general theory of government resource allocation. Above all, it is a decision technique whose aims are, first, to take all effects into consideration and, second, to maximize the present value of all benefits less that of all costs, subject to specified constraints. This brings into focus the major principles of cost/benefit analysis:

1. What are the objectives and constraints to be considered?
2. Which costs and benefits are to be included?
3. How are the costs and benefits to be valued?
4. What are the investment criteria to be used?
5. Which discount rate should be used?

Objectives and Relevant Constraints of Cost/Benefit Analysis

The main objective of cost/benefit analysis is to determine whether a particular expenditure is economically and socially justifiable. The basic criterion used is an efficiency criterion. One such criterion is that of Pareto optimality. A program is said to be Pareto-efficient if at least one person is made better off and no one is made worse off. The criterion is too impractical for cost/benefit analysis given that few programs are likely to leave some individuals better off and no one worse off. A weaker notion of efficiency, known as the Kaldor-Hides criterion, is generally used for cost/benefit analysis. Under this criterion, also known as the "potential" Pareto improvement criterion, a program is acceptable if it is Pareto-optimal or if it could redistribute the net benefits to everyone in the community so that everyone is at least as well off as he or she was before initiation of the program.[46] Basically, a program is efficient and should be undertaken if its total discounted societal benefits exceed the total discounted costs.

Besides the objectives of cost/benefit analysis which are basically to maximize society's wealth, it is important to recognize some of the constraints. Eckstein provided a helpful classification of constraints.[47] These include:

1. *Physical constraints*: The program alternatives considered may be constrained by the state of technology and more generally by the production function, which relates the physical inputs and outputs of a project.

2. *Legal constraints*: The program alternatives considered must be done within the framework of the law. Examples of legal constraints include property rights, time needed for public inquiries, regulated pricing, the right of eminent domain, limits to the activities of public agencies, and so on.

3. *Administrative constraints*: Each of the alternative programs requires the availability and hiring of individuals with the right administrative skills.

4. *Distributional constraints*: Any program is bound to generate gainers and losers. The unfavorable effects on income distribution may be alleviated by expressing the objective of cost/benefit analysis as either maximizing the excess of total benefits less costs of particular groups, or maximizing the net gain (or minimizing the net loss) to a particular group subject to a constraint relating to total benefits and costs.

5. *Political constraints*: Political considerations may act as constraints, shifting the decision from what is *best* to what is *possible*. Regional differences and presence of various competing interest groups are examples of actors bound to create political constraints on the choice of the best program.

6. *Budgetary constraints*: Capital rationing and evaluating may act as constraints, shifting the objective function from maximizing to suboptimizing of net benefit given a target budget.

7. *Social and religious constraints*: Social and religious taboos are bound to act as constraints, shifting the decision from what is *best* to what is *acceptable*.

Enumeration of Costs and Benefits

Enumeration of costs and benefits is important because it deals with the question of determining which of the costs and benefits of a particular project should be included in a cost/benefit analysis. Benefits of a project are either direct or indirect. Direct (primary) benefits of a project are those benefits which "accrue directly to the users of the service provided by the project." They consist of "the value of goods or services that result from conditions with the project as compared to condition without the project."[48] Indirect (secondary) benefits are those benefits accruing to entities other than the users of the service provided by the project. They are of two types:

real (technological) benefits or pecuniary benefits.[49] Real benefits are those benefits resulting from changes in total production possibilities and consumption opportunities. For example, if a dam causes a reduction of flooding and a more pleasant scenery, these benefits are real benefits. Pecuniary benefits are those benefits which alter the distribution of total income without changing its volume. They generally take the form of lower input costs, increased volumes of business, or changes in the land values. Only direct real benefits should be included; pecuniary benefits should be excluded from the enumeration of benefits of a project. Other benefits, of an intangible nature and difficult to specify, should be also considered. Costs of a project are also either direct or indirect: Direct costs are those which are incurred directly by the users of the service provided by the project. They include the capital costs, operating and maintenance costs, and personnel expenses required by the project. They may also be either real or pecuniary. Again, only the real secondary costs should be counted in the cost/benefit analysis.

Briefly, in enumerating the costs and benefits of a project, the analyst must be careful to distinguish their allocative effects from their pecuniary or distributional effects. In fact, the confusion of pecuniary and allocative effects constitutes a primary defect in many analyses of the efficiency of public projects. The only effects that should be taken into account in enumerating the costs and benefits of a public project are the real or technological externalities, that is, those that affect total opportunities for production and consumption, as opposed to pecuniary externalities, which do not affect production or consumption.

Valuation of Costs and Benefits

In general, *benefits* should measure the value of the additional goods or services produced or the value of cost savings in the production of goods or services, while *costs* should measure the value of real resources displaced from other uses.

Assuming a competitive economy, the benefits and costs are valued on the basis of the observable market prices of the outputs and inputs of the program. More precisely, the benefits are valued in either the market price of the output of the program or on the amounts the users are willing to pay if they were charged (that is, the consumers' surplus, which is the difference between the aggregate willingness to pay and the costs of the projects).

Where market prices do not accurately reflect the value of market transactions to society as a result of externalities, shadow prices, as adjusted or input prices, may be used. The general principle for estimating shadow prices for the output of public projects is to simulate what users would be willing to pay if they were charged as if the goods were sold in perfectly competitive markets.

Investment Criteria

Cost/benefit analysis is a method used to evaluate long-term projects. As such, the benefits and costs of each project have to be discounted to be comparable at time 0 when evaluation and decisions on the projects have to be made. There is a need to rely on some form of discounting in the choice of investment criteria. There are three possible investment or decision criteria. The first is the net present value method. Under this method the present value of a project is obtained by discounting the net excess of benefits (B_t) over costs (C_t) for each year during the life of the project back to the present time using a social discount rate. More explicitly,

$$V = \sum_{t=1}^{\alpha} \frac{B_t - C_t}{(1 + r)^t}$$

where

B = Value of the project
B_t = Benefit in year t
C_t = Cost in year t
r = Social discount rate
α = Life of the project.

Basically, a project is found acceptable if the present value V is positive. If there are binding constraints on a project (for example, budget appropriation, foreign exchange, private investment opportunity foregone), then the following model proposed by Steiner[50] would be more appropriate:

$$V = \sum_{t=1}^{\alpha} \frac{B_t - C_t}{(1 + r)^t} - \sum_{j=1}^{n} p_j k_j,$$

where

P_j = Shadow price of a binding constraint
k_j = Number of units of a constrained resource.

Second is the benefit/cost ratio. Under this method the decision criterion is expressed in terms of the ratio of the present value of benefits to the present value of costs (both discounted at the social discount). More explicitly, the benefit/cost ratio is:

$$\frac{\displaystyle\sum_{t=1}^{\alpha} \frac{b_t}{(1 + r)^t 1'}}{\displaystyle\sum_{t=1}^{\alpha} \frac{c_t}{(1 + r)^t}} = 0.$$

Basically, all projects that are not mutually exclusive with a benefit/cost ratio in excess of 1 are acceptable.

Last is the internal rate of return. Under this method the decision criterion is expressed in terms of the internal rate of return; that is, the discount rate will equate the net benefits over the life of the project with the original cost. In other words, 2 is the rate of interest for which

$$\sum_{t=1}^{\alpha} \frac{b_t}{(1 + r)^t} - \sum_{t=1}^{\alpha} \frac{c_t}{(1 + r)^t} = 0.$$

Basically, all projects with an internal rate of return which exceeds the closer social discount rate are deemed acceptable.

Choice of a Discount Rate

The choice of a discount rate is important for at least two reasons. A high rate will mitigate against the firm or the government undertaking the project while a low rate may make the project more acceptable from a return point of view. Furthermore, a low discount rate tends to favor projects yielding net benefits further into the future relative to projects yielding more current net benefits. Choosing the appropriate interest rate becomes therefore an important policy question. There are several possible alternative rates.

The first is the marginal productivity of capital in private investment. Given that the discount rate allows the allocation of resources between the public and private sectors, it should be chosen so that it indicates when resources should be transferred from one sector to another. This means that the discount rate should represent the opportunity cost of funds withdrawn from the private sector to be used in the public sector. As Baumol states, "The correct discount rate for the evaluation of a government project is the percentage rate of return that the resources utilized would otherwise provide in the private sector."[51]

The following considerations enter into the choice of the marginal productivity of capital as a discount rate: an effort to minimize governmental activity, a concern for efficiency, and a belief that the source of funds for government investment in the private sector or that government investment will displace private investment that would otherwise be made.[52]

Second is the social rate of time preference, which expresses a concern for future generations in the sense that the welfare of the future generations will be increased if investments are made now. It follows that the discount rate should be the social rate of time preference, that is, the compensation required to induce consumers to refrain from consumption and to save. One study committee argued that the federal government should use the "administration's social rate of time discount" to be established by the president in consultation with his advisors such as the Council of Economic Advisers.[53] The strongest argument for the social rate of time preference was made by Pigou when he suggested that individuals were short-sighted about the future ("defective telescopic faculty") and the welfare of future generations would require governmental intervention.[54]

Advantages and Limitations of Cost/Benefit Analysis

There are thousands of cost/benefit analyses of government projects. The popularity of the method is a witness to some of its advantages; there are also some limitations well recognized in the literature. Among the advantages are the following: (1) It has been pointed out that cost/benefit analysis is most effective in dealing with cases of intermediate social goods.[55] (2) It establishes a framework for a reasonably consistent evaluation of alternative projects, especially where the choice set is narrow in the sense that the projects are not only similar but generate the same volume of externalities. (3) It allows decisions to be made which are most advantageous in terms of the objectives accepted. Among the limitations are: (1) There are limits within which social objectives can be measured in money terms. An example of nonefficiency objectives which are not measurable in dollar terms is an equitable distribution of income. (2) Cost/benefit analysis falls under what is known as partial equilibrium analysis. It is useful in evaluating only those projects which have negligible impact outside the immediately affected areas of the economy. (3) There are obvious problems of enumeration and evaluation of the costs and benefits of particular projects.[56] A committee of the U.S. House of Representatives, pointing to the difficulty inherent in estimating the direct effects of a policy and assigning dollar terms to them, argued that such estimates are seldom accurate.[57] Similarly, Baram cites an inappropriate treatment of factors that transcend economies.[58]

STANDARDIZED ACCOUNTING AND ECONOMIC DEVELOPMENT

Given the important role of accounting in economic development in general and development planning and project appraisal in particular, there may be a need to ensure that the developing countries develop accounting systems capable of providing efficient and organized economic and financial data. One way of achieving this general objective is to simplify and unify all aspects of accounting information systems in order to improve the reliability and consistency of information. That is exactly the role of standardized accounting. It has been adequately defined as follows: "It [standardization] involves establishing methodological standards of definition and terminology; criteria for the identification, collection, measurement, and processing of data, and for the layout of accounts and tables, procedures for integrating information into cohesive models; and standards for evaluating and communicating such information."[59]

Various schemes for standardizing accounting are already in practice, for example, the French "Plan Comptable General," the Belgian Plan Comptable (Plan Raymond Mayer), the German framework of accounts (Kontenrahmen), and the various EEC "directives" to achieve harmonization of financial statements. These schemes are aimed at achieving better comparability among financial statements; better consolidation and integration of data at the corporate, sectoral, and national levels; better formulation of development and economic policies and plans; effective fiscal policy and administration; enhanced accounting theory; better-run small organizations; easier internal and external control and auditing of accountings by private accountants and governmental agencies; and a more specifically oriented training of personnel to administer the accounting system.[60]

ACCOUNTING EDUCATION AND ECONOMIC DEVELOPMENT

Given the importance of the role of accounting in development planning in general and project appraisal in particular, accounting education in the Third World appears to have a major importance. There is obviously a need for systematic accounting education in connection with technical-assistance programs to give a better chance for development planning to be effectively implemented.

The actual situation of accounting education in the developing countries is far from compatible with what should be required for an effective implementation of development planning. There are various accounting practice problems and accounting education problems which need to be effectively handled before accounting education in the developing countries could be considered adequate in its role of facilitating economic development. A recent survey of experts gives a rough ordering of the relative importance of the major accounting practice and education problems and their causes in the developing countries and showed that many of the most important accounting problems are believed to result from important causes deeply rooted in accounting education.[61] A list of these problems and their extremely important contributing problems are presented as Exhibits 11.1 through 11.4.

EXHIBIT 11.1 EVALUATION OF IMPORTANCE OF ACCOUNTING
PRACTICE PROBLEMS

		Importance of Problems			
	Total Responses	*Interna-tional Organiza-tions Canada & U.S.A.*	*Far East*	*Latin America*	*Medi-terranean and Africa*
Shortage of qualified accountants at all levels and in all areas of accounting.	Extreme	Extreme	Moderate	Extreme	Extreme
Accounting information is either not available in the proper form, or is received by users too late to be useful.	Extreme	Extreme	Extreme	Extreme	NI
Accounting information is not utilized advantageously for internal management purposes.	Extreme	Extreme	Extreme	Extreme	Extreme
Lack of adequate financial reporting and auditing standards.	Extreme	Moderate	Extreme	Extreme	NI
Lack of strong national associations of accountants.	Extreme	Extreme	Extreme	NI	NI
Lack of adequate accounting in government agencies and government owned businesses.	Extreme	Extreme	Extreme	Extreme	Extreme
Accountants and the accounting profession have significicnatly lower status than other professions.	Moderate	Moderate	Moderate	Moderate	NI
The lack of legislation relating to accounting and auditing standards and procedures.	Moderate	Less Important	Extreme	Moderate	Extreme
Accounting practices are viewed and utilized primarily as a means for helping companies evade taxes and manipulate financial reporting.	Moderate	Extreme	Extreme	NI	NI
Accounting practice tends to be proce-dures oriented.	Moderate	Moderate	Moderate	Moderate	NI
Accountants and accounting do little to improve government tax collection.	Moderate	Moderate	Moderate	Moderate	NI
Some accountants try to apply concepts and techniques imported from advanced nations regardless of their suitability for the local conditions and immediate needs.	Moderate	Moderate	Moderate	NI	NI
Lack of adequate inflation accounting, currency translation techniques and financial disclosure requirements.	Moderate	Moderate	Extreme	Extreme	Moderate
Conflict between national and inter-national accounting firms.	Less Important	Moderate	Less Important	Moderate	Less Important

NI: Not Included.

SOURCE: Committee on Accounting in Developing Countries, 1973-1975, "Report of the
Committee on Accounting in Developing Countries," *The Accounting Review*,
Supplement to Volume XLXI, p. 203. Reprinted with permission.

EXHIBIT 11.2 EVALUATION OF IMPORTANCE OF ACCOUNTING EDUCATION PROBLEMS

	Importance of Problems				
	Total Responses	International Organizations Canada & U.S.A.	Far East	Latin America	Mediterranean and Africa
Locally-authored textbooks are inadequate.	Extreme	Extreme	Moderate	Extreme	NI
Inadequate teaching of accounting subjects at the college level.	Extreme	Extreme	Extreme	Extreme	Extreme
Lack of qualified accounting instructors at the college level.	Extreme	Extreme	Extreme	Extreme	Extreme
Lack of professional development opportunities for accounting educators and practitioners.	Extreme	Extreme	Moderate	Extreme	Extreme
Inadequate accounting education for managers and prospective managers.	Extreme	Extreme	Extreme	Extreme	Moderate
Inadequacy of translated accounting textbooks for the local environment.	Moderate	Moderate	Moderate	NI	Moderate
Lack of translated accounting literature of advanced nations.	Moderate	Moderate	Moderate	Moderate	Moderate
Poorly organized college educational accounting programs and curricula.	Moderate	Moderate	Extreme	Extreme	NI
A bookkeeping and procedural approach to accounting education with very limited emphasis on the theoretical grounds of accounting discipline.	Moderate	Extreme	Moderate	Extreme	NI
Inadequate accounting libraries and other educational resources in colleges and universities.	Moderate	Moderate	Moderate	Moderate	Moderate
Lack of an educational program tailored to qualifying examinations for entrance to the profession.	Moderate	Moderate	Moderate	Moderate	NI
Lack of inadequate distinction between financial, managerial and tax accounting nature and role in college accounting curricula.	Moderate	Moderate	Moderate	Moderate	NI

NI: Not Included.

SOURCE: Committee on Accounting in Developing Countries, 1973-1975, "Report of the Committee on Accounting in Developing Countries," *The Accounting Review,* Suplement to Volume XLXI, p. 204. Reprinted with permission.

345

01 *Shortage of Qualified Accountants at All Levels and in All Areas of
Accounting & Practices*
Extremely Important reason:
01.1   Inadequate college educational training of accountants
03 *Accounting Information is Either Not Available Or Is Not Available in the
Proper Form, Or Is Received By Users Too Late to Be Useful.*
Extremely Important reasons:
03.1   Educational training lacks the emphasis on managerial accounting and on
developing accounting systems.
03.2   Accounting information systems are poorly organized and under-developed
for managerial accounting and on developing accounting systems.
03.2   Accounting information systems are poorly organized and under-developed
for managerial purposes.
04 *The Failure to Utilize Accounting Information Advantageously for Internal
Management Purposes*
Extremely Important reasons:
04.1   Managers lack general training and education about the nature and role
of accounting information for managerial functions.
04.2   Accounting reports are not adequate for use by management because of
improper form or because they are received by the user too late to be
useful.
06 *Lack of Legislation Relating to Accounting and Auditing Standards and
Procedures*
Extremely Important reason:
06.2   The accounting profession has not been united and forceful in developing
and enforcing reporting and auditing standards beyond the legal minimum.
08 *Lack of Strong National Associations of Accountants*
Extremely Important reason:
None
10 *Lack of Adequate Accounting in Government Agencies and Government-Owned
Businesses*
Extremely Important reasons:
10.1   Accountants' educational training does not emphasize the role of
accounting in planning and control of social goals and achievement or
the differences between governmental, quasi-governmental, and private
enterprise accounting.
10.2   Engineers and economists who are managing state-owned enterprises lack
appreciation of management accounting and lack understanding of the
often complex government accounting systems.
NOTE: The two and three digit numbers above represent, respectively,
the number of the primary problem and of the contributing problem in the
second round questionnaire. For example, problem number 06 was the
sixth primary accounting practice problem listed, and 06.2 was listed
second as a contributing problem for the sixth primary problem.

SOURCE: Committee on Accounting in Developing Countries, 1973-1975, "Report of the
Committee on Accounting in Developing Countries," *The Accounting Review*,
Supplement to Volume XLXI, pp. 204-5. Reprinted with permission

EXHIBIT 11.4 EXTREMELY IMPORTANT ACCOUNTING EDUCATION
PROBLEMS AND THEIR EXTREMELY IMPORTANT CONTRIBUTING
PROBLEMS

01 *Locally-Authored Accounting Textbooks Are Inadequate*
Extremely Important reason:
01.4 The accountants most qualified to write texts are too busy with other
concerns.
05 *Inadequate Teaching of Accounting Subjects at the College Level*
Extremely Important reason:
05.1 Accounting instructors often occupy several other positions in companies, government, and public accounting firms for the purpose of sup-
lementing their low teaching salaries and they do not have time for
adequate class preparation.
06 *Lack of Qualified Accounting Instructors at the College Level*
Extremely important reasons:
06.1 There is a general shortage of qualified accountants and educators.
06.4 College teaching careers are not adequately rewarded financially and
this has discouraged many qualified individuals from teaching careers.
09 *Lack of Professional Development Opportunities for Accounting Educators
and Practitioners.*
Extremely Important reasons:
None
10 *Inadequate Accounting Education for Managers and Prospective Managers*
Extremely Important reason:
10.1 The accounting education of the engineers and scientists who become
managers is limited to the bookkeeping aspects of accounting, or they
receive no accounting training at all.
NOTE: The two and three digit numbers above represent, respectively,
the number of the primary problem and the contributing problem in the
second round questionnaire. For example, problem 06 was the sixth
primary accounting education problem listed, and 06.4 was listed fourth
as a contributing problem for the sixth primary problem.

SOURCE: Committee on Accounting in Developing Countries, 1973-1975, "Report of the
Committee on Accounting in Developing Countries," *The Accounting Review,*
Suplement to Volume XLXI, p. 205. Reprinted with permission.

To improve accounting education in the developing countries and eliminate some of the problems identified in the exhibits, some foreign support is needed—not only as a matter of economic interest to the developed countries but also as a moral obligation. In this regard, a report to the U.S. Congress by former Comptroller General Elmer Staats, *Training and Related Efforts Needed to Improve Financial Management in the Third World*, states:

The absence of effective financial management is a major obstacle to the optimum use of resources, both internal and external, that are available to improve the standard of living in Third World countries. Effective financial management is essential because anything less dissipates available resources and thwarts development. To improve financial management developing countries must

1. Develop effective accounting and auditing practices.
2. Insure the presence of skilled personnel to effectively run their financial management systems.
3. Develop a comprehensive and up-to-date training program at both the national and regional level. . . .
4. Increase their commitment to the realization of an effective training development program.[62]

Various programs have been recommended for adoption by the developing countries. One noteworthy example is: A distinct body of knowledge, called "economic development accountancy," which is recommended as the way to cater effectively to the needs of socioeconomic development. "Economic development accounting can be described as the application of existing and potential accounting systems, techniques, procedures and data to enhance economic development within a nation and among nations."[63]

It is a concept more compatible with the requirements of development planning and of accounting for economic analysis, planning, and policies. It is intended to serve both micro and macro socioeconomic decisions.

Conclusions

This chapter has examined both economic development and the role of accounting in the developing countries. Economic development policies in the areas of growth, poverty and income distribution, unemployment, population growth, education, agricultural reform, international trade and development, foreign aid, and the new economic order offer various strategies to be included in any sensible development-planning programs. Accounting is seen as having a role in development planning in general and project appraisal in particular. Standardized accounting and effective accounting education appear as two solutions for an effective role of accounting in economic development.

Notes

1. Dennis Goulet, *The Cruel Choice: A New Concept in the Theory of Development* (New York: Atheneum, 1971), p. 23.

2. Michael P. Todaro, *Economic Development in the Third World*, 2d ed. (New York: Longman, 1977), p. 29. Copyright © 1977 and 1981 by Michael P. Todaro. Reprinted by permission of Longman Inc., New York.

3. Gunnar Myrdal, *Asian Drama* (New York: Pantheon 1968), Appendix 2.

4. Todaro, *Economic Development in the Third World*, p. 8.

5. Myrdal, *Asian Drama*, pp. 16-17.

6. Irma Adelman, "Development Economics: A Reassessment of Goals," *American Economic Review* (May 1975), p. 306.

7. W. W. Rostow, *The Stages of Economic Growth: A Non-Communist Manifesto* (London: Cambridge University Press, 1960), pp. 1, 3, 4, 12.

8. Named after Sir Harrod and Professor Avery Domar. In their model, growth is a result of the interaction between savings and the capital/output ratio, with capital as the engine of growth.

9. Todaro, *Economic Development*, p. 61.

10. Hans W. Singer, "Dualism Revisited: A New Approach to the Problems of Dual Society in Developing Countries," *Journal of Development Studies* 7, 1 (1970), pp. 60-61.

11. Todaro, *Economic Development*, p. 21.

12. M. S. Ahluwalia, N. Carter, and H. Chenery, "Growth and Poverty in Developing Countries," *Journal of Development Economics* 6 (September 1979), p. 306.

13. Todaro, *Economic Development*, pp. 146-49.

14. Edgar O. Edwards, *Employment in Developing Countries: Report on a Ford Foundation Study* (New York: Columbia University Press, 1974), pp. 10-11.

15. W. A. Lewis, "Economic Development with Unlimited Supplies of Labor," Manchester School, 1954. The model was formalized and extended in J.C.H. Fei and G. Ramis, "A Theory of Economic Development," *American Economic Review* 51, 3 (1961).

16. Michael P. Todaro, "A Model of Labor Migration and Urban Unemployment in Less Developed Countries," *American Economic Review* 59, 1 (1969), pp. 138-48.

17. Todaro, *Economic Development*, pp. 244-45.

18. David Fonguet, "Special Trade Zones Increase Despite Cities," *Chicago Tribune* (November 17, 1983), sect. 2, pp. 2-3.

19. Michael S. Teitelbaum, "Population and Development: Is a Consensus Possible?" *Foreign Affairs* (July 1974), pp. 754-55. Excerpted by permission of *Foreign Affairs*, July 1974. Copyright 1974 by the Council on Foreign Relations, Inc.

20. John Simmons, "Education for Development, Reconsidered," *World Development* 7 (1979), p. 1006.

21. Ibid.

22. Torsten Husen, "Problems of Securing Equal Access to Higher Education: The Dilemma between Equality and Excellence," *Higher Education* 5 (1976), p. 411.

23. Bruce F. Johnston, "Agricultural and Structural Transformation in Developing Countries: A Survey of Research," *Journal of Economic Literature* 8, 2 (1970), p. 374.

24. Todaro, *Economic Development*, pp. 278-80.

25. Pazos, Felipe, "Regional Integration of Trade among Less Developed Countries," *World Development* 1, 7 (July 1973), pp. 1-12.

26. Streeten, P. P., "Trade Strategies for Development: Some Themes for the Seventies," *World Development* 1, 6 (June 1973), p. 1.

27. Ibid., p. 2.

28. Ibid.

29. Adolf J. H. Enthoven, *Social and Political Impact of Multinationals on Third World Countries (and Its Accounting Implications)* (Dallas: Center for International Accounting Development, The University of Texas at Dallas, 1976), p. 2.

30. Keith Griffin and J. L. Enos, "Foreign Assistance: Objectives and Consequences," *Economic Development and Cultural Change* (April 1970), pp. 313-27.

31. William S. Gand, "Foreign Aid: What It Is, How It Works, Why We Provide It," *Development of State Bulletin* 59, 1537 (1968).

32. A thorough description of each of these demands and the history of its origination is provided in E. Laszlo, Robert Balser, Jr., Elliot Eisenberg, and Venkata Ramen, *The Objectives of the New International Economic Order* (New York: Pergamon Press, 1978).

33. T. L. Wilkinson, "United States Accounts As Viewed by Accountants of Other Countries," *The International Journal of Accounting Education and Research* (Fall 1965), pp. 11-12.

34. Quotations from Richard J. Briston, "The Evolution of Accounting in Developing Countries," *The International Journal of Accounting Education and Research* (Fall 1978), p. 113. Reprinted with permission.

35. Irving L. Fantl, "The Case against International Uniformity," *Management Accounting* (May 1971).

36. J. M. Samuels and J. C. Oliga, "Accounting Standards in Developing Countries," *The International Journal of Accounting Education and Research* (Fall 1982), p. 72.

37. Briston, "The Evolution of Accounting," pp. 117-18.

38. UN, *Planning the External Sector: Techniques, Problems and Policies* (New York, September 1965), p. 12.

39. Derek T. Healey, "Development Policy: New Thinking about an Interpretation," *Journal of Economic Literature* 10, 3 (1973), p. 794.

40. Todaro, *Economic Development*, p. 430.

41. Adolf J. H. Enthoven, *Accountancy and Economic Development Policy* (Amsterdam: North-Holland Publishing Company, 1973), p. 149.

42. Jan Tinbergen, *Development Planning* (New York: McGraw-Hill Book Company, 1967), p. 76.

43. This approach differs from the one taken by Enthoven, who foresees a role of accounting in the first two phases as follows:

(a) macro-phase-focal accounts and their components (e.g. national income, consumption, investments. Production functions data will be particularly relevant to this phase, although also extensively used in the subsequent phase.

(b) middle-phase-focal accounts broken down by sector and region on product and income, price indices, wage rates, and labor productivity. Input-output data by sector tend to be of special value in this phase. Shadow price estimates are also useful.

Enthoven, *Accountancy and Economic Development Policy*, p. 168.

44. A. R. Prest and R. Turvey, "Cost-Benefit Analysis: A Survey," *The Economic Journal* (December 1965), pp. 683-735.

45. The major components of a PPBS are presented in this chapter.

46. Another test for potential Pareto improvements is that everyone in society could be made better off by means of a costless redistribution of the net benefits.

47. Otto Eskstein, "A Survey of the Theory of Public Expenditure Criteria," in *Public Finances: Needs, Sources and Utilization*, ed. James M. Buchanan (Princeton, N.J.: Princeton University Press, 1961).

48. Jesse Burkhead and Jerry Miner, *Public Expenditure* (Chicago: Aldine-Atherton, 1971), p. 225.

49. R. N. McKean, *Efficiency in Government through Systems Analysis* (New York: John Wiley and Sons, 1958), chap. 8.

50. George A. Steiner, "Problems in Implementing Program Budgeting," in *Program Budgeting*, ed. David Novic (Cambridge: Harvard University Press, 1965), pp. 87-88.

51. William J. Baumol, "On the Discount Rate for Public Projects," in *Public Expenditures and Policy Analysis*, ed. Robert and Julius Margolis (Chicago: Markham, 1970), p. 274.

52. Burkhead and Miner, *Public Expenditure*, p. 232.

53. Report of Panel of Consultants, Bureau of the Budget, *Standards and Criteria for Formulating and Evaluating Federal Water Resources Development* (Washington, D.C., 1961), p. 67.

54. A. C. Pigou, *The Economics of Welfare*, 4th ed. (London: Macmillan, 1932).

55. R. A. Musgrave, *Fiscal Systems* (New Haven, Conn.: Yale University Press, 1969), pp. 797-806.

56. Prest and Turvey, pp. 729-31.

57. U.S. House of Representatives, 94th Cong., 2d Sess., Committee on Interstate and Foreign Commerce, Subcommittee on Oversight and Investigations, *Federal Regulation and Regulatory Reform* (1976), Chap. 15. (Subcommittee print)

58. Michael S. Baram, "Cost Benefit Analysis: An Inadequate Basis for Health, Safety, and Environmental Regulatory Decision-Making," *Ecology Law Quarterly* 8 (1980), pp. 473-531.

59. Adolf J. H. Enthoven, "Standardized Accountancy and Economic Development," *Management Accounting* (February 1976), p. 19.

60. Enthoven, *Accountancy and Economic Development Policy*.

61. Committee on Accounting in Developing Countries, "Report of the Committee on Accounting in Developing Countries," *The Accounting Review*, Supplement (1975).

62. Elmer Staats, *Training and Related Efforts Needed to Improve Financial Management in the Third World*, ID 79-46 (Washington, D.C.: General Accounting Office, 1979), p. 1.

63. Enthoven, *Accountancy and Economic Development Policy*, p. 168.

Bibliography

Adelman, I. "A Reassessment of Development Economics: Development Economics—A Reassessment of Goals," *American Economic Review* 65, 2 (1975), pp. 302-5.

Briston, Richard J. "The Evolution of Accounting in Developing Countries," *The International Journal of Accounting Education and Research* (Fall 1978), pp. 105-20.

Chenery, Hollis B. "The Structuralist Approach to Development Policy," *American Economic Review* 65, 2 (1975), pp. 310-15.

Committee on Accounting in Developing Countries. "Report of the Committee on Accounting in Developing Countries," *The Accounting Review*, Supplement (1973), pp. 198-212.

Committee on International Accounting. *Accounting Education in the Third World* (Sarasota, Fla.: American Accounting Association, 1929).

Elliot, Edward L. *The Nature and Stages of Accounting Development in Latin America* (Urbana, Ill.: Center for International Education and Research in Accounting, 1968).

Engelmann, Konrad. "Accounting Problems in Developing Countries," *The Journal of Accountancy* (January 1962), pp. 53-62.

Enthoven, Adolph J. H. *Accountancy and Economic Development Policy* (Amsterdam: North Holland Publishing, 1973).

_____. *Accountancy Systems in Third World Economies* (Amsterdam: North Holland Publishing, 1977).

_____. "Standardized Accountancy and Economic Development," *Management Accounting* (February 1976), pp. 19-23.

_____. "U.S. Accounting and the Third World," *The Journal of Accountancy* (June 1983), pp. 110-18.

Healey, Derek T. "Development Policy: New Thinking about an Interpretation," *Journal of Economic Literature* 10, 3 (1973), pp. 757-97.

Johnston, Bruce F. "Agricultural and Structural Transformation in Developing Countries: A Survey of Research," *Journal of Economic Literature* (1970), pp. 369-404.

Lall, Sanyaya. "Is 'Dependence' a Useful Concept in Analyzing Underdevelopment?" *World Development* 3, 11 and 12 (1975), pp. 799-810.

_____. "Less-Developed Countries and Private Foreign Direct Investment: A Review Article," *World Development* 2, 4 and 5 (April-May 1974), pp. 43-48.

Palma, Gabriel. "Dependency: A Formal Theory of Underdevelopment or a Methodology for the Analysis of Concrete Situations of Underdevelopment?" *World Development* 6 (1978), pp. 881-924.

Pazos, Felipe. "Regional Integration of Trade among Less Developed Countries," *World Development* 1, 7 (July 1973), pp. 1-12.

Samuels, J. M., and J. C. Oliga. "Accounting Standards in Developing Countries," *The International Journal of Accounting Education and Research* (Fall 1982), pp. 69-88.

Seidler, Lee J. *The Function of Accounting in Economic Development* (New York: Frederick A. Praeger, Publishers, 1967).

Simmons, John. "Education for Development, Reconsidered," *World Development* 7 (1979), pp. 1005-16.

Singer, Hans W. "Dualism Revisited: A New Approach to the Problems of Dual Society in Developing Countries," *Journal of Development Studies* 7, 1 (1970), pp. 60-75.

Streeten, P. P. "Trade Strategies for Development: Some Themes for the Seventies," *World Development* 1, 6 (June 1973), pp. 1-10.

Teitelbaum, Michael S. "Population and Development: Is a Consensus Possible?" *Foreign Affairs* (July 1974), pp. 742-60.

Tinbergen, Jan. *Development Planning* (New York: McGraw-Hill Book Company, 1967).

Wilkinson, T. L. "United States Accounts As Viewed by Accountants of Other Countries," *The International Journal of Accounting Education and Research* (Fall 1965), pp. 11-12.

INDEX

ABOUT THE AUTHOR

AHMED BELKAOUI is Professor of Accounting at the University of Illinois' Chicago campus. He is the author of *Industrial Bonds and the Rating Process, Socio-Economic Accounting* (Quorum Books, 1983, 1984), *Accounting Theory, Conceputal Foundations of Management Accounting,* and numerous articles.